CONTROLLING
STATE
CRIME

CONTROLLING STATE CRIME

Second Edition

Jeffrey Ian Ross
editor

Transaction Publishers
New Brunswick (U.S.A.) and London (U.K.)

New material this edition copyright © 2000 by Transaction Publishers, New Brunswick, New Jersey. Originally published in 1995 by Garland Publishing, Inc.

This book is printed on acid-free paper that meets the American National Standard for Permanence of Paper for Printed Library Materials.

Library of Congress Catalog Number: 00-026701
ISBN: 0-7658-0695-9
Printed in the United States of America

Library of Congress Cataloging-in-Publication Data

Controlling state crime / Jeffrey Ian Ross, editor.—2nd ed.
    p.cm.
Includes bibliographical references and index.
ISBN 0-7658-0695-9 (paper : alk. paper)
1. Political crimes and offenses. 2. Political corruption I. Ross, Jeffrey Ian.

HV6273 .C66 2000
364.1'3—dc21   00-026701

Contents

Introduction to the Second Edition

Almost five years have passed since the original publication of *Controlling State Crime*. I hoped that the book would stimulate not only scholarly research and debate, but also encourage progressive minded policy makers and practitioners, who work for both governmental and nongovernmental organizations, to at least pause and reflect upon the methods they advocate or use to minimize state transgressions.

With respect to the academic field, not only does work continue in the sub-fields of state crime (i.e., human rights abuses, corruption, etc.), but a number of scholars have published pieces that draw or build upon controlling state crime research (Glasberg and Skidmore, 1998; Israel, 1998; Situ, 1998; Leavitt, 1999; Vaughn, 1999). Not only is this work appearing in the academic journals, but monographs on the subject have appeared. David Friedrichs (1998), for example, edited a two-volume compendium of previously published articles on state crime, and David Kauzlarich and Ron Kramer (1998) applied the concept to the study of American nuclear policy. Needless to say, my academic work has continued, in whole (Ross, 1998, 1999; 2000; Ross et al., 1999) or in part, on the problem of state crime (Ross, 2000).

Unfortunately, state crimes continue to occur. We need look no further than today's headlines to read about Rwanda where government troops massacred countless Hutus and Tutsis, governmental atrocities in Kosovo, at the hands of the Yugoslavian Army, and East Timor where both individuals and property have been decimated, largely perpetrated by the Indonesian military.

In general, the reviews of *Controlling State Crime* were quite favorable (e.g., Webster, 1995; Israel, 1996; Gould, 1997; Klein, 1997; Stewart, 1997). One reviewer, for instance, called the book "the most ambitious and informative book of its kind" and suggested that *Controlling State Crime* "breaks new ground conceptualizing state crime from an international perspective (Klein, p. 103). And another commentator said that I "found a sizeable gap in the work of criminologists." He also suggested that the book goes "beyond 'appreciation' of crime and pursue[s] some vision of social justice" (Israel, p. 171) and "Ross' book is an important step in introducing the state into the crime prevention literature as an offender rather than simply as a victim, mediator or punisher of crime" (Israel, p. 172). Other reviewers were simply descriptive (e.g., Seabury, 1995), lukewarm (Weiss, 1995), or downright hostile (Cohen, 1996).

My work and thinking on state crime have been aided by a variety of persons, some of whom are friends, including Bruce Arrigo, Gregg Barak, Dorothy Bracey, Henry Brownstein, Natasha Cabrera, Jeff Ferrell, David Friedrichs, Ted Robert Gurr, Donna Hale, Victor Kappeler, David Kauzlarich, Peter Kraska, Otwin Marenin, Gary Marx, William McDonald, Stephen Richards, Larry Travis, Kenneth Tunnell, Austin Turk, and Mike Vaughn. Not only have they provided me with valuable advice, but they have been very collegial.

Although I was glad that the first edition of the book was published as part of Frank P. Williams III and Marilyn McShane's well received series "Current Issues in Criminal Justice," for Garland Publishing, the cost of the book was prohibitive, allowing mainly only libraries and diehard scholars to afford its purchase. I'm happy that Irving Louis Horowitz, Distinguished Professor, Rutgers University, and Editorial Director, Transaction Publishers adopted the book, made it available in soft cover with a price that is in line with competing works, and within the reach of most students and other consumers. This broader dissemination of the book will expand the debate and increase awareness of the problem of state crime and the difficulties and opportunities for its control.

Jeffrey Ian Ross

REFERENCES

Cohen, Stanley, (1996) Review of *Controlling State Crime, British Journal of Sociology*, Vol. 47, pp. 733-734.
Friedrichs, David, ed. (1998) *State Crime*, Aldershot, England: Ashgate, Vols. I and II.
Glasberg, Davita S. and Dan L. Skidmore, (1998) "The Role of the State in the Criminogenesis of Corporate Crime," *Social Science Quarterly*, Vol. 79, No. 1, pp. 110

Gould, Larry A, (1997) Review of *Controlling State Crime, The Social Science Journal* Vol. 34, No. 2, pp. 263-265.

Israel, Mark, (1996) Review of *Controlling State Crime* Vol. 2, No. 2, pp. 168-173.

Israel, Mark, (1998) "Crimes of State—Victimization of South African Political Exiles in the United Kingdom," *Crime, Law and Social Change* Vol. 29, No. 1, pp. 1-29.

Kauzlarich, David and Ronald Kramer, (1998) *Crimes of the American Nuclear State*, Boston: Northeastern University Press.

Klein, Lloyd, (1997) Review of *Controlling State Crime,* Vol. 21, No. 1, March, pp. 103-104.

Leavitt, G. (1999). "Criminological Theory as an 'Art Form,' *Crime and Delinquency,* Vol. 45, No. 3, pp. 389-399.

Ross, Jeffrey Ian, (1998) "Situating the Academic Study of Controlling State Crime," *Crime, Law and Social Change* Vol. 29, No. 4, December, pp. 331-340.

Ross, Jeffrey Ian, (1999) "State (Organized) Crime, Its Control, Unintended Consequences, and Suggestions for Future Research," in Stan Einstein and Menachim Amir (eds.) *Organized Crime: Uncertainties and Dilemmas* Chicago, IL: Office of International Criminal Justice, pp. 407-422.

Ross, Jeffrey Ian, (2000) *Making News of Police Violence* Westport, CT: Praeger Publishers.

Ross, Jeffrey Ian, et al. (1999) "The State of State Crime Research: A Commentary," *Humanity and Society,* Vol. 23, No. 3, August, pp. 273-281.

Ross, Jeffrey Ian, (ed.) (2000) *Varieties of State Crime and Its Control,* Monsey, NY: Criminal Justice Press.

Seabury, Elizabeth, (1995) Review of *Controlling State Crime, Journal of Crime and Justice,* Vol. 23, No. 5, pp. 493-497.

Situ, Y. (1998) "Public Transgression of Environmental Law," *Deviant Behavior,* Vol. 19, 2, pp. 137-155.

Stewart, James G. (1997) "State Crime," *The Journal of Conflict Studies*, Spring, pp. 148-155.

Vaughn, Michael S. (1999) "Police Sexual Violence: Civil Liability Under state Tort Law," *Crime & Delinquency,* Vol. 45, n. 3, pp. 334-357.

Webster, Andrew, (1995) "Battling the Armada," *Washington City Paper*, July 14, p. 43.

Foreword

Few if any would question the observation that governments often do harm to their own citizens as well as other people. But there is no consensus on specifics: (1) the definition of particular outcomes or conditions as harms; (2) the characterization of harms as intended or inadvertent, avoidable or inevitable; (3) the causal linkage of harms to governmental actions; (4) the possibility and methods of controlling the crimes of governments and their agents. Introducing the concept of *state crime* serves both to bring the issues into sharp focus and to signal a preference for certain positions rather than others.

The diversity of views on whether and how the notion of state crime should be used is well represented in this volume. One contributor argues that the concept is useless because it is indiscriminately applied to anything objectionable to whomever uses the term. The word *nasty* is not synonymous with *criminal*. Some contributors, including the editor, try (unsuccessfully, though informatively) to come up with a definition that is neither too indiscriminate nor too limiting. Most contributors discuss some putative form of state crime without much explicit attention to the definitional problem. Consequently, the book as a whole tends to confirm the skeptical view of the concept as almost entirely subjective, while also providing a wealth of information on a variety of outcomes and conditions that the authors see as examples or effects of state crime.

Whether analyzing crimes of education, crimes against labor, or offensive conduct by military, police, or intelligence agencies, the common theme or assumption is that the harm is evident and avoidable, and is the direct or indirect result of deliberate actions by government. In many instances, such as the historical efforts to subjugate and exploit workers, the harms are not only indisputable but by now readily shown to result from governmental policy decisions favoring the interests of capitalists and the wealthy over workers and the poor. However, in some instances (e.g., the critical discussion of education in America), both the criminal nature of the harm and the responsibility of the state for it are highly debatable.

To most readers, I suspect, the term *state crime* will be most applicable to the lawbreaking of officials and agencies charged with the responsibilities of making, implementing, and enforcing the criminal and civil laws. The expected chapters on police, military, and security agency crimes are here, with extremely thoughtful efforts by the authors to suggest how such crimes might be controlled. A novel, though nonetheless pertinent, contribution is the informative chapter on environmental damage resulting from military operations.

Although the informational value of this book is considerable, its primary success is in articulating and confronting the problems of controlling state crime however defined. Here again the picture is of diversity rather than uniformity of views. The anarchist conclusion is that reforming the state may be a more utopian notion than abolishing it. One contributor finds that states cannot police themselves, while another observes that no state ever has been, or is likely to be, prosecuted under international law. In any case, regardless of the level and type of control examined, the effective control of state crime—even blatantly illegal police misconduct—appears to be a distant and problematic goal in light of the findings and conclusions of even the most hopeful and determined contributors. Still, undaunted, the editor has done a masterly job of formulating a series of propositions hypothesizing the conditions under which control efforts at various levels are likely to be more and less successful. At the very least, he and his collaborators have set the research agenda for anyone willing to tackle the problems of defining, documenting, explaining, and controlling state crime.

Austin T. Turk
University of California, Riverside

Acknowledgments

This project began in the fall of 1990, when I started to edit a series of books entitled Comparative Approaches to Controlling State Crime and to organize a number of panels for the American Society of Criminology, Academy of Criminal Justice Sciences, and Canadian Association for Security and Intelligence Studies. This present project depends on the contributions of a team of respected political scientists, sociologists, criminologists, educators, and lawyers, many of whom are activists who improve our ability to control state crime in a variety of contexts.

Attempts were made to include the views of well-respected scholars, experts, and activists in the field who represent different genders, nationalities, and racial, religious, and ethnic groups, and almost every conceivable subtopic was considered for coverage. Unfortunately, the latter objective was not possible. Approximately eleven subjects could not be covered because I could not locate individuals to write the manuscript, because some who promised me papers never produced them, or due to resource constraints, I could not write them myself. Had I waited any longer to fill in the missing gaps, this book may never have been published.

During the course of the organization of this book, I incurred a series of debts. First, I would like to thank my contributors for their scholarship, diligence, and patience. Second, I would like to thank Paul Bond and Sam Matheson for capable research assistance. Third, thanks to anonymous volunteer internal reviewers (i.e., other contributors to the book) who took time from their busy schedules to provide thoughtful and helpful criticism on the chapters. Fourth, the wise counsel and encouragement of Natasha J. Cabrera and Kenneth D.

Tunnell was useful at several critical stages of this project. Fifth, special thanks goes out to Marilyn McShane and Frank Williams III, the series editors, for their patience and encouragement and for allowing this project to move forward. Sixth, the kind folks at Garland, including Phyllis Korper and Amy DeAngelis, who managed to keep the project on track. Seventh, the love, affection, and support of my wife, who helped make this project possible.

This book is dedicated to my parents, Marvin and Harriet Ross, who taught me to constantly question individuals' and institutions' motivations that may on the surface seem benign but on further examination are quite coercive.

Controlling State Crime

Controlling State Crime: Toward an Integrated Structural Model*

Jeffrey Ian Ross

Introduction

Until recently, the majority of academic research on crime has focused on the illegal actions of individuals and organizations (i.e., syndicates and corporations). When state crime, interchangeably labeled governmental crime, delinquency, illegality, or lawlessness, official deviance and misconduct, crimes of obedience, and human rights violations, is addressed, it largely is treated as a consequence of, or as a response to the presence of, insurgent violence, threats to national security, or a phenomenon endemic to authoritarian countries in second/transitional and third world/lesser developed contexts.[1] State crime, however, is pervasive and committed, with varying frequency, by all types of countries (Barak, 1990: 6). Moreover, the state is often the initiator rather than just the mediator or target of crime.[2] Although private institutions may wield coercive power, the state holds an exclusive legal authority to coerce. In fact, many important scholars (e.g., Marx, Weber, MacIver, Mann) have noted the importance of coercion and state crime to various manifestations of power held by states. Thus, state crime has existed since the first country was created, and it is argued that it may, in fact, be necessary for the creation of states (Gurr, 1988; Tilly, 1985).

The biggest impediments to the study of controlling state crime are definitional, conceptual, theoretical, and methodological in nature as well as lacking in the design of practical methods to abolish, combat, control, decrease, minimize, prevent, or resist this type of behavior. The author reviews these shortcomings, then develops a tentative model of the process to control state crime.

Definitional and Conceptual Problems with State Crime

There is much opposition to the concept of state crime. Sharkansky (this volume) argues that while many states violate laws they themselves created, academics who study state crime have used the term so indiscriminately as to render it useless. Through an examination of the literature on state crime, power of the state, and an application to the Israeli case, in particular, he argues that the state crime concept, and by implication the research agenda of controlling state crime, has only emotional weight. By extension, he argues for concept contraction rather than expansion.

In the same vein, Friedrichs (this volume) argues that governmental crime, like no other type of crime, including white-collar crime, is characterized by conceptual and typological confusion. His resolution to this conceptual messiness is to distinguish among "those governmental or political actions prohibited by the state's laws, those defined as criminal by international law, and those actions regarded as criminal by some other criteria of harmfulness." He uses *governmental crime* as a broad term that includes "the whole range of crimes committed in a governmental context." In contrast, he uses the term *state crime* to mean "activities carried out by the state or on behalf of some state agency," and the term *political white-collar crime* to include "illegal activities carried out by officials and politicians for direct personal benefit."

Perhaps the most comprehensive definition of state crime is offered by Barak (1991: 274). He lists twenty-three actions, including coverup, disinformation, unaccountability, corruption, "the general violation of both domestic and international laws . . . [as well as] behaviors which cause social injury and therefore violate universally defined human rights" (p. 274),[3] for a definition that is both under- and overinclusive.[4] Simply put, the difference between human rights violations and state crimes (e.g., Barak, 1990: 9) is that state crime is a broader and more inclusive concept than is the concept of human rights violations.

State criminality also cuts to the center of the debate between crimes that are *mala in se* and those that are *mala prohibita*. *Mala prohibita crimes* refer to those actions that are bad because they have been prohibited by law. For example, traffic violations, gambling, and violating various municipal ordinances are "not viewed as inherently bad in themselves but are violations because the law defines them as such." These laws are designed to make people's lives more predictable and orderly; breaking them carries little, if any, stigma and only minor sanctions (Hagan, 1990: 9). On the other hand, *acts mala in se* are acts that are bad in themselves, and there is widespread consensus on the illegitimacy of such behaviors. "The universality of [certain] laws against murder, rape, assault, and the like, irrespective of political or economic systems, bears witness to the lack of societal conflict in institutionalizing such laws" (Hagan, 1990: 9). Henry (1991), building on the philosophical and ideological belief that states have certain moral and ethical obligations to its citizenry, and adding another layer of complexity to the concept distinguishes between state crimes that are considered either crimes of commission or crimes of omission.

State crime then incorporates acts both *mala in se* and *mala prohibita*, as well as those behaviors that have not reached the point where a formal law prohibits them. While the appropriateness of states' responsibilities can and has been debated historically, this author's definition of state crime includes crimes of commission and omission (Henry, 1991), governmental crime, state crime, and political white-collar crime (Friedrichs, this volume).

In an effort to focus future research and policy, state crime, as defined here, is limited to coverups, corruption, disinformation, unaccountability, and violations of domestic and/or international laws. It also includes those practices that, although they fall short of being officially declared illegal, are perceived by the majority of the population as illegal or socially harmful (e.g., worker exploitation). This definition recognizes that legal systems are highly normative, slow to enact legislation, and often reflect elite, upper-class, or nonpluralistic interests. This definition also addresses and mitigates criticisms from the political right that state crime theorists are simply semanticians and should temper the left, who suffer at times from ambiguous and unrigorous usage of terms and methods.

Literature Review

Of the books focusing on political crime, the majority (e.g., Bassiouni, 1975; Ingraham, 1979; Roebuck and Weeber, 1978; Schafer, 1974; and Turk, 1982) primarily concentrate on oppositional political crimes, whereas a minority (e.g., Barak, 1991; Comfort, 1950; Proal, 1898/1973; Tunnell, 1993b) address, to some extent, state political crimes.[5] Still other monographs occupy a middle ground. Turk (1982: Chapter 4), for example, discusses "Political Policing" and outlines the activities that police may take to manipulate the public order. He stops short, however, of labeling these actions as state crimes. Others (e.g., Ingraham, 1979) fail to consider oppositional political crimes as such and focus the bulk of their discussion on crimes against the state.[6] Additionally, some of these efforts (e.g., Sink, 1974) serve as manuals to aid professionals charged with defending individuals with political crimes.

To date, the majority of the academic literature on state crime has concentrated on definitional issues (e.g., Friedrichs, this volume; Barak, 1991: Chapter 1 and Prologue; Bohm, 1993), its types (e.g., Proal, 1898/1973), and cataloguing its causes and effects in the context of case studies of state crime (e.g., Grabosky, 1989: Chapters 2–18; Aulette and Michalowski, 1993; Caulfield and Wonders, 1993). Unlike the voluminous literature on individual and organized crime, there is little material that aims at developing a model or theory of state crime, and much less that addresses and systematically analyzes methods for abolishing, combatting, controlling, decreasing, minimizing, preventing, and/or resisting, state crime.

Granted, some researchers present a list of factors important in the control of particular state criminogenic institutions or state crimes. Hurwitz (1981), for instance, examines regular and administrative courts; ombudsmen, or citizen protectors; parliamentary political activity; the European Convention on Human Rights; and Amnesty International as methods to improve governmental accountability primarily in the western countries. Kuper (1985), for example, analyzes methods to punish offenders and prevent genocide, and Klitgaard (1988), in particular, examines methods to control corruption. A subfield of political science examines human rights violations and in some cases their control in various nation-states as well as other contexts (e.g., Stunton, Fenn, and Amnesty International, 1991; World Watch, 1992). Kelman and Hamilton (1989) outline a series of factors to help "Break the Habit of Unquestioning Obedience" that contributes to the commission of state crimes. While important contributions in their own areas, and stepping-stones for future work, no one has integrated this diverse literature on specific criminogenic agencies into a testable model or theory for controlling state crime.

Additionally, some academics have articulated dominant factors in the process of state criminality. Comfort (1950) claims that "the delinquencies of states arise at two levels—in the psychopathology of publics, and in the psychopathy of individuals expressing their own and their culture's aggression through the mechanism of power" (p. 109). In particular, he articulates and discusses a series of causes of state delinquency, including the notion that delinquents occupy positions of political power, that delinquency is centralized and primarily found in urbanized communities, and the notion that perpetrators "have failed to achieve [power] through the normal mechanisms of dominance" (p. 20).

With respect to remedies to state delinquency, Comfort (1950) dismisses revolution (including anarchism, "biotechnic civilization," "para-primitive society," and "free society"), incentive, punishment, and world society. On the other hand, he advocates five groups of solutions to state delinquency: "education," "experiments in communal living and control of resources;" "pressure towards controlled break-up of large city aggregates, increased workers' control in industry, with decentralization of large units;" "propaganda to introduce sociality into the places where character formation takes place;" and, "individual psychiatry" (pp. 105–107). He suggests that the bulk of our energy should be focused on the individual, particularly those "who initiate state policy, and to the subjects who support them" (p. 109). While sensitizing us to the criminological interpretation of government delinquency and outlining a series of factors that are important in the commission of state delinquency that are essential to model building,[7] Comfort's book has a number of problems. The most important, for this researcher's purpose, is that he does not develop a theory or a model of controlling state crime.

Grabosky (1989: 294–299) presents a sophisticated treatment, which he calls "a provisional theory of state crime," and then outlines outcomes, including methods for control. First, his theory of government illegality involves seven principle factors: weak external oversight, powerlessness of victims, poor leadership, strong goal orientation, inadequate supervision, rapid organizational expansion, and communications breakdown. While a competent and parsimonious beginning, these factors are somewhat ambiguous, have many exceptions, do not explain state crime in non-western societies, and do not relate to control options.

Second, his tentative theory is accompanied by six basic outcomes of state crime: "deterrence," "rehabilitation," "victim compensation," "denouncing the misconduct in question," "reaffirming the rule of law," and "experienc[ing] the threat (or reality) of draconian punishment" (pp. 17–18; pp. 303–308). Finally, based on the understanding that given the diversity of official misconduct, there can be no single intervention or control of the problem, Grabosky includes seven methods of controlling state crime: "internal oversight," "organizational redesign," "external oversight," "whistleblowing," "criminal prosecution," "civil litigation," and "participatory democracy" (pp. 308–331). Although Grabosky has sensitized us to the need for more analytical techniques, and no one else has matched his work, Grabosky's factors can be criticized on a number of grounds. While of debatable utility, it is not clear why he did not simply suggest the converse of his theory of causation, which would entail: strong external oversight, empowering of victims, improving leadership, weakening goal orientation, improving supervision, slowing down organizational expansion, and improving communication. Since Grabosky does not outline interactions among the variables, he neither develops testable hypotheses nor a generalizable model to explain the control of state crime. Additionally, his research is also based on an unrepresentative sample, namely Australian cases. Finally, some of the variables he outlined can be criticized on a number of points. His conceptualization of external oversight is too narrow. For example, Grabosky neglects those organizations external to actual countries, such as the International Court of Justice and Amnesty International. Nonetheless, his work is an important starting point in the academic effort to understand the control of state crime and to prevent the abuse or to secure the proper use of state power.[8]

Many criminologists have concluded that certain types of crime require better control than currently available (Pepinsky, 1980: 4). A minority (e.g., Berkman, 1971; Pepinsky, 1980) oppose current crime control efforts on ideological (Berkman, 1971) or empirical grounds (Pepinsky, 1980; Walker, 1985). Those opposed on empirical grounds to crime control methods cite our inability to specify what exactly we should be controlling, the inadequacy of data on and methods to study conventional crime, and the processes utilized to deter or reform criminals. Pepinsky (1980: 271), for example, criticizes existing criminological research on the grounds that it overemphasizes etiology and rehabilitation of criminals. Those opposed on ideological grounds to controlling crime believe that since crime is a manifestation of a criminal (or illegitimate) state, we are only furthering the power of that state by controlling those actions that the entity deems illegal. Both of these types of critiques have been made in the context of conventional crime; however, they fail to consider as a separate issue controlling state crime.

Others are pessimistic on structural grounds about the possibility of controlling the state. Wilson and Rachel (1977) suggested that it is easier to control private rather than public institutions because governmental organizations, in particular, have at their disposal more resources to rely on as needed. Although this may be true, it should neither serve as a signal for failure nor imply that we automatically abandon efforts to control state crime. Controlling state crime can be accomplished through sound theoretical conceptualization that both identifies the criminal actions committed by the state as well as the mechanisms that sustain those criminal actions and devises methods to control these illegalities and hence to minimize the abuse of coercive power.

The control-of-state-crime agenda assumes that, much like the search for the causes of traditional crime in general (e.g., property, occupational, violent, public order, white-collar, organized, etc.), the search for the causes of state crime may have limited utility in the ability to control state crime. As with conventional crime, we do not have good measures of state crime, nor will we have them in the foreseeable future. The problem is compounded because there is considerable debate over a definition of state crime that would identify perpetrators, processes, and rates. For example, organizations like Amnesty International and databases on specific types of state crime such as genocide (e.g., Harff and Gurr, 1988), which provide analyzable data, have been criticized for their accuracy, validity, and reliability (e.g., Stohl and Lopez, 1984: final chapter).

Criticism, while important, is not enough; we need to go beyond the criticism to salvage what is good and offer improvements (e.g. De Bonno, 1979: 35–39). Moreover, even though proposing solutions is relatively easy, suggesting those that are realistic and practical for minimizing state crime are not simple. Mechanisms for control must be implemented so that they do not unnecessarily frustrate the prosocial nature of the organizations' original mission. The author argues that a model or theory of control might help us understand how to minimize the amount, frequency, and intensity of state crime. Useful to academics, activists, policymakers, and line personnel, the model proposed here builds on and goes beyond the strongest features of past research by incorporating new data. To support this model, research must examine efforts to control the state in general and the principal state actors that engage in state crime and the processes that they use, in particular. This research must look at victims' (or survivors') methods of controlling state crime. Victims of state crime can be individuals and groups or organizations and processes, although this distinction is not clear-cut. Because there is a certain amount of interdependence among these factors, we can specify what works and what does not and under what conditions only through analysis of all these factors.

Contributions to this volume go beyond the standard documentation and diagnoses of state abuses by providing proven practical methods that combat state crime. Additionally, these researchers examine both internal (state-controlled) and external (both state- and nonstate-controlled) mechanisms for controlling the opportunity, ability, desirability, and, by extension, frequency of states to engage in crimes.

Moreover, control, as distinguished from influence,

> refers to that form of power which A has authority to direct or command B to do something. Influence is a more general and pervasive form of power than control. When B conforms to A's desires, values, or goals on such grounds as suggestion, persuasion, emulation, or anticipation, then A exercises influence over B. . . . To exercise control, A must have authority in the sense of having access to the inducements, rewards and sanctions necessary to back up commands. (Kernaghan and Siegel, 1987: 252–253)

This latter process is subsumed under the concept of "authority of position," or "position power." Central to authority of position is A's ability to exercise influence as a result of "the rule of anticipated reactions."[9]

Actors that can control others' actions "have at their disposal sanctions and inducements formalized by law and the organization chart" (p. 253). On the other hand, "Influence over administrative organizations and . . . bureaucrats within these organizations can be exercised by those who do not have legally or formally sanctioned power to command or supervise" (p. 253). However, Kernaghan and Siegel argue that "such influence cannot be as [or more] effective as control. . . . Thus influence can be exercised by those without either authority of position or authority of leadership through a variety of means, including persuasion, friendship, knowledge, and experience" (pp. 253–254).

It must also must be understood that

> [p]ower relations between administrative organizations and other actors flow in two directions. Bureaucrats are not defenseless against pressures brought to bear on them by actors outside the bureaucracy. An examination of the real or potential impact of controls and influences over the bureaucracy must take account of the potent resources which bureaucrats can use to resist pressure and to exert power over others. (p. 257)

Based on the existing extensive public administration, public policy, and organizational theory literature, the following are four covering propositions (CP), or hypotheses, that will guide the model of controlling state crime:

CP1:   The greater the amount of resources (including sanctions), the greater the control.

CP2:   The greater the quality of resources, the greater the control.

CP3:   The better the ability to use resources, the greater the control.

CP4:   The greater the availability of resources, the greater the control. [10]

In this context, resources for controlling state crime can consist of expertise, experience, budgetary allocations, information (confidential or otherwise), and discretionary powers to develop and implement policies, programs, and sanctions (Kernaghan and Siegel, 1987: 257).

As Tunnell (1993b) warns, however,

> strategies offered here represent simply a starting point. . . . Because there is such wide variance in nation-states and the types of crimes that emanate from . . . states these strategies are best served if presented as loose designs for controlling state transgressions . . . rather than a blueprint for action. . . . Also, we must be mindful that

> strategies for controlling a particular . . . state's misdeeds may not be generalizable to other nation-states. Particular culture and ways of life play significant roles in giving rise to specific strategies for controlling state crime. (p. 24)

Having outlined the nature of the dependent variable, it is necessary to review the previously mentioned areas of the model and then develop a series of hypotheses and the tentative model.

Method Used to Construct the Integrated Model of the Control of State Crime

One of the main difficulties in the study of state crime is that this behavior is hidden from the public and the media (Barak, 1990: 15). Governments and states conceal their deviant behaviors as prudent measures to prevent their instability and downfall. Various methods are used to study state crime. In controlling this type of social and policy problem, relevant actors and processes and specific relationships must be identified and a time period must be specified. In general, these steps can be enhanced by utilizing a variety of methodologies, integrating qualitative and quantitative processes, and borrowing the techniques of researchers in cognate fields. A particularly important period to focus on is the past thirty-year period (i.e., since 1960) because the greatest expansion of states has taken place since this time. The author identifies, in model form, a series of controls on state crime and specifies propositions for further testing (Figure 1). This model is then explicated in the remainder of this chapter.

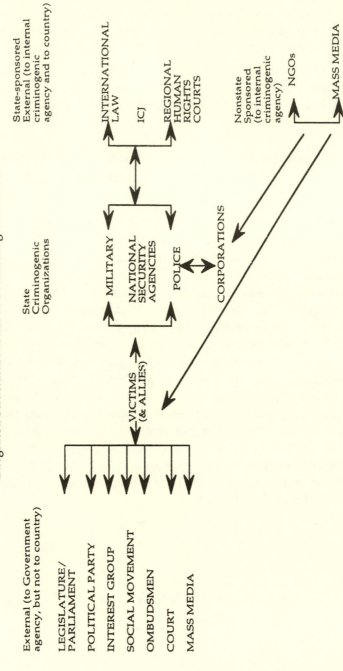

Figure 1
Integrated Structural Model of Controlling State Crime

State-sponsored
External (to internal
criminogenic
agency and to country)

State
Criminogenic
Organizations

INTERNATIONAL
LAW

ICJ

REGIONAL
HUMAN
RIGHTS
COURTS

MILITARY

NATIONAL
SECURITY
AGENCIES

POLICE

CORPORATIONS

Nonstate
Sponsored
(to internal
criminogenic
agency)

NGOs

MASS MEDIA

VICTIMS
(& ALLIES)

External (to Government
agency, but not to country)

LEGISLATURE/
PARLIAMENT

POLITICAL PARTY

INTEREST GROUP

SOCIAL MOVEMENT

OMBUDSMEN

COURT

MASS MEDIA

Causes and Perpetrators of State Crime

Introduction

At the core of each state are a number of powerful individuals and organizations capable of or actually engaging in a considerable and disproportionate amount of crime against their own citizens and external adversaries, sometimes as part of their policy and other times as a consequence of their mission. As Comfort (1950) has put it:

> Tolerated delinquents appear . . . at two distinct levels. They may enter and control the machinery of legislative and political power, as policy-makers and rulers. They may also be found, and tend in general to be more numerous, in the machinery of enforcement which intervenes between the policy-maker and the citizen. We owe our present recognition of the presence and the role of these tolerated delinquents, and of their capacity for mischief, to the rise of totalitarian states, but the reappearance of delinquency and military tyranny as socially accepted policies in civilized states has led, and must lead, to a scrutiny of similar mechanisms within the social democracies. (p. 13)

The principal state criminogenic actors who engage in state crime are the military, national security organizations, and various police agencies. While many excellent case studies on all of these institutions have been conducted, there is a dearth of academic literature analyzing how these institutions are controlled, who controls them, and the efficacy of these measures. Coterminously, this research is often ideographic, limited to one particular agency, country, or time period. Controlling these organizations, without frustrating their prosocial mission, is crucial in combatting state crime. Although there are general principles of control developed in the organizational theory, public administration, and public policy literature and sometimes used in practice, each type of organization demands special controls.

State Criminogenic Institutions and Processes

National security, the military, and police organizations, hereafter referred to as *state criminogenic organizations*, have been criticized for violating criminal laws as well as fundamental civil and human rights. Over the past three decades, national security agencies in many countries have broken the law or engaged in practices considered to be state crimes. Gill (this volume), for example, analyzes mechanisms that have recently been utilized to improve controls over national security in Anglo-American intelligence/national security agencies. His typology of "structural, legal, or institutional" controls and oversights on these organizations is broken down into levels, form of control, institutions of control, and institutions of oversight. In particular, he examines this process with respect to the Federal Bureau of Investigation, Canadian Security Intelligence Service, Australian Security Intelligence Organization, and MI-5 (Military Intelligence 5). He then reviews mechanisms of control that these organizations use, including how they define security threats, issues of recruitment, and publicity of violations of mandates.

Since the creation of the first army, concerned members of the public, politicians, and policymakers have witnessed, experienced, or chosen to address crimes committed by the military of various states. Ross (this volume) reviews, in general, various forms of violent and nonviolent actions and the more general violations of international law and war crimes. Several mechanisms have been advocated, many of which have been introduced, to control the armed forces and its ability to engage in these crimes. While many of these control mechanisms have been articulated before, no one has conceptualized them under the control of state crime literature. The chapter "Controlling Crimes by the Military" (Ross, this volume) provides a preliminary framework for this conceptualization.

A similar analysis is provided by Menzies (this volume), who argues that control of the police should concentrate on organizing them so that they "maintain a culture of 'responsible humanism' (i.e., "a culture that retains an awareness of the tension between the responsibility to the community and a humanistic concern for those who break the law)." To accomplish this goal both the police and the public must be educated "about the political dimension of policing"; the police must be rewarded "for citizen respecting actions"; "social jurors" must be created "to report regularly on the police"; and "political control of the police" must be divided among jurisdictions.

Most public educational systems and processes are tragically flawed and hence demand improvement. As Cabrera argues (this volume), our educational system reproduces the social order by reinforcing the meritocratic myth by appealing to an instrumentalist approach to literacy. The development of critical thinking is an important approach to controlling state crime. Building on the work of Freire, Giroux, and others, researchers suggest that critical literacy is one of the most effective ways of ending the "pedagogy of the oppressed" instituted by Western democracies as a means of controlling its citizens.

Another influential actor on state criminogenic organizations is large corporations. Corporations and states have created a liaison because they often pursue the same objectives and often engage in criminal actions to achieve mutual goals. Indisputably, this relationship should be controlled when it transgresses criminal laws. A number of practices, including boycotts, lobbying, and legal recourse, have been used by the public, interest groups, social movements, other corporations, and states, including regulatory bodies/agencies and advisory boards, to control such actions. The public and/or their representatives, through the use of these methods, can seek some retribution from state crimes caused or colluded by corporations.

There is considerable debate over which forms of control are better at restraining governmental organizations. Internal oversight and control have been criticized because they tend to protect the interests of the government. Undoubtedly, organizations in general have greater capacity than outsiders to supervise and control the behavior of subordinates. Grabosky argues that self-regulation is the mechanism by which organizations in the public sector maximize their autonomy. For example, employees may experience organizational pressure to identify and reveal unethical or illegal conduct (Grabosky, p.

308). The implementation of such mechanisms has the added advantage of increasing personnel "familiarity with the practices and procedures of the organization" (pp. 308–309). For Grabosky, internal organizational watchdog bodies can be both preventive and reactive. While reactive oversight bodies are utilized only "when they receive a complaint of alleged misconduct, preventive bodies can initiate investigations without just cause." A combination of reactive mobilization and preventive patrol is the more effective strategy of internal oversight bodies (p. 309).

The mere existence of internal control mechanisms, Kaufman (1973) argues, are necessary but insufficient to combat state crimes. Unless reinforced by independent external oversight bodies, internal control mechanisms are inefficient, can be co-opted, and can remain largely symbolic and hence lose credibility (p. 33). Moreover, lack of control or inadequate self-regulation make organizations vulnerable to outside attention. It follows then that the most effective organizational safeguards against state crimes are internal control mechanisms both reactive and preventive, that are subject to the scrutiny of external oversight bodies (Grabosky, 1989: 311).

Internal and external controls are implemented not only to prevent state criminogenic institutions from engaging in crimes, but also for organizational survival and public relations purposes.

Under internal institutional controls (IIC), the following propositions can be deduced:

> Proposition PIIC1: The greater the representation of various segments of society in state criminogenic institutions, the greater the control over the organization's state crimes.
> PIIC2: The greater the training in human rights and civil liberties that members of state criminogenic institutions receive, the greater the control over their ability to engage in state crimes.
> PIIC3: The greater the independence of internal oversight to line management, the greater the tendency to report directly to the chief executive, and the greater the control over state crime.

PIIC4: The stronger the supervision and leadership of state criminogenic organizations, the greater the control over their opportunity to engage in state crimes.

PIIC4A: The greater the internal supervision of state criminogenic organizations, the greater the control over their proclivity to engage in state crimes.

These general principles of internal control should be utilized by state organizations and victims in their attempt to control state crime or to set up external controlling organizations.

Victims' and Their Allies' Methods for Controlling State Crime

Introduction

The other side of the state crime equation is the manner in which outsiders, to state criminogenic organizations, have controlled this type of crime. State crimes have been committed against individuals, classes, groups, entire populations (i.e., racial, ethnic, and religious groups, etc.), and processes (i.e., the market, etc.).[11] Since government targets can be extensive, both a group and its actions (i.e., processes) can be targeted by state agencies. Grabosky (1989) argues that although government offenses, whether they are violations of democratic principles or mismanagement (i.e., waste and inefficiency in the expenditure of public funds), are offenses against all citizens. In many of the cases, the victims of official misconduct come from disadvantaged backgrounds (p. 284). His data suggest that, at least in Australia, the young, the poor and visible minorities are more likely than privileged people to be victims of state crime. The disadvantaged have fewer psychological, political, or financial resources "with which to defend themselves" than those of higher socioeconomic status (p. 285). The following section reviews the actions of many individuals and groups who, rather than remaining passive, have taken steps proactively and reactively to combat state crime.

Individuals and Classes

Traditionally, state crimes are committed by men against women. Feminist efforts, such as lobbying, protest, educational initiatives, and research, have influenced many states to take a more punitive approach to many of these crimes. Women's organizations and general public awareness of such crimes against women have made some progress, but not enough to identify and minimize such state misconduct. Nevertheless, empirical research demonstrates that various state agencies still fail to take appropriate actions to minimize domestic and sexual assault/abuse, underpaid work, and sexual harassment against women. It is clear that more effective legal and social reforms are needed to minimize state crimes against women in these contexts.

Other individuals and classes of victims (e.g., people with alternative life-styles; victims of war crimes; ethnic, racial, and religious groups; prisoners; etc.) have also utilized a number of methods to combat state crime. Some of these strategies include war crime tribunals and the enactment of hate crime legislation, methods that should also be examined and integrated into further iterations of the model.

Organizations and Processes

Alternatively, organizations and processes have been victims of state crimes. Tunnell (this volume) grapples with the problem of state crime against labor. He reviews typical public reactions to state crimes against labor and then presents a series of methods by which organized workers have countered this exploitation. According to Tunnell, some of the strategies used by labor include discontinuing state and province rights of corporate self-governance, the state resuming its role of caretaker rather than taskmaster, and a more proactive labor movement.

State crime against the environment is examined by Zilinskas (this volume). While waging war or pursuing a purported good (i.e., economic development) in times of peace, states often violate a collective good, namely the health of the environment (e.g., threatening biodiversity) to the detriment of the world's inhabitants. These actions are never branded as environmental or state crime. Zilinskas documents major incidents of state crimes against the environment and focuses on attempts to control this sort of abuse.

From the preceding discussion, and from research on group, social movement, interest group, and political party theory, one can discern a number of propositions connected to methods that individual victims (IVC) use to control state crime:

> Proposition PIVC1: The greater the number of victims (and their allies) affected, the greater the opportunity to control state criminogenic organizations and state crime.
>
> PIVC1A: The greater the power victims have, the greater the opportunity to control state criminogenic organizations and state crime.
>
> PIVC1B: The greater the resources victims have, the greater the ability to exert control over state criminogenic organizations and state crime.
>
> PIVC1C: The greater the organizational capabilities of victimized groups, the greater the control over state criminogenic organizations and state crime.
>
> PIVC1D: The better the communication between victims and internal and external control organizations, the greater the control over state criminogenic organizations and state crime.

Summary

Research on state crimes against individuals and classes of victims suggests that a number of other organizations and processes (e.g., political parties, social movements, interest groups, the arts, intellectual freedom, etc.) need to be examined. The inclusion of grievances from other victimized groups will give us a broader perspective on the victims of state crime and their attempts to overcome the incursion of state crime.

Organizational Controls

Introduction

While many organizations transcend state boundaries, controls that are instituted against the state generally can be found both inside the state and outside. The effectiveness of these controls is difficult to determine in light of government's self-preserving policies. Ultimately, most states want to preserve their integrity at home and in the international community, and try to utilize their internal organizations and structures for control before external ones get involved. Alternatively, they engage in public relations exercises.

Internal Controls: State Organizations and Processes

To address state crime, governments have at their disposal a number of mechanisms, external to state criminogenic actors, to influence reactively and in some cases control state crime. These processes are, from least to most important, in terms of their suitability and impact, freedom of information legislation, colored papers, advisory councils, royal and other types of commissions and inquiries, ombudsmen, and oversight and watchdog organizations.

Colored papers, advisory councils, task forces, commissions, and legislative committees provide the executive- and senior-level bureaucrats "with alternative sources of policy advice beyond that provided by public servants" (Kernaghan and Siegel, 1987: 231). "A common characteristic of all the[se] forms . . . is that they are more involved in consulting or researching than implementing or doing" (p. 23).

Governmental watchdog agencies exist in many countries and have similar functions. For example, ombudsmen "investigate citizens' complaints about improper, unfair, or discriminatory administrative treatment. . . . If he or she believes that certain complaints are justified, the public servants involved will be requested to remedy the mistakes." Typically, "the ombudsmen . . . present an annual report . . . describing the cases that have been dealt with by his or her office and the progress that has been made in redressing any administrative injustices" (p. 350).

Also, courts may use a number of common-law or ancillary remedies "after grounds for judicial review have been established" (p. 371). These are used "when no other form of relief is available, convenient or effective [and] include the prerogative remedies, namely certiorari, prohibition, mandamus, habeas corpus, and quo warranto, as well as the remedies of injunction, declaration and damages" (p. 371).

A number of propositions about state mechanisms involved in controlling state crime (SMC) summarize this discussion:

> Proposition PSMC1: The greater the autonomy of internal state controllers, the greater the control over state crime and state criminogenic organizations.
>
> PSMC2: The greater the number of internal state controllers, the greater the control over state crime and state criminogenic organizations.
>
> PSMC2A: The greater the number of internal state controllers with overlapping jurisdictions, the greater the control over state crime and state criminogenic organizations.
>
> PSMC3: The better the training of internal controllers, the better the control over state crime.
>
> PSMC4A: The greater the external supervision of state criminogenic organizations, the greater the control over their proclivity to engage in state crimes.
>
> PSMC4B: The greater the nongovernmental supervision of state criminogenic organizations, the greater the control over their proclivity to engage in state crimes.
>
> PSMC4C: The greater the multiparty supervision of state criminogenic organizations, the greater the control over their proclivity to engage in state crimes.
>
> PSMC5: The greater the number of state inquiries (regardless of the level of government) over state criminogenic organization activities, the greater the control over their proclivity to engage in state crimes.

PSMC6: Preventive and reactive controls are more effective than reactive controls on state crimes.

PSMC7: The greater the number of supervisory agencies over state criminogenic organizations, the greater the control.

External Controls: State-Sponsored and Private Organizations and Processes

The doctrine of *raison d'état* or sovereignty, holds that states are exempt from international intervention. It implies that governments are above the law because, by their very nature, they are lawmaking not lawbreaking institutions. However, many political philosophers have argued that states can be held responsible for their actions. To facilitate this process, politicians, policymakers, activists, and scholars have been instrumental in establishing international law and related organizations in order to monitor a series of state crimes. Several state-sponsored organizations as well as documents (e.g., UN resolutions) to control state crime have been created.

Despite recent developments encouraging identification and prosecution of state crimes under formal international law, Molina (this volume) argues, the likelihood of international prosecutorial regimes being created in the near future is nil. First, he argues that the most effective sanctions against offenders will emerge under the auspices of human rights regimes and initiatives. Molina demonstrates how the international legal system has not played any role in achieving "international condemnation of states allowing or promoting consensually reprehensible acts." Second, to overcome the definitional and practical problems embedded in a concept of state crime, including international enforcement, Molina outlines a philosophical explanation for the circumvention of these problems. Third, he describes "situations in which human rights procedures, not criminal proceedings, have effectively addressed normatively criminal acts by violative states." Finally, Molina "discuss[es] current formal, legal, and human rights–based international developments and instruments which may eventually form part of a comprehensive approach to curtail state actions which are both crimes and human rights violations."

It has been argued that regional human rights organizations and reports documenting human rights abuses are better able to have an influence over human rights violations than global ones (Akehurst, 1987). For example, Hurwitz (this volume) analyzes the European Convention on Human Rights as one of the principal international state-sponsored organizations to control state crime and offers a compelling argument:

> Even though several societies have made available domestic avenues of redress against state illegality . . . there still exists situations in which individuals have their civil-political human rights violated by state action and the domestic procedures are not able to validate the complaint.

Hurwitz reviews two cases that made their way to the European Court of Human Rights: *Ireland v. United Kingdom*, and *Denmark, Norway, Sweden and the Netherlands v. Greece*. Both cases had differential results in their ability to control state crime.

Yarnold (this volume), in "A New Role for the International Court of Justice: Adjudicator of International and State Transnational Crimes," suggests that states in the world community are prompted to circumvent international extradition procedures because of inadequate current extradition treaties. She buttresses her point by citing the 1960 kidnapping of Adolf Eichmann by Israeli security forces, the American invasion of Panama to capture Manuel Noriega, and the disguised extradition of Irish fugitives by the United States through the use of immigration procedures. She argues that "these extralegal extradition practices by states involve territorial violations of state sovereignty and violations of international treaty obligations. As such, they threaten the maintenance of world peace and security." These types of events, she argues, is reason enough to give authority to the International Court of Justice (ICJ) over the adjudication of international crimes and state transnational crimes (i.e., crimes in which a fugitive in one state flees to another state). She proposes a model for the adjudication of international and state transnational crimes by the ICJ. This model entails proposals for the substantive laws and procedures that would apply in such cases, the penalties that could be imposed by the ICJ, the creation of international juries and prisons, and other related matters.

Alternatively, a number of external nongovernmental agencies attempt to assist the process of resisting state crimes. Some of these include the human rights work of Amnesty International, the sanctions work of antiapartheid groups, the work of international lawyers, and divestment campaigns such as EIRES and others that use ethical investment. Other examples include the direct challenge by groups such as CAAT and the Omeaga Foundation that expose external agencies responsible for supporting tyrants with new technologies of repression.[13]

In "Eliminating State Crime by Abolishing the State," Martin (this volume) examines five possible visions of a world without states as well as methods for achieving these goals. Among the alternative visions he analyzes are communism, world government, small size, libertarianism, and anarchism. In each case, Martin discusses the likelihood of a particular goal and strategy to reduce or eliminate state crime. He concludes that abolishing the military should be the first step toward any of these objectives.

A number of propositions can be derived from the preceding discussion of international controls on state crime (ICSC):

> Proposition PICSC1: The greater the number of external controls, the greater the control over state criminogenic organizations and state crime.
>
> PICSC2: The greater the number of nation-states that participate in external control, the greater the control over state criminogenic organizations and state crime.
>
> PICSC3: The greater the number of private organizations that monitor state crimes, the greater the control.
>
> PICSC4: The greater the resources of external controllers, the greater the control over state crime.
>
> PICSC5: Regional external institutions control state crimes under their jurisdictions better than universal state organizations.

PICSC6: The greater the sanctioning power of external controls, the greater the control over state criminogenic organizations.

PICSC7: The better the communication among external controllers, the greater the control over state criminogenic organizations.

PICSC8: Nongovernmental organizations are more effective than nation-states at controlling state crimes in other countries.

Summary

To the already mentioned external processes for controlling state crime, others should be added. For example, the role of mass media and international organizations for press freedom, which has often been described as the fourth branch of government, can provide a forum for publicity of state crimes and ultimately another means to control state crime. Researchers must examine these other processes so that a comprehensive analysis of controlling state crime can be formulated. This analysis will help lay a foundation for more effective control of state crime.

The Future of Controlling State Crime: A Research Agenda

Causal modeling of the type developed here should be regarded as an iterative process. First-generation control models in a field of inquiry such as state crime, which is descriptively rich but analytically barren, will provide the foundation for future and more complex models. In order to make a preliminary test of the propositions of this model, researchers should choose a methodology that would allow for the comparative testing of these processes.

Future research on controlling state crime must build on previous efforts. In this chapter the author has identified topics that are lacking research. The next step is to individually examine the methods that private and government organizations have used to control state crime in different countries.[12]

An analysis of state crime in individual countries would provide a better contextual and more comprehensive approach to the subject of controlling state crime. Research of this nature represents the basis of all further theory development, testing, analysis, and, perhaps most important, policy formation and implementation. In short, this type of research should soon be recognized as an important building block in the emerging study of state crime and in the broader area of political crime.

Finally, as more evidence accrues on the subject of state crime, more-refined models may be constructed and hypotheses of those models can be tested. Increased shifting of governmental priorities in a rapidly changing world and an increase in rights-based ideology will provide added motivation to study and advocate solutions for controlling state crime well into the twenty-first century.

NOTES

* An earlier version of this chapter was presented at the Annual Meeting of the American Society of Criminology, New Orleans, November 5, 1992. Special thanks to Natasha J. Cabrera, Brian Martin, and anonymous internal reviewers for comments, and Paul Bond for research assistance.

1. See, for example, Becker and Murray (1971); Chambliss (1976); Clinard and Quinney (1978); Douglas and Johnson (1977); Lieberman (1972); Simon and Eitzen (1991).

2. In this context the state is not only the elected government; it also includes opposition members and those who work in and for the public administration.

3. For a review of Barak see Ross (1992).

4. It ignores torture and disappearance, and includes such processes as counterterrorism, secrecy, and destruction of "whole economies." Torture and disappearance can be subsumed under

behaviors that cause social injury. When practiced within the confines of most democratic and international laws, antiterrorism is perceived to be appropriate state behavior. If this is not the correct interpretation, it is unclear whether or not Barak is suggesting that all forms of response to oppositional terrorism constitute a crime by the state. Coterminously, given the reality of sovereignty and national security, most states, regardless of their ideological foundations or political-economic system, could not survive without some form of secrecy, espionage, and deception. The question is, at what point does it break a domestic law. And whole economies have been destroyed in the course of wars that have been deemed legitimate. Yet Barak does not entertain the possibility that dismantling the capitalist state, as well as the dire consequences of openness, would result from a government that has unlimited access to itself. In lacking clarity, his definition suggests that all government business decisions that lead to the decline of an economic sector are criminal acts. It is also somewhat redundant; murder, rape, burglary, illegal wiretap, illegal breakin, kidnapping, piracy, assassination, exporting arms illegally, obstruction of justice, perjury, fraud, and conspiracy (behaviors that Barak lists in his definition) can be subsumed under general violations of domestic laws.

5. An alternative, but complementary, distinction involves "political crimes against the state," "domestic political crimes by the state," and "international political crimes by the state" (Beirne and Messerschmidt, 1991: Chapter 8).

6. For a content analysis of the coverage of political crime by criminology and criminal justice texts see Tunnell (1993a).

7. Other problems include the following: first, the author's writing is pretentious, pompous, and longwinded (e.g., "It should, however, be clear that the fundamental criticism of modern society is its lack of organic growth, and the absence of scope for normal human biology and initiative") (p. 104). Second, many assertions are unsupported (e.g., "It is essentially the socially maladjusted civilian who is happiest in wartime—his problems are shelved") (p. 50). Third, he makes simplistic characterizations (e.g., "how much sexual content we find in these infantile attitudes will depend to some extent on our definition of sexuality" (p. 81). Fourth, the book is vague in its prescriptions (e.g., "Responsible sociology must recognize however, a sense of urgency"). Fifth, there is too much overgeneralization (e.g., "Psychiatry and social anthropology have not yet existed for a full century as independent disciplines. Within that independent . . . they have already brought about a greater revolution in human self consciousness than any other brand of discovery") (p. vii). Sixth, the

manuscript is sociological and social psychological centric (e.g., "If work of this kind is to continue it imposes a new type of obligation upon sociologists"). Finally, the author utilizes too many vague concepts (e.g., power).

    8. Grabosky (1989: 4) outlines a series of reasons why studying state crime is important that can be applied in this situation too, including "breaches of the law by governments can entail very great cost, in financial as well as in human terms"; "personal embarrassment" of elected officials and governments; violations of rights; and "attacks on the rule of law."

    9. According to Kernaghan and Siegel (1987: 253), "Application of this rule is evident in the innumerable instances in which administrative officials 'anticipate the reactions' of those who have power to reward or constrain them. Officials tend to act in a fashion that would be applauded—or at least approved—by those whose favour they seek."

    10. Many of these propositions are derived from Sherman (1978: 14).

    11. Grabosky identifies aboriginal peoples, criminal defendants, and ordinary Australians.

    12. A similar process was established with Stohl and Lopez (1984).

    13. Personal communication with Steve Wright, December 1990.

BIBLIOGRAPHY

Akehurst, Michael (1987) *A Modern Introduction to International Law.* London: Unwin Hyman.

Aulette, Judy Root, and Raymond Michalowski (1993) "Fire in Hamlet: A Case Study of a State-Corporate Crime," in Kenneth D. Tunnell (ed.), *Political Crime in Contemporary America*. New York: Garland Publishing, pp. 171–206.

Barak, Gregg (1990) "Crime, Criminology and Human Rights: Towards an Understanding of State Criminality," *Journal of Human Justice* 2, 1 (Autumn): 11–28.

————. ed. (1991) *Crimes by the Capitalist State: An Introduction to State Criminality.* Albany: State University of New York Press.

Bassiouni, M. Cherif, ed. (1975) *International Terrorism and Political Crimes*. Springfield, IL: Charles C. Thomas.

Becker, Theodore, and Vernon Murray, eds. (1971) *Governmental Lawlessness in America*. New York: Oxford University Press.

Beirne, Piers, and James Messerschmidt (1991) *Criminology*. Toronto: Harcourt, Brace, Jovanovich.

Berkman, Alexander (1971) *ABC of Anarchism*. London: Freedom Press.

Bohm, Robert (1993) "Social Relationships That Arguably Should Be Criminal Although They Are Not: On the Political Economy of Crime," in Kenneth D. Tunnell (ed.), *Political Crime in Contemporary America*. New York: Garland Publishing, pp. 3–29.

Caufield, Susan L., and Nancy Wonders (1993) "Personal and Political: Violence Against Women and the Role of the State," in Kenneth D. Tunnell (ed.), *Political Crime in Contemporary America*. New York: Garland Publishing, pp. 79–100.

Chambliss, William J. (1976) "The State and Criminal Law," in William J. Chambliss and M. Mankoff (eds.), *Whose Law, What Order?* New York: Wiley, pp. 66–106.

Clinard, Marshall, and Richard Quinney (1978) "Crime by Government," in David Ermann and Richard Lundman (eds.), *Corporate and Governmental Deviance*. New York: Oxford University Press, pp. 137–150.

Comfort, Alex (1950) *Authority and Delinquency in the Modern State*. London: Routledge and Kegan Paul.

De Bonno, Edward (1979) *Future Positive*. New York: Penguin.

Douglas, J., and J.M. Johnson, eds. (1977) *Official Deviance*. Philadelphia: Lippincott.

Grabosky, Peter N. (1989) *Wayward Governance: Illegality and Its Control in the Public Sector*. Canberra: Australian Institute of Criminology.

Gurr, Ted Robert (1988) "War, Revolution and the Growth of the Coercive State," *Comparative Political Studies* 21, 1: 45–65.

Hagan, Frank (1990) *Introduction to Criminology*. Chicago: Nelson Hall.

Harff, Barbara and Ted Robert Gurr (1988) "Toward Empirical Theory of Genocides and Politicides: Identification and Measurement of Cases Since 1945," *International Studies Quarterly* 32: 359–371.

Henry, Stuart (1991) "The Informal Economy: A Crime of Omission by the State," in Gregg Barak (ed.), *Crimes by the Capitalist State*. Albany: State University of New York Press, pp. 253–272.

Human Rights Watch (1992) *Human Rights Watch World Report, 1993*. New York: Human Rights Watch.

Hurwitz, Leon (1981) *The State as Defendant*. Westport, CT: Greenwood Press.

Ingraham, Barton L. (1979) *Political Crime in Europe*. Berkeley: University of California Press.

Kaufman, Herbert (1973) *Administrative Feedback*. Washington, DC: Brookings Institution.

Kelman, Herbert C., and V. Lee Hamilton. 1989. *Crimes of Obedience*. New Haven, CT: Yale University Press.

Kernaghan, Kenneth, and David Siegel (1987) *Public Administration in Canada*. Toronto: Methuen.

Klitgaard, Robert (1988) *Controlling Corruption*. Berkeley: University of California Press.

Kuper, Leo (1985) *The Prevention of Genocide*. New Haven, CT: Yale University Press.

Lieberman, Jethro (1972) *How the Government Breaks the Law*. Baltimore: Penguin.

Pepinsky, Harold E. (1980) *Crime Control Strategies*. New York: Oxford University Press.

Proal, Louis (1898/1973) *Political Crime*. Montclair, NJ: Patterson Smith.

Roebuck, Julian, and Stanley C. Weeber (1978) *Political Crime in the United States*. New York: Praeger.

Ross, Jeffrey Ian (1992) Review of Gregg Barak, *Crimes by the Capitalist State. Justice Quarterly* 9, 2 (June): 347–354.

Schafer, Stephen (1974) *The Political Criminal*. New York: Free Press.

Sherman, Lawrence (1978) *Scandal and Reform*. Berkeley: University of California Press.

Simon, David R., and D. Stanley Eitzen. (1991) *Elite Deviance*, 3rd ed. Boston: Allyn and Bacon.

Sink, John M. (1974) *Political Trials: How to Defend Them*. New York: Clark, Boardman Co.

Stohl, Michael, and George Lopez, eds. (1984) *The State as Terrorist: The Dynamics of Governmental Violence and Repression*. Westport, CT: Greenwood Press.

Stunton, Marie, Sally Fenn, and Amnesty International (1991) *The Amnesty International Handbook*. Claremont, CA: Hunter House.

Tilly, Charles (1985) "War Making and State Making as Organized Crime," in Peter B. Evans, Dietrich Rueschemeyer, and Theda Skocpol (eds.), *Bringing the State Back In*. Cambridge, Eng.: Cambridge University Press, pp. 169–191.

Tunnell, Kenneth D. (1993a) "Political Crime and Pedagogy: A Content Analysis of Criminology and Criminal Justice Texts." *Journal of Criminal Justice Education* 4, 1 (Spring): 101–114.

————, ed. (1993b) *Political Crime in Contemporary America*. New York: Garland Publishing.

Turk, Austin T. (1982) *Political Criminality*. Beverly Hills, CA: Sage.

Walker, Samuel (1985) *Sense and Nonsense about Crime: A Policy Guide*. Monterey, CA: Brooks/Cole.

Wilson, James Q., and Patricia Rachel (1977) "Can the Government Regulate Itself." *The Public Interest* 46: 3–14.

World Watch (1992) *Human Rights Watch World Report, 1993*. New York: Human Rights Watch.

A State Action May Be Nasty But Is Not Likely to Be a Crime

Ira Sharkansky

There is no doubt that some state officials act in ways that are illegal and/or distasteful to domestic and foreign observers. Yet there are no clear linkages between terms like *distasteful* or *nasty* on the one hand and *criminal* or *illegal* on the other. Not all official actions that are distasteful are illegal, and not all that is illegal is distasteful. Moreover, some actions committed by state officials are clearly not those of the state. Some violations of the laws by state officials are the rogue actions of individuals at the bottom of administrative hierarchies. Others may not be officially declared as policy, but may be perceived as having at least the tacit encouragement of policymakers.

Illegal actions by officials range from the prosaic and harmless, through a wide spectrum of actions that are intermediate in the controversies they provoke, to those that are truly nasty. At the prosaic end are traffic officers who allow drivers to exceed the speed limit or park in prohibited zones. In the middle range are environmental control agencies that permit industries to exceed legal standards of pollution, perhaps to allow a marginally profitable concern to remain open in a region already beset with high unemployment. At the nasty extreme are security agencies that liquidate individuals viewed as undesirable.

This chapter asks if there is anything to the concept of state crime beyond citing states for doing nasty things. It concludes that it is better to avoid the label of state crime or its close relations (e.g., government crime) and to stay with the simpler and more useful terms of nasty actions and their numerous synonyms.

Two primary reasons lead to the conclusion that state crime is not a useful concept. First, the state itself controls the definition of what is criminal (Molina, this volume). The state can indicate either explicitly or implicitly that actions of its servants are legal or acceptable exceptions from normal behavior or the unsanctioned actions of individual officials who will be disciplined. Second, academic practitioners in the field of state crime have gone to such extremes in their usage as to deprive the term of any significance. *Crime* implies an action that invites an authoritative response. However, many activities described by the label of *state crime* in the literature are not appropriate to such expectations. They include detentions, searches of property and persons, censorship, and physical and psychological pressures that state critics may call criminal but which the laws of the state permit its authorities. Therefore, it seems better to use one of the other condemnatory adjectives for actions or inactions that are deemed highly undesirable. The list includes such terms as abominable, appalling, atrocious, bad, beastly, cruel, deplorable, despicable, disagreeable, disgraceful, disgusting, dreadful, foul, hateful, horrible, ignoble, immoral, improper, insufferable, lamentable, loathsome, malicious, mean, nasty, odious, obnoxious, offensive, painful, repellent, reprehensible, repugnant, repulsive, rueful, shameful, shameless, terrible, ugly, vicious, vile, and villainous.

The Power of the State

Its power usually excuses the state from the label of criminal. Classical conceptions of the state give it the authority to define what is legal within its borders and a monopoly of physical force to enforce its laws and protect its existence (Lindsay, 1943: Chapter 8). Violence is part of stateness. Its practice is likely to be ugly and to attract condemnation from some observers. Von

Clausewitz's epigram that war is "a political instrument, a continuation of political commerce, a carrying out of the same by other means" suggests that violence occurs when the usual conduct of politics, diplomacy, or public administration does not achieve results that are acceptable to the participants (1832/1968: 119). Even in enlightened democracies violence is likely to be somewhere, to be used against citizens who will not pay their taxes or obey other rules voluntarily. When authorities feel themselves pressed, they may suspend certain laws under provisions of emergency legislation. In the absence of emergency provisions, officials may declare that the protection of the state or its residents justifies unusual actions.

There is no simple correspondence between the terms *state actions* and *lawfulness*. State officials do not enforce every detail of their states' laws. Implementation is a lively area in the social sciences. Academic researchers warn that programs are administered imperfectly and sometimes in ways that contrast with explicit law or policy (Mazmanian and Sabatier, 1983). Problems of implementation are likely to include insufficient resources, poorly designed programs, or insensitive authorities (Mazmanian and Sabatier, 1983). Such issues are more political or administrative than criminal, to be repaired by additional money, legislation, or rule-making, or to lose out in the ongoing competition for policymakers' commitments. Where individual administrators are accused of corruption or malfeasance, or where citizens demand compensation for officials' actions or inactions, the issues are judged in state courts, according to the judges' reading of state law and the relevant facts.

It has been known at least since biblical times that some proceedings of these kinds are corrupt. Two passages from the Hebrew Bible are:

> You shall not be led into wrongdoing by the majority, nor, when you give evidence in a lawsuit, shall you side with the majority to pervert justice. (Exodus 23:2)

> If you witness in some province the oppression of the poor and the denial of right and justice, do not be surprised at what goes on. (Ecclesiastes 5:8)

To use another phrase from the Book of Ecclesiastes, there is nothing new under the sun if it is found that some employees of the state are criminals.

When officials are prosecuted and punished for misconduct, the punishment is likely to seem lenient to some observers. But if the punishment is carried out by administrative superiors or judicial authorities, the leniency may not be illegal in a technical sense. If the punishment of errant officials is only symbolic, then it may be the case that state officials view the action as only a symbolic violation of the laws. Critics of the state may use the word *crime* for what has transpired. Authors of the Bible used the term *abomination* for the activities of some kings, as in the case of Manasseh (II Kings 21:2). According to a rabbinical tale, the king had the prophet Isaiah sawn in two because of the prophet's criticism (Urbach, 1987: 559). The widespread and highly placed origin of the loathsome actions suggest that they were not the isolated activities of errant officials. Manasseh's critics might have thought him guilty of state crime. Even in such cases, however, the label of state crime seems likely to begin arguments between state officials and their supporters on the one side and critics on the other side, and not to produce judicial proceedings appropriate to a crime.

To be sure, even the issue of state crime may be subject to change. International forums have worked to expand the concepts of law and rights. World and regional bodies make proclamations and enact legislation for states. The United Nations 1948 Universal Declaration of Human Rights has been incorporated into numerous other enactments by international and state bodies. International courts adjudicate between contending parties. International citizen groups lobby in national and international forums in order to expand the corpus of law and bring censure or punishment to bear on offenders (Cingranelli, 1988; Hevener, 1981; Vincent, 1986). However, the bulk of enactments must be implemented by states in order to have force. The governments of some countries that are targeted for censure or punishment have had considerable success in making the case to their own populations that those actions of foreign organizations should not be accorded the status of legitimacy. Israel, for example, has denounced a number of enactments directed against it by the United Nations General Assembly or UN affiliated bodies, like UNESCO, on the ground that the international bodies are chronically biased against Israel or are moved to act by temporary majorities of hostile forces.

The legal definition of a crime and the incidence of prosecutions varies from place to place and from one period to another within states or locales (Weisser, 1979). Scholars have found no action that is universally deemed to be criminal. Gurr et al. demonstrate in their comparative study of crime that even murder is hedged by the concepts of killing, manslaughter, wrongful death, self-defense, and justifiable homicide. What is prosecuted as homicide in one locale may be similar to what is treated as a lesser offense, or no offense at all, elsewhere (1977: 15). There is little doubt that political considerations influence what is considered criminal, and what ought to be prosecuted. It is difficult to escape the conclusion that class interests are among the factors that influence definitions and judgments about crime and the punishments that are appropriate for various transgressions and transgressors (Foucault, 1979; Turk, 1982). The color and the culture of the perpetrator are likely to affect authorities' responses to behavior. Classic is the epigram that the person who steals a goose from the common in order to obtain food is hung as a thief, while the person who establishes a family fortune by stealing the common from under the geese is honored as an aristocrat.

A number of scholars have sought to define the concept of state crime, but the issue is especially sticky (Barak, 1991a; Friedrichs, this volume; Henry, 1991; Menzies, this volume). Scholars have produced a boundless array of actions that might be labeled as state crimes, but the term has been so broadened as to render it just another epithet for *undesirable activities.*

Barak and Henry are prominent among those guilty of this intellectual transgression. Barak extends the concept of state crime to states whose eighteenth-century practices of slavery and other oppressions violated what were later viewed as fundamental human rights (Barak, 1991b: 9). Henry develops the concept of a state crime of omission to the point that a state's failure to assure adequate resources, housing, and other services is held responsible for pushing certain citizens to crimes against one another and against property. Henry goes even further to condemn policies of progressive taxation by virtue of their providing taxpayers a sense of legitimacy for the possession of after-tax resources, which they might use for socially undesirable activities (1991: 257). By Henry's standard of unintended but undesirable consequences, there hardly seems anything that could not be labeled a state crime. Henry thereby assures that whatever legitimacy the concept might have has disappeared into the netherworld, where there are no boundaries. If everything can be a state crime, then nothing is a state crime.

Hurwitz (this volume) makes a valiant and technically successful effort to rescue the concept of state crime from the likes of Barak and Henry. As Hurwitz concedes, however, the provisions for holding a state responsible for its own lawbreaking are difficult in the extreme for a plaintiff to master. Moreover, they have been implemented by only a tiny number of petitioners against a small and unrepresentative sample of the world's states. Molina (this volume) is more explicit in taking a limited view of state crime. He refers to the concept as "almost, but not quite, an oxymoron, a legal absurdity." Like Hurwitz, he finds only a limited number of cases, with unusual traits, where state authorities have conceded that actions of their state have been illegal.

The chapter by Martin, in this volume, is bold and pessimistic. He writes that crime may be so integral to stateness as to warrant the consideration of the radical alternative of abolishing the state. The chapters by Gill, Yarnold, and Zilinskas are modest in assessing particularistic instrumental reforms designed to expose or contain certain kinds of state activities. Their ideas may be useful against certain of the nasty things that some states do, while allowing us to avoid the argument as to whether they are crimes per se.

The problematic definition of state crime renders it open to exploitation by policymakers. Often it seems little more than an epithet to be used against international rivals. Critics of the Jimmy Carter administration have written that the President "stumbled across the human rights theme on his way to the

White House" (Falk, 1981). They describe the concern of that administration for the crimes of other states with terms like *pious posturing, cynical resignation, naive optimism* (Hevener, 1981: Introduction), *opportunistic* (Falk, 1981), *crabbed*, and *clumsy* (Borosage, 1981). A favorable review of U.S. foreign policy against state crime concludes that actions have been taken against states that violate human rights when there is a clear pattern of consistent offenses, which implies governmental complicity or tacit consent; when there are no local remedies available to those who suffer; and when state actions are "gross" (Hevener, 1981). A more cynical conclusion is that current political interests of the White House prevail over the conclusions of professionals in the U.S. State Department unit concerned with analyzing human rights and influence the formal evaluations that are announced each year for the countries under review.

The Israeli Case

Perhaps the problematic issues of state crime are best illustrated in the context of Israel, a country that aspires to the highest norms of morality yet faces vexing problems at the interface of self-defense and the use of force. While similar analysis might be offered for the problems of other states with chronic problems of terrorist attacks against civilian targets (Zuckerman, 1989), the Israeli case is most familiar to the author. There is no intention here to justify or condemn. As in other sections of this chapter, the emphasis is on the problems involved in the concept of state crime, as they are apparent in the difficult conditions faced at several layers of the Israeli state.

Israel has been accused of state crimes or related sins for the illegal occupation of territory, the repression of a conquered population, illegal detentions, torture, censoring the media, and piracy (Barak, 1991b; Georges-Abeyie, 1991). Israeli officials explain their actions as legitimate self-defense that falls within Israeli law or Israeli interpretations of international law. They admit that some officers exceed Israeli norms, but assert that such actions are subject to investigation and discipline according to Israeli law (O'Brien, 1991).

The background is well known, emotional, and relevant to the judgment of state crime. Much of the country's political elite matured during a period when German authorities embarked on a campaign to liquidate the Jewish people, and succeeded in killing some 40 percent of the world's Jews. Other advanced societies refused to accept more than a symbolic number of European Jews who sought refuge or to act directly against the genocide, even to the extent of bombing the death camps or the railroads leading to them (Abella and Troper, 1983). Such bombing was requested by Jewish leaders as a way of disturbing the industrialized transport and killing even if some Jews already on the railroads or in the camps would die in the process. The Allies consistently rejected the request, citing their priorities for more important targets. The establishment of the Israeli state in 1948 was the culmination of a Zionist movement that identified a Jewish state as essential for the protection of a people that had long suffered from being stateless. The presence of Holocaust memorials in numerous Western capitals does not erase the feeling among numerous Israelis that they have no allies who are truly reliable.

The Jewish state is powerful. Its budget, plus those of quasi–governmental entities, account for a higher proportion of the economic resources within its border than in almost any other Western democracy (Sharkansky, 1987). Its security forces are strong, and the state has legal advantages in dealing with individuals accused of wrongdoing (Hofnung, 1991). All of this owes much to the people's concern to protect themselves with a strong state. It also reflects something about the origins of most state founders in central and eastern Europe, where states are stronger than in the Anglo-Saxon tradition (Horowitz and Lissak, 1978).

The feeling of catastrophic threat is reinforced by a struggle that has been with Israel since its independence. Only in 1977 did Egypt become the first Arab state to renounce a policy of liquidating Israel. In light of the 1993 accord between Israel and the Palestine Liberation Organization (PLO) that commits the parties to work out their conflicts in peaceful negotiations, Israel finally may be entering a period of genuine peace with its neighbors. However, many Israelis look at their history and ask if the PLO is sincere and if Israel can control groups of Palestinians and other Arabs intent on scuttling the peace process through continued violence.

Israel is a feisty democracy that aspires to the highest norms of morality. Its elites concede their imperfections and worry publicly about their aspirations and practices in the face of vexatious conditions. The prestige of regime critics recalls the prophet Jeremiah (Sharkansky, 1991: Chapter 4). When some wanted to kill him for opposing the foreign policy of his regime and urging Jerusalem's soldiers to desert their posts in the face of the besieging Babylonians, the king provided him refuge in the palace (Jer. 38:10–16). Jeremiah's antiregime sentiments, plus those of other prophets, earned a revered place in the Hebrew Bible.

Israel's state comptroller is empowered to criticize governmental activity not only with respect to the conventional criteria of "economy, effectiveness, and efficiency," but also with regard to the open-ended criteria of "moral integrity." The state comptroller has criticized the police for excessive use of force and for detentions that violate what the comptroller has viewed as elementary human rights (State Comptroller, 1985: 435–457).

Prominent Israelis criticize the quality of their polity, especially the extent to which a self-described "Jewish state" limits opportunities for its non-Jewish citizens (Yaniv, 1993). Yehoshafat Harkabi is a former head of military intelligence and professor of international relations at the Hebrew University of Jerusalem who received a prestigious Israel Prize in 1993 from the Ministry of Education and Culture. Much of Harkabi's recent work has been historical and contemporary analysis that predicted disaster, perhaps even the destruction of the Jewish people, if there would not be a change in policy with respect to the territories occupied in 1967 and a willingness to negotiate with the PLO (Harkabi, 1983; 1988). Yeshayahu Leibowitz is an elderly religious Jew who was also designated a winner of the Israel Prize in 1993. He declined the award when his designation generated a wave of condemnation. Much of the commotion was directed at Leibowitz's use of the term *Nazi* to describe Israel's actions (Leibowitz, 1988). For a society built on the ashes of the Holocaust, that defined an outer limit of what is acceptable. The commotion was not directed at silencing Leibowitz's severe criticism of the state, but at giving an award to a critic whose use of adjectives was offensive and seemed unjustified to a population whose members had suffered at the hands of the real Nazis.

Israel has a formal policy to use only the degree of force that is appropriate in protecting the state and its citizens. Security forces conduct active programs of education among their personnel with respect to the norms of democracy and human rights, supervise their personnel, and hold individuals responsible for actions that violate the formal norms. The security forces examine and revise their orders with respect to the use of force, sometimes in direct response to episodes when the force seems to have been unnecessarily harsh. Israeli as well as foreign critics have charged that state supervision of the security forces, and punishments meted out to wayward members of the forces have not been sufficiently severe. Shulamit Aloni, the leader of a left-of-center political party and a minister in the governing coalition, was quoted on Israeli radio (July 8, 1993) as asking at a party gathering, "How many children does the army have to kill in order to capture one suspect?" Others have said that the punishments for the excessive use of force are too severe and do not take account of the problems of functioning in a security role under pressure. The plight of the individual soldier was captured by a newspaper cartoon that showed a hapless recruit facing an oncoming crowd of stone-throwers and leafing through his rule book to learn when he was allowed to open fire. Moreover, special commissions of inquiry have judged and censured ranking policymakers for their actions. Most prominent was the Kahan Commission that resulted in the resignation of Minister of Defense Ariel Sharon after the massacres in Sabra and Shatila while the Israeli army occupied Beirut in 1982.

The Jewish population of Israel supports its security forces. Young men aspire to join elite units that win media attention for heroic efforts and high rates of casualties. Yet the society is not militaristic in the sense of enforcing a narrow conception of security or lionizing a military point of view. Upon their retirement from the military, prominent generals are recruited as political candidates by left- as well as right-wing political parties. Some have been prominent in urging far-reaching concessions to Israel's adversaries (Horowitz, 1982).

High on the list of prestige military units during 1992–1993 were those that worked in the occupied territories disguised as Arabs. They attracted publicity for their record in seizing or killing Palestinians sought for killing Jews or other Palestinians. These units have a higher than average rate of casualties, with at least some of them inflicted by friendly fire. This is due, in part, to the fact that the participants are all dressed as Arabs and that much of their activity takes place at night. There have been more volunteers for these units than the army can accept. High school students from well-heeled families pay to join pre-army private training groups that promise to improve their chances to pass the physical and psychological tests used to select candidates. Some critics accuse the units of being liquidation squads. The Israeli Defense Force asserts that they operate by the same rules as other units as to when they are allowed to open fire and has brought charges against some personnel of these units for the excessive use of force. Critics of another kind accuse the military of being too selective in choosing candidates for these units. These critics feel that only well-educated youths or those able to afford the pre-army training courses can pass the tests for acceptance, and they want a chance for themselves or their children to participate. In a society that is preoccupied with security and considers itself egalitarian and democratic, a demand for equal opportunity to risk oneself in national defense is an issue likely to attract attention. The chief of the general staff addressed this concern when he appeared on television to assure parents that applicants to these units could be selected even if they did not undergo private premilitary training. Although some might accuse the units of state crime, the official nature of their activity as well as the widespread public support would seem to neutralize the accusation.

The work of a commission of inquiry (Landau Commission) is symptomatic of the security problems facing Israel, the subtleties with which policymakers attempt to deal, and their inability to satisfy all critics. The Commission, headed by retired Justice Moshe Landau of the Israeli Supreme Court, was appointed by the cabinet in 1987 to inquire into the investigative methods of the Israeli General Security Service. Ranking members of the service had been accused of lying to a judicial inquiry about the use of physical pressure to extract confessions.

The *Report* of the Landau Commission accepts the need for the protection of the state against those who would destroy it (*Israel Law Review*, 1989: 173). It sanctions the "use of moderate physical pressure" in interrogations, which it defends with principles of necessity and the balance of evils:

> A person may be exempted from criminal responsibility for an act . . . provided that he did no more than was reasonably necessary for that purpose and that the harm caused by him was not disproportionate to the harm avoided. (*Israel Law Review*, 1989: 169; see also Hofnung, 1991: 270)

Torture is widely held to be outside the pale of actions that are morally defensible. Yet the concept is not without its problems. A dictionary definition is "the infliction of severe physical pain as a means of punishment or coercion" (*American Heritage Dictionary*, 1986). But how much is severe? May not some degree of pain be administered when a detainee is thought to have information of life and death character? What about a captured terrorist who will not reveal if there is another bomb hidden in a crowded place? The Landau Commission was not so daring as to deal with the concept of torture head-on, but it sought to define acceptable pressure. It identified five general principles for its sanction of moderate physical pressure. Note the avoidance of the concept of torture per se:

1. Disproportionate pressure is inadmissible and should never reach a level of physical torture, grievous harm to the subject's honor or deprivation of human dignity.
2. Officials must consider the use of less serious measures.
3. Physical and psychological means of pressure must be defined and limited in advance by binding directives.
4. There must be strict supervision of interrogators.
5. Superiors must react swiftly and firmly against deviations from what is permissible. (*Israel Law Review*, 1989: 175)

The Commission admitted to going beyond what U.S. courts grant in the administration of justice. It notes that Israeli law allows the prosecution to submit some information to the judges (there are no juries in Israeli trials) that is kept secret from the defendant and his/her attorneys and that Israeli courts admit the use of evidence that U.S. courts would exclude as tainted as a result of improper police behavior.

The Commission also justified keeping secret certain sections of its *Report*, in order to aid the state in combating those who would destroy it. These include specification of the degree of physical pressure allowed, the conditions under which it is permitted, and procedures for supervising interrogating officers.

The tendency to sharp criticism within Israel's elite has not spared the *Report* of the Landau Commission. When Itzhak Zamir was attorney general (the state's chief legal officer, responsible to the Cabinet), he challenged the handling of the charges against the Israeli General Security Service and was forced to resign during the developments that led up to the appointment of the Landau Commission. He returned to his position as professor of law at the Hebrew University and later contributed an essay to a volume of the *Israel Law Review* dedicated to the *Report* of the Landau Commission. Like a number of other commentators, Zamir avoided simplistic condemnation or praise. He asserted that there is an ongoing conflict between issues of national security and human rights that is impossible to resolve with simple legal formulations (Zamir, 1989).

Another contributor to the *Israel Law Review* praised the Israeli government for dealing with "issues that virtually every government confronts, but almost no government discusses officially and openly" (Dershowitz, 1989). Some commentators made the point that it was not only a question of moderate pressure in the face of severe danger (e.g., slapping a suspect's face against the possibility of saving civilians from a terrorist's attack) and doubted that a policy of moderate physical pressure could coexist with human rights they would identify with a truly enlightened country. One writer called the Commission's conclusions "the most lawless of legal doctrines." He conceded that there are instances that would justify extraordinary means, but is convinced that they are less frequent than security officials contend (Dershowitz, 1989). Another worried that the dynamics of a campaign against terror and other police actions would produce an escalation upward from moderate physical pressure (Kremnitzer, 1989). Torture during an investigation also leaves the courts unable to evaluate the truth of a confession (Zuckerman, 1989). Another commentator concluded that the moral ban against torture disappears for those who cause the need for physical pressure by planting bombs that must be located and disarmed. However, he would extend the doctrine of moderate physical pressure only to cases of imminent harm and not to cases where security forces sought to obtain convictions (Moore, 1989).

Several experts admitted their ambivalence. One wrote about "a search for the impossible," and conceded that dirty work is required for the protection of a society that does not lend itself to clear definitions of right and wrong (Zuckerman, 1989). Another wrote that there was a "smell of hypocrisy" about the principles that he articulated, but saw them as integral to the difficult balancing of contending norms. He would accept the morality of cruel practices under extraordinary circumstances but would not give them the protection of explicit law. In his view, this subtle distinction would require the justification of individual cases that present the need for extraordinary action and tilt the game against those who would too easily engage in cruel practices (Kadish, 1989).

The Landau Commission's standard of moderate physical pressure has continued to trouble Israel's political establishment. As the final version of this chapter was being prepared in 1993, the policy came under attack by prominent members of centrist as well as left-wing parties. The head of the governing body for Israeli physicians indicated that he would bring charges for violating professional ethics against physicians who facilitated the application of the policy by the Israeli General Security Services. Then there was a bus hijacking in Jerusalem that resulted in the death of two hostages. The event seemed to be the work of a Moslem fundamentalist organization opposed to the peace talks between Israel, the Palestinians, and Arab governments. The topic of the Landau Commission left the agenda of the mass media. It remained unclear how the policy of moderate physical pressure would play itself out against the continued reminder of a security threat.

The Individual's Refuge

The point of this chapter is not the quality of justice shown by policies or practices in Israel or elsewhere, but the quality of the concept, *state crime*. The discussion of the Israeli case is relevant to this topic insofar as it shows the legality, within Israel, of actions that local and foreign critics call criminal, and the knotty problems of balancing the evils of nasty things done by a state in self-defense and in defense of its population, against the nasty things done by enemies of the state.

States do undesirable things. Many perform actions that are nastier than those of Israel and are unrestrained by open debates about what is necessary or moral. However, much of what is undesirable in the actions of any state falls within the range of what the state's laws permit, or what state officials justify as forms of defense against conditions that are even less desirable. To be sure, there are cases when state nastiness seems designed only to support the current regime or its officeholders. Individual citizens who care about such things will seek to avoid contamination from excessive nastiness, either as one of the functionaries who carry out the activities or as a target of them.

An outsider should be wary of recommending that insiders engage in heroic opposition to a regime that seems nasty but is well entrenched. It is admirable to suffer for justice, but in a just world there is no obligation to volunteer for harm or commit suicide. Moreover, many insiders are likely to tolerate or even justify what outsiders consider to be criminal. The freedom to criticize may be the elementary feature of a state that is not criminal in its essence. Where criticism is feasible, however, it does not add much to call an action a crime if it is not a violation of laws as generally implemented by the state in question. Other adjectives are equally powerful and save the critic the charge of implying a judicial remedy where none is likely to be available.

REFERENCES

Abella, Irving, and Harold Troper (1983) *None Is Too Many: Canada and the Jews of Europe, 1933–1948*. New York: Random House.

American Heritage Dictionary (1986) Boston: Houghton Mifflin.

Barak, Gregg (1991a) *Crimes by the Capitalist State: An Introduction to State Criminality*. Albany: State University of New York Press.

———— (1991b) "Toward a Criminology of State Criminality," in Gregg Barak (ed.), *Crimes by the Capitalist State: An Introduction to State Criminality*. Albany: State University of New York Press, pp. 3–16.

Borosage, Robert L. (1981) "Domestic Consequences of United States Human Rights Policies," in Natalie Kaufman Hevener, *The Dynamics of Human Rights in U.S. Foreign Policy*. New Brunswick, NJ: Transaction Books, pp. 53–62.

Cingranelli, David Louis (1988) *Human Rights: Theory and Measurement*. New York: St. Martin's Press.

Davies, Peter (1988) *Human Rights*. London: Routledge.

Dershowitz, Alan M. (1989) "Is It Necessary to Apply 'Physical Pressure' to Terrorists and to Lie About It?" *Israel Law Review* 23, 2–3: 192–200.

Falk, Richard A. (1981) "Ideological Patterns in the United States Human Rights Debate: 1945–1978," in Natalie Kaufman Hevener, *The Dynamics of Human Rights in U.S. Foreign Policy*. New Brunswick, NJ: Transaction Books, pp. 29–52.

Foucault, Michel. (1979) *Discipline and Punish: The Birth of the Prison*. Translated by Alan Sheridan. New York: Vintage Books.

Georges-Abeyie, Daniel E. (1991) "Piracy, Air Piracy, and Recurrent U.S. and Israeli Civilian Aircraft Interceptions," in Gregg Barak (ed.), *Crimes by the Capitalist State: An Introduction to State Criminality*. Albany: State University of New York Press, pp. 129–144.

Gurr, Ted Robert, Peter N. Grabosky, and Richard C. Hula (1977) *The Politics of Crime and Conflict: A Comparative History of Four Cities*. Beverly Hills, CA: Sage.

Harkabi, Yehoshfat (1983) *The Bar Kokhba Syndrome: Risk and Realism in International Relations*. Translated by Max D. Ticktin. Edited by David Altshuler. Chappaqua, NY: Rossel Books.

——— (1988) *Israel's Fateful Hour*. Translated by Lenn Schramm. New York: Harper & Row.

Henry, Stuart (1991) "The Informal Economy: A Crime of Omission by the State," in Gregg Barak (ed.), *Crimes by the Capitalist State: An Introduction to State Criminality*. Albany: State University of New York Press, pp. 253–272.

Hevener, Natalie Kaufman (1981) *The Dynamics of Human Rights in U.S. Foreign Policy*. New Brunswick, NJ: Transaction Books.

Hofnung, Menachem (1991) *Israel—Security Needs vs. the Rule of Law*. Jerusalem: Nevo Publishing (Hebrew).

Horowitz, Dan (1982) "The Israeli Defense Forces: A Civilianized Military in a Partially Militarized Society," in R. Kolkowich and A. Korbonski (eds.), *Soldiers, Peasants and Bureaucrats*. London: G. Allen, pp. 77–105.

———, and Moshe Lissak (1978) *Origins of the Israeli Policy: Palestine Under the Mandate*. Chicago: University of Chicago Press.

Israel Law Review (1989) Spring–Summer 23, 2–3.

Kadish, Sanford H. (1989) "Torture, the State and the Individual." *Israel Law Review* 23, 2–3: 345–356.

Kremnitzer, Mordechai (1989) "The Landau Commission Report—Was the Security Service Subordinated to the Law, or the Law to the 'Needs' of the Security Service?" *Israel Law Review* 23, 2–3: 216–279.

Leibowitz, Yeshayahu (1988) *On Just About Everything: Talks with Michael Shashar*. Jerusalem: Keter Publishing House (Hebrew).

Lindsay, A.D. (1943) *The Modern Democratic State*. New York: Oxford University Press.

Mazmanian, Daniel A., and Paul A Sabatier (1983) *Implementation and Public Policy*. Glenview, IL: Scott, Foresman.

Moore, Michael S. (1989) "Torture and the Balance of Evils." *Israel Law Review* 23, 2–3: 280–344.

O'Brien, William V. (1991) *Law and Morality in Israel's War with the PLO*. New York: Routledge.

Sharkansky, Ira. (1987) *The Political Economy of Israel*. New Brunswick, NJ: Transaction Books.

—— (1991) *Ancient and Modern Israel: An Exploration of Political Parallels*. Albany: State University of New York Press.

State Comptroller (1985) *Annual Report #35*. Jerusalem: State Comptroller (Hebrew).

Turk, Austin T. (1982) *Political Criminality: The Defiance and Defense of Authority*. Beverly Hills, CA: Sage.

Urbach, Ephraim E. (1987) *The Sages: Their Concepts and Beliefs*. Translated by Israel Abrahams. Cambridge, MA: Harvard University Press.

Vincent, R.J. 1986. *Human Rights and International Relations*. Cambridge, Eng.: Cambridge University Press.

Von Clausewitz, Carl (1832/1968) *On War*. London: Penguin.

Weisser, Michael R. (1979) *Crime and Punishment in Early Modern Europe*. Hassocks, Sussex, Eng.: Harvester Press.

Yaniv, Avner, ed. (1993) *National Security and Democracy in Israel*. Boulder, CO: Lynne Rienner Publishers.

Zamir, Itzhak (1989) "Human Rights and National Security." *Israel Law Review* 23, 2–3: 375–406.

Zuckerman, Adrian A.S. (1989) "Coercion and the Judicial Ascertainment of Truth." *Israel Law Review* 23, 2–3: 357–374.

State Crime or Governmental Crime: Making Sense of the Conceptual Confusion*

David O. Friedrichs

Controlling state crime—the focus of this volume—will surely be one of the premier challenges of the twenty-first century. The premise of the present chapter is that any coherent effort to control state crime must be rooted in a clear understanding of the relevant concepts and terms. The principal objective of this chapter is to contribute to the discourse on controlling state crime rather than to focus on the specific strategies that might be adopted to achieve such control. A series of conceptual clarifications will be proposed.

Today a good deal of confusion surrounds the use of the concept "state crime" or "governmental crime." Although the term *state crime* is perhaps the more familiar of these two terms (as is reflected in the title of this book, and in other chapters), the choice here is to adopt the broader term *governmental crime* and then to treat state crime as a subtype of this larger category. The term *state* refers to a political entity with a recognized sovereignty occupying a definite territory, whereas the term *government* refers to the political and administrative apparatus of such an entity (Plano and Greenberg, 1979). Government may also refer to the administrative apparatus of lesser political entities, such as municipalities. The term *state crime* suggests crime committed on behalf of a state (federal or not), while the term *governmental crime*, in my interpretation, can more naturally be applied to crimes committed within a governmental context on any level, and not necessarily on behalf of the state. In this chapter the term *governmental crime* will be used as a broad term for the whole range of crimes committed in a governmental context. The term *state crime* will be applied to activities carried out by the state or on behalf of some state agency, whereas the term *political white-collar crime* will be applied to illegal activities carried out by officials and politicians for direct personal benefit.

The term *crime* itself can, of course, have many meanings, including: "legalistic" and "international legalistic": that which is prohibited by criminal (or international) law (statutory) or the finding of a criminal (or international) court (adjudicated); "humanistic" and "moralistic": those activities that involve demonstrable harm to human beings or are at odds with a higher eternal law; and "political" and "popular": acts offensive to those in power or the focal point of public interest. In this chapter, several of these different meanings will be reviewed, with the specific meaning suggested by the context in which the term is used. The conventional acceptance of state definitions of crime is clearly limiting, insofar as much state criminality avoids being classified as crime (Kauzlarich, Kramer, and Smith, 1992). The discussion that follows, then, begins with a consideration of governmental crime generally.

The concept "governmental crime" may initially seem paradoxical to some. Government is, after all, the entity that produces, implements, and administers the law. People generally like to think the government is there to protect them from crime, and to deter, incapacitate, punish, and rehabilitate criminals. But one can quite confidently assert that the worst crimes—in terms of physical harm to human beings, abuse of civil liberties, and economic loss—have been committed by individuals and units acting in the name of the state, as the most consequential form of governmental crime. Quite conservative estimates attribute between 100 million and 135 million deaths of human beings during the twentieth century alone to the deliberate actions of the state. The far larger proportion of these deaths resulted from genocides, massacres, and mass executions, rather than war (Markusen, 1992). A large number of the inhabitants of the earth, then, have been killed during this century by government criminality (Glaser and Possony, 1979). In his recent survey of studies of genocide and war Markusen (1992: 119) cites findings attributing some 95 percent of twentieth-century violence (at least through 1975) to structural violence ("violence created by social, political, and economic institutions"), with a total (as of 1989) of some 1.6 billion deaths, or approximately 19 million per year. In addition, a great deal of nonviolent crime with major consequences is committed by governmental officials, either for political or economic gain.

Governmental crime is not always crime in the narrower legal sense of the term. One must distinguish between those governmental or political actions prohibited by the state's laws, those defined as criminal by international law, and those actions regarded as criminal by some other criteria of harmfulness not necessarily recognized by either the state's laws or international law.

Governmental Crime, Political Crime, and White-Collar Crime

Governmental crime is commonly classified as a form of political crime, a term which has been labeled a "broad and ill-defined category" (Allen, Friday, Roebuck, and Sagarin, 1981: 201). It has most typically been associated with crimes committed against the state, including assassination, sabotage, terrorism, insurrection, treason, sedition, disobedience of mandated service (e.g., draft dodging), and illegal protests (Turk, 1982). It should be stressed, however, that terrorism (including assassination, torture, and kidnapping), although most typically thought of as committed by individuals and groups outside the government, has also often been carried out by agents of the state, on behalf of the state (Stohl and Lopez, 1984). "Wholesale" acts of terrorism waged against independence or revolutionary movements by the state may be much more consequential, but receive less scholarly attention than do conventional forms of "retail" terrorism (Barak, 1990: 14; Herman, 1982). In the early 1980s, for example, it was estimated that some 90,000 people in Latin America "disappeared" at the hands of state forces (Herman, 1982: 12). These numbers may understate the scope of the crimes involved, however. In Guatemala alone it has been estimated that up to 150,000 people have been murdered by government-connected forces since the CIA-sponsored coup in 1954 (Agee, 1988: 11–12). While wholesale, or state, terrorism was carried out in countries in many parts of the world, including communist countries (e.g., the former Soviet Union), it is clear that the United States has engaged in some forms of such terrorism, and has supported many regimes carrying out state terrorism on a massive scale (e.g., see Simon and Eitzen, 1993). More specifically, American attacks on Panama and Libya, insofar as innocent civilians were killed, could be cited as examples of state terrorism. The Senate Intelligence Investigation of the 1970s identified various assassination plots directed by the CIA (Johnson, 1985). The United States has sold billions of dollars of arms and ammunition to "client states" all over the world that have used these munitions for state terrorist activities, and has trained hundreds of thousands of military and police personnel from such countries (Herman, 1982: 127). In El Salvador in the early 1980s, for example, well over 10,000 people in a single year were murdered by government forces supported by the United States, and as many as 70,000 may have been kidnapped and tortured to death between 1981 and 1988; it is far from clear that the countless murders carried out by "death squads" in El Salvador and other American "client states" can simply be attributed to "out of control" security forces (Herman, 1982: 182; Agee, 1988: 11–12). The United States was also heavily implicated over an extended period of time in the crimes of the Somoza regime against the Nicaraguan people, and the subsequent activities of the Contras (in violation of the UN Charter) (Kauzlarich, Kramer, and Smith, 1992). Without in any way belittling the crimes of conventional, retail terrorists—including the airplane saboteurs, car bomb drivers and kidnappers operating in the Middle East and elsewhere in recent years—it should be recognized that the term *terrorist* has been used by Western governments as a semantic tool against those engaged in antistate activities, although much of the worst terrorism is carried out on behalf of the state (Chomsky and Herman, 1979: 85–87). As Herman (1982: 84) argues,

> Retail terrorists do not deprive large numbers of their subsistence and produce hunger, malnutrition, high infancy mortality rates, chronic diseases of poverty and neglect, and illiteracy. This is all done by state terrorists.

Some political crime is committed specifically to advance a political ideology or to intervene against a political movement, such as the activities of the Ku Klux Klan and neo-Nazis, and is likely to be directed at minority groups rather than at the government.

An important distinction has to be made between those who commit crimes against the state from without, and from within. The former fit into the traditional conception of political crime; the latter are engaged in various forms of political corruption (some crimes—e.g., sabotage—may be carried out either from without or within the state). Political corruption is often regarded as a form of white collar crime. Geis and Meier (1977: 207) have advanced the term *political white collar* crime to refer to illegal actions carried out by political officeholders in the context of their offical duties. As suggested earlier, it seems to make conceptual sense to restrict this term to actions carried out for direct personal benefit, rather than on behalf of a state goal. Admittedly, one cannot in all cases clearly draw a sharp line of demarcation between state and personal objectives, but it still seems useful to differentiate between, for example, genocidal actions and political corruption (ranging from killing peasants to obtain their land to simply accepting bribes). Michalowski (1985: 380) has produced a typology differentiating between political crime committed by those in political power and those outside government, benefiting individuals or organizations, including government, and those committed for economic gain or political gain. Those with political power, for example, can accept bribes, steal government property, or use campaign funds for personal benefit; these acts for personal economic gain can be distinguished from lax enforcement of regulatory laws, legislative favoritism, and imperialist policies that provide economic benefits for the government or one of its divisions. People outside government, on the other hand, may pay bribes (sometimes in the form of illegal campaign contributions) for economic benefits for themselves personally, or on behalf of a private organization (e.g., a business). In a parallel vein those in government may abuse power for personal political gain (e.g., "dirty tricks" against a political opponent) or engage in repression for the perceived benefit of the government or one of its agencies. People outside government may seek political power or office, or representation, on their own behalf or for the benefit of their organization or business.

It is necessary to recognize, then, that crimes committed by (or on behalf) of the government have been classified as a type of political crime (Clinard and Quinney, 1973; Roebuck and Weeber, 1978). Such crime goes beyond Sutherland's original conception of white collar crime, but has so close a generic relationship with it, and is so often interrelated with it, that no survey of white collar crime can neglect it. Indeed, Roebuck and Weeber (1978: iv) "consider government crime and corporate crime to comprise one unit of political criminal behavior because we see the government as an extension and instrument of the economic system—a system dominated by the corporate structure." Some students of white collar crime (e.g., Simon and Eitzen, 1993) subsume both corporate and high-level governmental offenses under the heading of "elite deviance," with the latter at least as serious as the former. Other students of white collar crime (e.g., Coleman, 1989; Green, 1990) classify internal (e.g., corruption) political crime and crimes committed on behalf of the state, or some state entity, as forms of organizational or individual occupational or white collar crime, or treat it separately as a form of "state authority" occupational crime, depending on the context in which it occurs. The broad category "governmental" crime (as opposed to political or white collar crime) is adopted here to clearly differentiate this activity from crime carried out by individuals or ideological groups with no governmental status.

Governmental crime does indeed have a close generic relationship with white collar crime carried out by corporations, professionals, retailers, and others. The parties involved have a respectable status, occupy a position of trust, are most typically middle or higher income, and do not regard themselves as criminals. There are also, as indicated, many interrelationships and interlocks between the public (governmental) and private (corporate and business) sectors. It is clear that there is a symbiotic relationship between much governmental and traditional white collar crime, and a mutual interdependence (Simon and Eitzen, 1993). Political white collar crime is often motivated, as is much white collar crime, by the desire for financial benefit. But the extension or maintenance of power plays a much larger role in political white collar crime, and is central to governmental crime (Barak, 1991; Chambliss, 1989). In addition, when violence occurs as an element of state crime it is likely to be much more direct than the violence of corporate crime (Kauzlarich, Kramer, and Smith, 1992). Although the violation of trust is a key element in governmental crime and white collar crime generally, in the former case the violation of a public trust occurs, whereas corporate and occupational crime involve a violation of a trust that is essentially private. In this sense, some would regard governmental crime as worse than corporate and occupational crime precisely because the breach of a public trust is a more serious matter than the breach of a private trust (Thompson, 1987). The enormously harmful acts carried out on the orders of high-level government officials may well escape a formal designation as criminal, due to the great power concentrated in the hands of these officials. And the prosecution of governmental crime may involve some unique difficulties, especially when those accused of crimes are also part of the lawmaking and law-implementing apparatus. Indeed, the claim that governmental crimes have been carried out is especially vulnerable to the charge of ideological bias, and at least some governmental actions will be characterized in dichotomous terms, either defended as a desirable policy or castigated as a criminal form of repression. It is also important to recognize that governmental crime, when it is exposed, can receive sensationalistic media attention and becomes the focus of great public interest and outrage (Geis and Meier, 1977). The Nuremberg trials, the Watergate inquiries, and the Iran/Contra arms hearings are just three obvious cases of governmental crime that generated very high levels of public interest.

Traditionally, the study of governmental crime has been relatively neglected by criminologists, perhaps even more than the study of corporate and occupational crime (Barak, 1990, 1991; Roebuck and Weeber, 1978; Tunnell, 1993). In part, this relative lack of attention can be attributed to the challenge of gaining access to the politically powerful, their ability to conceal many of their crimes, the complexity and broad scope of the illegalities involved, and some ideological resistance to regarding government officials as criminals. This chapter can provide only an outline and brief review of some principal elements of such crime.

Governmental crime is usefully classified as a cognate form of white collar crime. In some criminology and criminal justice programs a separate and autonomous political or governmental crime course may be offered. Or governmental crime may be dealt with as one element of a white collar crime course, or in a more limited way as an element of a criminology course.

In view of the great confusion surrounding the term *political crime*, an argument can be made for restricting this term to criminal acts directed specifically against the state. Governmental crime, then, is the favored term for those crimes emanating from within the state, or committed by those who hold government office. A provisional typology of governmental crime, including state crime and political white collar crime, is offered below. A consideration of some basic premises and terms must precede identification of the different types of governmental crime.

First, it should be noted that the matter of governmental crime is linked with two of the more enduring and complex issues in political philosophy: the question of the nature of a legitimate political order, and the nature of the obligation to comply with the laws and commands emanating from a political order. A political order that is not legitimate—for example, a totalitarian dictatorship established by brute force—may be regarded as inherently criminal. But even a political order that came into being by fundamentally legitimate means—for example, the Nazi state—may be regarded as illegitimate by some other criteria. On the other hand, there is the difficult question of the duty to obedience. The whole tradition of civil disobedience—including the actions of Thoreau, Gandhi, and Martin Luther King—is premised on the idea that one has a moral obligation to *dis*obey some laws. There are also circumstances in which state agents are morally and sometimes legally obliged not to comply with commands of higher state authority. While these very large issues cannot be explored here in any depth, they must at least be introduced into any discussion of governmental crime.

Governmental Crime: Some Basic Terms

Some governmental crime terminology should be defined, insofar as these terms are used in quite different ways. *Abuse of power* is perhaps the broadest charge associated with governmental crime, but it has no fixed meaning. In one attempt at a definition Dussich (1991: 691) writes of "the violation of a standard in the use of forces such that persons are injured physically, mentally, emotionally, economically, or in their rights, as a direct and intentional result of the misapplication of these forces." The most obvious, least problematic instances of abuse of power occur when the state or agents acting for the state violate the laws to accomplish some improper or prohibited objective. The broader meaning of the term *abuse of power* links it with the state's assumptions of and exercising of power it ought not to have. When agents of an American government agency such as the Federal Bureau of Investigation engage in surveillance or break-ins specifically prohibited by law, abuse of power in the first sense is involved. When a government, such as that of South Africa, institutes an emergency act that enables it to arrest and detain dissidents, abuse of power in the second sense is involved. The full range of abuses of power that can be carried out in a governmental context is very broad. Barak (1991: 274) writes,

> Crimes by the state involve violence and property and include such diverse behaviors as murder, rape, espionage, coverup, burglary, illegal wiretapping, illegal

break-in, disinformation, kidnapping, piracy, assassination, counter- and state terrorism, bankrupting and deporting arms illegally, obstruction of justice, perjury, deception, fraud, conspiracy, and the general violation of both domestic and international laws. They also include behaviors which cause social injury and therefore violate universally defined human rights (e.g., food, shelter, self-determination, etc.).

Although the broad term *abuse of power* certainly includes acts of economic corruption, it would probably limit some confusion if the term were used only for acts involving the extension or maintenance of power, and the *crimes of omission* were treated separately.

A second basic concept associated with governmental crime is "corruption." In the English language of Shakespeare's time the expression "to corrupt" was used in both a sexual and a political sense: to seduce a young woman and to seduce an official from duty (Noonan, 1984: 319). Contemporary dictionaries offer many definitions of corruption, which have been classified as physical (e.g., decomposition), moral, and the perversion of anything from an original state of purity (Heidenheimer, 1977: 20). Corruption in a political context most typically suggests the misuse of political office for material advantage, although it also encompasses acts undertaken for political advantage; it has been applied both narrowly (i.e., the violation of specific laws, typically in response to some form of payment) or more loosely, as deviation from ideal or expected patterns of behavior (*Corruption and Reform*, 1986). The essence of political corruption has been defined as "stealing through deception in a situation which betrays a trust" (Alatas, 1990: 2). While the term *corruption* ordinarily has negative connotations, the argument is sometimes made that a certain level of political *corruption* is both inevitable and functional (Huntington, 1968; Lieberman, 1972: 20). This argument, however, has been criticized as inherently amoral and insensitive to the full range of harmful consequences of corruption (Alatas, 1990). Political corruption in some form can be found in all societies above the most primitive level. We have records of such corruption from the earliest times (e.g., Hammurabi of Babylon in 1200 B.C., and the Book of Exodus in the Old Testament) (Alatas, 1990: 13). But it is important to recognize that standards for defining corruption vary historically and cross-culturally, and actions that might be defined as corrupt by one standard are regarded as acceptable practices by another. Hope (1987: 127) writes, "widespread corruption has reached epidemic proportions in most developing states and is now regarded as a norm of their societal functioning," and Medard (1986: 115) writes, "What is loosely called 'corruption' is at the heart of the functioning of the African state and society." While the rhetorical condemnation of corruption is commonplace among politicians in such countries, the same parties are often deeply involved in corrupt practices themselves.

Bribery is probably the single activity most closely associated with political corruption. Noonan (1984: xi) states that "the core of the concept of a bribe is an inducement improperly influencing the performance of a public function meant to be gratuitously exercised." Bribery is specifically a legal concept, but the term itself has different levels of meaning: as defined by moralists, by written law, by law in practice, and by commonly accepted practices (Noonan, 1984: xii). Although the specific definition of bribery varies between societies, Noonan has established that the concept has deep-seated historical roots, and cuts across virtually all existing societies.

Finally, the concept of the "political scandal" is important to the understanding of governmental crime and political white collar crime. The process of exposing major forms of such crime tends to differ between totalitarian (or authoritarian) and democratic political systems. In a totalitarian system governmental crime can be exposed only from within by dissident groups that cannot publicize the crime openly, or from without the system (e.g., by exiles). Such crimes can be prosecuted only when the regime is defeated in an international war or overthrown from within. In a liberal democratic society major governmental crime is likely to be exposed in the context of a political scandal, and in one reading a political scandal is possible only in such a society (Markovits and Silverstein, 1988). Such scandals are most likely to occur when there is a basic division of power in society, when there is an absence of a major external threat to the society, and when politicians violate widely supported norms about proper conduct in political office (Neckel, 1989). The political opposition and the media, in a democratic society, play the major role in creating and sustaining a political scandal. Despite the enormous publicity and "orchestrated outrage" focused on such political scandals as Watergate and "Sewergate" (the Reagan administration's Environmental Protection Agency), on Harbourgate in Canada, and the serious consequences for some of the targeted individuals (loss of position and incarceration), the ongoing impact on how the political system operates is usually modest or limited (Szasz, 1986). Because political scandals tend to be person-centered they do not necessarily undercut the legitimacy of a political state and may even enhance it if the perceived wrongdoers are swiftly and justly punished (Logue, 1988: 264). If the political scandal is an important element of the response to major episodes of governmental corruption, the "sound and fury" of such scandals should not be confused with fundamental, enduring reforms, which are a possible but hardly an inevitable consequence of such scandals.

Governmental Criminality and Crimes of the State

In the view of one ideological tradition, anarchism, government itself is inherently aggressive and fundamentally unnecessary (Krimerman and Perry, 1966; Shatz, 1971; Wolff, 1976). It is at least implicit if not explicit in the anarchist tradition that government is by nature a criminal enterprise. But the extreme view of anarchism has not been adopted by very many political activists or ordinary citizens.

If depriving people unjustly of their property, their land, their way of life, and their life itself is regarded as criminal, then imperialistic conquests, and wars carried out by governments, are governmental crimes of extraordinary scope. Indeed, in one interpretation the European settlement of America and the establishment of the American nation was a massive criminal enterprise. The "discovery" of America by Christopher Columbus in 1492 has been celebrated by many generations of Americans, with the five hundredth anniversary of the discovery in 1992 the occasion for large-scale commemorations. Columbus's name has been attached to numerous geographical landmarks in North and South America, from the District of Columbia to Columbus, Ohio, from British Columbia to the country Colombia. But for over 200 years dissidents have argued that the widely populated Americas of the fifteenth century were not "discovered" by Columbus in any meaningful sense of the term, and his journeys are better characterized by the title of Sale's (1990) book, *The Conquest of Paradise*. For this author and other critics of the Columbian mythology, his voyages and the settlements he established in the "New World" initiated a long trend of despoiliation of a beautiful natural environment and the enslavement and genocide of its people. Others (e.g., Krautheimer, 1991) argue that on balance Columbus's discovery initiated a noteworthy advance for American civilization by introducing a more enlightened form of government, with a strong tradition of promoting human liberty, and this culture is superior in many respects to the civilization of the Aztecs and other indigenous American tribes. But if the opening of America to European settlement by Columbus is regarded as the first American white collar crime (stretching the concept somewhat!), it is especially ironic that the original chairman of the presidential commission coordinating the international celebration of the quincentennial of Columbus's first voyage was forced to resign the position in 1990 due to alleged financial improprieties concerning money raised for the celebration (Stanley, 1991). There is, of course, a formidable literature documenting many of the state-sponsored crimes committed by those who came after Columbus, especially the destruction of the world of Native Americans and the slavery trade involving African blacks (e.g., Brown, 1971; Davidson, 1961; *International Social Science Journal*, 1992). In one view, then, the very roots of American development involved various forms of state crime.

Earlier in this chapter it was noted that structural violence has perhaps been the principal source of premature death due to human actions, and surely the destruction of life and property over time due to imperialistic, colonialist, and mercantilist endeavors has been incalculably large (Markusen, 1992). The waging of war, however, has been an especially intense type of deliberately destructive governmental activity that can be regarded as a cognate form of white collar crime with devastating consequences. Tilly (1985) prefers to equate war-making with organized crime, carried out by "racketeer governments." He argues that "war makes states. . . . Banditry, piracy, gangland rivalry, policing and war-making all belong on the same continuum" (p. 170). Over time, according to Tilly, the state became the largest scale and most efficient user of violence, a capability it originally shared with bandits and pirates. No single private entity has come close to achieving the scale and scope of destructiveness caused by major states in more recent history. In the twentieth century alone, tens of millions of people have died in wars, and hundreds of billions of dollars have been expended or lost due to war. Pacifists, of course, regard all wars as criminal, but this is not the position that has been adopted by the countries of the world. Philosophers and theologians have made distinctions between just wars and unjust wars; the notion that there are good and bad wars has in fact been quite widely adopted (e.g., Walzer, 1977). The American involvement in World War II, and more recently in the Persian Gulf, was rationalized as the only available means to respond to the criminal actions of Germany and Japan, and Iraq, respectively. More recently still, military intervention in Bosnia has been called for on the same grounds. Since the middle of the nineteenth century various countries have joined together to ratify agreements prohibiting or outlawing particular acts of war, including the imposition of needless suffering, the mistreatment of prisoners of war, and the use of chemical and biological weapons (Falk, Kolko, and Lifton, 1971). Inevitably, however, only those who have lost wars and been captured have been brought to account for war crimes. Some of the surviving leadership of Nazi Germany and Japan was tried and convicted of war crimes after World War II; had the United States and Great Britain lost the war their surviving leadership might have conceivably been tried for war crimes relating to the bombing of Hiroshima and Dresden. The American involvement in the Vietnam War was widely condemned as criminal by many people all over the world, and by a significant number of Americans themselves during the course of the war (Young,

1991). Tons of bombs were dropped on Vietnam during the course of the war; millions of Vietnamese were killed, wounded, orphaned, or uprooted by the war; hundreds of thousands of American soldiers were wounded and traumatized, and tens of thousands lost their lives. In one view, the American engagement in the Vietnam War was illegal by American law, because Congress never specifically declared war as called for by the Constitution (although it did pass resolutions and appropriate funding for the war). Among the specific illegalities that the American forces have been accused of, by those persuaded of the criminality of the American involvement in Vietnam, are the following: dropping napalm during air strikes; chemical warfare; torturing of suspects; burning of villages; illegal detaining of suspects; bombing of hospitals and civilian areas, and dikes; moral corruption; and sabotaging of the economy. Millions of arable acres and hardwood forests were destroyed (see Zilinskas, this volume). The 1968 massacre of some 100 Vietnamese men, women, and children in the village of My Lai (more correctly, Son My), by Lt. William Calley and his troops, is the single most famous episode of American illegality in Vietnam. The subsequent trial and conviction of Lt. Calley (who served 35 months of house arrest on a military base) was widely criticized as deflecting attention from the far more substantial crimes of those higher in the chain of command, including the President and his associates. No American President, Cabinet officer, or other high-level civilian or military official involved in the pursuit of the Vietnam War has ever been required to provide a formal defense for the policy, and none ever stood trial for war crimes.

More recent American military ventures—including the invasions of Grenada and Panama, the mining of the Managua (Nicaragua) harbor, and the war against Iraq—have all been condemned in various quarters as illegal or criminal, although these actions have been widely endorsed by the American people. Despite some history of antiwar mobilization—most conspicuously during the Vietnam War—the more enduring strain in American culture has been one of resistance to the imputation of criminality to American acts of war. The American political leadership has traditionally rejected, and is likely to continue to reject, judgments of an international judiciary concerning its military actions, even if it supports an international criminal court with more limited jurisdiction (Cavicchia, 1992). Nevertheless the need for a truly effective and widely accepted international court with broad jurisdiction should become increasingly evident in the foreseeable future (see Yarnold, this volume).

The Threat of Nuclear War as Crime

The initiation of a nuclear war might be regarded as the penultimate form of governmental crime. A study in the mid-1980s by the World Health Organization estimated that a war involving just half the Soviet and American nuclear arsenal would kill some one billion people outright, and another billion would die within a year from radiation and other consequences of such a war (Markusen, 1992: 120). A nuclear war, in the worst case scenario, has the potential to create a "nuclear winter," which would utterly destroy the human environment, would lead to the obliteration of humanity (the "death of death"), and the "murder of the future" (Schell, 1982). Although the breakup of the Soviet Union and the officially proclaimed end of the Cold War has alleviated some of the anxiety over a superpower nuclear war, it has also led to new sources of instability and potential nuclear proliferation, and has hardly eliminated the long-term threat of nuclear war itself.

The whole issue of nuclear arms and the possibility of nuclear war has, of course, generated an enormous literature and a range of endlessly complex questions about the objectives of developing and producing nuclear weapons, their impact on international relations, and the best strategy to minimize the possibility of a nuclear war. It is quite remarkable, however, that the vast criminal potential in the use of nuclear weapons has been almost wholly neglected by criminologists and criminal justice practitioners (Friedrichs, 1985; Harding 1983). Although possession of nuclear weapons has not been prohibited by international law, the threatened use of such weapons, and their actual use, is prohibited by international law and the UN Charter

(Kauzlarich, Kramer, and Smith, 1992). The traditional nuclear weapons policy of the United States can certainly be interpreted as being in violation of such codes, charters, and historic agreements on the laws of armed conflict. At a minimum, those concerned with white collar crime should consider how involvement with nuclear arms relates to and is distinctive from governmental crime generally, and corporate crime specifically. How would the motivations of those who might launch a nuclear war parallel, and differ, from those of white collar criminals of all types? Does it make any sense to even raise the issue of nuclear warfare in the context of a survey of white collar crime?

State Criminality and the Criminal State

State criminality (as a specific subtype of governmental crime) takes many forms and occurs on various levels. When some form of state criminality becomes a dominant force in the operation of the state it may be justified to label the state a "criminal state," or use some related such label. Such a label conveys the view that broadly recognized criminality has become a central project of the state. In one view a criminal state is simply a state successfully labeled as such by one or more other states that are victorious over it, or that have the political power to impose such a label. Libya, under the leadership of Muammar Qaddafi, was frequently denounced as a criminal state, or as guilty of state criminality, by the United States and other Western countries. Jenkins (1988) suggests that the focus on Libyan state criminality was more a reflection of that country's relative impotence than an objectively supported determination that its involvement with international terrorism was greater than that of many other states, including the more powerful and strategically important Syria. In modern history Nazi Germany may be the single most familiar case of a state widely labeled as "criminal." But there have been many other candidates for this designation, from Stalin's Soviet Union to Hussein's Iraq. As late as the 1980s President Ronald Reagan characterized the Soviet Union as an "Evil Empire." In the early 1990s President George Bush compared Iraq's Hussein to Hitler, both leaders of criminal enterprises. South Africa in recent decades was treated as a pariah and a criminal state by many other countries in the world due to its formalized system of racism, apartheid. Of course in American history the Confederacy was regarded for all practical purposes as a criminal state by the Union. And as noted above, the United States itself has been characterized as a criminal state by many as a consequence of its actions in Vietnam and more recently in the Persian Gulf. For example, Iran's Khomeini and other Muslim fundamentalists in the Middle East characterized the United States as "the Great Satan." Finally, antinuclear weapons activists may in some respects be seen as labeling both the United States and Russia as criminal states as long as they continue to produce or simply hold nuclear weapons and lead the world toward the possibility of the ultimate crime, the obliteration of humanity itself in a nuclear war.

It is important, then, to acknowledge that any labeling of state criminality is ultimately interpretive, and likely to incorporate an ideological dimension. With that in mind, distinctions will be made below between the criminal state, the repressive state, the corrupt state, and the negligent state. It should be stressed, however, that these terms are "ideal types" only intended to capture an essential dimension of a state's criminality; further, predatory criminality, repressiveness, corruption, and negligence often coexist, in varying degrees, within a single state. The illustrative cases, then, highlight a particular form of state criminality.

An Abbreviated Consideration of Further Dimensions of Governmental Crime

For the purposes of this chapter, some useful conceptual distinctions, excerpted in a very abbreviated form from a much larger work in progress (provisionally entitled "Trusted Criminals: White Collar Crime and the Justice System") can be made. To begin with, one can differentiate between a criminal state, a repressive state, a corrupt state, and a negligent state. A *criminal state* is one whose central purpose is a criminal enterprise, such as a state policy of genocidal actions (e.g., Nazi Germany); a *repressive state* is one that engages in fundamental denial of basic human rights (e.g., totalitarian dictatorships in many parts of the world, and the former South Africa as a classic, special case); a *corrupt state* is one where the state is used as an instrument to enrich its leadership (e.g., the Philippines under Marcos); and a *negligent state* is one that willfully fails to act to prevent unnecessary tragedies (e.g., the United States, in its response to work-related diseases, AIDS, black infancy mortality, and homelessness). These concepts are, of course, not mutually exclusive, and obviously the application of any such concepts is necessarily contentious and controversial, but it seems useful to attempt to differentiate the essential ways in which a state, as a whole, may be regarded to engage in "crime" in the broad (nonlegalistic) sense. When all forms of harmful state activity are conflated into a broad category of state criminality the perceived validity of the whole notion of governmental crime may be compromised. There are, however, several formulations relating to state or governmental crime that require some specific attention here.

First, *state-corporate crime* has been usefully identified and defined by Kramer and Michalowski (1990: 3) as "illegal or socially injurious actions that occur when one or more institutions of political governance pursue a goal in direct cooperation with one or more institutions of economic production and distribution." This concept focuses attention on the important reality that a significant form of high-level criminality involves a cooperative effort between the state and one or more corporate entities (in socialistic states such as the former Soviet Union there is, of course, no meaningful separation between the state and economic institutions). The exploitation of slave labor in the Nazi concentration camps by I.G. Farben and other major German corporations is one historical example of this type of crime (Borkin, 1978). More recently, in the American context, at least some of the pervasive corruption involving defense contracts is best understood as a cooperative endeavor between high-level Pentagon officials and defense contractors. The well-publicized Wedtech case, involving a small Bronx-based defense contractor that fraudulently undertook major defense projects that were secured for the corporation by well-placed, corrupt politicians, is one specific example of this type of crime. And Kramer (1992) identifies the tragic explosion of the *Challenger* space shuttle as a consequence of the agenda of a government agency (National Aeronautics and Space Administration, or NASA) and a private corporation (Morton Thiokol). It is quite clear, in fact, that any consideration of governmental or state crime must attend to this hybrid type, state-corporate crime.

Another important concept in this context is state-organized crime. According to Chambliss (1989: 184) *state-organized crimes* are "acts defined by law as criminal and committed by state officials in pursuit of their job as representatives of the state." Chambliss specifically excludes criminal acts that benefit individual officeholders. State-organized crime is carried out on behalf of a government entity. As with much other white collar crime, however, the lines between individual and organizational benefit cannot always be so easily drawn. Douglas and Johnson (1977) promoted the term *official deviance* to encompass a wide range of governmental and political acts of corruption and usurpation of power. It has been proposed here to use the term *political white collar crime* to refer to illegal and improper acts of public officials carried out essentially for personal gain. Chambliss (1989) has identified piracy as an early form of state-organized crime, with state complicity in assassinations, criminal conspiracies, spying on citizens, diverting funds illegally, selling arms to blacklisted countries, and supporting terrorists as some contemporary manifestations. These forms of state-organized crime (while hardly new) are today especially likely to be carried out under the auspices of state agencies with investigative powers, such as the Central Intelligence Agency (CIA), the Federal Bureau of Investigation (FBI), and the Internal Revenue Service (IRS). Of course some of the activities carried out by the Richard Nixon White House in the 1970s (e.g., the "White House Plumbers" operation) and by the Reagan White House in the 1980s (e.g., the Iran/Contra arms operation) would fit under this category. State-organized crime can be carried out on all governmental levels, not simply on the federal level, but on the state and local level as well, down to improper actions of municipal policemen. State-organized crime on the federal level will generally have more pernicious and far-reaching consequences than will state-organized crime on the state and local level, simply because the federal government has extraordinary resources and its actions impact on far more people nationally and internationally. One issue with state-organized crime is the degree to which it is sanctioned by state authority figures, or is carried out quite autonomously by state agents. A second issue is the extent to which this type of crime is motivated by a disinterested commitment to the perceived interests of the state, or government, or is motivated by personal career-related aspi-rations.

It is useful to distinguish between state-organized crime, as defined above, and political white collar crime, or the abuse of elected or appointed governmental office for purely personal gain. In this category we naturally have a vast amount of illegal activity, ranging from a corrupt vice president, such as Spiro Agnew, accepting payoffs from contractors interested in doing business with the government, down to local police accepting bribes not to enforce certain laws. A somewhat parallel type of activity can be labeled "politician crime," which refers to illegalities committed by incumbent political officeholders and their associates for partisan advantage. Watergate and Harbourgate are, of course, two prominent examples from recent American and Canadian history. One of the most unusual features of the Watergate affair, which virtually all commentators agree upon, is the remarkably limited role of personal avariciousness in the whole range of Watergate-related activities. Politician crime encompasses various election law violations, and the corrupt dealings of politicians seeking to maintain their office and ensure their reelection. It must be noted, however, that a significant amount of politician crime is committed by those who do not hold, but aspire to, political office or a governmental position. Strictly speaking, such activity might be classified as a marginal or residual case of governmental crime. Most observers would probably agree that law violators in this category have far more in common with political officeholders who commit crimes than they do with assassins, terrorists, and protesters who

commit illegal acts against the government. A second point that
has to be reiterated here is that political and personal motives for
crimes in this category cannot be so easily disentangled.

Conclusion

An argument has been advanced here for adopting the term
governmental crime as the broad, all-encompassing term for a
range of illegal and demonstrably harmful activities carried out
from within, or in association with, governmental status. The
conventional term *political crime* has been used to embrace crimes
committed by those within the government and by those acting
against the state, and is probably more readily associated with
the latter type of activity. The term *state crime*, which has been
quite widely adopted in more recent times, refers only to one
major class of crimes that can be committed by those acting from
within a government. But if there is anything that conceptually
links the acts of genocide committed on behalf of the state with
the petty bribes accepted by the low-level official, it is this: they
are committed within a governmental context, and facilitated by
governmental power.

A second thesis of this chapter is that governmental crime
is best regarded as a cognate form of white collar crime. It has
both important parallels with traditional forms of white collar
crime—in its corporate and occupational forms—and not
infrequently important interlocks and interconnections with such
crime. Yet governmental crime was not what Sutherland had in
mind when he formulated the white collar crime concept, and it
is not what most of those who invoke the term today have in
mind. And the violation of a public trust, with its special forms
of power and responsibility, has some unique dimensions that
make it somewhat distinct from conventional forms of white
collar crime.

The specific nature of the interrelationship between
governmental crime and white collar crime, as here defined, has
been understudied. Governmental crime can clearly produce
structural conditions and generate an ambience that facilitates or
promotes various forms of white collar crime. The notion of

state-corporate crime, referred to earlier, is an important conceptual advance, insofar as it allows for a much clearer exploration of the symbiotic relationship between major forms of governmental crime and white collar crime.

Finally, as was stated at the outset, the conceptual distinctions advanced in this chapter can contribute to the ongoing discourse on controlling state (or governmental) crime. Clearly the different forms of governmental crime require different responses. Historically, perceived state crimes have sometimes inspired, as ultimate forms of control, revolution (or popular uprising) from within, and war (or military attack) from without. Political white collar crime, on the other hand, has been more fully controlled by formal governmental processes, mass media exposés, and civil suits. Controlling governmental or state crime on all levels requires a more substantial development of international law on the one hand, and transformation of domestic governmental entities on the other hand. Any serious and broad-ranging consideration of governmental crime inevitably confronts us with a deep-seated realization of certain inherent limitations of the traditional reliance upon the state as the primary means for responding to and controlling such crime. What are the optimal means of minimizing the harm done by governmental crime (as well as white collar crime) that avoids overreliance upon governmental institutions, which are themselves quite vulnerable to corrupting influences? The proper answer to this question is one of the major challenges facing those who study crime, criminal justice, and politics.

NOTE

* This chapter is based upon a paper presented at the Annual Meeting of the Academy of Criminal Justice Sciences, Pittsburgh, March 10–14, 1992. A University of Scranton Faculty Research Grant, for research and preparation of this chapter, is gratefully acknowledged.

The author also wishes to thank the editor of this volume, Jeffrey Ian Ross, and three anonymous reviewers for extensive, helpful comments on earlier drafts of the chapter.

REFERENCES

Agee, Philip (1988) "Remarks: The Role of the CIA, Anticommunism and the U.S. Institute for Media Analysis," Harvard University, November 11–13.

Alatas, Syed Hussein (1990) *Corruption: Its Nature, Causes and Functions.* Aldershot, UK: Avebury.

Allen, H.E., P.C. Friday, J.B. Roebuck, and E. Sagarin (1981) *Crime and Punishment.* New York: Free Press.

Arendt, Hannah (1963) *Eichmann in Jerusalem—A Report on the Banality of Evil.* New York: Viking Press.

Barak, Gregg (1990) "Crime, Criminology, and Human Rights: Towards an Understanding of State Criminality." *Journal of Human Justice* 2: 11–28.

——— (1991) *Crimes by the Capitalist State—An Introduction to State Criminality.* Albany: SUNY Press.

Borkin, Joseph (1978) *The Crime and Punishment of I.G. Farben.* New York: Free Press.

Brown, Dee (1971) *Bury My Heart at Wounded Knee.* New York: Holt, Rinehart & Winston.

Cavicchia, Joel (1992) "The Prospects for an International Criminal Court in the 1990s." *Dickinson Journal of International Law* 10: 223–261.

Chambliss, William J. (1989) "State-Organized Crime." *Criminology* 27: 183–208.

Chomsky, Noam, and Edward Herman (1979) *The Washington Connection and Third World Facism.* Nottingham, Eng.: Spokesman.

Clinard, Marshall, and Richard Quinney (1973) *Criminal Behavior Systems: A Typology.* New York: Holt, Rinehart & Winston.

Coleman, James William (1989) *The Criminal Elite*, second edition. New York: St. Martin's.

Corruption and Reform (1986) "Corruption and Reform: An Editorial Essay." *Corruption and Reform: An International Journal* 1: 3–11.

Davidson, Basil (1961) *The African Slave Trade*. Boston: Little, Brown.

Douglas, J., and J.M. Johnson, eds. (1977) *Official Deviance*. Philadelphia: Lippincott.

Dussich, John P.J. (1991) "Some Theoretical and Pragmatic Observations on the Abuse of Power," in G. Kaiser, H. Kury & J.-J. Albrecht (eds.), *Victims and Criminal Justice: Particular Groups of Victims*. Freiburg, West Germany: Max Planck Institute for Foreign and International Penal Law, pp. 677–688.

Falk, R., G. Kolko, and R.J. Lifton, eds. (1971) *Crimes of War*. New York: Vintage.

Friedrichs, David O. (1985) "The Nuclear Arms Issue and the Field of Criminal Justice." *The Justice Professional* 1: 5–9.

Geis, Gilbert, and Robert Meier (1977) *White Collar Crime*. New York: Free Press.

Glaser, Kurt, and Stefan T. Possony (1979) *Victims of Politics—The State of Human Rights*. New York: Columbia University Press.

Green, Gary S. (1990) *Occupational Crime*. Chicago: Nelson Hall.

Harding, Richard (1983) "Nuclear Energy and the Destiny of Mankind—Some Criminological Perspectives." *Australian and New Zealand Journal of Criminology* 16: 81–92.

Heidenheimer, A.J. (1977) "Definitions, Conceptions and Criteria of Corruption," in J. Douglas and J.M. Johnson (eds.), *Official Deviance*. Philadelphia: Lippincott, pp. 19–26.

Herman, Edward S. (1982) *The Real Terror Network: Terrorism in Fact and Propaganda*. Boston: South End Press.

Hope, Kempe Ronald (1987) "Administrative Corruption and Administrative Reform in Developing States." *Corruption and Reform* 2: 127–147.

Huntington, Samuel (1968) *Political Order in Changing Societies*. Cambridge, MA: Harvard University Press.

International Social Science Journal (1992) "The Americas: 1492–1992." *International Social Science Journal* 134: 457–606.

Jenkins, Philip (1988) "Whose Terrorists? Libya and State Criminality." *Contemporary Crises* 12: 5–24.

Johnson, Loch K. (1985) *A Season of Inquiry: The Senate Intelligence Investigation*. Lexington: University Press of Kentucky.

Kauzlarich, David, Ronald C. Kramer, and Brian Smith (1992) "Toward the Study of Governmental Crime: Nuclear Weapons, Foreign Intervention, and International Law." *Humanity & Society* 16: 543–563.

Kramer, Ronald C. (1992) "The Space Shuttle Challenger Explosion: A Case Study of State-Corporate Crime," in Kip Schlegel and David Weisburd (eds.), *White-Collar Crime Reconsidered*. Boston: Northeastern University Press, pp. 214–243.

———, and Raymond J. Michalowski (1990) "State-Corporate Crime." A paper presented at the Annual Meeting of the American Society of Criminology (Baltimore), Nov. 7–12.

Krautheimer, Charles (1991) "Hail, Columbus, Dead White Male." *Time* (May 27): 74.

Krimerman, Leonard I., and Lewis Perry, eds. (1986) *Patterns of Anarchy*. New York: Anchor.

Lieberman, Jethro K. (1972) *How the Government Breaks the Law*. Baltimore, MD: Penguin Books Ltd.

Logue, John (1988) "Conclusion," in A. Markovits and M. Silverstein (eds.), *The Politics of Scandal: Power and Process in Liberal Democracies*. New York: Holmes and Meier, pp. 254–265.

Markovits, Andrei, and Mark Silverstein (eds.) (1988) *The Politics of Scandal: Power and Process in Liberal Democracies*. New York: Holmes and Meier.

Markusen, Eric (1992) "Genocide and Modern War," in M. Dobkowski and I. Wallimann (eds.), *Genocide in Our Time*. Ann Arbor, MI: Pierian Press, pp. 117–148.

Medard, J.F. (1986) "Public Corruption in Africa: A Comparative Perspective." *Corruption and Reform* 1: 115–131.

Michalowski, Raymond J. (1985) *Order, Law and Crime*. New York: Random House.

Neckel, Sighard (1989) "Power and Legitimacy in Political Scandal: Comments on a Theoretical Framework for the Study of Political Scandals." *Corruption and Reform* 4: 147–158.

Noonan, John T. (1984) *Bribes*. Berkeley: University of California Press.

Plano, J.C., and Martin Greenberg (1979) *The American Political Dictionary*. New York: Holt, Rinehart & Winston.

Roebuck, Julian, and Stanley C. Weeber (1978) *Political Crime in the United States*. New York: Praeger.

Sale, Kirkpatrick (1990) *The Conquest of Paradise*. New York: Knopf.

Schell, Jonathan (1982) *The Fate of the Earth*. New York: Avon.

Shatz, Marshall S. (1971) *The Essential Works of Anarchism*. New York: Bantam.

Simon, David, and D. Stanley Eitzen (1993) *Elite Deviance*, fourth edition. Boston: Allyn & Bacon.

Stanely, Alessandra (1991) "The Invasion of the Nina, the Pinta and the Santa Maria." *New York Times* (June 2): E4.

Stohl, Michael, and George A. Lopez, eds. (1984) *The State as Terrorist: The Dynamics of Governmental Violence and Repression*. Westport, CT: Greenwood Press.

Szasz, Andrew (1986) "The Process and Significance of Political Scandals: A Comparsion of Watergate and the "Sewergate" Episode of the Environmental Protection Agency." *Social Problems* 33: 202–217.

Tilly, Charles (1985) "War Making and State Making as Organized Crime," in P. Evans, D. Rueschmeyer, and T. Skocpol (eds.), *Bringing the State Back In*. Cambridge, MA: Harvard University Press: 169–191.

Thompson, Dennis F. (1987) *Political Ethics and Public Office*. Cambridge, MA: Harvard University Press.

Tunnell, Kenneth D. (1993) "Political Crime and Pedagogy: A Content Analysis of Criminal Justice and Criminology Texts." *Journal of Criminal Justice Education* 4: 101–114.

Turk, Austin (1982) *Political Criminality*. Beverly Hills, CA: Sage.

Walzer, Michael (1977) *Just and Unjust Wars: A Moral Argument*. New York: Basic Books.

Wolff, Robert Paul (1976) *In Defense of Anarchism*. New York: Harper Torchbooks.

Young, Marilyn (1991) *The Vietnam Wars: 1945–1990*. New York: HarperPerennial.

Controlling State Crimes by National Security Agencies

Pete Gill

During the last twenty-five years the activities of security intelligence agencies in liberal capitalist states have been exposed as never before. In some countries, such as Australia, Canada, and the United States, wide-ranging judicial or legislative inquiries confirmed that state agencies had both surveilled and disrupted lawful political activities (Church, 1976; Hope, 1977, 1985; McDonald, 1981a, 1981b; Pike, 1977). In the United Kingdom, on the other hand, even more serious allegations have been made, for example, of state agencies mounting disinformation campaigns against elected governments (Dorril and Ramsay, 1991; Leigh, 1988: 215–255) and summarily executing people believed to be engaged in serious political violence against the state (Kitchin, 1989, Stalker, 1988). Yet the government of the UK sought to limit the damage of these allegations by instituting a series of internal inquiries with narrow terms of reference. In 1992, however, the courtroom confessions of a former government minister that the government had misled the House of Commons regarding arms sales to Iraq led to the establishment of a judicial inquiry that started to shine some unaccustomed light into the murkier recesses of the British state, including its security intelligence agencies.

A State of Several Levels

The primary concern of this chapter[1] is to suggest a model for
the control and oversight of security intelligence agencies that
incorporates the various institutional experiments carried out in
liberal democracies in recent years. There has been a general
move toward both greater political, or ministerial, control and
the development of a variety of oversight or review mechanisms.
The implications of the model are that effective control and
oversight require some mechanism at each level. It does not
specify that any particular institutional form will be universally
superior; such mechanisms must be rooted within their own
culture.

The model is constructed on the assumption that it is less
useful to view the state as a whole as "authoritarian," "coercive,"
or "weak" than it is to see the state as an entity that always
operates on different levels. Jessop (1990), for example,
suggested that research into the state should include an
exploration of how the boundaries of the state are established
through specific practices. It should not be assumed, he wrote,
that the "core" of the state "is a unified, unitary, coherent
ensemble or agency." Rather, he says,

> In many cases we can expect to find several rival emergent
> "states" corresponding to competing state projects with no
> overall coherence to the operations of the state system.
> (Jessop, 1990: 366)[2]

Explorers of the terrain of security intelligence have already
discovered such phenomena. In the United States, Wise and Ross
(1968) characterized "The Invisible Government" as the "loose
amorphous grouping of individuals and agencies drawn from
many parts of the visible government." Although centered on
the intelligence community, it extended also into the private
sector (p. 9). Later, discussing the origins of the Watergate affair,
Wolfe (1976) identified the emergence since about 1960 of two
states: the first, formal and legal, which contained all the
elements of liberal democracy and exercised a symbolic
importance. The second state was covert, unaffected by changes
in elected officials and unconcerned with constitutional niceties.

The "vigilantes" of the covert state were initially concerned with foreign affairs, but later turned their attention to domestic politics. Overall, he argued, Presidents John F. Kennedy, Lyndon Johnson, and Richard Nixon all showed that they were prepared to break any laws that stood in the way of the national interest as they perceived it and had relied upon a covert state to achieve that end subject only to its own discretion (Wolfe, 1976: 46).

E.P. Thompson, the British historian, writing in 1979, developed a similar theme regarding the UK when he suggested that

> . . . the growth of an unrepresentative and unaccountable state within the State has been a product of the twentieth century. Its growth was, paradoxically, actually aided by the unpopularity of security and policing agencies; forced by this into the lowest possible visibility, they learned to develop techniques of invisible influence and control. (1979: 9)

Thompson identifies a number of causal factors, for example, two world wars habituating people "to arguments of national interest," and facilitating much interchange between academics and intelligence agencies; the retreat from the Empire leaving security, military, and police agencies with colonial experience looking for new fields of application; and the legacy of "McCarthyism" in Britain, which, while not producing anything as stringent as the Berufsverbot in West Germany, resulted, through the positive vetting system, in a "moderate" orthodoxy in the higher reaches of the civil service (1979: 9–10).

The rules, policies, and practices relating to information, power, and decision-making at the different levels of the state are frequently quite different; indeed each of these has its own discourse (Farson, 1989: 129–130). So, within the "secret state" there is a predominant "insider" view concerned more with the need for effective operations and a belief that law and oversight mechanisms inhibit these, while outside, in the public discourse, there is likely to be more concern with the propriety of operations and with legal rights (Gill, 1991: 89–91).

A number of factors explain how these different levels and their discourses continue along their contradictory paths. First, the public may well be aware of the liberal democratic rhetoric of the public discourse, but because of secrecy, it will not be aware of the specific details of agencies' operations. As long as these details remain secret, their only connection with law will be with the Ways and Means Act; it will be only if those operations become public that it will become necessary to provide post hoc rationalizations of the actions that were taken. Second, McBarnet's (1981) exploration of how the law simultaneously sets out to achieve crime control while maintaining the ideology of due process of law can be usefully applied to the security intelligence area. Part of her explanation is structural; she suggests that "[t]he doctrine of the separation of powers provides a multi-headed state and with it the potential to extol the rhetoric in one sector and deny it in another" (159). The other part lies in techniques of judicial reasoning. Specifically, judges will routinely reiterate the rhetoric of due process in general but will decide particular cases in ways that deny that due process to individuals (p. 159).

For the purposes of the present analysis three levels of the state are identified. The first—the "secret state"—includes the security intelligence agencies and related bodies such as the Canadian Cabinet Committee on Security and Intelligence (CCSI), U.K. Joint Intelligence Committee (JIC), and the U.S. National Security Council (NSC). The second level is the executive branch, which incorporates both the government, or "political executive," and the permanent bureaucracy. The third level will include legislative assemblies, the judiciary, and other bodies appointed by the executive but formally operating independently thereof. The fourth level of analysis, outside the state, is society made up of citizens or, in the UK, subjects.[3]

Two concepts assist in modeling the relationship between society and these different levels of the state. First, autonomy, which is the process whereby particular institutions maintain control over the determination of their ends and means (e.g., Keller, 1989: 21), and, second, penetration, which incorporates the idea of institutions seeking information about and exercising power over institutions and people at other levels. Autonomy and penetration thus represent opposite sides of the same process—a group is autonomous to the extent that it is able to resist the penetration of others. Struggles concerning the control and oversight of security intelligence agencies can thus be characterized as struggles between individuals, groups, and institutions to maintain or increase their autonomy and to resist penetration. These struggles are conducted by a variety of strategies of power (e.g., Foucault, 1983: 310) and information control (e.g., Wilsnack, 1980).

Liberal democracy is based, in part, on the premise that states enjoying excessive autonomy are prone to abuses of power that, whether or not they are actually in breach of specific laws, might be characterized as "state crime." In the security intelligence area the extent to which state actions are defined as crime or not itself reflects the outcome of struggles in terms of the definition of law. What follows is based on the proposition that a reduction in state autonomy by way of increased democratic penetration (control and oversight) is a necessary condition for minimizing state crime.

Principles of Control and Oversight

An important consideration in this discussion of structural, legal, or institutional means of controlling security intelligence is the significance of political will and the danger of faith in the "structural fix" (Betts, 1981: 248; Oseth, 1985: 185–187). Elegant structures of control and oversight may be erected but may be quite worthless if those responsible for them see their role as providing no more than a modicum of public reassurance that previous problem areas of government are now under control. The general propensity of reforms to be directed in part at "symbolic reassurance" has been noted by Edelman (1964); in an area of government operations as secretive and intrinsically difficult to control as security intelligence, this is an even greater danger. This should alert us to the possibility that some working inside security intelligence agencies may embrace reform as a means of staving off more thorough changes.

Whatever oversight structures are developed, the preconditions for them to have some real rather than purely symbolic impact are that they have adequate resources, including full access to information, and the political will to use them (e.g., Gill, 1989b). Oversight structures lacking the necessary resources and will are worse than just useless, however. By providing an apparent channel for accountability they may provide an extra protective layer for the inner state as it resists democratic penetration. Even in the United States, where oversight would seem to be most energetic, there are suggestions that the Congress was pulling its punches in the case of the Iran/Contra deals (Hersh, 1987: vii–viii).

The following principles of control and oversight should be treated as hypotheses that might be used heuristically. They might be used as a benchmark against which to compare historically the lack of control and oversight procedures and by which to evaluate the adequacy of reforms introduced more recently. First, both managerial control and external oversight are required at each of the different levels that were identified above (see Figure 1). Second, the same positions should not be responsible for both control and oversight. This is not to say that those responsible for the control of security intelligence agency operations should not consider the desirability that those operations are carried out properly and without infringing the law and civil rights, but, rather, that it is naive to believe that ministers or officials will be able to subject their own actions to effective oversight. This skepticism forms the basis of political control of bureaucracy in general in liberal democracies.

Third, those positions responsible for control of security intelligence agencies should draw up standards and guidelines that will be public insofar as is compatible with fundamental security needs, and that will increase in specificity the nearer the level of control is to the agency itself (Supperstone, 1987: 219).

At the highest level of generality will be the manifestos adopted by outside groups and political parties that are likely to cover questions of overall oversight structures as well as security intelligence mandates. Next will be the statutory mandate as established by the legislative assembly. Also relevant at this level will be those court decisions that, if they occur at all, establish case law regarding the basic powers of security intelligence agencies. Based on the statutory mandate, more specific guidelines and directions should be issued by the relevant (politically appointed) minister, and finally, the most

Figure 1

Model of Control and Oversight of Security Intelligence Agencies

LEVEL OF CONTROL/ OVERSIGHT	1	2	3	4
	INTERNAL TO THE AGENCY	THE EXECUTIVE BRANCH	OTHER STATE BODIES	CITIZENS AND GROUPS
FORM OF CONTROL	GUIDELINES	MINISTERIAL DIRECTIONS	STATUTORY MANDATE	MANIFESTOES
		DRAWN UP BY →	→	→
INSTITNS OF CONTROL	e.g., DIRECTOR	→ e.g., ATTORNEY GENERAL	→ LEGISLATIVE ASSEMBLY	→ POLITICAL PARTIES
	←	← REPORT TO	←	←
INSTITNS OF OVERSIGHT	e.g., PROFESSIONAL RESPONSIBILITY OFFICE (FBI)	e.g., INSPECTOR GENERAL (CAN)	e.g., SIRC (CAN) LEGISLATIVE COMMITTEES (USA, AUS, CAN)	PUBLIC INTEREST GROUPS

specific guidelines of all will be those generated internally by the agency to give effect to ministerial guidelines and directions.

Fourth, each control position will be accountable or responsible to that at the next level moving away from the agency, in conformity with the usual principle of political control. Fifth, the primary role of each oversight institution will be to report to the control institution at the same level. For example, an oversight institution that is outside the security intelligence agency itself but within the executive branch should report initially to the minister who is responsible for control at that level. In addition, in order to augment the accountability of each control position to that at the next level, each oversight institution should make as much of its findings as possible available also to the oversight institution at the next level. Since control and oversight should rest, ultimately, with the people, the discussion will begin and end at level four (see Figure 1).

Level Four Control

Military and police agencies must be controlled by civilians who are themselves subject to control by the "institutions of polyarchy" (Dahl, 1991: 82). Johnson (1991a) identifies a number of areas in which the political parties—the main "institutions of polyarchy"—in the United States have debated intelligence controversies, for example, the role of the CIA in Vietnam, Watergate, and Iran/Contra, and that of the FBI in domestic political surveillance. During the 1980s the aggressive foreign policies of the Ronald Reagan administration led to more clear-cut party divisions in the congressional intelligence committees (pp. 59–60). In the United Kingdom the political parties took no obvious position over security intelligence matters until the 1980s, when both the Labour and (then) Liberal parties published extensive discussion documents. Their specific proposals foundered in the 1980s on the rocks of Thatcherite majorities in the Commons. The Security Service was placed on a statutory footing in 1989, but the inspiration for this was the threat of an adverse decision in the European Court on Human Rights (see Hurwitz, this volume), and therefore it was more a measure aimed at legalizing Security Service activities than the kind of rights-oriented proposal being advanced by Labour and Liberal Democrats.

Elsewhere the clearest party view was found in Australia where the Labour Party sought to bring about change via Justice Hope's commissions and subsequent legislation. In Canada the divisions between the Progressive Conservatives and the Liberals, the two largest parties until 1993, were based far more on historical and regional rather than ideological factors and the only consistent party position—one of skepticism toward the need for a separate domestic security intelligence agency—was provided by the New Democratic Party.

Level Three Control

It is easy for governments to exploit the connection between their own survival and that of the state in order to increase their leverage over internal politics (Buzan, 1991: 89), and it becomes easier as the definition of *national security* broadens. Historically, the term has been used to increase the discretionary power available to political executives. For example, examining the U.S. Legal Code for 1970, Relyea (1987) found that about 240 of 390 references to national security were descriptions of grants to the President of extensive discretionary authority.

> In none of these instances was national security defined, but the cumulative effect, nevertheless, was one of giving the Executive Branch overwhelming latitude to determine national security and, accordingly, what actions could appropriately be taken regarding it. (p. 19)

Regarding domestic security, Watergate revealed the extent to which this condition had reached an apotheosis in the 1970s. The congressional inquiries that, first, culminated in the impeachment and resignation of Richard Nixon and then investigated the FBI and CIA, gave the starkest examples of the use and abuse of the notion of national security.

The implications for policy are that clear criteria be established for determining how information is to be gathered as to what threats exist and, then, for assessing which threats are of sufficient intensity to require countering action (Buzan, 1991: 141). However, clearer legislative mandates for security intelligence agencies are prone to two main types of vulnerability. On the one hand, highly detailed statutes that seek to minimize the discretion of those to whom the law will apply may not provide a workable framework for security intelligence agencies. This was one argument against a comprehensive charter for the FBI in the late 1970s. On the other hand, a statute enunciating general principles, which may be the only practical way of proceeding, is likely to be particularly vulnerable to having the gaps filled in by those not entirely sympathetic to the intentions of the legislators. The general law would provide a source of ideological strength, by demonstrating that security intelligence activities were now governed by law, while the actual gaps and ambiguities in that legislation would be a source of operational strength for the security intelligence agencies.

As a result of the McDonald inquiry into the Royal Canadian Mounted Police's (RCMP) activities in the 1970s, the Canadian Security Intelligence Service (CSIS) Act (1984) created the CSIS out of the former RCMP Security Service and also attempted a more specific definition of threats to national security. Section 2 of the CSIS Act provides a "negative" definition of national security in terms of threat,[4] and, subsequently, the government announced in 1989 its five priority national security concerns on which the CSIS should concentrate its security intelligence effort (Blais, 1989).

Within the general idea of national security, there are particular concepts that have provided rationales for security intelligence activities. The one that has been most extensively used and abused during the twentieth century is subversion. The CSIS Act defines subversion as

> activities directed toward undermining by covert unlawful acts, or directed toward or intended ultimately to lead to the destruction or overthrow by violence of, the constitutionally established system of government in Canada. (s.2(d))

In 1987, the Security Intelligence Review Committee (SIRC) having carried out research into the activities of CSIS's countersubversion branch, concluded that individuals were targeted mainly because of their relationship with some domestic political group, and that CSIS overestimated the influence of such groups and the likelihood of violence. SIRC concluded that the valid work of this branch was actually concerned with two main threats, foreign manipulation and political violence. Therefore, said SIRC, the branch should be closed and this work split between the counterintelligence and counterterrorism branches (SIRC, 1987a, 34–40; Gill, 1989b). The branch was closed, and there was a major decrease in the number of countersubversion investigations. Since 1988, those that remain have used only open sources, and there have been none of the ministerial authorizations necessary for CSIS to use intrusive measures for an investigation solely under s.2(d). SIRC and, in 1990, the Commons Committee reviewing the operation of the CSIS Act, recommended that the national security mandate be narrowed by the removal of s.2(d), but the government refused to do so (SIRC, 1989: 1; Special Committee, 1990: 23–24; Solicitor General, 1991: 40–41).

In Australia, Hope (1977) noted that there was an inherent danger that investigations could infringe basic democratic rights if dissent or nonconformity were mistaken for subversion, and therefore proposed that the definition be confined to activities involving violence or illegality (§§62–66). After further examination of the question, Hope recommended in his 1985 report that the term *subversion* be dropped (Hope, 1985: 69–70). Therefore, in the Australian Security and Intelligence Organization (ASIO) Amendment Act (1986), the term *politically motivated violence* replaced both *subversion* and *terrorism* as objects of security concern (Hanks, 1988: 131).

In the United Kingdom the 1989 Security Service Act defines subversion as: "actions intended to overthrow or undermine parliamentary democracy by political, industrial or violent means" (s.1(2)). This definition clearly includes political and industrial activity that is both peaceful and lawful. Pressed in the Commons on the inadequacy of this, the Home Secretary responded with an interpretation of the definition that excluded those

> who have views on the structure or organisation of
> Parliament, or if they are involved in seeking to change

industrial practices in this country or to negotiate a better
deal if they are members of trade unions, or if they seek to
challenge or change the Government's policies relating to
defence, employment, foreign policy or anything else.
(Hurd, 1989: col. 218)

But the Home Secretary said this was not a declaration of
ministerial policy, nor would it be incorporated into the bill
(Hurd, 1989: col. 219). Thus the government sought to maintain
the maximum flexibility.

Level Two Control

There are two extreme possibilities with respect to
ministerial control, both of which pose considerable dangers:
either a complete lack of control or ministerial direction in the
partisan interests of the governing party. Historically, security
intelligence agencies have enjoyed almost complete autonomy
from ministerial guidance. Ministers seem to have taken the
position that ignorance is, if not bliss, certainly preferable to
becoming implicated in security operations. Pierre Trudeau,
former prime minister of Canada, for example, enunciated this as
Canadian policy in 1977 (Edwards, 1980: 94). The McDonald
inquiry examined the extent to which ministers had given tacit
assent to the RCMP to engage in illegal surveillance activities
after the October Crisis of 1970. McDonald concluded that senior
members of the RCMP had tried to have the question of illegal
acts discussed by the cabinet but that ministers had failed to
resolve the question one way or another; that is, they had neither
directed the RCMP to continue nor instructed them to desist
from such activities (McDonald, 1981b: 63–68).

In the United States, once FBI Director J. Edgar Hoover
had his authorization for the surveillance of subversive activities
from President Franklin Roosevelt and Secretary of State Cordell
Hull in 1936, he neither troubled attorneys general (his formal
superiors) with further requests for authorization nor informed
them of what the FBI was doing unless he decided that there was
some particular reason for doing so. At the same time, he
safeguarded his direct access to successive presidents with
judicious use of the information gathered by the Bureau so that

he became the real "untouchable" in Washington. Only one attorney general, Robert Kennedy, was able to prevent Hoover from bypassing him, but only while his brother was President (Schlesinger, 1978: 259).

Security intelligence agencies are now generally subject to greater ministerial direction. In Canada, since 1984 over fifty separate ministerial directions have been issued to CSIS (Solicitor General, 1991: 11–16). The Australian legislation not only permits but actually obliges the minister to give ASIO directions regarding investigations of politically motivated violence (ASIO Act, 1979, s.8A(2)). In 1976 the United States Attorney General Edward Levi produced guidelines for the conduct of FBI investigations, which were subsequently relaxed somewhat in 1983 by Attorney General William Smith (e.g., Poveda, 1990: 132–141). In the United Kingdom ministerial reluctance to intervene has been reinforced historically by the general mystification surrounding intelligence matters (Andrew, 1985: 500–506). This has been ameliorated slightly by the passage of the Security Service Act (1989), which requires ministers to sign warrants authorizing Security Service "interference with property" (s.3). However, the prime determinant of the extent of ministerial interest in the Security Service remains the press of events, for example, some major incident or scandal resulting in public arousal will increase ministerial interest above the normally minimal level. Therefore, it might be suggested that there is a direct relationship between the autonomy of the security intelligence agency and public ignorance or apathy. Of course, to the extent that security intelligence matters remain shrouded in unnecessary secrecy, being publicized normally only through state (dis)information policies, then this autonomy will be self-reinforcing.

On the other hand, serious problems may arise if there is either too much ministerial direction or direction of a particular kind. Since ministers are amateurs, it is said, their guidance should be restricted to a clear enunciation of government intelligence priorities and overall questions of organization and budgets. Second, as stated in the UK Maxwell-Fyfe Directive of 1952, it is wrong for elected politicians to make use of this particularly sensitive part of the state apparatus to achieve some political advantage, and officers must be protected from attempts to use them in this way:

> It is essential that the Security Service should be kept absolutely free from any political bias or influence and nothing should be done that might lend colour to any suggestion that it is concerned with the interests of any particular section of the community, or with any other matter than the Defence of the Realm as a whole. (Reproduced in Denning, 1963: §238)

This might be compared with the 1989 Security Service Act that refers only to a prohibition of work in support of a political party and says nothing about working against parties (s.2(2)(b)). Morton Halperin, director of the ACLU, has argued that most of the abuses of civil liberties by security intelligence agencies in the United States came from Presidents seeking to spy on and manipulate their political opponents rather than from career officials; for example, Roosevelt's orders to the FBI to investigate those wanting to preserve U.S. neutrality in World War II, Kennedy's orders to the FBI to investigate the sugar industries, and Johnson's orders to the FBI to spy on people at the 1964 Democratic Party Convention (Moore, 1985: 52).

However, the issue goes deeper. Maxwell-Fyfe's view depends on an assumption that, whereas particular governments may have partisan views, the state reflects some overall consensus about the goals of and threats to society. This assumption is rarely justified; whatever the view taken of the debate about the partisan nature of the state in general, there can be no doubt that security intelligence agencies in North America and the United Kingdom have all behaved in a highly partisan fashion. This has resulted not just from a minister issuing orders to an otherwise neutral agency, but also because shared assumptions between particular governments and its security intelligence agencies have made formal partisan direction unnecessary.

Level One Control

The forms of control within security intelligence agencies will be dependent on internal processes of communication and power. In hierarchically organized agencies such as the police, the main problem will be the distortion of information as it moves between levels; while in smaller security intelligence agencies the compartmentalization of knowledge—"need-to-know" procedures—will be more significant.

The question of recruitment to security intelligence agencies is particularly important because, if it merely reflects the political dominance of certain classes or groups, partisan direction of agencies may be unnecessary. For example, in the FBI the only black agents for many years were Hoover's personal servants and his racism permeated the Bureau (Powers, 1987: 323–324, 367). In Canada the RCMP, including its security service, was dominated by Anglophones, and the issue of the status of Francophone agents continued to dog the new CSIS in its early years (SIRC, 1987b). Some of the greatest controversies surrounding the FBI and the RCMP concerned their respective investigations of the black civil rights movement in the United States and the separatist movement in Québec.

A central feature of modern states is that recruitment to their administrative apparatuses becomes based less on patronage and more on impersonal and competitive educational criteria (Dandeker, 1990: 53–54). Until the late 1970s the UK Security Service was apparently able to resist this trend. Recruitment between the wars was by personal introduction, which was believed to be the best guarantor of loyalty and integrity, and most recruits were middle-aged retired men from the public services, whose pensions cushioned them against the low salaries (Hinsley and Simkins, 1990: 10). During the postwar period most recruits were ex-police officers, armed forces personnel, and former officials from the declining colonial service. Porter concludes his historical survey by suggesting that security service officers

> had always been an odd bunch . . . socially and politically entirely untypical of the nation as a whole, eccentric and

often not very bright. This does not seem to have changed
appreciably by the 1970s. (Porter, 1989: 213)

This autonomy from developments in the rest of the state was
both cause and effect of a certain backwardness in the Security
Service.In 1976, in an effort to broaden the recruitment base to
MI5, James Callaghan and Merlyn Rees insisted that the Service
go through Civil Service Commission procedures, which appears
to have had some impact (Ingram, 1984: 349). More recently,
faced with recruitment problems, the Security Service com-
missioned a private personnel firm to examine its policy and
sought ways of discreetly advertising for recruits (Simpson,
1992: 10). ASIO has made use of an advertising agency (ASIO,
1989: 40), and CSIS has recruited openly via over 100
newspapers (SIRC, 1990: 51).

In common with the rest of the state sector, women have
been underrepresented in security intelligence agencies and have
tended to be concentrated in clerical and administrative jobs.
Two-fifths of ASIO staff in 1988 were women, but whereas three-
quarters of clerical staff were women, only 17.5 percent of
intelligence officers were (ASIO, 1989: 44). CSIS has been
attempting to detach itself from the white Anglophone male
image of the days of the RCMP. The Commons' Special Review
Committee reported that the proportion of Francophones
recruited to CSIS had increased significantly since 1984, although
it noted also continuing complaints of discrimination against
Francophone employees (Special Committee, 1990: 54–56). The
proportion of women in CSIS increased from 36 to 43 percent
between 1984–1991, and from 7 to 20 percent among intelligence
officers (CSIS, 1992: 24–25) but the Parliamentary Committee
was critical of the minimal improvement in the representation of
women at supervisory levels (Special Committee, 1990: 56).

Regarding recruitment from minorities, federal privacy
requirements in Canada prevent ethnic monitoring (SIRC, 1990:
52), but CSIS reported that between 1988 and 1991 "visible
minorities" increased from 0.6 to 2.45 percent of employees
(CSIS, 1992: 25). In Australia, ASIO reported that 7.2 percent of
its employees were from non-English-speaking backgrounds,
compared with 12.1 percent in the Australian public service as a
whole (ASIO, 1989: 44). Under Hoover the FBI was notoriously

an organization dominated by white men, and when William Webster became director in 1978 there were still only 91 women agents (just over 1 percent) (Phillips, 1984: 74). Table 1 shows the changes that occurred in the FBI during the 1980s.

TABLE 1

Minorities and Women Special Agents in the FBI, 1978 and 1989

	Native American		Asian American		African American		Hispanic American		Women		Total Number of Special Agents Employed
	No.	%	No.	%	No.	%	No.	%	No.	%	No.
1978	23	0.3	40	0.5	185	2.3	173	2.2	147	1.9	7,900
1989	39	0.4	120	1.2	432	4.5	482	5.0	910	9.4	9,650

Source: Adapted from House of Representatives, 1990: 475.

The U.K. Security Service has now revealed that just over half of its 2000 employees are women, but it has not given their proportion among intelligence officers, nor has it given any information regarding minority recruitment (MI5, 1993: 9–10).

However, more broadly based recruitment is not a panacea. Problems will result from people's self-imposed conformity in the face of some perceived organizational "dominant ideology" as identified in the U.K. Security Service by Ingram (1984: 349–350). On the other hand, Emerson (1992) shows how such conformity may be imposed from above, as in the CIA's analytical directorate in the 1980s. Another, more subtle, process is "groupthink" to which security intelligence agencies might seem to be particularly vulnerable. According to Janis (1972),

> The more amiability and esprit de corps among the members of a policy-making in-group, the greater is the danger that independent critical thinking will be replaced by groupthink, which is likely to result in irrational and dehumanizing actions directed against out-groups. (p. 13)

This might even degenerate into the kind of paranoia that seems to have inflicted the U.K. Security Service at various times, most notoriously in giving rise to the "mole hunts" against senior members of the Service (e.g., Knightley, 1986: 340–363; Mangold, 1992: 323–347).

Level One Oversight

Historically, such internal oversight mechanisms as have existed in security intelligence agencies had low status and made very little impact. Within the CIA, for example, there were a variety of offices with internal auditing functions including the Office of Inspector General, which was to investigate anything from employees' affirmative action complaints to allegations of unlawfulness and impropriety. Yet the Office was unaware of any of the wrongdoings disclosed by the Church Committee, and the later Iran/Contra affair. As the CIA became embroiled in congressional investigations of its history, William Colby, then CIA director, indicated the importance of the inspector general by reducing its staff from fourteen to five (Johnson, 1989: 239). The significance of internal oversight can be further gauged by the failure of a number of detailed histories of the CIA even to mention the Office in their indexes (e.g., Jeffreys-Jones, 1989; Ranelagh, 1987).

The inadequacy of formal internal mechanisms for oversight highlights the potential significance of ethical resistance; however, the protection for whistleblowers varies among states. In the United States it has always been difficult to prosecute civil servants for leaking information, except in the relatively narrow case of espionage, because of the First Amendment protection of the freedom of speech.In 1978, the U.S. Congress passed the Civil Service Reform Act, which set out to protect whistleblowers who leaked information that they believed revealed "mismanagement, a gross waste of funds, an abuse of authority, or a substantial and specific danger to public health or safety" (Michael, 1985). In other countries, notably the United Kingdom, prosecuting public officials has been far easier. But, short of prosecution, the main hazard faced by civil servants everywhere has been the variety of internal administrative punishments that might be inflicted upon them.

Holroyd (1989), a military intelligence officer, alleged a variety of countering operations by the security forces in

Northern Ireland during 1974–1975, including assassination. He was taken under guard to the army psychiatric hospital in Netley (pp. 70–105). Cathy Massiter, who joined MI5 in 1970, complained to the head of her section, her assistant director and then the personnel branch that her work in providing briefing material to the Ministry of Defence about CND was outside the Maxwell-Fyfe Directive. She was told to see a psychiatrist, who had clearance to see members of the Security Service, and eventually it was made clear to her that she would have to resign. She left the Service in February 1984 (*Observer*, February 24, 1985: 1–2).

Public officials must be viewed as citizens rather than merely as employees (Swan, 1989: 173–174), and in security intelligence agencies, where both the formal and informal pressures to maintain secrecy are greatest, some systematic provision for whistleblowers is needed. This would assist the general oversight of such agencies and reduce the likelihood of leaks being even more damaging if they go directly to the media. In Canada, the McDonald Commission proposed that security intelligence employees should be encouraged to disclose, without penalty, questionable activities to the independent review body that it proposed (McDonald, 1981b: 749), but the CSIS Act places an obligation only on the director of the Service to disclose to the solicitor general and attorney general unlawful activities (s.20). These reports will be passed to SIRC. Under Attorney General Levi, FBI officials and agents were ordered to report any requests made to the Bureau or practices within the Bureau "which may be improper or which present the appearance of impropriety" (Elliff, 1979: 182).

Level Two Oversight

In the United Kingdom the government has attempted to maintain a strict doctrine of ministerial responsibility, that is, ministers can both control and oversee security intelligence agencies. Elsewhere the weakness of this argument has been recognized and the main innovation intended to provide ministers with some means of oversight is the Office of Inspector General. In Canada, the inspector general (IG) monitors and reviews the operational activities of CSIS with particular reference to their compliance with ministerial policies, legality, and reasonableness (CSIS Act, 1984: §§30–33). The IG has access to all the information under CSIS control, subject to the same exclusion as SIRC regarding cabinet confidences (§31). She provides the minister with a certificate regarding CSIS, having monitored and reviewed the Service's activities.

Formal and informal dealings with SIRC have played a crucial part in determining the inspector general's workload. In the early years, because of the pressure on resources felt both in SIRC and the IG's office, considerable efforts were made to avoid the duplication of effort, for example, by coordinating future projects. Even in cases where SIRC issues the IG with a formal direction to carry out a review, there is prior consultation as to the scope and wording of the direction, and interchange will continue throughout on refining the scope of the study as new information emerges (De Rosenroll, 1988).

In Australia, following the recommendation in Justice Hope's second report, the Inspector General of Intelligence and Security Act (1986), provided for an inspector general within the executive branch and gave the Office a potentially wider remit than that in Canada. In Australia it covers not just the domestic security intelligence agency, ASIO, but also the Secret Intelligence Service (ASIS), the Defence Signals Directorate (DSD), the Joint Intelligence Organisation (JIO), and the Office of National Assessments (ONA). At the instigation of a minister, a complainant, or on his own volition, the inspector general can inquire into compliance of the agencies with the law and ministerial guidelines and the propriety of their activities as well as employee grievances, though the inspector general's powers are more restricted with respect to the last two agencies. The inspector general has full access to documents and may compel responses from officials, overriding secrecy provisions in other statutes. All of his reports go to the responsible minister, and he can only respond to a complainant in terms approved by the minister. His annual report goes to the Prime Minister and is to be laid before Parliament (Hanks, 1989: 47–48). On paper, therefore, the Australian inspector general appears to combine the review functions of the Canadian inspector general and SIRC.

However, whereas they cover just one agency and have between them twenty-four staff, the Australian inspector general covers five agencies and has three staff! In the first four and a half years, the Office received forty-six complaints, all against ASIO, and "the vast majority" were said to be unfounded (Holdich, 1991: 13). He also investigated some allegations that appeared in the media but most of the workload concerned employee grievances. Although the Office has carried out spot checks into records where ASIO has conducted intrusive surveillance with a ministerial warrant, its agenda would seem to be primarily reactive compared with the greater element of a proactive oversight agenda in Canada.

Level Three Oversight

Regarding the possibilities of legislative oversight in parliamentary systems, the Canadian debate in the 1980s involved three different arguments. The first was the fundamental principle of liberal democracy that the accountability of permanent bureaucracies was to elected representatives in Parliament and that, though security intelligence raised particular problems, it should not be exempted from that principle. The second accepted the principle but argued that it was not practicable, while the third argued that external review would actually be more effective if carried out by a nonparliamentary body.

In Canada, the government accepted the second argument. The only opportunity envisaged for parliamentary discussion would be the consideration of SIRC's annual report by the Standing Committee on Justice and the solicitor general. The Special Committee set up by the Canadian House of Commons to carry out the five-year review of the CSIS Act during 1989–1990 represented Parliament's first systematic review of the security intelligence system. Although this Committee pursued a nonconfrontational strategy toward the government over the question of access to information, it was not successful in obtaining much of the material it sought. For example, neither the IG nor the SIRC would release reports that had been made to the minister. Time constraints on the Committee to complete its work ruled out any judicial challenge to the government, who, it appears, quite consciously delayed the Committee on this issue (Farson, 1991a). The Commons has attempted to maintain the momentum achieved by the Special Committee by establishing in June 1991 a permanent subcommittee on national security.

In Australia, both Hope's reports in 1977 and 1985 recommended against a parliamentary committee, but the Labour government announced that it intended to establish a joint committee of its house of representatives and senate to oversee ASIO. Legislation was passed in 1986, but it was August 1988 before the new committee started work. The committee has seven members appointed by each house (three from the senate, four from the house) after consultation with all party leaders. It is precluded from reviewing certain matters: foreign intelligence, matters that are "operationally sensitive," matters not affecting Australian citizens or permanent residents and individual complaints (which are the business of the IG). It can require the production of documents and the giving of evidence, but it must give five days' notice, and the minister may issue a nonreviewable certificate preventing any person or document from going to the committee (Cain, 1991: 123; Hanks, 1989: 51–53). In other words, the committee's powers are highly restricted, and by 1992 it had conducted only one inquiry (Cain, 1993: 87).

In the United Kingdom, the House of Commons Select Committee on Home Affairs has recently advised that it should be granted a role in the oversight of Security Service policy and budgets, but not operations (1993), but the government made it immediately clear that it had no intention of following this advice (Home Office, 1993).

Oversight by judges presents a second possibility at level three. According to the rule of law, government officials are subject to the same rules of law and conduct as citizens. This should provide one of the main checks on the abuse of power by the state. However, judges are involved in pronouncing on the activities of security intelligence agencies only on a rather haphazard and ultimately restricted basis. They may be requested to make decisions in press freedom cases or criminal trials in which security intelligence agencies and questions of national security are involved. Alternatively, judges may become involved through specific measures established for the granting of warrants for wiretapping and bugging, or as part of some scheme for the review of the security intelligence apparatus as in the U.K. Security Service Act 1989.

There are a number of general factors accounting for the hesitancy of the courts to deal with national security in all countries. Comparing the contribution of courts with that of legislatures and judicial commissions, Hanks (1988) suggests a number of structural factors. Commissions such as those by McDonald in Canada and Hope in Australia have had broader terms of reference regarding the organization and policies of domestic security intelligence agencies, while the courts have been faced with diverse and specific issues, for instance, the publication of government information, security intelligence officers' memoirs, and the question of trade unions within security intelligence agencies. Also, a wide variety of views and options are available to commissions, whereas courts possess only a limited repertoire of remedies with which to deal with the specific aspects of the case before them. However, concludes Hanks, whether courts' reluctance to become involved in national security questions is because of judicial unwillingness to deal with difficult issues or because of institutional constraints, the consequence of their unwillingness to challenge executive definitions has been to endorse an authoritarian view of the state (1988: 132–133).

Special review bodies are a third possibility at this level, for example, SIRC in Canada. Established in Canada in 1984 to provide external oversight of CSIS, its five privy councillors are appointed by the government after consultation with other parties. Those appointed are not necessarily already privy councillors, which can help to avoid such a committee becoming a sinecure for ex-ministers. They work part-time but have the support of a full-time staff of about a dozen in carrying out their dual functions of reviewing CSIS and sitting as an appeals body against refusals of security clearances and hearing other complaints against the actions of the CSIS.

It is reasonable to conclude that SIRC has had some real impact on CSIS operations. In the years following the closure of the countersubversion branch in 1987, 54,000 of its 57,562 files were destroyed or packed for the national archives. Of the remainder, only a "small percentage" (SIRC, 1988: 13) were reallocated to the counterterrorism or counterintelligence branches for active investigation, and by 1991 the remaining "residue" of countersubversion files had been recategorized, or allocated either for destruction or for the archives (SIRC, 1990: 44; 1991: 24). Another measure of the impact of SIRC has been the extent to which it has been prepared to make public its criticisms of CSIS. Certainly this upset a number of insiders, but it is clear that the use of publicity was necessary in order to induce the CSIS to make changes that it was otherwise resisting, for example, improving the status of civilian recruits compared with those from the RCMP (Gill, 1989a).

SIRC's initial reporting responsibility is to the minister. So, in terms of the oversight model developed here, SIRC, operating at level three, is to report to the minister at level two. This has brought SIRC into conflict with Parliament. Since the IG also reports to the minister, the question arises as to how far SIRC and the IG cover much of the same ground in terms of reviewing CSIS. This issue became quickly apparent to the Special Committee on the Five Year Review of the CSIS Act, which reported in 1990. SIRC requested access to both the IG's certificates and those reports that SIRC had made to the minister but that had not been made public. In both cases access was denied to the Special Committee. The Special Committee proposed additional powers for SIRC and recommended that SIRC report directly to Parliament rather than through the minister (Farson, 1991b: 34–6). Some members of SIRC itself clearly felt that they should be able to report directly to Parliament (Farson, 1991a: 23).

Level Four Oversight

Publicity is a significant weapon in the struggle to control bureaucracies in general (Peters, 1984: 242–243) and access to files is the very center of attempts to exercise real control over security intelligence agencies. In the United States the first major inroads into the files of the FBI were made by the Church Committee, and many were reprinted as part of their hearings. Further documents have been obtained by various means. In 1973 the Socialist Workers Party (SWP) and the Young Socialist Alliance (YSA) filed a lawsuit seeking damages for the illegal acts they had suffered and an injunction to halt any further FBI countering actions. Pretrial proceedings lasted eight years and produced hundreds of thousands of pages from FBI files. The trial itself lasted three months in 1981, and the decision was announced in 1986. The FBI was found guilty of violations of the plaintiffs' constitutional rights and was ordered to pay $264,000. A year later an injunction against any further use of FBI files by the SWP or YSA was granted. The Justice Department did not appeal (Jayko, 1988: 5–7).

Also, there have been many requests under the Freedom of Information Act. These have been so extensive that the FBI's Office of Congressional and Public Affairs published a guide to researchers wishing to access FBI records. Material that has been processed already under the Freedom of Information Act can be read and copied at the FBI Headquarters Reading Room, and staff will assist with the making of further FOI requests where necessary. Researchers are even advised that the previous "Do Not File" memoranda may now be accessed through the central records system! (FBI, 1984: 6). These files have formed the basis of a number of biographies of Hoover and other studies (e.g., Churchill and Vander Wall, 1990; Davis, 1992; Keller, 1989; Powers, 1987; Theoharis and Cox, 1989).

On the other hand, much material has been deleted from some released documents because it is covered by one of the exemptions permitted by the legislation. In the case of the FBI this is likely to be either "national security" or "law enforcement," and in some cases has led to the deletion of entire files, for example, 95,000 pages relating to the Ethel and Julius Rosenberg case in the 1950s. More recently, similar struggles over access have taken place in Canada. The Access to Information Act was passed in 1980 and has granted rights of access to citizens and shifted to the government the burden of proving that material falls within exempted categories. A number of Canadian scholars have benefited from this greater access; for example, Whitaker (1989) and Kealey tried and failed to gain access to the RCMP Security Service's historical counter-subversion files, but were able to obtain access to the RCMP internal intelligence bulletins for the period from the early 1920s to mid-1950s.

Under the Australian Freedom of Information Act (1982), all ASIO documents are exempt, although if materials supplied by ASIO to other agencies is incorporated into their documents, it is not automatically exempt and ASIO has to argue its case. However, it is clear that of much greater concern to ASIO was the Archives Act of 1983, which allowed public access to all records over thirty years old. ASIO could claim exemption for material relating to the identity of informers, interception methods, information provided by foreign agencies, and internal procedures but clearly does not like being subjected to a general thirty-year rule and has proposed that it be exempted (ASIO, 1989, 15–18). The attorney general asked the Parliamentary Joint Committee to investigate the matter, and they reported in 1992. The government decided that ASIO was not to be exempted from the Act and that the attorney general should act as arbiter in disputes about the release of ASIO records (Cain, 1993).

Whatever the variations in practice throughout North America and Australia, they present a clear contrast with the situation in the United Kingdom. Security intelligence information has become available to scholars in an entirely haphazard way, and the reform of the Official Secrets Act in 1989, whatever else it was, was not a freedom of information measure. Since then William Waldegrave, the minister responsible for the Citizen's Charter, has announced a government intention to increase the flow of information to the public, including an invitation to historians to make proposals to him for the release of intelligence material such as JIC assessments (BBC, June 25, 1992). However, a general right of access to information is still rejected, and reliance on ministerial intentions is more likely to reinforce than challenge traditional information control processes in the United Kingdom.

Even in the United States, where, it might be argued, there are important examples of oversight being exercised at level four, it is clear that the "polyarchical" processes of organized group politics do not penetrate very often into the secret state and do not constitute democratic control over intelligence policy (Johnson, 1991a: 59). Finally, there is always the possibility that the absence or failure of oversight institutions will provoke more dramatic and direct forms of oversight. The breaching of the Berlin Wall in 1989 remains the best-remembered symbol of the collapse of the East German regime, but equally significant was the invasion and occupation by citizens of offices of the Stasi in Berlin, Leipzig, and elsewhere in January 1990. The subsequent liberation of the agency's files under the control of a special commission headed by Joachim Gauck, a Lutheran minister, has proved highly controversial. Hundreds of thousands wrote in to seek access to their files, but the subsequent identification of Stasi informers has proved extremely painful for many people, and the extensive exposures have been contrasted with the treatment of Nazi supporters (Gauck, 1991).

Western states have not been immune from similar direct action. In March 1971 a group presumed to be anti–Vietnam War activists broke into the FBI office in Media, Pennsylvania, and stole about 1000 classified documents detailing COINTELPRO operations. Calling themselves the Citizens' Commission to Investigate the FBI, they subsequently copied the documents in batches to the news media and legislators. The full story of COINTELPRO subsequently emerged from the Socialist Workers Party legal action against the FBI, but the media burglary has been credited with causing Hoover to cancel all COINTELPRO operations shortly thereafter (Davis, 1992: 1–24).[5] In the absence of effective institutions, such commissions may be the only effective oversight.

Conclusion

As struggles to form new political institutions take place in eastern Europe and South Africa, the activities, control, and oversight of security intelligence agencies are central to attempts to construct states that are more democratic. A variety of structural forms for the control and oversight of these agencies have been developed in liberal capitalist states in recent years. This brief survey has indicated that some of the mechanisms have had real impact on the autonomy and behavior of security intelligence agencies, while others seem to have been created to protect them from more radical reforms.

The objective of the model outlined here is to facilitate further comparative analysis of these developments. This is not with a view to identifying institutional forms that might have universal applicability because institutions are culturally specific and simply cannot be transplanted between states. Rather, it is a view to generating more specific propositions as to the most effective democratic structures and the conditions required for their sustenance.

NOTES

1. This chapter is drawn from a larger study (Gill, 1994) that seeks to develop a framework for the analysis of security intelligence agencies and apply it particularly to the United Kingdom.

2. See also Buzan (1991), who talks of "many layers of sub-state actors" existing within the state (p. 349). Similarly, Sim et al. (1987) describe how "the state comprises a series of relations which exist at different levels" (p. 62).

3. These four levels correspond to the categories identified by former CIA director Stansfield Turner, as those that focused the intelligence debate in the United States in the 1970s (Oseth, 1985: 182).

4. The CSIS Act was "negative" in the sense that it did not define what "national security" is. For examples of such definitions see Buzan (1991: 16–18).

5. Between 1983 and 1985 the FBI carried out an investigation of the Committee in Solidarity with the Peoples of El Salvador (CISPES) that broke the attorney general's guidelines and paralleled in many respects COINTELPRO activities. However, it should be noted that the operation was, first, halted by the operation of Justice Department (level two) review procedures and subsequently publicized as a result of a Freedom of Information lawsuit (level four) (Stern, 1988).

REFERENCES

Andrew, Christopher (1985) *Secret Service*. London: Heinemann.

ASIO (1989) *Report to Parliament, 1987–88*. Canberra: Australian Government Printing Service.

Betts, Richard (1981) "American Strategic Intelligence," in Robert L. Pfaltzgraff et al. (eds.), *Intelligence Policy and National Security*. Basingstoke, Eng.: Macmillan, pp. 245–267.

Blais, Pierre (1989) "Accountability and Effectiveness: National Requirements for Security Intelligence in the 1990s." Notes for a speech, Ottawa, September 29 (unpublished).

Buzan, Barry (1991) *People, States and Fear*, 2nd ed. Hemel Hempstead: Harvester Wheatsheaf.

Cain, Frank (1991) "Accountability and the ASIO: A Brief History," in Stuart Farson et al. (eds.), *Security and Intelligence in a Changing World: New Perspectives for the 1990s*. London: Frank Cass, pp. 104–125.

——— (1993) "The Right to Know: ASIO, Historians and the Australian Parliament." *Intelligence and National Security* 8 (1) January: 87–101.

Church, Frank (1976) *Final Report of the Select Committee to Study Governmental Operations with Respect to Intelligence Activities*, Book II, *Intelligence Activities and the Rights of Americans*. Washington, DC: United States Senate.

Churchill, Ward, and Jim Vander Wall (1990) *Agents of Repression: The FBI's Secret War Against the Black Panther Party and the American Indian Movement*. Boston: South End Press.

CSIS (1992) *Public Report, 1991*. Ottawa: Minister of Supply and Services.

Dahl, Robert (1991) *Modern Political Analysis*, 5th ed. Englewood Cliffs, NJ: Prentice-Hall.

Dandeker, Christopher (1990) *Surveillance, Power and Modernity*. Cambridge, Eng.: Polity Press.

Davis, James (1992) *Spying on America: The FBI's Domestic Counter-Intelligence Program*. New York: Praeger.

Denning, Lord (1963) *Report of the Inquiry into the Profumo Affair*, Cmnd 2152. London: HMSO.

De Rosenroll, Michael (1988) Interview with Acting Inspector General, May, Ottawa (unpublished).

Dorril, Stephen, and Robin Ramsay (1991) *Smear! Wilson and the Secret State*. London: Fourth Estate.

Edelman, Murray (1964) *The Symbolic Uses of Politics*. Urbana: University of Illinois Press.

Edwards, John L. (1980) *Ministerial Responsibility for National Security*. Ottawa: Minister of Supply and Services.

Elliff, John (1979) *The Reform of FBI Intelligence Operations*. Princeton, NJ: Princeton University Press.

Emerson, Stephen (1992) *The CIA and the Politicization of Intelligence in the 1980s*. Paper for International Studies Association Conference, Vancouver, April.

Farson, Stuart (1989) "Propriety, Efficacy and Balance," in Peter Hanks and John McManus (eds.), *National Security: Surveillance and Accountability in a Democratic Society*. Cowansville, Québec: Les Éditions Yvon Blais, pp. 127–155.

——— (1991a) *Parliament's Capacity to Conduct a Comprehensive Review: Weak Link in the Chain of Accountability*. Paper for SIRC seminar, Vancouver, February.

——— (1991b) *Problems of Political Oversight*. Paper for CASIS Conference, Queen's University, Kingston, Ontario, June.

FBI (1984) *Conducting Research in FBI Records*. Washington, DC: FBI Office of Congressional and Public Affairs.

Foucault, Michel (1983) "Power, Sovereignty and Discipline," in David Held et al. (eds.), *States and Societies*. Oxford, Eng.: Martin Robertson, pp. 306–313.

Gauck, Joachim (1991) *Die Stasi-Akten*. Reinbek bei Hamburg: Rowohlt. (German)

Gill, Peter (1989a) "Defining Subversion: the Canadian Experience Since 1977." *Public Law* (Winter): 617–636.

——— (1989b) "Symbolic or Real? The Impact of the Canadian Security Intelligence Review Committee." *Intelligence and National Security* 4 (3) (July): 550–575.

——— (1991) "The Evolution of the Security Intelligence Debate in Canada Since 1976," in Stuart Farson et al. (eds.), *Security and Intelligence in a Changing World: New Perspectives for the 1990s*. London: Frank Cass, pp. 75–94.

——— (1994) *Policing Politics: Security Intelligence and the Liberal Democratic State*. London: Frank Cass.

Hanks, Peter (1988) "National Security—a political concept." *Monash University Law Review* 14: 114–133.

—— (1989) "Accountability for Security Intelligence Activity in Australia," in Peter Hanks and John D. McManus (eds.), *National Security: Surveillance and Accountability in a Democratic Society.* Cowansville, Québec: Les Éditions Yvon Blais, pp. 43–54.

Hersh, Seymour (1987) "Foreword," in *The Chronology: The Documented Day-by-Day Account of the Secret Military Assistance to Iran and the Contras*. New York: Warner Books.

Hinsley, Harry, and Anthony Simkins (1990) *British Intelligence in the Second World War*, Volume Four, *Security and Counter Intelligence.* London: HMSO.

Holdich, Roger (1991) "The Work of the Australian Inspector General of Intelligence and Security," *CASIS Newsletter*, No. 16, University of Montreal.

Holroyd, Fred (1989) *War Without Honour*. Hull, Eng.: Medium Publishing.

Home Office (1993) *Accountability of the Security Service*, Cm 2197. London: HMSO.

Hope, Justice R.M. (1977) Royal Commission on Intelligence and Security, Fourth Report, *Australian Security Intelligence Organisation.* Canberra: Australian Government Printing Service.

—— (1985) *Report on the Australian Security Intelligence Organization.* Canberra, Australia: Commonwealth Government Printer.

House of Commons (1993) Home Affairs Committee, First Report, *Accountability of the Security Service*. London: HMSO.

House of Representatives (1990) Hearings Before the Subcommittee on Civil and Constitutional Rights, Committee on the Judiciary, *FBI Oversight and Authorization Request for Fiscal Year 1991.* Washington, DC: U.S. Government Printing Office.

Hurd, Douglas (1989) House of Commons Debates, January 17.

Ingram, Miranda (1984) "Trouble with Security." *New Society* (May 31): 349–350.

Janis, Irving (1972) *Victims of Groupthink: A Psychological Study of Foreign Policy Decisions and Fiascoes*. Boston: Houghton Mifflin.

Jayko, Margaret, ed. (1988) *FBI on Trial: The Victory in the SWP Suit Against Government Spying*. New York: Pathfinder.

Jeffreys-Jones, Rhodri (1989) *The CIA and American Democracy*. New Haven, CT: Yale University Press.

Jessop, Bob (1990) *State Theory: Putting Capitalist States in Their Place.* Cambridge, Eng.: Polity Press.

Johnson, Loch (1989) *America's Secret Power: The CIA in a Democratic Society.* New York: Oxford University Press.

——— (1991a) "Controlling the CIA: A Critique of Current Safeguards," in Glen Hastedt, ed., *Controlling Intelligence.* London: Frank Cass, pp. 46–78.

——— (1991b) "Strategic Intelligence: An American Perspective," in Stuart Farson et al. (eds.), *Security and Intelligence in a Changing World: New Perspectives for the 1990s.* London: Frank Cass, pp. 46–68.

Keller, William (1989) *The Liberals and J. Edgar Hoover: Rise and Fall of a Domestic Intelligence State.* Princeton, NJ: Princeton University Press.

Kitchin, Hilary (1989) *The Gibraltar Report.* London: Liberty.

Knightley, Phillip (1986) *The Second Oldest Profession: The Spy as Bureaucrat, Patriot, Fantasist and Whore.* London: Pan.

Leigh, David (1988) *The Wilson Plot: The Intelligence Services and the Discrediting of a Prime Minister.* London: Heinemann.

McBarnet, Doreen (1981) *Conviction: Law, the State and the Construction of Justice.* Basingstoke, Eng.: Macmillan.

McDonald, Justice D.C. (1981a) *Certain RCMP Activities and the Question of Governmental Knowledge.* Commission of Enquiry Concerning Certain Activities of the Royal Canadian Mounted Police, Third Report. Ottawa: Minister of Supply and Services.

——— (1981b) *Freedom and Security Under the Law.* Commission of Enquiry Concerning Certain Activities of the Royal Canadian Mounted Police, Second Report. Ottawa: Minister of Supply and Services.

Mangold, Tom (1992) *Cold Warrior.* New York: Simon & Schuster.

MI5 (1993) *The Security Service.* London: HMSO.

Michael, James, et al. (1985) *The Ponting Dilemma: Secrecy, the Civil Servant and the Public Interest.* London: Policy Studies Institute.

Moore, John, et al. (1985) "National Security and Civil Liberties." *Center Magazine* 18 (May–June): 46–64.

Oseth, John (1985) *Regulating U.S. Intelligence Operations.* Lexington: University Press of Kentucky.

Peters, B. Guy (1984) *The Politics of Bureaucracy*, 2nd ed. New York: Longman.

Phillips, David A. (1984) *Careers in Secret Operations: How to Be a Federal Intelligence Officer*. Bethesda, MD: Stone Trail Press.

Pike, Otis (1977) *CIA: The Pike Report*. Nottingham, Eng.: Spokesman Books.

Porter, Bernard (1989) *Plots and Paranoia*. London: Unwin Hyman.

Poveda, Tony (1990) *The FBI in Transition*. Pacific Grove, CA: Brooks Cole.

Powers, Richard (1987) *Secrecy and Power*. New York: Free Press.

Ranelagh, John (1987) *The Agency: the Rise and Decline of the CIA*. New York: Simon & Schuster.

Relyea, Harold (1987) "National Security and Information." *Government Information Quarterly* 4(1), pp. 11–28.

Schlesinger, Arthur M. (1978) *Robert Kennedy and His Times*. London: Andre Deutsch.

Sim, Joe, et al. (1987) "Introduction: Crime, the State and Critical Analysis," in Phil Scraton (ed.), *Law, Order and the Authoritarian State*. Milton Keynes, Eng.: Open University Press.

Simpson, John (1992) "The New Espionage." *The Spectator* 22 (February): 9–11.

SIRC (1987a) *Annual Report 1986–7*. Ottawa: Minister of Supply and Services.

—— (1987b) *Closing the Gaps: Official Languages and Staff Relations in the CSIS*. Ottawa: Minister of Supply and Services.

—— (1988) *Annual Report 1987–8*. Ottawa: Minister of Supply and Services.

—— (1989) *Amending the CSIS Act: Proposals for the Special Committee of the House of Commons, 1989*. Ottawa: Minister of Supply and Services.

—— (1990) *Annual Report 1989–90*. Ottawa: Minister of Supply and Services.

—— (1991) *Annual Report 1990–1*. Ottawa: Minister of Supply and Services.

Solicitor General (1991) *On Course: National Security for the 1990s*. Ottawa: Minister of Supply and Services.

Special Committee on the Review of the CSIS Act and the Security Offences Act (1990). *In Flux but Not in Crisis*. Ottawa: Canadian Government Publishing Center.

Stalker, John (1988) *Stalker*. London: Harrap.

Stern, Gary (1988) *The FBI's Misguided Probe of CISPES*. Washington, DC: Center for National Security Studies.

Supperstone, Michael (1987) "The Law Relating to Security in Great Britain," in Ken Robertson (ed.), *British and American Approaches to Intelligence*. Basingstoke, Eng.: Macmillan, pp. 218–243.

Swan, Ken (1989) "Whistle-blowing and National Security," in Peter Hanks and John D. McManus (eds.), *National Security: Surveillance and Accountability in a Democratic Society*. Cowansville, Québec: Les Éditions Yvon Blais, pp. 171–181.

Theoharis, Athan, and John Cox (1989) *The Boss: J.E. Hoover and the Great American Inquisition*. London: Harrap.

Thompson, Edward P. (1979) *The Secret State*. London: Independent Research Publications.

Whitaker, Reg (1989) "Access to Information and Research on Security and Intelligence: The Canadian Situation," in Peter Hanks and John D. McManus (eds.), *National Security: Surveillance and Accountability in a Democratic Society*. Cowansville, Québec: Les Éditions Yvon Blais, pp. 183–195.

Wilsnack, Richard (1980) "Information Control: A Conceptual Framework for Sociological Analysis." *Urban Life* 8: 467–499.

Wise, David, and Thomas Ross (1968) *The Invisible Government*. London: Mayflower.

Wolfe, A. (1976) "Extralegality and American Power." *Society* (March–April): 44–47.

Controlling Crimes by the Military

Jeffrey Ian Ross

Introduction

Since the creation of the first army, activists, military officers, politicians, and policymakers have witnessed, experienced, or chosen to address crimes committed by the military of various states.[1] Several mechanisms have been advocated, many of which have been implemented, to control the armed forces, in general, and its ability to engage in these types of crime in particular. Although many of these control mechanisms have been articulated before, they have not been conceptualized under the control of state crime literature, nor in a relatively comprehensive manner. This chapter provides a preliminary framework for this orientation.

In all countries the military is a powerful state actor.[2] In some authoritarian, totalitarian, or developing states, the armed forces even run the bureaucracy (Fidel, 1975: 1; Nordlinger, 1977: Chapter 1). The military of most countries has enormous resources,[3] in particular weapons, which, in some countries, are used to promote and/or enforce their corporate interests. These resources are both a source of power and the means that enable the armed forces to commit state crimes.

In general, the problem of "crime and deviant behavior in the military context," regardless of the state, "has been largely ignored and/or neglected by" academics (Bryant, 1979: 6). Where it has been addressed, the general focus is in the context of work-deviance relationships or the criminal behavior of soldiers in combat situations (Bryant, 1979: 359). Consequently, it is only natural that a literature on controlling crimes by the military is also underdeveloped.

In order to build on this research, the author briefly reviews the work on what can be conceptualized as crimes by the military (also labeled "khaki-collar crime") (Bryant, 1979); examines the mechanisms advocated (some of which have been implemented) to minimize, prevent, and ideally control these crimes; and suggests additional processes to control the military and prevent or deter it from engaging in state crimes. This analysis, although broad in scope, will help individuals, groups, and states implement existing mechanisms or suggest other more effective controls on crimes by the military.

Before proceeding, a number of definitional and conceptual vagaries should be clarified. In the main, the military is a collectivity of professional individuals (e.g., soldiers, officers, etc.)[4] responsible for the protection and defense of their country or others they are ordered to protect or defend. Their services are used to counter external and occasionally internal real or perceived threats. Specifically, the military is sanctioned to use physical force to maintain the state's national security and achieve foreign policy objectives. In general, they are distinct from a state's national security/intelligence agency and police forces, but may interact with and perform similar functions as these governmental agencies.[5]

Even though the armed forces throughout the world share similarities (e.g., command structures, discipline, military culture, rank systems, etc.), they also differ from one context (i.e., cultural, economic, ideological, political, etc.) and country to another (e.g., Janowitz, 1977). Consequently, the manner by which the armed forces is controlled varies from one context and country to another (e.g., Willimett, 1980: 250). Nevertheless, a number of general statements can be made regarding military crimes and their controls.

The General Literature on Crimes by the Military

The academic literature on military crimes and its control is embedded in seven traditional subtopics, including "civil-military relations," "civil supremacy over the military," "armed forces political activities," "antiwar movement," "military intervention in politics," "national security studies," and "military government." This research has several commonalities. For instance, most of the work utilizes individual case studies or cross-national statistical research methods. Although case studies are primarily descriptive in nature, quantitative studies disproportionately focus on coups d'etats. Both types of analyses are prevalent in a variety of mediums including governmental reports, academic monographs, and journal articles.

Even though specific focus on crimes by the military in the previously mentioned literatures is uncommon, a comparison between war-making and organized crime has been made. Tilly (1985), for example, suggests that "[a]t least in the European experience of the past few centuries, a portrait of war makers and state makers as coercive and self-seeking entrepreneurs bears a far greater resemblance [to organized crimes] than do its chief alternatives" (p. 169). He argues that the army, as a group of organized criminals, is responsible for the interdependent and complementary acts of war-making, state-making, protection, and extraction (pp. 181–183). Tilly, however, does not go beyond this distinction to offer solutions for controlling these activities.[6]

Most of the critical analyses of the role of the military draws on the work of a number of so-called conflict theorists or progressive social scientists (e.g., Lasswell, 1941; Mills, 1956). Mills, for example, argued that, at least in the United States, a military-industrial complex exists that encourages the growth and conservatism of the military and fuels capitalism through the manufacture and sale of weapons. This theory, however, was later challenged by several researchers who, while admitting that a process like this could be discerned, argued that the military industrial complex was simply a caricature and a product of its time and place (e.g., Moskos, 1974).

Central to this counterargument was the evidence that

> The military is not necessarily a conservative and rigidly
> obedient instrument; . . . it can be a dynamic means for
> inducing and compelling change. It can [as the experience
> of many lessor developed countries attests], support
> revolutionary parties or it may be revolutionary itself.

Moreover, "military forces, despite their supposed discipline and
cohesion, are themselves factionalized even before they
intervene as rulers or coalition forces" (Bienen, 1968: xx). Finally,
the armed forces "are not socially indivisible or ideologically
coherent. There is diversity, especially between the ranks"
(Martin, 1984: 191).

Alternatively, Lasswell (1941; 1962), in the garrison state
hypothesis, advanced another "conspiracy type" analysis. He
suggested that power relations in advanced industrialized
democracies were changing "from the relatively mixed elite
pattern of [the] nineteenth century to military-police dominance
in the impending future" (1962: 51). According to him, in the
garrison state,

> (1) the power elites value power enough to resort to large-
> scale coercion when they . . . [believe it will help support]
> their ascendancy; and (2) the elites . . . [believe] that the
> retention of power during at least the immediate and
> middle range future depends upon capability and
> willingness to coerce external or internal challengers.
> (1962: 53)

Specifically, Lasswell argued that elites attempt to exert their
coercive power through the military. Even though Lasswell's
theory is compelling and a number of studies have tested some
of his hypotheses (e.g., Fitch, 1985; Walker and Lang, 1988), this
research has been narrow in its focus. Regardless of how and
why the military exerts power, more important are the criminal
consequences of that power.

In general, studies examining the connection between the
military and crimes have been content simply to describe those
criminal actions (e.g., Liebknecht, 1917; Bryant, 1979); develop
typologies of crimes by the military (Bryant, 1979: Chapters 3–5);
and review its causes (e.g., Bryant, 1979: Chapter 2; Hakeem,
1946; Lunden, 1952; Tracy et al., 1971; Wagley, 1944). This

literature, however, rarely discusses methods to control this type of organizational behavior.

First, as early as 1917, Liebknecht (1917: Chapter 4) discussed five "cardinal sins of Militarism," including maltreatment of soldiers, the costs of supporting a military, being "a weapon [used] against the proletariat in the economic struggle," being a "weapon against the proletariat in the political struggle," and as "a menace to peace." Although sophisticated for its time, Liebknecht's "sins" are narrow in scope and ideological focus, and are therefore limited in applicability. Others (e.g., Bryant 1979) identify "fragging an officer, looting, malingering, going to sleep on duty, insubordination, mistreating prisoners of war, or failing to clean one's weapon" (p. x). All of these crimes have been studied separately as well as in relationship to the military. Moreover, they are not unique to the military; police forces and national security agencies may engage in similar criminal actions.

In addition to these classifications, some critical theorists also categorize military spending as criminal in itself because it diverts resources from other prosocial policy areas (e.g., health, education, etc.) (e.g., Barnet, 1969). This argument, however, is perhaps an overextension of the term *crime*. Additionally, during and after coups d'etats, the military may engage in crimes (Nordlinger, 1977). However, classifying all coups as crimes would be misleading because some ameliorate coercive conditions where crimes by the military exist.

Second, some theorists offer a typology to classify military crimes. Bryant suggests two systems. The first consists of three broad categories: "(1) crimes against property; (2) crimes against persons; and (3) crimes against performance" (p. 8). The second, perhaps the more sophisticated one, classifies crimes according to context: "Intra-occupational," "Extra-occupational," and "Inter-occupational." Intra-occupational crime refers to a violation of "norms internal to the military itself" (p. 8). These actions "may involve theft or misuse of government property, interpersonal violence, and inappropriate military behavior" (p. 11). Extra-occupational crime refers to "interaction or behavior" by military personnel that transgresses "the civilian normative system, abuses of or offenses against civilians or their property, or the social activity between the members is judged to be inappropriate or detrimental to the military or offensive to civilian authorities" (p. 8). Finally, Inter-occupational crimes include "violations of norms concerning correct and appropriate behavior in regard to the enemy" (p. 11).

Alternatively, crimes committed by the military could be categorized as nonviolent and violent. Those actions comprising the nonviolent end of the continuum are corruption, nonviolent illegal arrests, and nonviolent maltreatment of soldiers. At the violent end of the spectrum are various forms of violence, such as property destruction, kidnapping, assault/brutality (including rape), torture, murder/assassination, sanctioned massacres, and genocide. Meanwhile, violations of international law and war crimes can encompass both violent and nonviolent acts.

Military crimes can also be classified as crimes of commission or omission. In the main, crimes of commission may include "intimidation of the civilian authorities" and "threats of non-co-operation with or violence towards civilian authorities" (Finer, 1962: 140), illegal violence, and violation of international law. On the other hand, crimes of omission may encompass "failure to defend the civilian authorities against violence" (p. 140).

Third, although some studies of morale, discipline, and courts-martial have advanced causal theories, no hypotheses, models, or theories concerning the causes of military crime in general have been advanced. Nevertheless, a number of general factors have been identified as being important, including "the opportunity structure of the military system;" "the sociocultural and geographical settings in which the military normally operates;" "the informal pressures and strains inherent in military culture;" "the structured subversion of organizational goals frequently component to military enterprise" (Bryant, 1979: 7); the detachment between user and victim of military weapons and equipment" (Bryant, 1979: 354); and, "equipment may be so complex that in certain emergencies the individual in charge may not be able to control it properly" (Bryant, 1979: 355). Even though the types, typologies, and causes of military crimes are important to its study, more central to the purpose of this chapter is a consideration of the controls.

Literature on Controlling the Military

Periodically, informed observers of the military will selectively mention controls on crimes by the military. The most common types of controls that have been articulated are conventional civilian criminal codes, military law, and international treaties (Bryant, 1979: 6). Within these broad categories, some academics (e.g., Barnet, 1969; Galbraith, 1969: 52–60; Martin, 1984) have listed a number of alternative mechanisms to control the military. Although a necessary beginning, this literature lacks a theoretical framework, primarily focuses on the United States, and therefore may have limited applicability to other countries.[7]

Scholars Huntington (1957) and Nordlinger (1977), however, offer more sophisticated treatments, identifying types of controls on the armed forces that citizens can use. Huntington, for instance, offers two broad suggestions: an unstable process called "Selective Civilian Control: Maximizing Civilian Power" and a stable situation labelled "Objective Civilian Control: Maximizing Military Professionalism." Even though Huntington has sensitized us to the broad problems and contours of controlling the military, his work has been subjected to a series of critiques (e.g., Abrahamsson, 1972; Janowitz, 1960; Tilly, 1993) that he did not feel was necessary or has not been able to refute.

Alternatively, Nordlinger (1977) outlines three models of civilian control: traditional, liberal, and penetration. In the traditional model,

> military intervention presupposes a conflict between soldiers and civilian governors; and conflict in turn requires some differentiation between the two groups. [Thus] in the absence of significant differences between civilians and soldiers, the civilians may quite easily retain control because the military has no reason . . . to challenge them. (p. 11)

In the liberal model, Nordlinger argues that "civilian control is explicitly premised upon the differentiation of elites according to their expertise and responsibilities. Civilians holding the highest governmental offices . . . are responsible for and skilled in determining domestic and foreign goals, overseeing the administration of laws, and resolving conflicts" (p. 12).

Finally, in the penetration model, Nordlinger suggests that "Civilian governors obtain loyalty and obedience by penetrating the armed forces with political ideas (if not fully developed ideologies) and political personnel. Throughout their careers officers (and enlisted men) are intensively imbued with the civilian governor's political ideas" (p. 15).

According to Nordlinger, none of the models of control "can be applied in all types of polities and securely relied upon to ensure civilian supremacy" (pp. 10–11). Therefore, civilian control is problematic, and thus one would expect a high frequency of coups (p. 19). Even though Nordlinger has highlighted the variety of different types of civilian control, he has neglected other types of constraints, and his models of control lack a certain amount of specificity important when considering controls for the military.

Suggestions for Alternative or Improved Methods to Control Crime by the Military

Introduction

There are at least twenty-nine methods that analysts, military officers, and/or concerned citizens and organizations have suggested and/or implemented to control crimes by the military. These mechanisms can be grouped under five interrelated headings[8]: individual/self-control; control by the military establishment (e.g., internal controls), control by government institutions, control by foreign actors, and control by the public. Each of the mechanisms are reviewed separately but ordered, from least to most important, under each heading, in terms of their hypothesized importance. Moreover, it must be understood that these controls are not mutually exclusive; in other words some mechanisms may overlap with other strategies, and if they are not carefully implemented, they might even increase military crimes.

Individual/Self Control

Soldiers can minimize actions they consider criminal, committed by their organization, by disobeying orders given by their superiors. This, however, is particularly difficult for armed forces personnel because there are often severe consequences for insubordination. In an attempt to circumvent this dilemma, Kelman and Hamilton outline two basic recommendations by which soldiers can "(1) reduc[e] the impact of binding forces by counteracting the effects of rule and role orientation, respectively, and (2) enhanc[e] the impact of opposing forces by buttressing the effects of value orientation" (1989: 321–322). Their discussion of specific suggestions, however, seem extremely difficult to implement in traditional military settings where authority is centralized.

Alternatively, in most armies, there is an internal or external complaints system that allows soldiers and officers the opportunity to file grievances. In some armed services it is an effective organization, while in others it is simply a public relations mechanism. In the United States, for example, the Inspector General of the army, a staff organization, "receive[s] complaints of any kind from all personnel. All Army personnel, enlisted men and officers alike . . . have a right to register complaints directly with an Inspector General officer instead of taking them up with their immediate superiors" (Evan, 1962: 189). This unit is "an organizational anomaly in granting all Army personnel a legal right to lodge complaints directly with IG officers, for, in effect, it sanctions the circumventing of the chain of command in certain circumstances" (p. 190). Despite armed forces personnel's use of this process, there are a number of obstacles to due process with this system (pp. 191–194).

Control by the Military Establishment

There are six types of internal controls that military organizations can utilize to minimize or prevent crimes by members of their organization. They are, from least to most important, in terms of predicted importance, proper training, improving soldiers general level of education in nontraditional subjects, discipline, professionalism, fostering interservice rivalry, and threatening or using warnings, counseling, and court-martial.

Initially, armed services train their personnel in a variety of skills, functions, and methods of carrying out particular orders. "When new recruits are going through training, they are learning how to live in a totally different world. The drill sergeants and other instructors are basically working a clean slate. Everything that that private learns is from them. Whatever they put on that slate, either good or bad, will most likely influence that soldier in the future."[9] The amount of training and the emphasis on different techniques varies from one context to another. In general, one can predict that the greater the training, the more effective soldiers will be in their duties.

Additionally, soldiers should be taught and trained in such nonmilitary subjects as civil and human rights, ethics, and international law. These efforts, however, might simply train them to better conceal their activities or prepare more sophisticated arguments to justify their crimes.

Discipline, hierarchy, and the chain of command are also important organizational attributes of the military. "This involves the ordering of virtually all the statuses of the Army in a strict hierarchy and specifies that all communication, upward and downward, shall be through channels" (Evan, 1962: 190). These processes not only can prevent individual soldiers and officers from engaging in military crimes but also can help those higher up in the chain of command force those subordinate to them to engage in unfavorable actions, including crimes.

Moreover, professionalism can serve to reinforce chains of command, hierarchy and prior training and can thereby minimize individual soldiers' and officers' acts of crime. Scholars, however, are divided about the so-called benign effects of professionalism. Some (e.g., Huntington, 1957) argue that professionalism serves as an important deterrent to military intervention in politics. Others (e.g., Abrahamsson, 1972; Stepan, 1973) suggest that it has a contradictory effect, thereby encouraging military lobbying, coups d'état, and processes that frustrate the control of military crimes.

Furthermore, interservice rivalry can serve as a control on military units (Huntington, 1961; Lang, 1972: 118–119). The competition over scarce resources among the navy, army, and air force often creates a situation in which one unit monitors the other's weaknesses in order to gain some sort of advantage when negotiating with other state agencies. On the other hand, concerned citizens must be on guard for "logrolling," which can serve to increase military expenditures and diffuse overall defense priorities.

Finally, "all military entities have attempted to enforce discipline and compliance with orders with regulated sets of norms and a system of sanctionative military justice" (Bryant, 1979: 26–27). Historically, the penalties, often quite barbaric, included flogging, burning the tongue with a hot iron, and death (Spencer, 1954: 61–78). Currently, most armed forces have a Code of Military Justice, manuals of military law, and judge advocates, all of which specify infractions and possible penalties (Ujevich, 1969). There are also nonjudicial punishments that superiors may administer. Some of these are admonition, reprimand, restriction, extra duties, reduction in rank, loss of wages, delay of pay, detention to barracks, correctional custody, and confinement on bread and water or diminished rations (Knudten, 1970: 481). The most severe sanction, however, are courts-martial. But given the similarity of some of these controls to those used in nonmilitary environments, it is doubtful that they are effective in deterring crimes.[10]

Government Control of Its Military

Most government organizations that control state crime exert their power at the state level, sometimes at great costs to their institutions and members. Seven strategies can be used by governments to control crimes by the military. These mechanisms, ordered from least to most important, include better regulations on lobbying by the military and their contractors, collecting accurate data on crimes by the military, strengthening human rights organizations, providing selective amnesty for soldiers and officers who commit crimes; reducing military spending and converting military industries, decreasing the size of the military, and abolishing the military.

First, with respect to lobbying, many corporations invest a considerable amount of money attempting to convince the military, and those responsible for overseeing this institution, of the necessity of purchasing more and better weapons of destruction (Thayer, 1969). Not only do corporations engage in lobbying, but the armed forces itself, using taxpayers' money, attempt to influence politicians (Fullbright, 1971; Goodspeed, 1962: 44; Parenti, 1983: 100–101). Even though many states have legislation concerning the proper conduct of lobbyists, informed observers of the military have argued that controls on this activity restricts access to timely and accurate information.

Second, given the closed nature of the military, data on individuals (i.e., soldiers, officers, etc.) and groups (e.g., military units) who engage in military crimes are difficult for the public and in particular researchers to obtain. Military actors are reluctant research subjects, and information obtained regarding their illegal actions is often obtained from insiders, such as disgruntled employees, and from nonmilitary sources, such as the victims themselves and from friends and families of victims and witnesses, whose reliability is questionable. Ethnographic studies of military involvement in crimes could improve this area of research. A careful analysis of information and propaganda distributed by the state and that obtained from other, nongovernmental sources would also be useful. Better and more comprehensive data could be collected if data sets of various monitoring agencies are combined. Regardless of the strategy, rarely is this type of work conducted.

Third, both domestic and international state- and nonstate-sponsored human rights organizations should be strengthened by increasing their resources. Efforts to combat human rights abuses have occurred at four major levels: national, international, regional, both governmentally and non-governmentally directed. In general, foreign human rights organizations are better at monitoring abuses that occur in another country because they are less likely to be co-opted by domestic agencies. Consequently, since resources are limited, the lion's share should be directed to external rather than domestic human rights bodies.

Fourth, those charged with committing military crimes could selectively be offered amnesty if they agree to inform on others who engaged in similar types of actions. This promise would encourage disgruntled people who work for regimes that practice or allow military crimes to occur to provide information to outside sources. Periodically, some criminogenic regimes of this type crumble (e.g., East Germany), and their records become accessible to the public for intensive analysis, judicial review, and remedy.

Fifth, military spending should be reduced and capped. Even though the Cold War is over, the military budgets of many countries in the world are increasing at exponential rates (Russett, 1970; Sivard, 1974–1988; Tilly, 1993: 209). According to Barnet (1969), because "the pursuit of national security through the arms race is a matter of faith rather than logic, arms spending is at present impossible to control" (p. 16). In order to decrease and limit military spending, respective units of the military should be encouraged to increase competition among themselves for the allocation of scarce resources (p. 188), the peace lobby should be strengthened, constituencies that do not economically depend on the military spending could spearhead the protest (Russett, 1970: 7), and taxpayers and soon-to-be taxpayers (e.g., students) should complain to their elected and appointed politicians and bureaucrats about this problem, ask them for specific solutions, and hold them accountable, particularly during election time or renewal of their contracts.[11]

Sixth, although an expensive process, more military industries should continue to convert to peaceful production (e.g., Martin, 1984). Many of the military suppliers have nonmilitary divisions that make products or provide services that are prosocial in nature. For example, military contractors such as Otis produce elevators, Litton manufactures office furniture and microwave ovens, Grumman produces canoes, and Lockheed and Boeing make airplanes for commercial use. Activists should continue to lobby resistant shareholders of these companies to encourage their boards to dedicate more of their production toward the nonmilitary sector.

Seventh, closely connected to decreasing military spending and conversion of military industries is reducing the size of the military. Most full-time military units consume a phenomenal amount of resources. An alternative strategy is to establish a "lower manpower ceiling" for the armed forces of each country. This option might mitigate political influence by the armed forces and place control back with legislators (Russett, 1970: 188). Downsizing the military should be coupled with disarmament, transarmament, and other arms control and reduction methods (Roberts, 1967a; 1967b; Galbraith, 1969: 52–60). Although historically it has been the practice of militaries to disarm their enemies, perhaps states could assume this task as an internal matter. Part of the way that this might be accomplished is by "remov[ing] weapons from the military budget" (Galbraith, 1969: 60). Nevertheless these processes should not be implemented so recklessly as to hinder the ability of the state to maintain internal and national security (Roberts, 1967a).

Last and perhaps the most radical suggestion, is to abolish the military (e.g., Liebknecht, 1917; Martin, 1984: 193; Martin, this volume). In the armed forces place, militias (e.g., Nicaragua after the fall of Somoza) can be organized. However, militias should not be interpreted as a panacea as they may tend to lack the discipline and training of standing armies and may thereby act as vigilantes, carrying out such things as personal, ethnic, and religious vendettas.

Control of the Military by Foreign Political Actors

There are at least five methods that foreign actors (e.g., agencies, institutions, and states) can pursue to minimize crimes by the military. These processes are, from least to most useful, the greater use of war crimes trials, minimizing the number of dependent economies, encouraging a more proactive media, preventing the creation of national security states, and cutting off economic support to countries where military crimes take place.

To begin with, only a handful of war crimes trials have occurred. They have helped bring to justice many individuals who have engaged in crimes against humanity. However, those trials that have taken place suffer from a number of problems. For example, "[d]efendants in war crimes trials often . . . [argue] . . . that they were carrying out the orders of a superior" (Akehurst, 1982: 278).[12] To aggravate matters, war crimes are poorly defined and "this failure of definition makes it highly [arbitrary] to impose responsibility on leaders of defeated nations" (Falk, Kolko, and Lifton, 1971: 45). There have also been a series of questions concerning procedure at these trials (e.g., Minear, 1971).

Additionally, dependent economies should be minimized or prevented from being established, because in these contexts the military is more apt to come to power. Such economies require the repression of the working- and lower-class and peasants. The military is the best candidate to accomplish this task due to its coercive ability (Evans, 1979). Additionally, in the process of increasing military spending, the typical capital deficiency leads the military to draw on foreign capital and to repress civilian economic demands in order to amass the necessary resources (Luckham, 1973a; 1973b). In sum, the penetration of foreign capital into dependent economies increases the military establishment's power and autonomy relative to other factions (Klare and Arnson, 1981).

Moreover, the media must be more vigilant in exposing crimes by the military and the links that states have in creating, maintaining, and influencing military crimes (Herman and Chomsky, 1988). Rarely do journalists (investigative or otherwise) expose military crimes. And those who do, in some contexts, have reason to fear for their lives. Reporters are logical targets for regimes afraid of exposure. Efforts must be made to make it safer for the press to document crimes by the military including giving journalists protection tantamount to diplomatic status. Also, tougher sanctions against regimes that threaten, injure, or kill journalists should be implemented. We must also encourage reporters to take a more investigative role in developing and researching news stories about military crimes. Journalists, if they are going to be effective in this area, must also improve their skills, by learning appropriate foreign languages, visiting foreign countries, and being on guard for self-censorship. With proper safeguards in place, it would be useful if a series of grants and awards were to be developed and distributed for reporting on military crimes.

Furthermore, in national security states the military is more likely to engage in crimes against real or suspected opponents to the regime. Activists and politicians must work harder to prevent the creation of these types of countries.[13] One way national security states are created is through support by foreign powers. Historically, militaries in national security states have been trained and funded by the superpowers (Tilly, 1993: 207). This relationship has established a precedent whereby weapons from the superpowers are donated or sold to the national security states that use them against their citizens. The superpowers should tie military support and sales of weapons not only to the human rights violations of client states, but also to improvement in reductions in the amount of military crimes.

Finally, and closely connected to controlling national security states, is cutting off economic aid to countries where military crimes are allowed to take place. The superpowers have supported (through financial assistance, low-cost loans, etc.) a series of authoritarian regimes (e.g., Brazil, Chile, Guatemala, etc.), whose militaries have routinely engaged in crimes against their own peoples (e.g., Herman, 1982: 23). Not only does this foreign financial support often get channelled into the coercive duties of the military, but it also draws money away from necessary prosocial government services at home. Once again, support must be connected to human rights performance and the commission of military crimes.

Control by the Public

Most importantly, the military must be controlled by the public. This process is generally referred to as civilian supremacy. According to this doctrine,

> the head of state and the apparatus of government should be civilian and, under no circumstances, be drawn from

serving members of the military or police. Sometimes,
however, principle and practice diverge, as when the
leaders of coups, or those associated with them, drop their
military rank and assume civilian status. (Willimett, 1980:
253)

In general, six controls by the public can be identified. They are,
from least to most important, public protest, draft evasion or
desertion, conscientious objection, challenging bureaucratic
truth, the support or establishment of public organizations to
monitor the military, and self-education.

First, public protest, ranging from demonstrations to
civilian defense, has been relatively effective in minimizing
military crimes (Tilly, 1985: 183). For example, during the 1960s
and early 1970s antiwar demonstrations were relatively
successful in stopping American involvement in the Vietnam
War. Additionally, during the early 1980s the "Mad Mothers of
the Plaza de Mayo" held a "silent vigil outside the Argentinean
Government House for their . . . children" who disappeared
during the "Dirty War" (Herman, 1982: 30). Because of the
international media attention and some books written about the
victims, this vigil was relatively helpful in releasing some of the
individuals who were held incommunicado or in letting the
mothers know where their children were buried. Moreover,
"civilian defense," which includes "non-cooperation with an
opponent's orders, obstruction of his actions, defiance in face of
his threats and sanctions, attempts to encourage non-compliance
among his troops and servants, and the creation of a parallel
system of government" (Roberts, 1967b: 9), was relatively
effective in frustrating the Nazi actions in occupied countries
during World War II.[14]

Second, draft evasion or desertion, which under most
criminal codes is a criminal offense, is another strategy to control
crimes by the military. The logic behind this suggestion is that
the lower the manpower of the armed forces, the less the number
of soldiers that could potentially engage in military crimes. By
the same token, an argument might be made that those
individuals who evade the draft or desert would be least likely
to engage in military crimes. Nevertheless, draft evaders and
deserters often engage or support protest. Some of the

individuals who evade the draft and are caught, however, are sent to prison and the power of their protest is curtailed. Others have immigrated to other states where they are relatively free and capable of protesting against their own country and its initiation or participation in war.

Third, those who are drafted or conscripted but who object to military service can, in some countries, claim conscientious objector status (Levi and DeTray, 1993). However, according to Levi and DeTray (1993), "For those who want to make a more forceful stand against a particular war or who cannot qualify for CO status but wish to remain citizens, draft resistance is likely to be the preferred option" (p. 427).

> Conscientious objection is neither the only nor necessarily the most prevalent form of refusing behavioral consent. Applications for draft exemptions and deferments may also reflect dissent; certainly draft evasion, draft resistance, and emigration to avoid conscription are other examples of refusing consent. However, only in the cases of conscientious objection, draft resistance, and possibly emigration is there a relatively clear statement about one's beliefs about the justness, and not just the personal inconvenience, of the war. (Levi and DeTray, 1993: 429)

Fourth, individuals could continuously challenge the propaganda or "bureaucratic truth that serves military power" (Galbraith, 1969: 17). Such messages include the necessity of arms races, the dangers of communism, anarchism, or foreign domination; the necessity of maintaining the global position of a country; and that individual interests should be subordinate to national interests (Galbraith, 1969: 17; Martin, 1984: 7).

Fifth, the public could establish or increase their financial support for nongovernmental organizations that monitor abuses against individuals by the military (e.g., Amnesty International, World Watch, etc.) and other crimes by the military. This would improve the resources of these organizations and hopefully the accuracy, reliability, and strength of their research and lobbying efforts.

Finally and perhaps most important is education of the public (Galbraith, 1969: 7–8). Universities and colleges could place more emphasis on courses dealing with the military, state violence, human rights, and international law. Besides the written medium, other means of education can be used including academic and international awareness conferences. For example, the first Latin American Congress of Relatives of the Disappeared, held in San Jose, Costa Rica, January 20–24, 1981, attracted considerable media attention and thereby increased its educational value (Herman, 1982: 8–17).

Summary

This review of control mechanisms on crimes by the military has been intended as an organizational tool in order to understand processes that have or could be implemented to prevent military crime as well as to identify those controls that need strengthening. In general, the greater the number of types of controls utilized, the less likely or often that soldiers and by implication the military will engage in crimes.

Further Research and Praxis

Since the range of controls articulated in this chapter is rather broad in scope, further research and specificity is warranted. To begin with, because it is difficult for researchers to penetrate or conduct ethnographic research on the military, perhaps the next and most fruitful step is to interview victims of crimes by the military and ask them what they believe would be the most important controls on military crimes. Alternatively, because the types of crimes that the military engages in vary in the degree of seriousness, solutions for each type of crime may have to be dealt with separately. Thus, perhaps individual researchers might choose one type of military crime and intensively explore both its causes and controls in a limited number of contexts (e.g., countries, armies, time periods). Moreover, a series of case studies might be assembled to determine the conditions under which each of these methods of control have succeeded or failed.

Citizens, politicians, and the military have an obligation to monitor crimes by the armed forces and to suggest or improve means by which military crimes can be controlled or prevented. While labeling abhorrent actions committed by the military as "crimes" may seem like a semantic device, it is a first step in reconceptualization and combatting these actions. This approach allows us to move beyond the traditional public administration and policy literature by examining these actions in the more critical literature found in other relevant fields, such as criminology, criminal justice, law, political science, and sociology. Crimes by the military should not be treated as business as usual but as transgressions that need to be addressed legally and morally and most important prevented from reoccurring.

NOTES

* An earlier version of this chapter was presented at the Canadian Association for Security and Intelligence Studies Annual Meeting, Calgary, June 11, 1994. Special thanks to Nancy Jacobson and Sam Matheson for research assistance, and to Tom Brewer, Paul Bond, Natasha J. Cabrera, David Charters, Frank Williams III, and anonymous internal reviewers for comments.

1. In this chapter, the author uses the expression "crimes committed by the military" and "military crimes" interchangeably. *Military crimes*, as articulated in this chapter, are those actions that, in general, violate a legalistic and a moral conception of crime. They also include the acts of mentally stable and unstable soldiers (e.g., Corporal Lortie's actions in the Québec National Assembly). Although some observers may suggest that the acts of mentally unstable individuals should be excluded, the military bears responsibility for supervising individuals in their employ.

2. According to Galbraith (1969: 23), at least in the United States, "military power is not confined to the [Armed] Services and their contractors—what has come to be called the military-industrial complex." Those who support the military power include intelligence agencies, foreign service officers, university scientists, "defense-oriented organizations as RAND, the Institute for Defense Analysis and Hudson Institute," and the Armed Services Committees of the Senate and House

of Representatives (Galbraith, 1969: 23–24). Additional supporters include veterans' associations (Liebknect, 1917: 170).

3. There are a variety of resources that militaries possess, including money, weapons, experience, personnel, and organization.

4. This definition builds on Huntington (1957: Chapter 1).

5. This chapter is not concerned with such mechanisms as the national guard; however, its proscriptions could well apply to this organization.

6. This idea might suggest that all war-making is wrong; however, my intention is simply to point out that war-making for expansionistic purposes is morally wrong.

7. It must also be recognized that some crimes, such as illegal drug use among soldiers, are dealt with more severely by the military of some countries than are the crimes that occur in the mainstream criminal justice system.

8. These controls, in turn, fall under two dimensions of control (form: formal and informal; and location; external and internal [e.g., Rycroft, 1975]).

9. Personal communication with Tom Brewer, November 1994.

10. See, for example, Bryant (1979: 31–33) for a review.

11. Reducing military expenditures or personnel can also lead to crimes; increases stress among military personnel, which in turn motivates them to engage in crimes.

12. This, Kelman and Hamilton (1989) call a crime of obedience.

13. Those preoccupied with the maintenance of national security.

14. See Roberts (1967a) for a series of excellent case studies where civilian resistance has been utilized.

REFERENCES

Abrahamsson, Bengt (1972) *Military Professionalism and Political Power*. London: Sage.

Akehurst, Michael (1982) *Introduction to Modern International Law*, 4th ed. Boston: Allen and Unwin.

Barnet, Richard (1969) *The Economy of Death*. New York: Atheneum.

Bennett, Jeremy (1967) "The Resistance Against German Occupation of Denmark, 1940–5," in Adam Roberts (ed.), *The Strategy of Civilian Defence*. London: Faber and Faber, pp. 154–172.

Bienen, Henry (1968) *The Military Intervenes: Case Studies in Political Development*. New York: Russell Sage Foundation.

Bryant, Clifton D. (1979) *Khaki-Collar Crime: Deviant Behavior in the Military Context*. New York: Free Press.

Evan, William M. (1962) "Due Process of Law in Military and Industrial Organization." *Administrative Science Quarterly* 7: pp. 187–207.

Evans, Peter (1979) *Dependent Development: The Alliance of Multinational, State, and Local Capital in Brazil*. Princeton, NJ: Princeton University Press.

Falk, Richard. A., Gabriel Kolko, and Robert Jay Lifton (eds.) (1971) *Crimes of War*. New York: Random House.

Fidel, Kenneth (1975) *Militarism in Developing Countries*. New Brunswick, NJ: Transaction Books.

Finer, Samuel E. (1962) *The Man on Horseback: The Role of the Military in Politics*. London: Pall Mall Press.

Fitch, J. Samuel (1985) "The Garrison State in America: A Content Analysis of Trends in the Expectation of Violence." *Journal of Peace Research* 22, 1: 31–45.

Fullbright, J. William (1971) *The Pentagon Propaganda Machine*. New York: Vintage.

Galbraith, John Kenneth (1969) *How to Control the Military*. Garden City, NY: Doubleday.

Goodspeed, D.J. (1962) *The Conspirators: A Study of the Coups d'Etat*. Toronto: Macmillan.

Hakeem, Michael. (1946) "Service in the Armed Forces and Criminality." *Journal of Criminal Law and Criminality* 37 (May–June): 120–131.

Herman, Edward S. (1982) *The Real Terror Network*. Boston: South End Press.

———, and Noam Chomsky (1988) *Manufacturing Consent*. Boston: South End Press.

Huntington, Samuel P. (1957) *The Soldier and the State*. New York: Random House.

———— (1961) "Interservice Competition and the Political Roles of the Armed Services." *American Political Science Review* 55, 40–52.

Janowitz, Morris (1960) *The Professional Soldier*. New York: Free Press.

———— (1977) *Military Institutions and Coercion in the Developing Nations*. Chicago: University of Chicago Press.

Kelman, Herbert C., and V. Lee Hamilton (1989) *Crimes of Obedience*. New Haven: Yale University Press.

Klare, Michael T., and Cynthia Arnson (1981) *Supplying Repression: U.S. Support for Authoritarian Regimes Abroad*. Washington, DC: Institute for Policy Studies.

Knudten, Richard D. (1970) "The System of Military Justice," in *Crime in a Complex Society: An Introduction to Criminology*. Homewood, IL: Dorsey Press, Chapter 19.

Lang, Kurt (1972) *Military Institutions and the Sociology of War*. Beverly Hills, CA: Sage.

Larson, Arthur D. (1974) "Military Professionalism and Civilian Control: A Comparative Analysis of Two Interpretations." *Journal of Political and Military Sociology* 2: 57–72.

Lasswell, Harold (1941) "The Garrison State." *American Journal of Sociology* 46 (January): 455–68.

———— (1962) "The Garrison State Hypothesis Today," in Samuel Huntington (ed.), *Changing Patterns of Military Politics*. New York: Free Press, pp. 51–70.

Levi, Margaret, and Stephen DeTray (1993) "A Weapon against War: Conscientious Objection in the United States, Australia, and France." *Politics and Society* 21, 4 (December): 425–464.

Liebknecht, Karl (1917) *Militarism*. New York: B.W. Huebsh.

Luckham, Robin (1973a) "Militarism: Arms and the Internationalization of Capital." *IDS Bulletin* 8, 3.

———— (1973b) "Militarism: Force, Class and International Conflict." *IDS Bulletin* 8, 3: 19–32.

Lunden, Walter (1952) "Military Service and Criminality." *Journal of Criminal Law, Criminology and Police Science* 2, 6 (March–April): 766–773.

Martin, Brian (1984) *Uprooting War*. London: Freedom Press.

Mills, C. Wright (1956) *The Power Elite*. New York: Oxford University Press.

Minear, Richard (1971) *Victor's Justice: The Tokyo War Crimes Trial*. Princeton, NJ: Princeton University Press.

Moskos, Charles C. (1974) "The Concept of the Military-Industrial Complex." *Social Problems* 21: 498–512.

Nordlinger, Eric (1977) *Soldiers in Politics: Military Coups and Government*. Englewood Cliffs, NJ: Prentice Hall.

Parenti, Michael (1983) *Democracy for the Few*. New York: St. Martin's Press.

Roberts, Adam (1967a) "Civilian Resistance to Military Coups." *Journal of Peace Research* 12, 1: 19–36.

—— (1967b) *The Strategy of Civilian Defence: Non Violent Resistance in Aggression*. London: Faber and Faber.

Russett, Bruce M. (1970) *What Price Vigilance? The Burdens of National Defense*. New Haven, CT: Yale University Press.

Rycroft, Robert W. (1975) "The Military Reform Movement: 1969–1972: The Development of Bureaucratic Control System." *Journal of Political and Military Sociology* 3 (Fall): 179–189.

Sivard, Ruth Leger (1974–1988) *World Military and Social Expenditures*. Washington, DC: World Priorities, Annual Publication.

Spencer, John C. (1954) *Crime and the Services*. London: Routledge and Kegan Paul.

Stepan, Alfred (1973) "The New Professionalism of Internal Warfare and Military Role Expansion," in Alfred Stepan (ed.), *Authoritarian Brazil: Origins, Policies, and Future*. New Haven, CT: Yale University Press, pp. 45–65.

Thayer, George (1969) *The War Business*. New York: Simon & Schuster.

Tilly, Charles (1985) "War Making and State Making as Organized Crime," in Peter B. Evans, Dietrich Rueschmeyer, and Theda Skocpol (eds.), *Bringing the State Back In*. New York: Cambridge University Press, pp. 169–191.

—— (1993) *Coercion, Capital, and European States*. Cambridge, MA: Blackwell.

Tracy, Robert G., et al. (1971) "A Study of the Relationship Between Military Service in the Armed Forces and Criminality." Criminal Justice Monograph, Vol. 3, No. 1, Institute of Contemporary Corrections and Behavioral Sciences, Sam Houston State University.

Ujevich, Robert M. (1969) *Military Justice: A Summary of Its Legislative and Judicial Development*. Washington, DC: Library of Congress.

Wagley, Perry (1944) "Some Criminologic Implications of the Returning Soldier." *Journal of Criminal Law and Criminology* 34, 2 (January–February): 313–314.

Walker, Stephan G., and S. Ivy Lang (1988) "The 'Garrison State Syndrome' in the Third World: A Research Note." *Journal of Political and Military Sociology* 16 (Spring): 105–116.

Willimett, Terry C. (1980) "Social Control and the Military in Canada," in Richard Ossenberg (ed.), *Power and Change in Canada*. Toronto: McClelland and Stewart, pp. 246–284.

State Crime by the Police and Its Control*

Ken Menzies

The concept of state crime recognizes that the state and its personnel violate the laws that are supposed to bind them. State crimes are "acts defined by laws as criminal and committed by state officials in pursuit of their job as representatives of the state" (Chambliss, 1989: 184). This concept draws attention to how state positions are a source of criminal opportunities (Green, 1990: 12–13). Like other white collar crime, state crimes may be committed for personal gain or on behalf of the employing organization, which is known as organizational crime (Coleman, 1989: 9). The dividing line between these two types of state crime is fluid; activities that benefit one's state agency often lead to the criminal's promotion and higher pay.

Causes

Once the possibility of state crime is acknowledged, the police can be seen to be in a highly advantageous structural position to commit such crimes (Clinard and Quinney, 1978: 140). The weak position of most suspects and the low visibility of arrest and interrogation have enabled police to deny suspects' legal rights (Corrado and Oliverio, 1988), extract confessions by force (Green, 1990: 159) and present false evidence in court (Marx, 1988: 134). The low visibility and high discretion involved in routine patrolling facilitates individual and systematic corruption (Misra, 1986; Lundman, 1980). Highly profitable victimless crimes like prostitution, gambling, and drug offenses have provided criminals with large funds for systemic corruption. Police dealing with these crimes are particularly prone to corruption (Coleman, 1989: 96; Knapp, 1973; Punch, 1985).

Occupational factors inherent to police organizations, such as the police officer's working personality and the loyalty internalized regarding police colleagues, also may facilitate state crime by the police. Skolnick (1966) argues that the realities of policing generate a police officer's working personality, which involves being authoritarian, suspicious, preoccupied with danger, and cynical. This personality may generate unnecessary violence (Green, 1990: 160). Brutality is particularly likely when a citizen fails to show what the police officer sees as "proper deference" to their authority (Lundman, 1980; Van Maanen, 1982). The dangers inherent in the role, the "us versus them" mentality, and the pressures of adapting to shift work generate strong loyalties to other police officers (Skolnick, 1966). At a minimum, this loyalty makes detecting police crime and convicting a police officer difficult, as the people most likely to know of his or her offenses are reluctant to report the offenses and testify against the fellow officer. At a maximum, occupational solidarity provides strong support for such state crime as systemic corruption (Knapp, 1973).

The police subculture can contribute to state crime. Police often see themselves defending the weak against the predatory, as the indispensable "thin blue line" defending a way of life (Reiner, 1985: 85–110). This can lead to police officers taking the law into their own hands because they feel the courts are too slow and/or lenient. It also makes police more willing to harass protest groups. For instance, in the United States, law enforcement officers have disseminated false information (Marx, 1979); hired agent provocateurs (Michalowski, 1985: 394–5); infiltrated and engaged in illegal surveillance of, for example, black militants, antinuclear groups, and even welfare mothers groups (Coleman, 1990: 62–65). In Canada, the police have destroyed membership lists and searched illegally for information (Keable Commission, 1981; McDonald Commission,

1981). Some South American police willingness to engage in death squad activities comes from their belief that they must defend their country's soul or essence against Godless opponents. Police, in their work, view the whole world as being at stake (Chambliss, 1989). When police culture is racist, the potential for state crime is augmented, as the video of the Los Angeles police beating of Rodney King reminds us. Similarly, the Manitoba Aboriginal Justice Inquiry raises worrying questions about Canada.

The structural, occupational, and cultural factors outlined above can facilitate state crime by the police. A major question democratic societies must resolve is how to ensure that the police uphold the law rather than subvert it. This chapter asks what policies and structures would best ensure that a police force acts within the law. The question is, What can help ensure a law-abiding police force in a country with substantial commitments to democracy?[1]

This chapter continues with a brief discussion of some background assumptions required for this thought experiment to be worthwhile. Then, it attacks the usual responses to the question. Next, the chapter argues that the police should be "responsible humanists," rewarded for actions that respect civilians, watched by "social auditors," and guided by several political masters.

Background Assumptions

If our question is not to be utopian, or stated alternatively, if our analysis is to be relevant to our societies today, then we must acknowledge that our communities have a substantial commitment to democratic process and the rule of law. It makes no sense to ask how the KGB or the Gestapo could have been made into law-abiding institutions. If a state accepts the use of terror against those it considers its enemies within (as Nazi Germany and Stalinist Russia both did), then one must change the whole sociopolitical structure to remove state terror, not simply change the police. A focus on how to foster a law-abiding police force requires the assumption that significant political forces support this ideal. To use the familiar analogy, if the police are the iron fist in the velvet glove of the dominant social forces, then we must make two assumptions: first, the fist fits in the glove, but not perfectly (note that it is possible that the police are more law accepting than dominant social forces); second, the glove has a substantial commitment to legality. If these two assumptions are true, then it may be possible to devise ways to increase the fist's commitment to legality. In short, a discussion of how to ensure that the police are not an instrument of state terror makes sense only if society and the police have a substantial commitment to democratic legality. It should be noted that the topic under consideration also logically requires that substantial state crime by the police can coexist with a substantial commitment by the police and society to democratic legality. A general commitment to legality with some state crime characterizes most Western democracies. We have something to build on. Thus, this chapter is reformist in tone, rather than speculative and revolutionary. However, to some people, some reforms may seem quite revolutionary.

If the potential for the police to be agents of state terror is to be taken seriously, then we must reject much of the theoretical framework of Ericson's police studies (e.g., 1981a; 1981b; 1982). His critical, symbolic interactionist framework presents the police as active creators of public order and crime labels for activities. He criticizes social commentators in general, and the police in particular, for reifying the law and seeing an abstraction, the law, as governing police activities. Ericson's view of the police as creators of public order are found within his symbolic interactionist premises. These premises frequently focus on people making meaningful choices and downplay the power of other people to restrict the choices available. Thus, people appear more in control of their activities, freer and less constrained, than they actually are (Farberman, 1975; Menzies, 1982: 43). Ericson's approach views legislation governing police powers of arrest and interrogation not as restricting the police, but as enabling them to do these processes. Unfortunately, this obscures important differences. It fails to distinguish laws that facilitate state crime from those that do not. For instance, Sparger and Giacopassi (1992) show that in Memphis, at least, restrictions on police use of weapons since the 1975 Garner decision have had an effect. Those restrictions permit police to shoot a fleeing felon only if he or she is a danger to the officers or others. Police shootings have been reduced, lives have been saved, and the inequality in the ratio of black to white suspects shot in less threatening situations has been reduced, though not eliminated. In short, the difference in what police are enabled to do is important, but Ericson's framework obscures it.[2]

Guarding the Guardians: Problems with Some Proposals

Who shall guard the guardians? The super-guardians. And who shall guard the super-guardians? The super-super-guardians. Wrong questions lead to an insoluble infinite regress. The correct questions are, What organization and ethos must a police force have, and how should the police relate to the rest of society so that the police act to fulfil their mission? What follows is a brief outline of three answers—utopian, local democratic control, and professionalism.

Utopian

Waddington (1987) argues that training the police in paramilitary techniques leads to less violence, as untrained police are more fearful of and less prone to violence than those with confidence in their ability to handle violence. Jefferson attacks this position as "idealistically abstract" (1990: 131) and advocates viewing the police from the perspective of those at the bottom of society, those driven to protest. Paramilitary tactics, he argues, amplify violence. Jefferson (1987) concludes that to deal with public order policing, "we have to combine the *political* control of decision-making in this area with a conception of *justice* compatible with the interests of the policed. Jointly, these would clearly identify paramilitarism as part of the problem" (p. 53).

Jefferson's analysis is attractive because he discusses police organization not in the abstract, but in an analyzed social context. Unfortunately, however, his neo-Marxist framework leads him to assume that protest must challenge an unjust imbalance. In addition, it assumes there is a social arrangement that everybody will accept. Jefferson thus engages in utopian dreaming about a conflict-free society. No matter how a modern society is organized, some group at some time will feel inclined toward protest. While Jefferson assumes that protests are responses to injustice, empirical evidence shows that many of them perpetuate injustice. A good society accepts both civil protest and the need to uphold the law until it is changed. As a last resort, police must be available to respond to protest and be prepared to use paramilitary techniques. It is clear that Jefferson objects to particular situations that the police have responded to in a paramilitary way. His mistake is to displace onto the police his moral repulsion with these situations and advocate an impractical general solution that does not favor a resolution seen as just by those being policed if this group supports a position that he views as immoral (e.g., racism).

Local Democratic Control

Lea and Young (1984) and Lustgarten (1983) argue that law-abiding policing depends centrally on enlisting local support. This is best realized, they maintain, if police policy is determined by locally elected politicians. Thus, the community should consult the police in formulating its policing needs instead of the police consulting the community in formulating their strategy. Local democratic control of the police is symbolically attractive. However, there are two major unresolved difficulties with this position: first, local democratic control may lead to a tyranny of the majority, not a concern for legality; second, the advocates of this position need to go beyond a process (democratic control) to spell out how police forces should be structured.

Stated abstractly, local control of the police sounds like a good formula for the police respecting the laws of the community and the people supporting the police. However, local control is always implemented by a select few in a given local area. If they are elected democratically, then they will accept the first imperative of democratic politics—obtain popular support. Due process and no prejudiced actions against minorities and/or the weak are central to policing that respects people. These concerns often clash. Majority support is often available for actions against weak minorities (e.g., punks) or disagreeable individuals (e.g., public drunks). Lea and Young (1984: Chapter 7) suggest that one possible objection to local democratic control is that unrepresentative local interest groups may gain control of the police. This underestimates the problem. Representative groups may control the police and use the police to impose a tyranny of the majority. For instance, in response to a community policing program, police in two American cities adopted aggressive tactics, especially illegal stops and frisks. The community demanded summary enforcement against "bad eggs" (Toch, 1976: 41). Aggressive, law-disregarding police action against groups seen as potentially dangerous may be very popular. Police under the direct control of the local power structure will be under pressure to reinforce that structure and rarely enforce the law impartially.

The second problem is that advocates of local democratic control present a value, a commitment to a type of process, without specifying concretely how it is to be enacted. Unanswered is, what process, and what reward system for police leads to street-level enactment of the wishes of a local government? Without spelling out how in practice the police will be locally controlled, the feasibility of this position cannot be assessed.

Professionalism

The police view improvements in their profession arising from increased professionalism and a further distancing from political control (Goldstein, 1990: 5–8). Thus, the police will be fully accountable to and in very substantial accord with the law when they become fully professional and completely removed from any political inference. They argue that this practice provides the best guarantee of policing that serves society. The occasional "bad apple" in the police department can be handled by internal disciplinary procedures and/or the criminal courts. Outside complaint or review boards are viewed as unacceptable and ineffective, as they force the police to close ranks and render them vulnerable to manipulation by the forces of evil (e.g., the mafia and/or civil rights activists).

Professionalism is an ideology that makes the technical aspects of work define the work itself. Seeing policing as a nonpolitical activity that can be done scientifically can reduce state crime by the police. Historically, increased professionalism has decreased corruption (Bayley, 1977; Chapman, 1982). Police corruption, brutality, racism, and sexism undermine police support by the groups discriminated against, cutting into the cooperation and information flow needed for police effectiveness (Lea and Young, 1984). Thus, policies that improve policing in general are likely to reduce state crime by the police. For instance, Bayley and Garofalo (1989) found that police officers identified by their peers as more skilled were more versatile in their tactics in handling violent situations. However, even observational studies that maximize the chance to observe violence have been ineffective in that the actual number of cases of observed police force was too small to demonstrate that the police who were viewed as more skillful actually were. These studies conclude that as violence is rare, that while officers need to be trained to avoid obvious provocations, the best way of improving the handling of violent situations is training to broaden police officers' range of tactical choices in all situations. In addition, good police administration through clear policy guidelines about concerns like violence and undercover operations helps reduce abuses (Green, 1990: 160; Marx, 1988: 181–89).

While adopting a professional ideology has helped reduce state crime by the police, this approach is limited in two major ways. First, it denies the need for accountability to the public. The problem is that if they lack this commitment and believe, for instance, that the importance of eradicating drug dealing justifies terror and illegality against drug users and dealers, then professionalism does not provide a check (Goldstein, 1990: 10). The second problem is that, although good policing requires not only professionalism, in the sense of a commitment to and faith in their ability to do good work, it needs both a constant awareness of the political nature of policing and accountability to various sociopolitical groups.

Law-Respecting Police

Not only will improved policing decrease state crime by the police, but a law-respecting police force will also (1) recognize the political aspect of their work and approach policing as "responsible humanists," (2) be rewarded for people-respecting actions, (3) be monitored by "social auditors," and (4) serve several masters. We turn now to each of these topics individually.

Responsible Humanism

Police professionalism asserts that police officers apply a body of specialized knowledge in their work. Yet this approach makes police difficult to question, as they are viewed as realists who are doing what needs to be done to protect society. However, policing at its best uses coercive means to achieve just ends (Muir, 1977). Police should be responsible humanists, concerned for the offenders while recognizing that this approach must be within a context of responsibility to the community, which seems to be a contradiction of principles. But, police who are responsible humanists act with an awareness of this tension among key values.

One resource police have for maintaining order is arrest (Ericson, 1982), but it should be a last resort and characterized by responsible humanism. For instance, if one member of a separated couple is removing property from a previously jointly owned house and the other phones the police to complain of theft, then a resolution of the property dispute is often more appropriate than an arrest. Because judicial and punishment processes do not usually benefit offenders, mild offenses should be kept from the formal social control system if others will not be harmed. Police now tend to accept this, though a shortage of personnel (Van Maanen, 1982) may be more causally important in producing this result.

Police should be tough-minded philosophers or active practical philosophers. This concept may strike readers initially as an oxymoron similar to the idea of a ten-mile "fun" run. However, it highlights central components of police work. If police see themselves as philosophers, then they recognize that their work is about debatable moral choices. But police cannot sit in their squad cars contemplating their choices for hours. They often must act quickly on limited information. The view of police as active practical philosophers recognizes that they act politically in ambiguous situations. A general public recognition that policing is political and filled with ambiguous choices will help illustrate the limits of policing and will facilitate the notion that society must tackle certain issues through other methods.

Police are expected both to obey the law and to stop crime. A police officer, however, will sooner or later confront the "Dirty Harry dilemma of either violating the rules or allowing offenders of whose guilt he is convinced to go free" (Reiner, 1985: 184). Occasionally disregarding somebody's legal rights is unfortunate, but not a major social concern. However, if the police culture institutionally tolerates such abuses of legal rights and then supports whatever is needed to get a conviction, then the police are participants in state crime. If the police were active practical philosophers engaged in making political choices in ambiguous situations, then they would be more accepting of not always being able to convict those they believe to be guilty. Furthermore, this less professional self-image would in turn lead to more modesty and a recognition of the limits of policing.

Training must encourage responsible humanism in policing. A major motivation now for becoming a police officer is the possibility of meaningful community service (Fielding and Fielding, 1987). This desire can be built on, especially as current police pay levels make policing attractive to people with and/or capable of advanced education. In the United States, police academies spend about 90% of their time on "crook catching," particularly the technical aspects of this (Meadows, 1987). Police training is short (usually three–six months) compared to that for other occupations such as social work with substantial power to intervene in people's lives (Bittner, 1983). First, police need more extensive training in criminology, penology, and law to help them understand more fully their place in society. By examining different styles of policing throughout the world, police trainees will learn that different choices in policing are available. Police training also needs to develop recruits' moral sensitivity so that they will become aware that their use of power is contestable. However, the strong theoretical reasons for more policing education must be approached with caution (e.g., Bittner, 1983; Green, 1990: 160). Simply suggesting a college education should be interpreted with caution. Empirical studies comparing college-educated to non-college-educated police in the United States (e.g., Sherman and Blumberg, 1981; Wycoff and Susmilch, 1979) find no consistent differences in any form of behavior including the willingness to use force.

Police Who Respect People

The antithesis of criminal acts against people is an attitude of respect for people. However, several factors may undermine police respect for civilians. The structural position of the police gives them power. The cliche "power corrupts" has truth. Their working personality facilitates authoritarian approaches, while their occupational culture says they should make definitive decisions. As they are also often under time pressures, the circumstances for overbearing behavior toward civilians to become routine are present. Yet respecting people is important as Wiley and Hudik (1980) show. They compared police stops of people where the police explained the purpose of the stop with cases where no explanation was offered. All were naturally occurring stops of people on suspicion of having committed an offense, but cases where no arrest resulted. Citizens were willing to spend more time helping the police when offered a reason for being stopped. In addition, people spent more time with and thereby helped the police if they believed the offense was more serious. In other words, politeness pays.

The more police are integrated into society, the more likely they are to treat civilians with respect. Unfortunately, the police are often socially quite isolated. For instance, the Royal Canadian Mounted Police in 1978 employed 19,000 people of whom only 4,800 were civilians (Mann and Lee, 1979: 154). The police should employ many more civilians on a part-time basis (e.g., doctors for medical evidence on child abuse and rape, accountants to help with fraudulent bankruptcy). Regular police involvement with civilian part-timers would help keep law enforcement values in line with the rest of society. Conversely, many people would become more understanding of the pressures on the police. Law enforcement officers would also be more socially integrated if police academies were located close to universities and/or community colleges so the police cadets (another less-military word would be needed) could take many of their courses at the university (Stark, 1972: 235–236). This would help integrate the police into the mainstream values of society. In addition, potential social workers and lawyers would learn about the police perspective on many issues and events.

The police individually and organizationally see their arrest rate as a success measure. One problem this creates is that "By narrowing their attention to something they can apparently control, the arrest rate, they have tied themselves to a socially determined process (crime) over which they have virtually no control" (Manning, 1977: 19). Police performance measures, particularly for individual police officers, should focus much more on what police do have control over. For instance, law enforcement officers should be assessed on how they arrest people, collect evidence, or provide advice on building security (Wycoff and Maunting, 1983). If we want police respect for people to be important, then it must count in the assessment of specific police activities (Goldstein, 1990). Police performance measures should include a component linked to how they treat a suspect, a victim, or someone offering assistance. There are many ways of collecting the relevant evidence; random follow-up on a selection of officers' calls would determine "customer satisfaction" (Manning, 1977: Chapter 10) and also provide increased accountability to victims of crime. Just as teachers are assessed in the classroom, so too should police be reviewed on the street, where inspectors would evaluate a police officer's skill at, say, handling a barroom brawl with a minimum of violence.

In light of the current vogue for community-based policing, it should be noted that people-respecting policing need not be community-based. A hierarchical, military-style police force focused on crime and not service functions could learn more about the people being policed and respect them. On the other hand, a decentralized police force with a strong emphasis on service roles and community involvement (Clairmont, 1991) could be manipulative and have only a public relations front of respect for the community. Nevertheless, some of the concerns that community-based policing is endeavouring to address such as the need to know the community and their values (a part of respecting people) is relevant to our concerns.

Social Auditors[3]

Social concern about state crime by police is often difficult to generate as the media on the whole is not a successful watchdog on the police (Skolnick and McCoy, 1985). The police exercise substantial control over crime and police news agendas in a variety of ways (Ericson, Baranek, and Chan, 1989). Reporters are highly dependent on the crime and police news sources, but when adverse publicity would hurt officers' crime-fighting ability, reporters are forced to pursue other stories (Fishman, 1980).

Social auditors trained in basic police observational methods and report writing should perform extensive observation of the police (e.g., Ericson, 1981a; Black, 1980). Social auditors should have access by law to whatever they wish. After a year the social auditors who had been observing a large metropolitan police force or a variety of smaller forces would get together and produce a report. If their experiences were different, then there could be one manuscript with several dissents or alternatively several reports if the differences were too large to reconcile into a single document.

Like trial jurors, social auditors could be cosen by lot. However, as it would involve about a year-and-a-half of a person's life, he or she could refuse. Just as with trial jurors, social auditors could for cause (for example, a criminal record) be rejected by the government agency running the program and a limited number of other reasons. Social auditors would be paid the police salary for a constable who has passed his or her probationary period. This would be attractive to many out of work, so it is to be expected that previously unemployed people would be overrepresented among social auditors. To ensure that social auditors would not be interested in doing a whitewash of police activities by the prospect of future employment, all social auditors would be barred from police employment for a substantial length of time.

Social auditors are a mechanism to do regularly what is now done sporadically by various specialized groups. For example, in parliamentary democracies there are ongoing royal commissions into police behavior. For instance, in Latin America there are human rights organizations staffed by courageous individuals whose exposure of police methods and death squad activities has helped bring international pressure to bear on various governments. Finally, social auditors would be like academics (e.g., Hazlehurst, 1991), and would write analyses exposing questionable social control practices to critical public scrutiny.

Social auditors will provide a regular source of newsworthy information about the routine realities of police work. Just as the auditor general's reports on government mismanagement generate a concern among bureaucrats not to misuse money and to correct identified wasteful practices, so too should social jurors' reports help keep the police law-abiding. However, as social auditors will be regular members of their societies, their reports will reflect public attitudes and values. Thus, the reports may say that the police are doing the best they can and are desperately short of resources. The reports may advocate more police powers, more police, and better equipment. Law enforcement officers will see this as public education, their critics as co-optation. Police critics, like liberal academics and civil rights lawyers, should remember in response to such reports, that the police always significantly, though not entirely, mirror their society. If more resources should be supplied to the police and fewer rights for suspects be given is the public view, then changing public opinion, not the police, should be the focus of those who disagree. Being in line with the popular will, and whether they are should be clear from social auditors' reports, means the police in one basic sense are democratic.[4]

Left realists (e.g., Jones, MacLean, and Young, 1986; Currie, DeKeseredy, and MacLean, 1990) have stressed that society needs independent information on police activities. The police cannot be controlled if all our information on policing comes from the police themselves. Left realists have advocated and implemented victimization surveys to map a community's policing needs. However, victimization is the product of many social processes of which policing is but one. Except for their questions about police brutality, these surveys do not address actual police behavior. The approach advocated here accepts the left realist argument that society needs independent information on the police to be in a good position to control them, but suggests that direct observation of the police is what is needed most. This is not to deny the utility of victimization surveys or that such techniques are much easier to get political acceptance for than social auditors would be.

Serving Several Masters

If a society has one strong centralized police force, then, should this police force become hostile to the society, it is in a good position to stage a coup. At a less extreme level, eliminating abuses of any type in the one force that people depend on for crime control is likely to be very difficult. If a single national police force is rejected for these reasons, and a strictly locally controlled one is accepted for the reasons outlined earlier in this chapter, then there should be not only a number of police forces, but their control should be divided among several political levels. There should be local control to ensure adaptation to local priorities, but this should be overseen by other governmental levels to ensure that societywide policing standards are maintained.

A police chief who is accountable to several masters, each of whom is in consequence a partial master, is forced to be sensitive to a wide range of political concerns. If the different political levels are in agreement, then he or she has to fall quickly into line. If politicians at the different political levels disagree, then he or she has more autonomy that probably will be used to continue as before, as is appropriate for a basically conservative institution such as the police. As long as the police chief remains sensitive to the different levels' political issues, he or she has substantial autonomy. In other words, making the police accountable to several masters means the police must accept long-run political conerns. They retain, however, independence from short-run issues that accountability to only one political master would entail. Multiple masters should make the police socially responsive without being politically partisan. In addition, with several groups able to demand an accounting, there is less chance that corruption or inefficiency will continue without arousing concern. Unfortunately, divided power may make eliminating corruption or inefficiency more difficult, as one level of government may frustrate another. However, given the unpopularity of police corruption, the willingness of politicians at some level of government should lead to an attack on corruption.

Both current Canadian and British situations ensure divided control. Savage (1984: 50) sets out the current English structure as being: "The Chief Constable is responsible for the *'direction and control'* of the force, the police authority [local but only partially elected] for the *'maintenance'* of the force and the home office (National Government for *'ensuring the efficiency'* of the force." Brogden (1982) concludes that English chief constables have considerable freedom of action with regard to how they direct their activities. However, the freedom is that "of a managerial negotiator, not that of an autocrat" (pp. 220–221). A police chief, by resisting the political objectives of local and national politicians, can increase his or her own autonomy in the short run. In the long run, however, he or she will produce a reaction that will curtail police autonomy. Thus, if police chiefs are competent administrators, politicians cannot interfere in the day-to-day operations of the police, yet the police are responsive to well-established social concerns.

The police should also be seen to be symbolically answerable to the law. To see that justice is done, there must be a neutral party who can ask the police to answer the law (Terrill,

1990). Consequently, local governments should appoint a civilian review board with its own nonpolice staff to investigate allegations against the police. In cases where the review board's commissioner is satisfied with police cooperation, the board works with the police's own internal disciplinary investigation. This provides an incentive for the police to cooperate. If the commissioner senses a cover-up, then he or she should work independently. The results of each investigation are reported to the police chief except if they directly concern him or her. An investigation of the police chief is submitted to the next political level. For some complaints, the commissioner will recommend internal police disciplinary procedures and must be informed of the outcome. In other cases, the commissioner will provide information to the public prosecutor for possible criminal charges.

A review board will give the press and whistle-blowers in the police a better chance to expose police abuses. However, its main value is symbolic. In practice, many valid complaints will not be substantiated for three main reasons. First, police solidarity means that the police will tend to cover up for each other. Second, many complaints will come from people in trouble with the law and often with previous convictions. Their credibility to the commissioner or a jury will be less than police officers'. Finally, civilian review boards being basically judicial provide substantial procedural safeguards for the accused. Internal disciplinary processes work to the civil standard of an administrative tribunal and are more likely to support complaints against officers (Kerstetter, 1985). The difficulty in obtaining convictions is one reason why the commissioner may prefer police internal disciplinary processes to the courts. The evidence may show very conclusively that the officer acted inappropriately and allow his or her dismissal, but may be insufficient to establish criminality.

Conclusion

The police's structural position, occupation, and occupational culture can facilitate state crime. Reducing this possibility is an important concern of democratic societies. The utopian and usual left- and right-wing approaches to this problem are inadequate. The key features of a good solution are a stress on the value of responsible humanism, rewarding the police for respecting people, having the police watched by social auditors, and dividing control of the police among several political levels. Until we can successfully implement these practices, policing will be plagued with undemocratic processes.

NOTES

*   An earlier version of this chapter was presented at the Annual Meetings of the Academy of Criminal Justice Sciences at Pittsburgh in 1991. I would like to thank two anonymous contributors to this book, Ron Hinch and Susan Reid-MacNevin, and Jeffrey Ian Ross for comments on a previous draft of this chapter.

1.   This chapter reflects the thinking involved in my current major project—outlining the social structure of as good a society as realistically possible in terms of the values of individual freedom, social equality, and people participating in the major decisions affecting their lives.

2   It should be noted that this is a criticism of Ericson's framework, not his data. His theoretical framework presents all processes as enabling.

3.   The initial formulation of this idea came from a conversation with Richard Henshel at the University of Western Ontario.

4.   The idea of social auditors has relevance to other social concerns. For instance, they could monitor the routine of the nuclear power industry, though here the pool of social auditors might have to be defined by certain educational criteria.

REFERENCES

Bayley, David (1977) "The Limits of Police Reform," in David Bayley (ed.), *Police and Society.* Beverly Hills, CA: Sage, pp. 219–236.

————, and James Garofalo (1989) "The Management of Violence by Police Patrol Officers." *Criminology* 37, 1: 1–23.

Bittner, Egon (1983) "Legality and Workmanship: Introduction to Control in the Police Organization," in Maurice Punch (ed.), *Control in the Police Organization.* Cambridge, MA: MIT Press, pp. 1–11.

Black, Donald (1980) "Production of Crime Rates," in Richard Lundman (ed.), *Police Behaviour: A Sociological Perspective.* New York: Oxford University Press, pp. 108–130.

Brogden, Michael (1982) *The Police: Autonomy and Consent.* London: Academic Press.

Chambliss, William (1989) "State-Organized Crime." *Criminology* 27, 2: pp. 183–208.

Chapman, Brian (1982) "The Canadian Police: A Survey," in Craig Boydell and Ingrid Connidis (eds.), *The Canadian Criminal Justice System.* Toronto: Holt, Rinehart and Winston, pp. 68–88.

Clairmont, Don (1991) "Community-Based Policing: Implementation and Impact." *Canadian Journal of Criminology* 33, 3–4: 469–84.

Clinard, Marshall, and Richard Quinney (1978) "Crime by Government," in M. David Ermann and Richard Lundmann (eds.), *Corporate and Governmental Deviance: Problems of Organizational Behaviour in Contemporary Society.* New York: Oxford University Press, pp. 137–150.

Coleman, James (1989) *The Criminal Elite: The Sociology of White Collar Crime.* New York: St. Martin's Press.

Corrado, Raymond, and Annamarie Oliverio (1988) "Political Deviance," in Vincent Sacco (ed.), *Deviance: Conformity and Control in Canadian Society.* Scarborough, Ontario: Prentice-Hall, pp. 284–322.

Currie, Down, Walter DeKeseredy, and Brian MacLean (1990) "Reconstituting Social Order and Social Control: Police Accountability in Canada." *Journal of Human Justice* 2, 1: 29–53.

Ericson, Richard (1981a) *Making Crime: A Study of Detective Work.* Toronto: Butterworth.

—— (1981b) "Rules for Police Deviance," in Clifford Shearing (ed.), *Organizational Police Deviance.* Toronto: Butterworth, pp. 83–110.

—— (1982) *Reproducing Order: A Study of Police Patrol Work.* Toronto: University of Toronto Press.

——, Patricia Baranek, and Janet Chan (1989) *Negotiating Control: A Study of News Sources.* Toronto: University of Toronto Press.

Farberman, Harvey (1975) "Symposium on Symbolic Interaction: An Introduction." *Sociological Quarterly* 16: 435–7.

Fielding, W., and J. Fielding (1987) "A Study of Resignation During British Police Training." *Journal of Police Science and Administration* 15, 1: pp. 24–36.

Fishman, Mark (1980) *Manufacturing the News.* Austin: University of Texas Press.

Goldstein, Herman (1990) *Problem-Oriented Policing.* Philadelphia: Temple University Press.

Green, Gary (1990) *Occupational Crime.* Chicago: Nelson-Hall.

Hall, Stuart, Chas Critcher, Tony Jefferson, John Clarke, and Brian Roberts (1978) *Policing the Crisis: Mugging, the State, and Law and Order.* London: Macmillan.

Hazlehurst, Kayleen (1991) "Passion and Policy: Aboriginal Deaths in Custody in Australia 1980–1989," in Gregg Barak (ed.), *Crime by the Capitalist State: An Introduction to State Criminality.* Albany, NY: State University of New York Press, pp. 21–47.

Jefferson, Tony (1987) "Beyond Paramilitarism." *British Journal of Criminology* 27: pp. 47–53.

—— (1990) *The Case Against Paramilitary Policing.* Milton Keynes, United Kingdom: Open University Press.

Jones, Trevor, Brian MacLean, and Jock Young (1986) *The Islington Crime Survey: Crime Victimization and Policing in Inner-City London.* Aldershot: Bower.

Keable Commission (1981) *Rapport de la Commission d'Enquête sur des Operations Policiers en Territoire Québeçois.* Quebec: Government de Québec Ministre de la Justice.

Kerstetter, Wayne (1985) "Who Disciplines the Police? Who Should?" in William Geller (ed.), *Police Leadership in America: Crisis and Opportunity.* New York: Praeger, pp. 149–181.

Knapp, Whitman (1973) *The Knapp Commission Report on Police Corruption.* New York: George Brazziler.

Lea, John, and Jock Young (1984) *What Is to Be Done About Law and Order*. Harmondsworth, Eng.: Penguin.

Lundman, Richard (1980) "Police Misconduct," in Richard Lundman (ed.), *Police Behaviour: A Sociological Perspective*. New York: Oxford University Press, pp. 163–180.

Lustgarten, Lawrence (1983) "Beyond Scarman: Police Accountability in Britain," in N. Glazer and K. Young (eds.), *Ethnic Pluralism and Public Policy*. Lexington, MA: D.C. Heath, pp. 236–57.

Mann, Edward, and John Lee (1979) *The RCMP vs. the People: Inside Canada's Security Service*. Don Mills: General Publishing Co. Ltd.

Manning, Peter (1977) *Police Work: The Social Organisation of Policing*. Cambridge, Mass.: MIT Press.

Marx, Gary (1979) "External Efforts to Damage or Facilitate Social Movements: Some Patterns, Explanations, Outcomes and Complications," in Mayer Zald and John McCarthy (eds.), *The Dynamics of Social Movements: Resource Mobilization, Social Control and Tactics*. Cambridge, MA: Winthrop Publishers, pp. 94–125.

——— (1988) *Undercover: Police Surveillance in America*. Berkley: University of California Press.

McDonald Commission (1981) *Commission of Inquiry Concerning Certain Activities of the Royal Canadian Mounted Police: Freedom and Security Under the Law*, Second Report Vols. 1 and 2. Ottawa: Ministry of Supply and Services Canada.

Meadows, Robert (1987) "Beliefs of Law Enforcement Administrators, Criminal Justice Educators Toward the Needed Skill Competencies in Entry-Level Police Training Curriculum." *Journal of Police Science and Administration* 15, 1: 1–9.

Menzies, Ken (1982) *Sociological Theory in Use*. London: Routledge and Kegan Paul.

Michalowski, Raymond (1985) *Order, Law and Crime: An Introduction to Criminology*. New York: Random House.

Misra, Shailendra (1986) *Police Brutality: An Analysis of Police Behaviour*. Delhi: Vikas Publishing House.

Muir, William (1977) *Police: Streetcorner Politicians*. Chicago: Chicago University Press.

Punch, Maurice (1985) *Conduct Unbecoming: The Social Construction of Police Deviance and Control*. London: Tavistock.

Reiner, Robert (1985) *Politics of the Police*. Brighton, Sussex, Eng.: Wheatsheaf Books.

Savage, Stephen (1984) "Political Control or Community Liaison? Two Strategies in the Reform of Police Accountability." *Political Quarterly* 55: 48–59.

Sherman, Lawrence, and Mark Blumberg (1981) "Higher Education and Police Use of Deadly Force." *Journal of Criminal Justice* 9: 317–331.

Skolnick, Jerome (1966) *Justice Without Trial: Law Enforcement in a Democratic Society.* New York: Wiley.

———, and Candace McCoy (1985) "Police Accountability and the Media," in William Geller (ed.), *Police Leadership in America: Crisis and Opportunity.* New York: Praeger, pp. 102–138.

Sparger, Jerry, and David Giacopassi (1992) "Memphis Revisited: Reexamination of Police Shootings After the Garner Decision." *Justice Quarterly* 9, 2: 211–225.

Stark, Rodney (1972) *Police Riots: Collective Violence and Law Enforcement.* Belmont, CA: Wadsworth.

Terrill, Richard (1990) "Alternative Perceptions of Independence in Civilian Overnight." *Police Science and Administration* 17, 2: 77–83.

Toch, Hans (1976) *Peacekeeping: Police, Prisons and Violence.* Lexington, Mass.: Lexington Books.

Van Maanen, John (1982) "The Disagreeable Complainant," in Norman Johnston and Leonard Savitz (eds.), *Legal Process and Corrections.* New York: Wiley, pp. 44–55.

Waddington, P. (1987) "Paramilitarism? Dilemmas in Policing Civil Disorder." *British Journal of Criminology* 27, 1: 37–46.

Wiley, Mary, and Terry Hudik (1980) "Police-Citizen Encounters: A Field Test of Exchange Theory," in Richard Lundman (ed.), *Police Behaviour: A Sociological Perspective.* New York: Oxford University Press, pp. 78–90.

Wycoff, Mary, and Peter Maunting (1983) "The Police and Crime Control," in Gordon Whitaker and Charles Phillips (ed.), *Evaluating Performance of Criminal Justice Agencies.* Beverly Hills, CA: Sage, pp. 15–32.

Wycoff, Mary, and Charles Susmilch (1979) "The Relevance of College Education for Policing: Continuing the Dialogue," in David Petersen (ed.), *Police Work: Strategies and Outcomes in Law Enforcement.* Beverly Hills, CA: Sage, pp. 17–35.

Control and Prevention of Crimes Committed by State-Supported Educational Institutions*

Natasha J. Cabrera

Introduction

Although the unsettling fact that Western democracies routinely engage in crimes against its citizens is well documented in scholarly journals and books (e.g., Barak, 1991; Gurr, 1988; Tilly, 1985; Tunnell, 1993), it is rarely acknowledged by the general public. This situation may reflect our general contentment with the way things are run, apathy, or a deeply held belief that aside from higher taxes, it does not affect us personally. Whether citizens' attitudes toward these types of crime support or control them is beyond the scope of this chapter. The point here is that when we think about crimes committed by the state, we seldom think of our own elected governments, let alone the institutions we hold sacrosanct: the police, the military, and national security agencies, who are here to serve and protect us; health institutions, which are created to heal us, or the schools, which are established to educate us. In essence, we conceive of the state and its agencies as protectors of our rights and freedoms, and we have come to depend on them for our welfare, much like we depend on our own families for security.

But when the state or state-run agencies violate the rights of individuals, which may or may not be illegal, a state crime has been committed (Barak, 1993: 209). Conceding to many definitional problems, Bohm (1993: 6) builds on definitions by the Schwendingers (1975) and Quinney (1977) to suggest that "persons, social relations [e.g., racism, sexism, poverty], and social systems that deny others' rights to realize their human potential" are state crimes because they "cause systematic abrogation of basic human rights." Such violations of human rights cause social injuries that affect, for example, life and health chances (Barak, 1991b: 274).

The obvious question is, Why does the state harm its citizens? Recognizing that "the state is both a crime-regulating and crime-generating institution," Barak (1993: 208) argues that there is an integral connection among class, race, gender, crime, social control, and the state. As a crime-generating institution, crimes committed by the state are political because they serve to "enhance or preserve political institutions and economic organization within society" (Michalowski, 1985: 379). Political crime subsumes both crimes committed against the state (e.g., treason, sedition) and crimes committed by the state (e.g., genocide). In general, political crime, Bohm (1993: 7) argues, is the product of individualistic, competitive, and materialistic pursuit of capital. This "capitalist accumulation model" (Dietrich, 1986: 50) entails Marx's (1967: 146–155) contention that the internal logic of the capitalist system is the continual expansion of production and profit.

The process by which capital accumulation is attained is criminogenic because it produces social harm. This process includes injurious social relations (Bohm, 1993), disinformation, unaccountability, and coercive social control, among other contentious behaviors, (Barak, 1991b: 274). Although not all these actions (e.g., social relations) are *mala prohibita* crimes, there is general agreement that they are illegitimate (Hagan, 1990: xx). For example, Bohm (1993: 7–8) successfully argues that social relations such as the grossly inequitable distribution of wealth, poverty, hunger, institutionalized racism and sexism, home-lessness, and intentional or criminally negligent killings are political crimes because they contribute to other dangerous or harmful behaviors. In other words, these social relations are political crimes because they deny others the right to realize their human potential and are preventable.

Similarly, disinformation, social control, and unaccountability are state crimes because they violate the state's moral and ethical obligations to its citizenry (Henry, 1991), and in doing so they cause social injury. In essence, the state or state-run agencies commit political crime when they use disinformation, reinforce coercive social control mechanisms, are unaccountable, and, through their economic and social policies, create social relations that are harmful to its citizens.

I argue that institutions of higher education,[1] as state agencies whose main function is to reproduce the capitalist class structure, engage in transgressions against its students. These violations deny the majority of citizens, who are or have been in schools, their right to realize their human potential and hence can be classified as state crimes. These actions amount to more than poor education because in order to fulfill their role of legitimizing the hierarchical structure of capitalism (Antonio, 1981), educational institutions indoctrinate students in the ideology of meritocracy, use various coercive mechanisms of social control, use a curriculum that teaches the inevitability of harmful social relations such as sexism, discourage excellence, and are academically unaccountable. This type of education affects people's life chances and how they fare in the marketplace. Underemployment, unemployment, and internalization of meritocratic justice are but some of the resulting social harms.

This chapter, then, broadens the scope of the study of state crime by including the actions of state-run educational institutions based on their role as reproducers of the current social order. The theses of this chapter are (1) institutions of higher education commit state crimes of omission (e.g., unaccountability, negligence, and intellectual marginalization) and crimes of commission (e.g., reinforcement of coercive social control mechanisms, disinformation, and use of biased curricula), and (2) the prevention of these crimes or at least their control lie in changing the system from within; educators and students must become responsible for the type of education they provide and obtain, respectively, by learning to question and challenge the system using critical thinking skills taught in a global education context.

Before discussing the types of transgressions that educational institutions engage in, I briefly review the function of public education since its inception, its role in our capitalist system, and the mechanisms by which it accomplishes its goals.

The Functions of Educational Institutions

Before institutions can fulfill their social, economic, and ideological functions they must survive. Thus educational institutions' main goal, much like other organizations, is to maintain their organization status (Van Scotter et al., 1991: 106–109). Secondary goals include the quality of survival, type of education students receive, and type of citizens they produce. To survive, institutions of higher education must have a high proportion of graduates (retainees); be competitive with other post-secondary institutions; and as social agencies, must enhance the process of socialization (p. 106).

Schools have at least five social functions: education, indoctrination, custodial care, social-role selection, and community activity (Reimer, 1971; Boulding, 1972). However, the most important functions schools have are economic and ideological. Schools are in charge of reproducing the capitalist structure by producing a work force that can uphold it (Antonio, 1981; Schecter, 1987).

To begin with, a distinction is made between the terms *education* and *schooling*. Education is not the sole responsibility of schools; rather, all social institutions take an active part in this process. In today's self-serving, profit-driven, corporate society (Greenberg, 1986), even church and family have relinquished their educative role to schools. The education of our youth has been placed by default on the shoulders of educational institutions. The consequences are dire. Schools, perceived to be the transmitters of knowledge, wisdom, and values, are expected to turn out productive individuals who can enhance and participate in our democratic system. In reality, students are exposed to other agents of socialization that encourage and foster values that compete with those of educational institutions (Van Scotter et al., 1991). One of these influences is the mass media, which communicate images of popular culture. Postman (1979) has called the subject matter people learn from the mass media the "first curriculum"; school is the second. Thus, the role of schools in educating its students occurs in a much broader cultural context.

Schooling, on the other hand, involves not only the learning of academic subject matter, the core curriculum, but also the values of the dominant class, of political and intellectual leaders, as well as traditional values (e.g., dignity, punctuality, honesty, responsibility, respect for property, sexual modesty, mastery, and achievement) and attitudes (e.g., competitiveness, individualism, and elitism coupled with egalitarianism, communalism, and cooper-ativeness). The transmission of traditional values ensures continuity and maintenance of our sociopolitical economic structures (Giroux, 1989a: xii). In the process of schooling, educational institutions are "perhaps the single most potent institutions shaping long-term views of the population" (Clayton, 1992). Educational institutions, therefore, shape not only our views but also our behavior and expectations. Hence, discipline, organization, obedience to authority, and learning to be content with one's lot in life are essential aspects of schooling. Schooling is then an institutionalized socialization process, one that uses group instruction, does not impart a love of learning, and argues for a dichotomized style of teaching, where students receive and teachers impart knowledge (e.g., Giroux, 1989a). It proscribes freedom and mirrors existing social conditions (Van Scotter et al., 1991: 24–60). Citizens must be schooled in order to both legitimize and perpetuate the existing social structure.

The role of education is fulfilled by teaching particular modes of communication (e.g., reading, writing, etc.), thinking (problem solving, scientific), knowledge, skills, values, attitudes, sensibilities, rational consent to being governed with materialism and capitalist economies, and many other cognitive and affective attributes (Van Scotter et al., 1991). These values, attitudes, and sensibilities betray a middle-class bias and are designed to make students believe that there are no "real" barriers to the entrance into this privileged socioeconomic class. Education as a process of indoctrination then involves the transmission of cultural and social values that overtly and covertly support the hierarchical structure of industrial societies (e.g., Carnoy, 1989). In so doing, Antonio (1981: 50) argues, "Modern education is an incredibly efficient tool of class domination because it is both a means of class stratification and the structural objectification of the ideology that legitimates stratification."

As custodians, the schools function as baby-sitters and provide this service for at least a quarter of a century. During this period, students are socialized along socioeconomic classes. Because social classes (statuses or social-role groupings), either ascribed or acquired, are stratified, members enjoy power, prestige and material goods according to the socioeconomic class to which they belong. The schools both reinforce ascribed status and provide a medium to gain acquired characteristics. That is, by rewarding some behaviors and punishing others, and by graduating, certifying, and sorting students into "either/or" for curricular or extracurricular activities, the schools play an important role in status allocation (Reimer, 1971). This practice, however, undermines the most important function, that of educating students (Reimer, 1971).

In pursuit of these goals, Carnoy and Levin (1985: 4) have argued that the education policy of the democratic capitalist state is necessarily contradictory. It both socializes and trains labor for capital production and fosters the development of democratic ideals including the belief that because education brings material comforts it should be accessible to all. Hence, they argue that American education is "a product of both 'reproductive' forces . . . and 'democratizing' forces" (p. 5). As part of the state, schooling contributes to both legitimation and accumulation functions. It reproduces the values of the dominant class while at the same time encouraging subordinates to participate in shaping their own future.

The economic and ideological functions of schools have been in place since the establishment of mass public education in Western industrialized societies (Antonio, 1981). Historically, Antonio argues, the origins and evolution of educational institutions parallel the establishment and development of a capitalist system. He periodizes capitalism and educational development into three phases: expansion, differentiation, and inflation.

During the first phase, educational expansion (1800–1890), the task of education was to transform rural, independent people into dependent wage laborers who would develop "proper industrial work habits," such as punctuality, obedience to authority, regular attendance, order, and cleanliness as well as help to promote industrial development (Antonio, 1981: 52–53). In the next phase, the educational differentiation (1890–1960), corporate capitalism gave rise to a bureaucratically controlled, hierarchical power structure that deepened the division of labor, and demanded more advanced technology and training (p. 54). This "differentiation," Antonio argues, was nothing more than the imposition of a "class-based 'tracking' system" and reflected and promoted the bureaucratization of American life. Using guidance counseling, vocational education, and educational testing, children were guided into careers that were consistent with their class backgrounds (p. 54). The last phase, educational inflation (about 1970 to the present), is characterized by a surge of professional, certified specialists in large bureaucracies where the college has become a form of mass education (p. 56). But this universal accessibility to higher education has produced a surplus of college graduates, who had been absorbed by "extensive bureaucratization and growth of the public sector" (p. 56). A college degree implicitly promises jobs that require "independent, responsible, creative labour"; the problem is that these jobs are slowly disappearing.

Antonio (1981) makes a poignant argument that with the culmination of mass higher education, the ideological function of schooling is a *fait accompli*. Universal higher education assures the inclusion of groups of people who had been previously denied access to higher education. This is taken to be not only proof of "equal opportunity," but it also suggests that that society is a "just meritocracy" (p. 57). However, as has been argued elsewhere (e.g., Schecter, 1987), higher education does not necessarily lead to economic mobility, but it provides "meritocratic legitimation for capitalism" (Antonio, 1981: 57). In fact, Antonio argues, the distribution of wealth in our society has not drastically changed (p. 57). The combination of indoctrination based on the ideology of meritocracy and the tokens of success have contributed to the general belief that our society is just and that success is attainable if one naturally deserves it.

In sum, the social functions of schools (i.e., education, indoctrination, social-role selection, and custodial care) are intimately connected with the economic function of reproducing the class structure. The economic function is concrete and ideological. Schools provide both "scientific means for placement in the division of labour . . . while at the same time legitimat[e] the process on the basis of natural inequality and technical competence" (Antonio, 1981: 57). Whereas quality education has a legitimizing effect for those who already belong to the economic and political elite (p. 68), it is only marginally important to those who have been shuffled into jobs at the lower strata. For both groups, however, formal schooling is still essential in inculcating "good behavior, external motivation, and social cooperation" (p. 57).

Crimes of Omission and Commission

Because schools are primarily a means for the reproduction of class hierarchy, the ideology of meritocracy that schools disseminate and on which they depend for survival is a myth. Although the myth of meritocracy has already been exposed (e.g., Antonio, 1981; Schecter, 1987), it has not been viewed as a crime that the state deliberately commits against its citizens. To reiterate, I argue that the implicit endorsement of this myth, or negligence in revealing this myth, unaccountability, intellectual marginalization, reinforcement of social control, and the use of biased curricula are state crimes because they result in social injury. This list is not exhaustive; there are other crimes that could have been included, for example, curtailment of academic freedom and propagation of disinformation. But because of length considerations, I focus only on the first six. By focusing on the transgressions that educational institutions commit, I do not imply that this is all schools do. Schools' positive impact on their students is, however, beyond the scope of this chapter.

In general, state crimes can be classified into crimes of omission and crimes of commission (Henry, 1991). Un- accountability and negligence are conceived as crimes of omission because by not being accountable and expecting minimal academic performance from the students, the educational system fails to fulfill part of its social contract to provide an education that allows individuals to realize their potential. Similarly, intellectual marginalization, use of biased curricula, and coercive social control are crimes of commission because they produce a recognizable social harm. I now turn to a discussion of crimes of omission committed by institutions of higher education.

Crimes of Omission

Unaccountability

Compared to public school teachers, college professors are not expected to teach anything other than their own specialization, however broadly that may be defined. Moreover, being part of the educational bureaucracy means that professors discover that academic success depends, partly, on the degree to which they can reproduce the existing system (e.g., Macedo, 1993: 186). Professors are not accountable for their students' academic failures in the way that public school teachers are. Failure to learn in a university setting is the sole responsibility of the students. Of course, institutions of higher education have a system of checks and balances to make sure that professors are doing what they were hired to do. These range from students' evaluations of professors to appeal processes by students. But none of these mechanisms are designed to assess whether or not professors have been successful in teaching students valuable skills and knowledge. On the contrary, these methods of accountability may, at times, have the reverse effect of lowering academic standards, encouraging cheating, and instituting grade inflation.

One way to hold professors accountable is through students' evaluations. The merit of evaluations has, however, long been questioned (e.g., Glass, 1975; Kerlinger, 1971). The content of students' evaluations as well as the process of administering them, however, are not only irrelevant but also unfair to both the student and the professor. Teachers' evaluations typically include a report on teachers' tardiness to class, organization, and bureaucratic style, among other things. While promptness is a trait valued in "punch-clock situations," it does not particularly comment on teaching ability and the quality of the professor. Moreover, most students have neither a set of valid criteria nor proper training to evaluate the performance of their teachers. For instance, some students may believe that journal writing is the best approach to being evaluated or that memorization is the only skill that should be tested. In the absence of a consensus of what characteristics good teachers should have, students use their own. For so-called Generation X students who are "television-reared," used to fast and diverse stimulation and expect to work little for rewards (Howe and Strauss, 1993), a good professor may be one who is entertaining, grades easier, and has talk show–like class discussions. For others, the grade they expect to obtain, their own learning style, teachers' personal appearance, and how he or she fares in comparison with other professors may be indices of good teaching. Typical evaluations, then, lack reliability and predictive validity.

Although the student is protected from the wrath of the teacher, anonymous evaluations can have the unwelcomed consequence of preventing professors from receiving honest, constructive, and tactful criticism. Instead of encouraging this type of skill, which is essential in maintaining healthy relationships either personally or in the workplace, institutions make students unaccountable for their actions. In sum, as Kerlinger (1971:13) writes, students' evaluations of their professors may result in "hostility, resentment and distrust" between professors and their students.

Regardless of the nature of criticisms, in general, professors learn about these only at the end of the semester. Neither the students nor the professors benefit from them. It is also doubtful whether these are relevant or have any value to the next batch of students who may have different learning styles, background knowledge, and expectations. Although admitting to the problems of validity and reliability of students' evaluations, many administration officials will keep them in the professor's file and, from time to time, use them for tenure or review decisions. This practice may, in turn, influence faculty, particularly untenured faculty, to accede to most, if not all, students' demands even if they are pedagogically of questionable merit.

Another way of holding professors accountable is through mechanisms such as the grade appeal process. Typically, students' learning is assessed with written examinations, essays, and assignments. If the discrepancy between the grade received and the grade deserved is mathematical or a misrecording of the grade, it is easily resolved between the student and the professor. If the issue is more subjective (e.g., essay grading) or the student does not agree with the professor's explanation, then the student may launch a formal appeal. Whatever the results,[2] grade appeals are more about the awarding of grades and less about accountability for what has been taught in the classroom. Although institutions have their own particular appeal process, it is generally a grueling experience, one that many professors and students ultimately find frustrating and not worth their time and effort. To avoid grade appeals professors may find themselves, consciously or unconsciously, lowering their academic standards, modifying their grading system, inflating grades, giving easier tests, expecting less from their students, and leaving nothing to chance to the point of bureaucratizing the way they conduct their courses. Admittedly, not all professors who avoid grade appeals adopt some or all of these measures. But, relaxing academic standards, coupled with the overall institutional policy of not being responsible for students after they graduate, has a positive short-term effect on the institution and the students, namely, happier students.

Although grade appeals and students' evaluations may make some professors relax their academic standards, these are not the only reasons for grade inflation. The causes vary from educational philosophy to the political economy of education.

Regular commentaries and editorials in scholarly magazines suggest that grade inflation is rampant in American colleges, and that not even the Ivy League schools have escaped it (e.g., Cole, 1993; Levine, 1994). For example, Cole (1993: A48) writes that particularly in the humanities, undergraduate institutions are rewarding mediocre or average work with high grades. In my experience, grade inflation appears to be a "hidden policy"[3] that is unaccepted but unchallenged.

Failure to discriminate between good and bad work and opt instead for inflated grades is, as Cole (1993) argues, rooted in the "opening up of the curriculum" that occurred in the late 1960s. He also writes that professors' laziness, their negative attitude toward teaching in general, and the belief that today's students are of poorer quality are the reasons for awarding grades without academic merit. It is also possible that somehow the system encourages professors to be lax about their academic standards. For example, professors are expected to teach a full load while at the same time produce academic work of high caliber and engage in service. Because few places award tenure on the basis of teaching alone, professors may be tempted to take shortcuts in teaching (e.g., using videos, multiple choice exams, etc.). Also, a professor who is seen as the only one who gives lower grades is vulnerable to students' negative evaluations. These pressures suggest that only tenured faculty are the ones in a position to challenge existing policies.

From the institutional perspective, grade inflation may be motivated by institutions' goal for "retention," that is, to increase the number of graduates per year. Retention rates are one, albeit misleading way, of holding institutions accountable to its consumers (Astin, 1993: A48). Astin argues that to maximize graduation rates, institutions may have to increase their entrance standards to weed out those students who are more likely to drop out and hence decrease actual retention figures.[4] However, in times of economic uncertainty and tight budgets, institutions of higher education cannot afford decreased enrollment. To circumvent the retention problem, some colleges may opt for lowering entrance standards while at the same time lowering academic standards.[5] This represents a shift of emphasis from providing a quality education to education as a "delivery service." This shift does not jeopardize schools' economic function because they are still training the workforce for the marketplace.

Although many have offered solutions to the problem of grade inflation (e.g., Levine, 1994), the problem of unfair grading remains. Inflated grades reflect professors' unaccountability for their evaluation methods and, by extension, their teaching. Moreover, by failing to discriminate honestly between good and poor work, professors are "abdicating one of the primary responsibilities of their profession" (Cole, 1993). Awarding unmerited high grades does not adversely affect an individual professor's career (e.g., Cole, 1993); in fact, it may help if this practice leads to good students' evaluations.

Grade inflation, however, negatively affects the student. Because high grades are equated with better job opportunities, students place a premium on them. In pursuing high grades, students may take courses from "easy" professors, outguess the professor, study hard, buy essays, cheat, and appeal low grades that are perceived to be undeserved. Although some of these behaviors (i.e., outguessing, studying hard, choosing easy professors) reflect practical intelligence (Sternberg, 1987), they do little to enhance the thinking skills of students. High grades also appeal to students' desire to "get the most for their money," to get results (i.e., high grades). The problem is that students are deceived. They are led to believe that their academic performance merits high grades.

Although there are some students who are aware of this practice, many truly believe that their work is of exceptional quality. For example, Levine (1994: B3) reports that the number of students with GPAs of A– or higher has quadrupled from 1969 to 1993, from 7 percent to 26 percent. Moreover, 60 percent of students surveyed believed that their GPAs understated the true quality of their work. If such students find themselves in a situation where they are awarded lower grades for the same quality of work, they may deem the test unfair or the professor unreasonable or, perhaps, resort to cheating and plagiarism (e.g., Fishbein, 1993). It is unthinkable that a student who received an A would launch an appeal because he or she feels that the grade is too high or that it is not deserved.

In essence, grade inflation is another stratification method. It particularly targets students with shaky academic credentials to ensure their future position in the lower strata by preventing them from acquiring the necessary cognitive skills that more prestigious jobs require. Because institutions are not accountable to anyone for how students fare in the "real world" once they have completed their education, by imparting a false sense of academic competency grade inflation is a way to retain those students who would have otherwise dropped out. It also relieves institutions from the arduous and resource-intensive task of implementing remedial classes for students who need them.

The negative effects of this false sense of competency are also evident later on when such students seek employment. Employers are not as willing as professors to reward work of poor quality with promotions or wage increments. Having bought into the ideology of meritocracy, some would believe that they deserve what they get, whereas others, at least the ones who are diligent, realize that they are less prepared than they were led to believe and that their education has cheated them.

By rewarding mediocrity, "schools discourage excellence" (Cole, 1993) and deceive students. This practice is criminogenic because it prevents some students from realizing their human potential and causes social harm. For example, a student who is used to doing little work for high grades will never benefit from the powerful motivating force that lower grades can have; the student will be cheated out of a proper education. This policy can also foster attitudes that may jeopardize the schools' economic function of producing honest, hard-working citizens.

Negligence

The current global recession and its dire consequences (e.g., downsizing, company closings, job phaseouts) has provided an impetus for retraining, returning to school, or staying in school longer yet. Despite timely news reports on the disproportionate number of recent college graduates who are unemployed, underemployed, or doing something other than what they were trained to do, scores of people are knocking on the doors of community colleges and universities. For many, the solution to unemployment is to get more education even though there is a large supply of highly educated labor and a low demand for such labor (Antonio, 1981). The schooling myth—more schooling means more upward mobility (Schecter, 1987)—continues to survive. This myth also suggests that obtaining a degree is not motivated solely by "learning for learning's sake." Higher education is seen as a sound financial investment (e.g., Alexander, 1993).

Anecdotal[6] and scholarly evidence suggest, however, that higher education is not enough by itself to achieve economic success (Schecter, 1987: 20). The question is if it is an employer's market and few good jobs, why is there such a demand for higher education? The answer lies once again in the meritocratic myth propagated by educational institutions (e.g., Antonio, 1981; Schecter, 1987). To achieve this goal, schools are negligent of exposing this myth and the complex relationship between economics and education.

The ideology of the modern capitalist state, composed of a specialized division of labor, is that rewards are distributed on the basis of merit (e.g., Antonio, 1981; White, 1987). In this system, "relations of domination (based on class, race, and sex) are seen as 'just' forms of inequality derived from differences in genes, motives, and morals" (Antonio, p. 50). Consequently, the unequal distribution of wealth is justified and a "just social order [is produced] not an egalitarian one" (p. 50). The meritocratic legitimating of this system is done through schools whose ideology implies that inequality based on merit is justified because external inequality (status, wealth, political power) has been eliminated (pp. 48–50).

Schools send the message that occupations and upward mobility are strictly a function of merit. Not only is this a simplification of the economic system, but it is also not true. For example, social class, family background, gender, noncognitive abilities, and other nonmerit factors have a role to play in the relationship between economic success and education.

The problem with the implicit promise that a college education is economically liberating and a ticket into the middle class is that the middle class is slowly disappearing (Greenberg, 1986). The employment worth of a bachelor's degree is not that of perhaps ten or twenty years ago. With more no-skill, manual jobs being done in developing countries, the previous working class has been reduced and in many cases replaced by those holding university degrees who would have been the middle class in other times. Moreover, educational requirements have increased without a significant corresponding change in skill demands in the marketplace (Antonio, 1981: 60). When new skills are needed, on-the-job training (Collins, 1971: 1003–1007) or experience gained on the job, not more formal education, are usually required by employers.

Not only is higher education promoted as essential for upward mobility, but so are grades. Despite evidence to the contrary (e.g., Bowles and Gintis, 1972/1973: 68; Sternberg, 1987), academic success, as measured by grades, is seen as a valid predictor of economic success. In general, the myth goes as follows: the higher the grade, the more intelligent one is, the richer one will be (Schecter, 1987: 47). This myth is perpetuated by institutions in the way students are socialized to believe in the omnipotence of high grades. Consequently, students are grade-rather than knowledge-driven. Few students do extra work, are curious, or are concerned about learning.

The myth has worked so well because, Schecter argues, it is partly true. Although good grades can mean that one is "smart" and hence that one can obtain a good-paying and personally satisfying job, it is not always the case (e.g., Sternberg, 1988). Economic success depends on the noncognitive factors (e.g., discipline) of schooling, which are systematically related to social class and economic success (Antonio, 1981: 61). Schooling and class have a much stronger relation to economic success than academic intelligence as measured by grades (p. 60). In the same vein, Sternberg (1988) argues that ability to manage oneself, maximize strengths and minimize weaknesses, shape the environment, as well as tacit knowledge and allocating time to problems properly are more important than IQ scores.

As a form of capital, the distribution of schooling approximates that of economic capital (Antonio, 1981: 61), which is based on class (Szymanski, 1981). Class inequalities in the educational system have been perpetuated by guidance counselors and tracking systems (Antonio, 1981; Schecter, 1987). While in high school, working-class children are generally advised to pursue "realistic" careers (e.g., two-year professional or nonprofessional) and are discouraged from nonprofitable academic paths (Antonio, 1981: 66). For example, more than half of community college students are from the lower classes (Karabel, 1972: 527). Community colleges provide vocational programs (e.g., golf course manager) and remedial programs that give students a sense of mobility (p. 556). Tracking students into careers consistent with their backgrounds, then, perpetuates class hierarchy and assigns occupations according to class.

Students from working-class backgrounds attending college, Antonio (1981: 64) argues, may not have well-developed middle-class values of punctuality, external motivation, and dependability that are neccessary for successful completion of higher education. Because of their inadequate preparation, these students have higher dropout rates (e.g., Astin, 1993) and, particularly in the United States, only a limited number gain entrance to prestigious colleges (Antonio, 1981: 62). Even when both rich and poor have access to the same educational institutions, the wealthier tend to fare better. Even when working-class students are diligent and studious, they encounter other class-related barriers. For example in Canada, higher education is subsidized for all, rich and poor. The wealthy, however, are more successful and experience less hardship because they have less financial or emotional pressures. Holding down part-time jobs leaves little or no time for extracurricular activities such as study groups, clubs, or committees. In other words, although our egalitarian society provides equality of opportunity, it does not provide equality of condition, and hence the gap between the rich and the poor is not minimized.

The importance of the family in their children's educational success is another important nonmerit factor in academic and economic successes. In general, working-class students not only lack economic resources, but they also do not benefit from "cultural capital," high expectations of success, and a stimulating environment that middle-class families can provide (Antonio, 1981: 62). Unlike working-class students, middle-class students have better chances of obtaining employment or of being aware of certain economic and political trends that may help their academic choices. These "mistakes and weaknesses of families," Antonio (p. 59) argues, cannot be overcome by schools, and so their promise of giving equal opportunity to all is false.

In fulfilling their custodial and economic functions, then, schools are largely negligent of informing students of the true relationship between economics and education and of the worth of a liberal arts education. By overemphasizing the economic benefits of education, educators neglect to advise students that economic success depends on diverse attributes and skills, not just academic degrees. Many universities do not have compulsory courses, workshops, lectures, or seminars on the political economy of education.[7] Consequently, students are unaware of economic trends and realities that may have affected the choices they made. For example, few graduates are aware that the creation of jobs is largely dictated by the needs of the global community (Kennedy, 1993). This means that job requirements as well as the structure of employment are in a state of flux. In today's economic climate, a bachelor's degree is a minimal requirement for employment, and jobs that many students are being trained for may be nonexistent by the time they graduate. Also the security that full-time employment brought is being replaced by uncertainty created by part-time, full-time/part-time contract employment, and piecework.

I am not suggesting that the function of universities, particularly of liberal arts education, should be to prepare students for specific jobs or occupations. My argument is that educational institutions are negligent when they fail to inform students of the capitalist ideology to which they ascribe. This negligence is purposive because it achieves at least two goals: (1) those with educational credentials have internalized norms and values that have convinced them that the distribution of jobs and rewards is legitimate and fair (Schecter, 1987: 53); and (2) it draws more people to higher education under economic pretenses.

This approach is criminogenic because it leads to a number of attitudes and behaviors that diminish one's chances to succeed in life. Believing that economic rewards are awarded on merit alone, most students are discouraged from developing other skills that are complementary to the degree, for example, establishing networks, working in job-related fields, and volunteering for relevant organizations. Instead, the majority of students concentrate on enjoying themselves, having fun, and studying. In the process, they do not understand the value of a liberal arts education (Fishbein, 1993), lack "street smarts" skills and are indirectly encouraged to pursue careers "believed to be profitable" but in which they have little or no interest.

Crimes of Commission

Intellectual Marginalization

An effective way to reproduce the capitalist order is through intellectual marginalization. Institutions of higher education achieve this by encouraging specialization, indoctrinating students to take their place in the hierarchy without challenging the status quo, using an instrumentalist approach to literacy (Macedo, 1993: 186), and relying on a curriculum that depicts relations of wealth and power that exclude minorities and women (Renzetti, 1993: 225). In order to better understand this process, I discuss the first of three processes that lead to intellectual marginalization; the effects of using a biased curriculum are discussed in the next section.

In producing the "specialist class" (e.g., college graduates, teachers, engineers, doctors, professors), both in community colleges and universities, even those that subscribe to a liberal arts program, students are encouraged to specialize in a particular field. Educational specialization is necessary to meet the needs of specific and specialized economic interests. To this end, students, mostly male, are generally steered away from a career in the humanities or the arts if their goal is to find employment (e.g., Hanrahan, 1987).[8] Consequently, there is an overemphasis on the "hard sciences" and a drifting away from the "soft sciences" (e.g., courses in arts and the humanities) (Macedo, 1993). The division is further assured when students "learn" that scientific rigor demands a separation of "hard sciences" from the uncertainty that "soft sciences" generate (p. 192). In the process students learn "scientism" based on the assumptions of "absolute objectivity" and the epistemological superiority of the scientific method (p. 192). This type of specialization, then, dichotomizes the world along disciplinary boundaries.

As one ascends the echelons of higher education, further specialization and, sometimes, hyperspecialization are required. This process requires expertise in a narrow area of study, which is accomplished by creating "false dichotomies rigidly delineated by disciplinary boundaries" (Macedo, 1993: 192). Despite intellectual justification for multidisciplinary studies, the majority of fields remain single-disciplined (e.g., Lefkowitz, 1994: B2). The purpose of hyperspecialization is twofold: (1) it encourages the fragmentation of knowledge and (2) it dislodges these pieces of knowledge from the larger social, economic, and political context that gave rise to them in the first place (Macedo, 1993: 193). The inability to relate various and diverse types of information impedes a "critical reading" of the world, which implies, according to Freire (1985: 131), "a dynamic comprehension between the least coherent sensibility of the world and a more coherent understanding of the world." This makes it possible, for example, to see state crimes as separate from the state that created them.

Macedo (1993) argues that a reductionist approach to the act of knowing results in what Ortega y Gasset (1964: 112) has called semiliterate specialists or "learned ignoramus." These individuals who have a narrow educational net or interest are largely ignorant of anything outside their specialty. Even if these specialists have sophisticated logical and thinking skills they tend to be, for the most part, domain-specific. An illustration of this point would be the separation of ethical consequences from scientific research (e.g., construction of nuclear bombs, gene therapy).

Whereas the problem of the "learned ignoramus" is at one end of the spectrum, the problem of people who cannot think reflectively is at the other end. The process of schooling is accomplished at the expense of procedural and broad declarative knowledge that would allow individuals to learn critically (e.g., Paul, 1990). For example, there are numerous reports,[9] many scholarly works (e.g., McGinty, 1994; Paul, 1990), and popular media reports that document the poverty of students' academic skills, thinking abilities, problem solving, and their inability to adapt to an ever-changing world. Most professors have neither the time nor the skills to teach thinking skills within their respective subjects, hence they rely on what is perhaps the only learning skills students enter college with, namely memorization. Learning through rote memory achieves the goal of mastering facts long enough to pass a memory-type test and to keep both students and professors content with the distribution of grades.

Another way to marginalize certain students is by treating every student, regardless of academic ability, in a similar fashion. While universities admit students with differing levels of academic abilities (as measured by their high school grades or community college upgrading scores), many do not have any institutionalized mechanism to help those students who were admitted with a C average and are hence beginning university less prepared than those who were admitted with a B or an A average. Although many students who did poorly in elementary schools do better in university, the majority do not.

This approach to education is quite consistent with the economic function of educational institutions. For example, institutions of higher education are gearing toward a "vocationalization of learning" (Giroux and McLaren, 1989: xvi), which is directly connected to employment. Similarly, Gutmann (1987: 172) argues that most colleges are doing what high schools should have done, that is, provide students with basic literacy for the sole purpose of helping them get a job. Because for many students the main purpose of education is to get a job and because the labor market is dichotomized into unskilled jobs and very specialized, technical jobs, educational institutions need only to graduate people who have the minimal skills to fulfill the jobs at the low end of the spectrum.

Specialization and lack of teaching of reasoning skills are directly related to illiteracy and indoctrination. The connection between indoctrination, which is typically accomplished at the expense of independent thought, and illiteracy has been made by Chomsky (1988). According to Chomsky (1988), the Trilateral Commission concluded that schools are institutions for indoctrination, "for imposing obedience, for blocking the possibility of independent thought and they play an institutional role in a system of control and coercion" (p. 671). He argues that because education is a form of indoctrination the less educated are less indoctrinated and therefore "tend to be more sophisticated and perceptive about [ideological] matters" (p. 708). On the other hand, the professional class must internalize and believe the "doctrinal system," Chomsky argues, because they have the obligation to reproduce it. Although the generality of Chomsky's claims is arguable, his conclusion that the main goal of educational institutions is to indoctrinate rather than to educate is compatible with the discussion presented so far.

Indoctrination is the result of an instrumentalist approach to literacy. Whether it be the "competency-based skills such as banking" for the poor or the hyperspecialization for the rich, the result is the same, namely, people who lack independent critical analysis and thought (Macedo, 1993: 188). In general, such literacy produces "functional literates" who have mechanically learned to read and write but are incapable of independent thought (p. 189).

An instrumentalist approach to literacy facilitates the "manufacture or engineering of consent" (Chomsky, 1988), and it is hence fundamental to maintaining the status quo. Indoctrination and an instrumentalist approach to literacy result in students graduating with inappropriate (e.g., memorization when understanding is required) and inadequate (e.g., lack of critical thinking skills) set of skills and dispositions. These students cannot be expected to participate critically in our or any other democracy because they lack "the necessary critical tools that would unveil the ideology responsible for [their] blinders" (Macedo, 1993: 186). The failure to graduate students with adequate cognitive skills is counterproductive even to "reproducing a class division of labour and capitalist relations of production" (Carnoy and Levin, 1985). Moreover, it perpetuates class inequalities and denies people the opportunity to improve their condition.

Biased Curriculum

An essential component of indoctrination is the type of curriculum used. A distinction can be made between the covert, or hidden, curriculum and the overt, or existing, curriculum.

Whereas "the hidden curriculum produce[s] a disciplined and stratified labour force so capital could reproduce with little social conflict" (Schecter, 1987: 46), the overt curriculum is designed to impart knowledge and skills. Typically, most school reform movements have targeted the overt curriculum; the hidden curriculum has been left practically intact. With few exceptions (Freire, 1985; Giroux and McLaren, 1989; Macedo, 1993), the ideological function of institutions of higher education is unchallenged.

Recent social, cultural, and economic developments, however, have prompted universities and colleges to provide a "new curriculum" that is more inclusive, pluralistic, and less Eurocentric. The "old curriculum" has been criticized for offering courses that are generally organized around disciplinary subject matter rather than how students learn (Alexander, 1993); teaching some subject matter (e.g., the history of the American West) from a perspective that confirms myth stereotypes (Shoemaker, 1993); and using a "core curriculum" that excludes issues concerning women and gender (Lynch et al., 1992). In short, there is an emerging powerful criticism that our curricula suffer from a Western white middle-class bias.

Indications of curriculum reform can be found in new buzzwords such as multiculturalism, politically correct curriculum, critical thinking, liberal education, return to the basics, minority studies, gender studies, and so on (e.g., D'Souza, 1991) and cover a whole spectrum of positions. For some, the "new curriculum" means a call to "cleanse" the curriculum of works by dead white males (e.g., Homer, Plato, Shakespeare, Locke, Rousseau, Jefferson, Marx) and replace them with works by oppressed, Third World ethnic groups, females, homosexuals, lesbians, and nonwhites (e.g., Gates, Jr., 1992). For the extreme minority, it means teaching material even if it is not supported with scholarly evidence.[10] Others want to uphold the canon the way it is and resist any change (e.g., Hirsch, 1987). Others still suggest that the core curriculum should be taught nontraditionally, that is, to include, not be replaced by, for example, feminist critique (Renzetti, 1993: 224). And there are those who argue for a middle-ground position. They value multicultural analysis and focus the debate over who should be included and added to the canon and how this inclusion would ultimately change the classical canon (Erickson, 1991: B1).

Some of these new proposals have been criticized on a number of levels. For example, Feinberg (1989: 69) has criticized calls for a return to the core curriculum because they have "quieted inquiry and dissent and have packed vocationalism as academic courses." Reports such as former President George Bush's "A Nation at Risk," he argues, contribute directly to "an ascending ideology of statism and control" (p. 70).

At a practical level, D'Souza (1991) has documented the changes that have occurred across American campuses since the "new curriculum" came into place. In many cases, Eurocentrism has been replaced by Afrocentrism, and other such "isms." The result has been the further segregation of people along the same old demarcations. D'Souza argues that neither the old curriculum nor the new curriculum encourage independent thought and critical understanding of the subject matter. What has happened in some cases is that rather than learning to examine critically scholarship according to a set of accepted criteria, we learn to use the arbitrary characteristic of gender, race, ethnicity or religion as a sole criterion to deem something worthy of value. The classics are out because they represent the oppressor, and the works by the oppressed are in because the oppressed have been wronged.

Ironically, this curriculum revolution may have little effect on loosening the "screw of social control" and has political liberalism under attack (Clayton, 1992: B2). Designed to be inclusionary, the new curriculum has, in some instances, become just as exclusionary as the old curriculum. For example, some advocates of this approach refuse to recognize that European civilizations, whatever their shortcomings, were also responsible for the best features of our society: political democracy, the rule of the law, individual liberty, cultural freedom, and human rights (e.g., D'Souza, 1991; Schlesinger, 1992). Recognizing these accomplishments in no way undermines minority and women's struggles for higher education that are less racist and more inclusive.

An argument can then be made that educational institutions are partly responsible for imposing a curriculum that dichotomizes and fragments rather than one that unites. Many university and college students are disinterested, bored, and, for example, have never heard of the Great Depression (although they may have seen a Hollywood movie about it), nor do they want to know. They specialize in women's studies, black studies, the sciences, or the humanities, and there is little cross-disciplinary thought. Some college programs disdain academic subjects for being "wishy washy" and encourage a technical or pragmatic approach where facts, rules, and principles are memorized. What we find, then, is that students do not want to know anything else other than their specialties, are not interested in learning how to think, and are mainly concerned with being able to maximize their role as consumers once they graduate.

Reinforcement of Coercive Social Control

Schecter (1987) argues that the history of school reform has been characterized by changes that have consistently tightened the screw of social control. The state exerts control over its citizens by socializing them into productive individuals, hence the need for mass public and, now, mass higher education. The establishment of a public school system, public school attendance, expansion of secondary and post-secondary education, democratization of higher education by gender and class, vocational and career education, guidance counseling, and progressive education (e.g., free schools, open classrooms, multiple streaming, and computer technology) have increased centralization of decision-making power in the elite spheres of government and bureaucrats (pp. 47–55). This centralization, in turn, helps ensure that school reform centers around progress, welfare, and meritocratic equality (p. 53).

As one of the state's agents of social control, Schecter (1987: 51) argues, schools have wedded the "autonomous domain of subjectivity to a statist framework" hence diminishing the opportunities to produce alternatives to the social order. This has established a "subtle cybernetic dialect" between subjectivity and autonomy and the "modern forms" of power assumed by the modern state, that is, to be in control of our lives (p. 52). Through manipulation of social activity, the state has created more freedom within socially defined limits. The more our choices in terms of consumer goods, recreational activities, years of schooling, the deeper the illusion of autonomy (e.g., Greenberg, 1986). Socialized by mass culture and consumer society (e.g., Kozol, 1993), students are sold on the notions of freedom, autonomy, and meritocracy. By creating a dependency on our consumerism habits and on the services that the state has to offer, our view to autonomy is nothing more than a selling pitch.

For a democratic capitalist state to function, social control must be total. To this end, the educational machine is responsible for controlling those who refuse to be socialized and indoctrinated (e.g., school dropouts, right- and left-wing extremists) (e.g., Nelsen, 1987). Right-wing extremists are, for the most part, looking for direction, hope, and trying to regain what they feel is being taken away from them by traditionally less powerful segments of society (Bell, 1962). On the other hand, left-wing extremists may opt for censorship of anything that might be offensive. Both groups, however, show authoritarian attitudes and in this sense share the same goal. To counteract the political unrest these groups may cause, the state invests in massive "going back to school" campaigns, and creates public awareness of the potential harm of dropouts. And, in response to the perception that dropouts find schools boring, educators motivate them with a less-than-taxing curriculum that leaves the hidden curriculum untouched (e.g., Nelsen, 1987).

The success of the hidden curriculum, as a means of social control, is that it shapes "all undesirables" and others into supporters of the status quo. For example, schooled people have acquired what Freire (1970) has called the "pedagogy of the oppressed," that is, oppressed groups who have internalized the values and norms of the oppressing class will, when given the opportunity to seize political or economic power, behave in the same manner as their oppressors. When this phenomenon occurs in Western democracies, it is a political triumph for the capitalist state, for it then is able to perpetuate itself.

Another method of social control is to segregate the masses rather than to promote unity. The new curriculum, as discussed earlier, has also been a catalyst for segregation rather than group cohesion. Even egalitarianism has not promoted respect for differences, instead it has disseminated the idea that we are all the same—the same as the dominant class, that is. It is not surprising then that school diversity and affirmative action or equal opportunity programs rather than closing the gap between the haves and have-nots have actually fueled the emergence of neoconservativism and neoliberalism, particularly in young people. It can be argued that these two extremes, one accepting the status quo and the other accepting multicul-turalism, have created two predominant groups of students, those on the extreme right and those on the extreme left of the political spectrum. Both groups are ethnocentric, less tolerant of others, and more segregated, yet both camps have assimilated the values of the dominant class (D'Souza, 1991). The potential proliferation of groups according to gender, race, ethnicity, or religion effectively deflects attention from criminogenic state institutions and focus it on ourselves. This segregation successfully creates racism and sexism, which, as Bohm (1993) has argued, are criminogenic social relations.

Control and Prevention

Because institutions of higher education play a key role in the capitalist state, the state has a quasimonopoly on them and, aside from a few cosmetic changes, has no reason to fundamentally alter the system. The onus for change, then, must be placed upon students and educators. Public-driven, or external, controls can help individuals wean themselves from the state's protective cloak.

The second thesis of this chapter is that prevention of these crimes or at least their control lie in changing the system from within; educators and students must become responsible for the type of education they provide and obtain, respectively, by learning to question and challenge the system using critical thinking skills and global education. These cognitive tools would enable students to question the underlying political and economic mechanisms of class inequalities, racism, sexism, and heterosexism, which make schooling non-egalitarian and exclusive.

School Reform and Other Controls

Not all that schools do is criminogenic. The economic opportunities that it can afford cannot be ignored. However, the social harms that it does cause are so pervasive that they must be addressed in order to empower and enlighten all students.

Transgressions committed by educational institutions have not been called crimes per se. Nevertheless, there has always been a belief that our educational system needs change. The change resulting from the various school reform movements, however, has not fundamentally altered the educational system (e.g., Adler, 1977; Antonio, 1981), and in fact, Kozol (1990) argues, schools have succeeded extremely well in their historic role of national indoctrination. Predictably, educational reform has not been able to "loosen the screw on social control" (e.g., Schecter, 1987). Even with the advent of mass higher education (Antonio, 1981: 57), which has been taken as proof of opportunity and calls for a new curriculum, these institutions continue to provide unequal access to higher levels of occupational, political, and social life (p. 66). So long as they continue to reproduce the social order, the distribution of income will remain the same and class inequalities will continue to exist (e.g., Jencks, 1972: 264). Even today when some of the barriers to educational equality have been exposed, it remains an "elusive goal" (Erwin and MacLennan, 1994).

Other efforts that could be categorized as controls or, at least, calls for change have targeted specific deeds that the state engages in, for example, coercive social control. To "unscrew social control," Schecter (1987: 55) proposes that educators must address the future of students, insist on the relevance of classic studies and sciences, seek alternatives that are more democratic, and preserve culture by inculcating a respect for what is valuable in our past. In general, his solutions call for a return to the basics accompanied with a pragmatic approach to education that would ensure the employability of graduates. Criticisms of returning-to-the-basics notwithstanding, this solution takes into account economic conditions but does not really "loosen the screw" of social control because it does not suggest ways that students can question and challenge the contradictions and inconsistencies of the system they are perpetuating.

An inevitable consequence of every type of crime is the victims it generates. The best solution to stop the victimization is to get rid of the aggressor. In the case of state crime, this would amount to dismantling the state as we know it (e.g., Martin, this volume). Ideally, it would be replaced by something more just, more democratic, perhaps. In the case of education, it would mean autonomous schools and the abolition of public schools. Apart from being utopian, this solution would mean that elementary education would no longer be compulsory. It is doubtful whether the state will ever relinquish control over educational institutions, even if they were all to become private. It is also against the best interests of powerful businesses to return to early pre-industrial times where fewer than half the children attended school and only a tiny minority attended secondary schools (e.g., Antonio, 181: 46–47).

Other, less-radical controls designed for other state crimes can be adopted or modified to prevent transgressions by educational institutions. For example, one of Grabosky's (1989) methods to control state crime is participatory democracy. The assumption is that some of the states' wrongdoings can be prevented if the public exercises its democratic right to demand accountability from the government. However, for political and institutional reasons, only a small percentage of the population actively participates in the political process in advanced industrialized democracies. Moreover, participation is not enough. Macedo (1993: 1991) argues that "the instrumentalist approach [of our educational institutions] views literacy as meeting the basic reading demand of an industrialized society." This approach leads to "functional literacy," both for the poor and the rich, which "prevent[s] the development of the critical thinking that enables one to 'read the word' critically and to understand the reasons and linkages behind the facts" (p. 188)

For participatory democracy to be used as an effective means of control, our educational approach must change from instrumentalist to critical literacy (e.g., Chomsky, 1988; Macedo, 1993). A critical literacy will allow individuals to avoid fragmentation of knowledge, which is the result of specialization; recognize contradictions in the system; and question and challenge the status quo as well as their role in preserving it. Without critical literacy, democratic participation has the potential of causing social harm. For example, in some parts of Canada and the United States, parental involvement in public education is pressuring politicians to ban classic works such as John Steinbeck's *Of Mice and Men* from the public school curriculum. The ban is proposed by those who find the novel's use of "profane language" per se offensive. This fragmentation of the act of reading and knowing may contribute to the "tyranny of the majority."

Types of Controls Available to Educators and Students

Although students and educators do not have official authority, that is, are not mandated to alter the system, they do have some control in the way they educate or receive education. I argue that rather than relying on the oppressor to change its tactics, the victims, specifically students and educators, should and need to disrupt the dialectic between the state and its citizens that created the crime in the first place. Becoming a critical participant allows us to take responsibility for our actions and for the role that our behaviors, or lack of them, may have in those transgressions. This perspective is based on the assumption that individuals have some degree of control in shaping their lives. I am not absolving the state; rather I am suggesting that the public should take the initiative to control the shaping of their lives.

To achieve this end, I propose that students and educators should actively and broadly use and develop critical thinking skills and dispositions as well as ascribe to a curriculum that is global rather than centrist.[11] This proposal is not new. Although many proponents of teaching critical thinking skills (e.g., Dewey, 1933; Giroux and McLaren, 1989; Macedo, 1993; Paul, 1990) and critical literacy have made great gains in establishing both the conduit and rationale for an education that is more democratic, it is still not a national trend.

To be a critical thinker is to be able to clarify, reveal assumptions, identify relationships among concepts, evaluate the strengths and weaknesses of evidence, and provide alternative explanations or hypotheses. In theory, a critical thinker is someone who uses the whole range (e.g., Dewey, 1933; Ennis, 1987; Lipman, 1984; McPeck, 1981; Paul, 1990; Siegel, 1988) of CTS and has the character traits and values to examine his or her own beliefs as well as those of others in light of a given context. This process of self-reflection, in turn, makes the critical thinker a certain type of person.

Aronowitz and Giroux (1991) propose an agenda for the transformation of school systems while focusing on questions of power relations. They argue that since the 1970s and 1980s, "education history can be told in terms of student dis-empowerment" (p. 5). This has been accomplished by giving students knowledge rather than by encouraging them to contest and challenge ideological messages (p. 181). They view "schooling and education as a form of cultural politics, as a discourse that draws its meaning from the social, cultural, and economic context in which it operates" (p. 187). Educators must "combine a democratic public philosophy with a postmodern theory of resistance" (p. 182). That is, from a postmodern educational criticism, "educators [need] to rethink the relations between the centers and the margins of power" (p. 194). The empowerment of students is the central value of postmodern education (p. 22).

How do we empower students? How do we de-indoctrinate them? How do we prevent the state, through its educational institutions, from imposing a dominant ideology? How do we encourage young people to become more responsible for their own learning, their own thinking, and, ultimately, their own actions? Empowerment, in the sense used by Aronowitz and Giroux, can be accomplished by teaching students how to critically examine knowledge claims. This can be accomplished by a systematic pedagogical approach that would have as one of its goals not only the teaching of declarative knowledge, but also the teaching of procedural knowledge. Insisting on the relevance and importance of teaching CTS and dispositions across the curriculum can be a good starting point.

While education can never be ideology-free, indoctrination can be avoided, or at least diminished, by teaching thinking rather than a set of concepts or principles (Van Scotter et al., 1991). Teaching of CTS can encourage students to question and challenge not only the material they are learning but also their own beliefs and the world around them. From a critical literacy point of view, the goal of education is to teach students a set of skills that help them analyze and evaluate evidence, question the truthfulness of propositions, provide alternative explanations, be self-critical, and, consequently, make judgments. Using these skills should be initiated by the critical person as an automatic cognitive approach to a particular situation, event, or problem. This process of inquiry affords the critical thinker the ability to distinguish a knowledge claim from a mere belief. Recognition of the epistemological assumptions (e.g., Kitchener and King, 1981; Perry, 1970) underlying propositions and the dynamic nature of knowledge are some of the outcomes of teaching CTS.

Teaching CTS should be accompanied by a curriculum that emphasizes a pluralistic world view. This type of curriculum has been labeled global education because it recognizes the cultural, social, and economic interdependece of the "global village." Global education is particularly important now that trade barriers are coming down (e.g., North American Free Trade Agreement, General Agreement on Tariffs and Trade, FTA) and the structure of the labor market has become more globalized. Understanding world cultures and traditions, speaking several languages, and learning to value the self-images, culture, and identity of other cultures and ethnic groups provides the opportunity to view the world and ourselves in a less simplistic and solipsist manner.

Global education conceives the individual not only as a citizen of a particular country but also as an important part of the "global village." In this process, it helps us to incorporate the histories and knowledge bases of other cultures into the curriculum. The purpose is then to provide students with many perspectives from which they can examine their own situations, help them understand their choices, unveil some of the political and social policies for which their governments are responsible, and help them become more democratic members of society.

Both CTS and global education can be used to make educators and students aware of their role in national and world political affairs. And for some, this may lead to a realization that they have some control to change conditions they are unwilling to support. For example, educators can increase their accountability by deflating grades and awarding marks on the basis of merit and hence discriminate between good and poor academic performance. By encouraging intellectual honesty and integrity in their students, educators teach students to become motivated rather than devastated by lower grades.

Additionally, professors should address the complex relationship between economics and education in appropriate contexts. These steps should help understand the meritocracy myth while at the same time encouraging students to develop their potential in whatever field of study they choose.

Educators should become acquainted with various discipline-specific ways to teach students to be critical about the material for which they are responsible. An introductory lecture or two at the beginning of the semester devoted to epistemological concerns, and how to develop CTS may be a good start.

In this effort, professors should make all attempts to include pop culture and to incorporate students' beliefs into lectures. In our information era, people acquire most of their information/knowledge from television, magazines, films, and videos. In these media, illogical reasoning and fallacious argumentation pass for facts (e.g., Johnson and Blair, 1983). Dorman (1994: 35) argues that the "media logic" of television encourages viewers to see the world as simple and certain, all events as having the same degree of importance, only simplified fragments of complex issues, and emotion and imagery at the expense of reason. Recognizing that when students come to class they already have a set of formed beliefs (whether or not they are supported by evidence) about almost anything would facilitate the teaching of active rather than inert knowledge. This approach aims to eliminate the fragmentation of knowledge by including interdisciplinary perspectives as well as considering the student as an active contributor to the act of knowing.

Students, for their part, with the help of their professors, should start to take responsibility for their own learning. Transferring CTS taught in one classroom to another context can help them to develop a predisposition to be critical and to seek arguments that can be analyzed, thought about, tested, and accepted or rejected.

In this process, the role of the educator is extremely crucial. As Freire (1967) has noted, the role of the educator is not to liberate the students but rather to guide them and structure their thinking so that they can liberate themselves. Educators must avoid playing the role of rescuer, for as Morrison (1992: xxv) writes, "the rescued have the problem of debt." In other words, educators cannot give students a "better" view to replace the old, outdated one. Telling students which is the better view is another form of social control, for it robs them of their right to use their thinking skills to discover, learn, create, and construct a world view that is not intellectually dissonant.

Ideally, then, the teaching of CTS should begin in kindergarten and continue through college and be infused across the curriculum as well as taught as a separate course (Ennis, 1989; Paul, 1990). Undeniably, this approach to education has an ideological bent. It assumes that once such skills are learned, students will be predisposed to use them in and out of the classroom to make decisions that are just, democratic, and compassionate. Given the current context of ideological extremes (the rise of the right and fundamentalist groups, on the one hand, and the newly found censorship on freedom of expression of many university campuses, on the other) (e.g., D'Souza, 1991), it appears that whatever educators have been doing so far to produce graduates who are capable of independent thought has been mainly unsuccessful.

In sum, CTS and global education should produce students who are less specialized, less indoctrinated, more empowered, more critical thinkers, encouraged to form a flexible and tolerant world view, and less intellectually marginalized. This, in turn, should help students prevent some of the crimes that educational institutions can commit against them.

Conclusion

Educational institutions are generally conceived as benevolent but misguided in their efforts to educate. It is not widely known that as state-run agencies, they fulfill their economic and ideological functions by committing a series of transgressions against their students. I have argued that these behaviors, including the effects of unaccountability, negligence in revealing the meritocratic myth, intellectual marginalization, reinforcement of coercive social control, and use of a biased curriculum, are state crimes because they cause social harm such as minimizing individuals life chances and preventing them from realizing their potential. These can take the form of underemployment, unemployment, and harmful social relations such as sexism and racism.

The state fails to provide an education that is liberating because it benefits from the intellectual marginalization and stratification of students along social class lines. Distribution of wealth and power according to meritocratic justice allows individuals to believe that our society is just and to accept their place in it. In the process of schooling, this is largely accomplished by inflating grades, using a narrow and fragmenting curriculum, failing to teach CTS and independent thinking, dissipating the meritocratic myth, and deceiving students about the relationship between education and economic achievements.

I argued that because these transgressions ensure the reproduction of the capitalist structure, the state has no reason to fundamentally alter the way it educates its citizens. Consequently, control or prevention of these transgressions has to come from the bottom up. One way to achieve this goal is by advocating an approach to literacy that is critical rather than instrumentalist. The development of CTS in a global educational context would provide students and educators with reasoning skills and dispositions that would enable them to challenge the system and make decisions that improve their chances of realizing their potential. In so doing, we will continue to realize that we can no longer expect the state to take care of us.

NOTES

* Special thanks to Jeffrey Ian Ross, Frank Williams III, and the anonymous internal reviewers for their helpful suggestions. The views expressed in this chapter are mine and are not necessarily those of the National Research Council or the National Academy of Sciences.

1. This chapter focuses on institutions of higher education, especially universities and colleges of advanced industrialized democracies, in particular those in Canada and the United States. The term *institutions of higher education* includes both public and private institutions. Although private institutions are only partly funded by the state, they still follow the goals of the capitalist state. Finally, in discussing the process of schooling, I refer to the time students spend in educational settings from elementary school to college or universities.

2. At the small liberal arts university where I taught on a sessional basis, the majority of grade appeals (the ones due to subjective reasons) are decided in favor of the student. Other colleagues have informed me that at their universities (more prestigious), the appeal system is stacked against the student. Perhaps smaller universities cannot afford to be tougher on students and do not have to maintain the same academic prestige that other, larger universities do.

3. During a personal conversation with the dean of arts and science at the university mentioned in the previous footnote, I was told that grade inflation at this university was a known fact. I was advised to go along with it.

4. Astin (1993: A48) argues that retention rates per se are misleading because they do not take into account the type of student admitted to an institution. "Expected rates" of retention depend on high school grades, admissions test scores, sex, and race of each entering student.

5. At the University of Lethbridge, Canada, admissions standards were recently lowered to 65 percent for high school students. At the same time, the dean of arts and science has designated two full-time academic advisors to help first- and second-year students advance to senior years.

6. One of my university friends, who has a BA in political science and a year experience in Uganda as an economic program coordinator, recently applied for a job that explicitly required a master's in social policy. Two people were shortlisted; she was one of them. Clearly, the graduate requirement was not strictly necessary.

7. As an academic advisor for the faculty of arts and sciences, University of Lethbridge, I have some understanding of the type of academic advice students receive. Despite good intentions and hard work, advisors do not have the appropriate training to advise students regarding the type of professions they should pursue, what jobs will be available, what types of skills should they develop; how to enter into particular fields, and what type of graduate work should they pursue. For the most part, students come to academic advisors for technical (i.e., curriculum or program prerequisites) advice. Although the National Academic Advising Association is fostering the professional development of academic advisors through conferences and journals, most advisors do not have the academic background to answer the questions posed above but rely on personal experiences when such questions come up.

8. Francis Slankey, science policy administrator for the American Physics Society, argues that to respond to the Bill Clinton administration proposed changes to make research universities engines for economic growth and make students ready for the workforce, universities should make their BSc and MSc programs more practical (*The Chronicle of Higher Education*, Volume XL, No. 19, Jan. 19/94, A48).

9. For example, "A Nation at Risk" (1985), President George Bush's address in Virginia (1989), and a report by the Canadian National Advisory of Science and Technology, "Learning to Win" (1991), emphasize the need to teach students to be better thinkers.

10. In "Combating False Theories in the Classroon," Mary Lefkowitz writes that under the name of Afrocentrism, many universities are allowing professors to teach material such as that "Europeans are 'ice people' who are genetically inferior to the 'sun people' of Africa, that the Greeks stole their philosophy from Egypt, and that Jews were primarily responsible for the slave trade" (*Chronicle of Higher Education*, Jan. 1994, No. 19, p. B1). However, in a response to Lefkowitz, Reginald Wilson points out that there are also those professors (e.g., Michael Levin, Arthur Jensen, Phillip Rushton, William Shockley), who teach, for example, that blacks are genetically inferior to whites and "propound erroneous racial theories" (Letters to the Editor, *Chronicle of Higher Education*, 1994, Vol. XL, No. 46, p. B3).

11. Teaching CTS is not a panacea for all educational ills; however, it is a start. For a review on some of the conceptual and methodological problems, see Baron and Sternberg (1987), Coles and Robinson (1989), Paul (1990), Siegel (1988), and deBono (1984).

REFERENCES

Adler, Mortimer J. (1977) *Reforming Education.* New York: Macmillan.

Alexander, Jeffrey (1993) "The Irrational Disciplinarity of Undergraduate Education." *Chronicle of Higher Education* (December 1): B3.

Antonio, Robert (1981) "The Political Economy of Education." In Scott G. McNall (ed.), *Political Economy: A Critique of American Society.* Glenville, IL: Scott, Foresman, pp. 46–71.

Aronowitz, Stanley, and Henry A. Giroux (1991). *Postmodern Education.* Minneapolis: University of Minnesota Press.

Astin, Alexander (1993) "College Retention Rates Are Often Misleading." *The Chronicle of Higher Education* 40, 5: A48.

Barak, Gregg, ed. (1991a) *Crimes by the Capitalist State: An Introduction to State Criminality.* Albany: State University of New York Press.

——— (1991b) "Resisting State Criminality and the Struggle for Justice," in Gregg Barak (ed.), *Crimes by the Capitalist State: An Introduction to State Criminality.* Albany: State University of New York Press, pp. 273–281.

——— (1993) "Crime, Criminology and Human Rights: Toward an Understanding of State Criminality," in Kenneth D. Tunnell (ed.), *Political Crime in Contemporary America: A Critical Approach.* New York: Garland Publishing, pp. 3–30.

Baron, Joan Boykoff (1987) "Evaluating Thinking Skills," in Joan Boykoff Baron and Robert J. Sternberg (eds.), *Teaching Thinking Skills.* New York: W.H. Freeman, pp. 221–248.

——— and Robert J. Sternberg, eds. (1987) *Teaching Thinking Skills.* New York: W.H. Freeman and Company.

Bell, Daniel (1962) *The Radical Right.* Garden City, NY: Anchor Books.

Bohm, Robert (1993) "Social Relationships That Arguably Should Be Criminal Although They Are Not: On the Political Economy of Crime," in Kenneth D. Tunnell (ed.), *Political Crime in Contemporary America: A Critical Approach.* New York: Garland Publishing, Inc., pp. 3–30.

Boulding, Kenneth (1972) "The Schooling Industry as a Possibly Pathological Section of the American Economy." *Review of Educational Research* 42, 1: 129–143.

Bowles, Samuel, and Herbert Gintis (1972–1973) "I.Q. in the U.S. Class Structure." *Social Policy* 3: 65–96.

Burbles, Nicholas (1986) "A Theory of Power in Education." *Educational Theory* 36 (Spring).

Carnoy, Martin (1989) "Education, State, and Culture in American Society," in Henry A. Giroux and Peter L. McLaren (eds.), *Critical Pedagogy, the State, and Cultural Struggle*. Albany: State University of New York Press, pp. 3–23.

———, and Henry M. Levin (1985) *Schooling and Work in the Democratic State*. Stanford, CA: Stanford University Press.

Chomsky, Noam (1988) *Language and Politics*. New York: Black Rose Books.

Clayton, Cornell (1992) "Politics and Liberal Education." *Chronicle of Higher Education* (April 8), B2.

Cole, William (1993) "By Rewarding Mediocrity We Discourage Excellence." *Chronicle of Higher Education* (January 6): A48–49.

Coles, Martin, and Will Robinson (1989) *Teaching Thinking*. Bristol Press.

Collins, Randall (1971) "Functional and Conflict Theories of Educational Stratification." *American Sociological Review* 36: 1002–1019.

deBono, Edward (1984) "Critical Thinking Is Not Enough." *Educational Leadership* 42, 1: pp. 16–17.

Dewey, John (1933) *How We Think*. Boston: D.C. Heath.

Dietrich, Heinza (1986) "Enforced Disappearances and Corruption in Latin America." *Crime and Social Justice* 25: 40–54.

Dorman, William (1994) "Mass Media and Logic: An Oxymoron?" *Educational Vision* 2: 35.

D'Souza, Dinesh (1991) *Illiberal Education: The Politics of Race and Sex on Campus*. New York: Vintage Books.

Ennis, Robert H. (1987) "A Taxonomy of Critical Thinking Dispositions and Abilities," in Joan Boykoff Baron and Robert J. Sternberg (eds.), *Teaching Thinking Skills*. New York: W.H. Freeman, pp. 9–26.

——— (1989) "Critical Thinking and Subject Specificity: Clarification and Needed Research." *Educational Researcher* 19, 4: 4–10.

Erickson, Peter (1991) "Rather than Reject a Common Culture, Multiculturalism Advocates a More Complicated Route by Which to Achieve It." *Chronicle of Higher Education* 37, 41: B1–B3.

Erwin, Lorna, and David MacLennan (1994). *Sociology of Education in Canada*. Toronto: Copp Clark Longman Ltd.

Feinberg, Walter (1989) "Fixing the Schools: The Ideological Turn," in Henry A. Giroux and Peter McLaren (eds.), *Critical Pedagogy, the State, and Cultural Struggle*. Albany, NY: State University of New York Press, pp. 69–91.

Fishbein, Leslie (1993) "Curbing Cheating and Restoring Academic Integrity." *Chronicle of Higher Education* 40, 15: A52.

Fowler, Richard, Bob Hodge, Gunter Kress, and Tony Trew (1979) *Language and Control*. London: Routledge and Kegan Paul.

Freire, Paulo (1985) *The Politics of Education*. South Hadley, MA: Bergin and Garvey.

Fullan, Michael (1982) *The Meaning of Educational Change*. New York: Teachers College, Columbia University Press.

Gates, Henry Louis, Jr. (1992) *Loose Canons: Notes on the Culture Wars*. London: Oxford University Press.

Giroux, Henry A. (1983) *Theory and Resistance in Education: A Pedagogy for the Opposition*. South Hadley, MA: Bergin and Garvey.

—— (1989a) "Introduction: Schooling, Cultural Politics, and the Struggle for Democracy," in Henry Giroux and Peter McLaren (eds.), *Critical Pedagogy, the State and Cultural Struggle*. Albany: State University of New York Press, pp. xi–xxxv.

—— (1989b) "Schooling as a Form of Cultural Politics: Toward a Pedagogy of and for Difference," in Henry Giroux and Peter McLaren (eds.), *Critical Pedagogy, the State and Cultural Struggle*. Albany: State University of New York Press, pp. 125–151.

—— (1992) *Border Crossings: Cultural Workers and the Politics of Education*. New York: Routledge.

——, and Peter McLaren (1986) "Teacher Education and the Politics of Engagement: The Case for Democratic Schooling." *Harvard Educational Review* 56: 213–238.

Glass, Gene (1975) "A Paradox About Excellence of Schools and the People in Them." *Educational Researcher* 4: 9–13.

Grabosky, Peter (1989) *Wayward Governance*. Canberra: Australian Institute of Criminology.

Greenberg, Edward (1986) *The American Political System: A Radical Approach*, 4th ed. Boston: Little, Brown.

Gurr, Ted Robert (1988) "War, Revolution and the Growth of the Coercive State." *Comparative Political Studies* 21, 1: 45–65.

Gutmann, Amy (1987) *Democratic Education*. Princeton, NJ: Princeton University Press.

Hagan, Frank (1990) *Introduction to Criminology*. Chicago: Nelson-Hall.

Hanrahan, Maura (1987) "Producing the Female Reserve Labour Force: Women and Schooling," in Terry Wotherspoon (ed.), *The Political Economy of Canadian Schooling*. Toronto: Methuen, pp. 117–140.

Henry, Stuart (1991) "The Informal Economy: A Crime of Omission by the State," in Gregg Barak (ed.), *Crimes by the Capitalist State: An Introduction to State Criminality*. Albany: State University of New York Press, pp. 3–16.

Hirsch, E.D., Jr. (1987) *Cultural Literacy: What Every American Needs to Know*. New York: Vintage Books.

Howe, Neil, and Bill Strauss (1993) *13th Gen: Abort, Retry, Ignore, Fail?* New York: Vintage Books.

Hurwitz, Leon (1981) *The State as Defendant: Governmental Accountability and the Redress of Individual Grievances*. Westport, CT: Greenwood Press.

Jencks, Christopher, et al. (1972.) *Inequality*. New York: Basic Books.

Johnson, Ralph H., and J. Anthony Blair (1983) *Logical Self-Defense*. Toronto: McGraw-Hill Ryerson Ltd.

Johnston, William B., and Arnold H. Packer (1987) *Workforce 2000*. Indianapolis, IN: Hudson Institute.

Karabel, Jerome (1972) "Community Colleges and Social Stratification." *Harvard Educational Review* 42: 521–562.

Kennedy, Paul. (1993) *Preparing for the Twenty-First Century*. Toronto: Harper Collins.

Kerlinger, F.N. (1971) "Student Evaluation of University Professors." *School and Society* 99: 353–356.

Kernaghan, Kenneth, and David Siegal (1987) *Public Administration in Canada*. Agincourt, Ontario: Methuen.

Kitchener, Karen, and Patricia King (1981) Reflective Judgment: Concepts of Justification and Their Relationship to Age and Education. *Journal of Applied Developmental Psychology*, 2: pp. 89–116.

Kozol, Jonathan (1990) *The Night is Dark and I Am Far from Home*. New York: Simon & Schuster.

——— (1993) "The Sharks Move In." *New Internationalist* (October): 1–3.

Lamy, Steven L. (1987) "The Definition of a Discipline: The Objects and Methods of Analysis in Global Education." *Global Perspectives in Education*, pp. 1–10.

Lefkowitz, Mary (1994) "Combating False Theories in the Classroom." *The Chronicle of Higher Education*, 40, 20: B1–B2.

Levine, Arthur (1994) "To Deflate Grade Inflation, Simplify the System." *The Chronicle of Higher Education* 40, 20: B3.

Lipman, Mathew (1984) "The Cultivation of Reasoning Through Philosophy." *Educational Leadership* 42, 1: pp. 51–56.

Liston, Daniel P., and Kenneth M. Zeichner (1987) "Critical Pedagogy and Teacher Education." *Journal of Education* 169: 17–137.

Lynch, Michael J., J. Huey, J. Santiago Nunez, B.R. Close, and C. Johnson (1992) "Cultural Literacy, Criminology, and Female–Gender Issues: The Power to Exclude." *Journal of Criminal Justice Education* 3, 2: 183–202.

Macedo, Donaldo P. (1993) "Literacy for Stupidification: The Pedagogy of Big Lies." *Harvard Educational Review* 63, 2 (Summer): 183–206.

McGinty, Sarah (1994) "Why Are Students Stumped by the Application Essay?" *Chronicle of Higher Education* XL, 18: A64.

McPeck, John E. (1981) *Critical Thinking and Education*. New York: St. Martin's Press.

Marx, Karl (1967) *Capital*. New York: International Publishers.

Mazurek, Kas (1987) "Multiculturalism, Education and the Ideology of the Meritocracy," in Terry Wotherspoon (ed.), *The Political Economy of Canadian Schooling*. Toronto: Methuen, pp. 141–164.

Merkle, Peter H., and Leonard Weinberg, eds. (1993) *Encounters with the Contemporary Radical Right*. Boulder, CO: Westview Press.

Michalowski, Raymond J. (1985) *Order, Law, and Crime: An Introduction to Criminology*. New York: Random House.

Morrison, Toni (1992) *Race-ing, Justice, En-gendering Power*. New York: Pantheon Books.

Nelsen, Randle (1987) "Books, Boredom, and Behind Bars: An Explanation of Apathy and Hostility in Our Schools," in Terry Wotherspoon (ed.), *The Political Economy of Canadian Schooling*. Toronto: Methuen, pp. 117–140.

Ortega y Gasset, Jose (1930/1964) *The Revolt of the Masses*. New York: Norton.

Paul, Richard (1990) *Critical Thinking: What Every Person Needs to Survive in a Rapidly Changing World.* (Edited by A.J.A. Binker). Rohnert Park, CA: Center for Critical Thinking and Moral Critique.

Perry, W.G., Jr. (1970) *Forms of Intellectual and Ethical Development in the College Years.* New York: Holt, Rinehart & Winston.

Postman, Neil (1979) *Teaching as a Conserving Activity.* New York: Dell Publishing.

Quinney, Richard (1977) *Class, State, and Crime: On the Theory and Practice of Criminal Justice.* New York: David McKay.

Reimer, Everett (1971) *School is Dead: Alternatives in Education.* New York: Doubleday.

Renzetti, Claire (1993) "On the Margins of the Malestream (or, They Still Don't Get It?): Feminist Analyses in Criminal Justice Education." *Journal of Criminal Justice Education* 4, 2: 219–234.

Roemer, Marjorie Godlin (1991) "What We Talk About When We Talk about School Reform." *Harvard Educational Review* 61, 4: 434–448.

Schecter, Stephen (1987) "Another Turn of the Screw: Education Reform in Progress." In Terry Wotherspoon (ed.), *The Political Economy of Canadian Schooling.* Toronto: Methuen, pp. 141–164.

Schlesinger, Arthur, Jr. (1992) *The Disuniting of America: Reflections on a Multicultural Society.* London: Viking.

Schwendinger, Herman, and Julia Schwendinger (1975) "Defenders of Order or Guardians of Human Rights? in I. Taylor, P. Walton, and J. Young (eds.), *Critical Criminology.* London: Routledge & Kegan Paul, pp. 113–146.

Shoemaker, Nancy (1993) "Teaching the Truth about the History of the American West." *The Chronicle of Higher Education* 40, 10: A48.

Siegel, Harvey (1988) *Educating Reason.* New York: Routledge.

Slakey, Francis (1994) "Science Students can Become 'Engines for Economic Growth.'" *The Chronicle of Higher Education* 40, 19: A52.

Sternberg, Robert (1987) "Teaching Intelligence: The Application of Cognitive Psychology to the Improvement of Intellectual Skills," in Joan Boykoff Baron and Robert J. Sternberg (eds.), *Teaching Thinking Skills.* New York: W.H. Freeman and Company, pp. 182–218.

——— (1988) *The Triarchic Theory of Mind.* New York: Basic Books.

Shor, Ira, and Paulo Freire (1987) *A Pedagogy For Liberation.* South Hadley, MA: Bergin and Garvey Publishers, Inc.

Szymanski, Albert (1981) "The Role of the State in Society," in Scott G. McNall (ed.), *Political Economy: A Critique of American Society*. Glenview, Illinois: Scott, Foresman and Company, pp. 156–188.

Tilly, Charles (1985) "War Making and the State Making as Organized Crime," in Peter B. Evans, Dietrich Reuschmeyer, and Theda Skockpol (eds.), *Bringing the State Back In*. New York: Cambridge University Press, pp. 189–191.

Tunnell, Kenneth D. (1993) "Prologue: The State of Political Crime," in Kenneth D. Tunnell (ed.), *Political Crime in Contemporary America: A Critical Approach*. New York: Garland Publishing, Inc., pp. xi–xxx.

Van Scotter, Richard D., John D. Haas, Richard K. Kraft, and James D. Schott (1991) *Social Foundations of Education*, 3rd ed. Englewood Cliffs, NJ: Prentice Hall.

White, R.D. (1987) "Education and Work in the Technological Age," in Terry Wotherspoon (ed.), *The Political Economy of Canadian Schooling*. Toronto: Methuen, pp. 99–116.

Crimes of the Capitalist State Against Labor*

Kenneth D. Tunnell

Definitional Debates

The criminological community often has engaged in debates over an inclusive definition of crime with some sides accepting rational-legal definitions and others desiring a redefinition to include behavior that, while socially harmful, presently eludes the criminal label. This latter camp has advanced a moral definition of crime inspired by, among others, the Schwendingers (1975), who maintain that any definition of crime is guided by moral standards. Their primary focus is human rights and individuals' freedom to advance their own human potential. Denying individuals the basic right of realizing their own potential, in this context, is considered criminal. Such an interpretation implies that individuals as well as organizations and social systems potentially are criminal (Bohm, 1993). Although many immoral social relationships and processes elude the criminal label, they, nonetheless, are harmful and are considered criminal within a more inclusive definition of crime.

Recently, the criminological community (with a few exceptions) seemingly has ignored this definitional debate, and legal definitions of crime are widely accepted (or at least remain largely unchallenged) (e.g., Bohm, 1993). However, to simply ignore this unresolved issue will not aid our understandings of crime, criminals, and their labeling, as well as various social harms that presently are not criminal. Furthermore, continuing to ignore such issues implies acquiescence to official definitions and labels of crime and criminal, and in effect, is an indictment of the criminological community for its unwillingness to advance, through public debate, a definition that includes moral transgressions that presently are not considered crime but nonetheless quite often cause greater physical and economic harm than street crime (e.g., Tunnell, 1995a).

One benefit from earlier definitional debates is that crime now is treated as a political act, and the criminal law, the embodiment of political decisions. Chambliss (1976: 101), perhaps, best stated this position:

> Crime is a political phenomenon. What gets defined as criminal or delinquent behavior is the result of a political process within which rules are formed which prohibit or require people to behave in certain ways. It is this process which must be understood as it bears on the definition of behavior as criminal if we are to proceed to the study of criminal 'behavior.' Thus to ask 'why is it that some acts get defined as criminal while others do not' is the starting point for all systematic study of crime and criminal behavior.

What is and what is not defined as crime does not occur in a social vacuum but in a political arena where decisions are made with an eye toward furthering capital accumulation, maintaining a particular social order, and providing state services to the citizenry. Within such an arena, the political agenda virtually ignores behavior that, while not defined as criminal, nonetheless results in significant social harm, especially the state's independent behavior and its collusive behavior with capital. While some harmful state and corporate behavior has been defined as criminal, typically such harms have been ignored by both the academic community and those in positions of legislation and law enforcement.

Although upperworld crimes (Geis, 1974; Morris, 1968) have received considerable attention from the criminological community, crimes of the state have received only sporadic coverage. More recently, progressive criminologists have extended earlier definitional debates of crime to the state's actions and its failure to act and treat such as crimes of commission and omission. For example, homelessness, typically regarded simply as the consequences of individual decisions or lean economic times, recently has been addressed as a crime of the capitalist state in its failure to adopt formal policies providing its citizens with a basic human need—shelter (Barak, 1991a). Likewise, social commentators point to the state's failure to address other social problems, including poverty, hunger, institutionalized racism, and institutionalized sexism, and treat such state inaction as moral transgressions, that is, state crime (e.g., Bohm, 1993; Caulfield and Wonders, 1993; Reiman, 1990). In fact, actions that are now recognized as state crimes against humanity often have been "in full compliance with the law" or simply have not violated existing law (e.g., slavery, racial segregation) (Barak, 1991b: 9).

As scholars have wrestled with the ambiguous term *state crime*, clearly defined conceptualizations only recently have emerged. Recent definitions have taken a moral position by focusing on transgressions of both commission and omission. For example, Henry (1991: 256) recently defined state crime as

> the material or physical harm on its citizens, a subgroup of citizens, or citizens of other nations resulting from the actions or consequences of government policy, mediated through the practice of state agencies, whether these harms are intentional or unintentional.

Notice that this definition is not bound by legalistic strictures. Nor does it focus on occupational state crime, that is, individualistic crimes committed by state agents. Rather the focus is on official government policy transmitted through state agencies—an organizational conceptualization—where harm occurs as a result of both commission and omission. As scholars envisage state crime in such broad terms, it has been applied to, among other cases, the United States' refusal to ratify human rights documents, which no doubt contributes to interminable human suffering (Barak, 1991b).

This chapter extends earlier discussions of state transgressions and describes acts of commission and omission that, although not officially labeled crime, cause catastrophic social harm to individuals' lives, health, economic security, and livelihoods. Such activities, as described in this chapter, are considered state crimes. Of central focus are state crimes against working-class men and women, that is, those who labor and on labor's attempts at controlling state transgressions.[1] Although various state crimes, as well as state actions and inactions that while not considered crime nonetheless produce social harm, have received coverage in recent years, little attention has been given to state crimes against labor. Although other types of state crime produce various harms, few are as far-reaching and consequential as state crimes against labor. The sheer number of potential victims is staggering as the majority of capitalist states' inhabitants are workers. Understanding this type of crime and its potential for harming countless millions of individuals is imperative for both a broader understanding of state crime and various means of controlling such harmful activities.

Three points of clarification are essential for this chapter. First, I focus on state crimes against labor, meaning the working class. The term *labor* is used interchangeably with *working class* to mean those who do not own the means of production and as a result of their relationship in the production process (i.e., as non-owners) must sell their labor power to those who do own, namely capitalists. It is the working class who labors for those who do not have to and the working class who is exploited as surplus value (i.e., profit) is expropriated from them (e.g., Wright, 1985; Wright et al., 1982). Second, although most of the emphasis in this chapter is on organized labor, unorganized labor also is the victim of state crime. A focus on organized labor is a logical one, since when the state engages in transgressions against the working class, as detailed in this chapter, such actions are almost always aimed at either organized or organizing labor. It is this activist part of the working class that most often is the recipient of the state's wrath as the latter ideologically and materially aligns with the interests of capital. Attention to unionized labor does not imply that nonunion labor is exempt from such state transgressions, for as the state discriminately engages in transgressions against organized workers and those attempting to organize, the working class as a whole is victimized. Third, although much attention is given to the state as criminal, we must be mindful that the state is composed of individuals who make decisions that affect workers' lives. While avoiding reification of the state, it is nonetheless treated as a structure through which the government and state managers act. Its functions are determined fundamentally by social structures rather than by individuals who occupy positions of state power (Gold, Lo, and Wright, 1975: 36). It is a "relatively autonomous plurality of institutions through which various social forces struggle for use of its apparatuses and agencies" (Henry, 1991: 253). Recognizing that access to the state is unequal and that the state is dependent on continued capital accumulation, the capitalist state functions as such, meaning it aligns itself most often with capital's interests through policies, laws, administration, and lastly force, when such is defined as appropriate.

The State in Capitalist Societies

The state's precarious responsibilities in capitalist societies, in part, explain its seemingly contradictory behavior, for it fulfills divergent functions—accumulation and legitimation. On one hand, it functions to further capital accumulation, or at least not hinder it, while, on the other hand, it functions to assure its subjects that a socioeconomic system with built-in inequities appears legitimate, fair, and in their own best interests. These accumulation-legitimation functions are difficult for the state to maintain and often demand that it exercise questionable practices that seemingly are not in the best interests of its subjects. Earlier theorists have described these contradictory state functions (e.g., Miliband, 1969) and remind us that a state cannot survive without maintaining legitimacy. One vehicle for doing such is the law and its appearance of neutrality, which is necessary for any semblance of legitimacy. However, there are occasions when laws, including those protecting workers, their right to organize, assemble, and strike, are incongruous with the state's and capital's interests. Thus, conflict between the state's legitimation and accumulation functions (including maintaining a particular sociopolitical order) oftentimes results in various state transgressions, acts of both omission and commission against workers (e.g., Chambliss, 1989). In the tradition of recent commentary, such activities addressed in this chapter are treated as state crimes against labor (e.g., Barak, 1991b; Bohm, 1993; Tunnell, 1995b).

State Crimes Against Labor

Labor histories in various countries are marked with violence, bloodshed, and death as laborers have engaged in overt conflict with representatives of capital, including the state and its apparatuses of force, law, and administration (e.g., Chicago's Haymarket Riots in 1886, Appalachian workers' struggles in forming the United Mine Workers Union, and labor's struggles with state-corporate police forces in the early twentieth century and detailed in Harring, 1981). In fact, U.S. labor history has been labeled the bloodiest in the industrialized world (Turk, 1982: 41). Across the histories of various nation-states, law has been created specifically to keep "labor relations . . . within safely conventional bounds" (Turk, 1982: 67), and by doing such, has the power to define insurgent labor groups as both criminal and subversive. As Turk (1982: 67) reminds us:

> Centuries of workers' resistance to expropriation of their lands and exploitation of their labor have led to relatively sophisticated legal devices by which class conflict may be managed without being resolved. Laws explicitly defining political criminality are distinguished by their politicality, vagueness, and permissiveness regarding enforcement procedures. Though the ideology of modern legal systems is democratic, this mystique is belied by the promulgation of laws overtly designed to facilitate the suppression of political opposition.

The state and its monopoly on legitimate force, law, and administration has the ability to define labor as "subversive" when workers, among other things: (1) are considered defiant toward the socioeconomic order, (2) threaten to engage in sympathy strikes, and (3) in the public sector consider striking. State managers often consider such labor movements antagonistic toward the best interests of capital, the state, and its (unstated) policy of upholding, what Chomsky called "the fifth freedom"—license to rob and exploit (Caulfield, 1991; Chomsky, 1988). Furthermore, the state's ability to designate workers as subversive has led to "moral panics," where those not involved directly in the conflict between labor and state/corporations demand that something be done about the subversives that, by definition, pose a threat to dominant economic and sociopolitical systems.

Even when dissidents' activities do not violate the law, they often are treated as if they had or were on the verge of doing so. For example, recent history has witnessed countless state-sanctioned counterintelligence operations designed to gather information on laborers and unions and on organizations considered collusive with labor and leftist politics, which, by definition, question legitimate socioeconomic order (e.g., Clinard and Quinney, 1978; Davis, 1992). Such state practices are not new developments. For example, in England in 1834, six members of the Tolpuddle Friendly Society of Agricultural Laborers were charged under a 1797 mutiny law for administering a union oath to a new recruit. They were convicted and sentenced to banishment in Australia for seven years. In the United States, in 1886, the Federation of Organized Trades and Labor Unions of the United States and Canada was determined to win a workday of eight hours. During a protest (now known as the Haymarket Tragedy) led by anarchists in Chicago, a police officer was killed. Although there were no witnesses, leaders of the city's anarchist movement were arrested, tried, and convicted. Four of the leaders were hanged. In 1918, labor leader Eugene Debs was indicted for sedition—for allegedly criticizing the U.S. government. Debs was convicted and sentenced to 10 years in prison, but was pardoned three years later (Christenson, 1991). These are but a few examples in a protracted history of conflicts between workers and the capitalist state.

The New Left in America, labor unions in the United States and Canada, sindicatos in Mexico, and labor parties in western Europe are often victims of covert and illegal counterintelligence operations officially sanctioned by state managers. Their organizations have been infiltrated by state agents, and as a result, their potential power for representing laborers weakened. In the United States, the Federal Bureau of Investigation (FBI) has attempted to disrupt both labor unions and the Communist Party by pitting one against the other and each against the Mafia. The FBI's objective during such times was to disrupt labor's (and the Communist Party's) activities, weaken their organizations, and thwart their sociopolitical strategies (Churchill and Wall, 1990). A recent examle of state forces infiltrating labor unions occurred during the 1984 national coal miners' strike in England, a strike that was viewed as both a threat to legitimate order and a rallying point for labor. The army, disguised as police, was used to squash the striking miners. Margaret Thatcher's conservative government, determined to defeat left-wing opposition within labor, used the state, its law, and force to crush what Thatcher labeled "the enemy within" (Brake and Taylor, 1984: 28). This case exemplifies that labor's concerns and problems, often directly produced by the incessant drive for increasing capital accumulation and the state's procapitalist economic policies, often are contained and left unresolved by the repressive arm of the state—the police and army (Brake and Taylor, 1984). Such official state behavior is treated here as a crime against workers, since the state both refused to intervene in ways that humanely address proletarian issues and that, in fact, acted against labor. Ironically, in the fall of 1992, the British Coal Company (a partly socialized company) was privatized amidst much public debate. As a result of the sale and subsequent restructuring within the company, an estimated 30,000 coal miners ultimately will lose their jobs. The state is complicitous in this decision and is a co-contributor to miners losing their livelihoods, a form of state crime against labor.

In the United States, working-class men and women have suffered harmful consequences because of official state policy. During the 1980s, U.S. workers continuously were pressured to accede to wage cuts associated with officially approved state policy. During that time, labor unions were defeated at nearly every turn—when bargaining for wage increases, health care, changes in workweeks, and new contracts that simply extended previous ones rather than wage hikes. In the United States, labor has experienced one beaten strike after another. On several

policies; and crimes of omission, as the state continued to allow corporations and capital to flee; all the while, voices of dissent, from across the political spectrum, decried such trade agreements.

By moving to countries where environmental and worker safety regulatory laws are weaker than in their home countries, corporations, often prodded by the state, are able to avoid regulation while reaping enormous profits. We now witness death, diseases, and birth defects as a result of corporations' unbridled disregard for the environment and individuals' lives. For example, in Matamoros, Mexico, just across the border from Brownsville, Texas, low-paid Mexican workers employed by the U.S. transnational corporation Mallory are now showing signs of environmental disease. Patterns of retardation and deformities in children have been linked to the corporate giant, for the children share a common bond—all their mothers, while pregnant, worked at Mallory. To date, sixty-seven afflicted children have been discovered and expectations are that more will be detected. Although Mallory is a U.S. corporation operating in Mexico, neither government has acted to enforce health and safety regulations in this industrial zone occupied by the unregulated *maquiladoras*—foreign-owned factories (Greider, 1992a). Their failure to act in ways to prevent future diseases and birth defects is yet another example of state crime of omission and, in some aspects, commission, since such tragic consequences have been predicted from the onset of various free trade talks.

Another relatively recent and tragic example is the release of deadly gases from Union Carbide's plant in Bhopal, India, in 1984. The gases killed between 2,000 and 5,000 persons and injured another 200,000. Long-term effects of exposure to such deadly chemicals remain unknown, but fertility problems have been on the rise (Mokhiber, 1988). The injured included workers and nonworkers, and responsibility for such is credited to both Union Carbide and the state. This is yet another example of state crime, as both the United States (the home of the parent corporation Union Carbide) and India failed in their obligations to protect workers and citizens by placing corporate activities and profits before human life.

218   *Kenneth D. Tunnell*

Thus, the capitalist state commits various transgressions against labor by engaging in activities and pursuing official policies that while not officially defined as crime are immoral and produce horrendous consequences for laborers. The state is involved in various infractions such as labeling dissident workers "criminal," preventing laborers from organizing, infiltrating legal organizations and engaging in covert surveillance of laborers, refusing to intervene on behalf of nearly powerless workers as they attempt to settle disputes between themselves and capital, engaging in official policies of breaking labor unions, and entering into negotiations that nearly all workers oppose because they believe jobs will be lost and capital will operate virtually unregulated. These actions have far-reaching consequences for laborers in capitalist states and are examples of the state's criminal activities against working-class men and women.

State-Corporate Crime

State-corporate crime is a more recent type of crime that is allowed, tolerated, and abetted by the state. *State-corporate crime* has been defined specifically as "illegal or socially injurious actions that result from a mutually reinforcing interaction between (1) policies and/or practices in pursuit of the goals of one or more institutions of political governance and (2) policies and/or practices in pursuit of the goals of one or more institutions of economic production and distribution" (Aulette and Michalowski, 1993: 175). State-corporate crime, a recent concept in further understanding upperworld crime, occurs when the state and its agencies, working in conjunction with capitalist production, either commit actions that result in social harm or fail to act in ways that would prevent socially injurious actions. First applied to the explosion of the U.S. space shuttle *Challenger* (Kramer, 1992), the concept is used here to explain further state actions that may be criminal or simply socially harmful, yet perhaps not defined as criminal. The state's complicitous role in state-corporate transgressions is especially pertinent as we consider acts of both commission and omission against workers (Friedrichs, this volume).

The explosion of the space shuttle *Challenger* technically resulted from faulty seals; however, the social causes are situated in the "hurry up" agenda of the National Aeronautic Space Administration (NASA) and the management of Morton Thiokol, the private producer of the seals. Although corporate engineers voiced misgivings over the scheduled flight of the shuttle, their concerns were overridden by both NASA and Morton Thiokol management—both desiring a series of space shuttle flights, as had been proposed by former President Richard Nixon and vehemently supported by then-President Ronald Reagan. The fatal consequences were the result of both private producers and state managers whose concerns for production, flight schedules, and a financially self-sufficient space shuttle program overshadowed those for human life (Kramer, 1992).

In September 1991, the U.S. public again was shocked by another state-corporate crime that directly victimized workers —the Imperial chicken processing plant fire in Hamlet, North Carolina. This case is yet another recent example of the state's failure to protect workers' safety while at the same time allowing businesses to increasingly accumulate wealth. In fact, North Carolina's history of regulatory failure by state and federal agencies contributed to the tragedy in Hamlet. North Carolina failed to fund (and to use available federal funds for) its own state Occupational Safety and Health Program—a program designed to protect workers' safety while on the job. Federal funding for its own OSHA program had decreased in the probusiness, antilabor political climate of the 1980s in America. North Carolina had promoted a social climate friendly to business and hostile to labor and corporate regulation. The state has its own right-to-work laws, which dilutes what little power organized labor holds there. The workers at Imperial were not unionized and likely would have remained that way. Furthermore, the majority were poor women, many of whom were single mothers working at slightly more than minimum wage (Shanker, 1992).

Regulatory inspectors knew that Imperial kept fire exit doors locked in order to prevent workers from stealing chicken parts. As a result, twenty-five workers died in the fire. The state, in this case, shirked its responsibilities of protecting workers (i.e., enforcing the law) and allowed a corporation to engage in illegal and ultimately deadly actions (Aulette and Michalowski, 1993). Although the company was fined $800,000 in civil fines (the largest in North Carolina history) for fifty-four "willful" safety violations and twenty-three "serious" violations, and the owner of the company recently was sentenced to prison for manslaughter, the state emerged unblemished. This case is but one example of the state's role in fostering a climate that solicits business and discourages workers from organizing, while failing to protect its citizens from working in life-threatening environments.

The state in such instances is not only involved in illegal and moral transgressions, but holds a unique position. On one hand, the state is the moderator of sociolegal conflicts, but on the other hand, is complicitous in the crime. The state, as coconspirator, continues to exercise its authority in its role then as investigator of the crime, prosecutor of itself, and fact finder/adjudicator (i.e., judge) about its own involvement in transgressions. The potential for escalating state-corporate crime activities is staggering and obviously is especially detrimental to labor's efforts at promoting labor unions and work settings that are safe from immediate and long-term life-threatening situations.

State Economic Crime

Progressive criminologists claim that economic woes are often the result of the state's proactive or ommissive policies (e.g., Barak, 1991a). Unemployment, for example, often results from both capital and the state engaging in activities to manipulate its rate. Corporations often blame unemployment on oversupplies, under-demands, or employee requests (Roebuck and Weeber, 1978: 61). Likewise corporate logic opposes state plans to create jobs, since the number of unemployed and hence corporations' control over the workforce would diminish. Corporations' opposition is manifest in their intensive lobbying of state managers and lawmakers regarding changes in the economy.

The state contributes to unemployment problems through its official policies of slowing down the rate of inflation, which often increases unemployment. Often, increasing prime interest rates contributes to unemployment, as new business investments usually slow down (Szymanski, 1978). For labor, unemployment results in both economic problems and a divided working class, as worker is pitted against worker competing for fewer and fewer jobs. As a result, work-place militancy rarely surfaces, and the status quo has a much broader appeal.

The state itself engages in other economic crimes against labor by regulating some wages, guaranteeing laborers for the market, and preventing industrial disorder and unrest. The state's educational agenda reproduces capitalism as legitimate while training prospective laborers for the workforce. Not only does the state educate individuals on skills pertinent to particular types of employment, but deference to supervision, authority, and legitimate order as well as appropriate responses to material incentives. Beyond this, the concept of wage labor is rarely criticized in capitalist education and becomes widely accepted as a fair and legitimate social arrangement. Such an arrangement is questioned as rarely as the ingestion of "soma" in Aldous Huxley's *Brave New World* and has similar results— acquiescence (e.g., Gaventa, 1980). In effect, the system reproduces itself through state-sanctioned education as state-approved curriculums foster widespread acceptance of the social relationships unique to a capitalist mode of production (e.g., Cabrera, this volume). Although not illegal, and in fact regarded as necessary for capitalism's continuity, these actions are treated here as state-sanctioned crimes, crimes that result in both harmful economic consequences for workers and the mindless acceptance of living with the widespread exploitative social relations particular to capitalism—both material and ideological manipulations.

Capitalism continuously has extended its tentacles into international markets, forging links with countries throughout the world and embracing them in an emergent world economic system (e.g., Wallerstein, 1974). The capitalist state and its agencies have played significant roles in these recent developmental activities. Workers and peasants of developing countries have been assured that with the introduction and expansion of capitalism, democracy would follow. State managers, when speaking of capitalism, almost without exception proclaim the virtues of democracy that allegedly evolve in tandem with capital expansion. But, in the late 1960s and early 1970s, while capital expanded in developing countries, democracy did not. Benefits and improved life-styles were not distributed to workers and the masses. Rather than a narrowing of income and life-style differences, increasing inequalities became the norm along with the disintegration of indigenous cultures. Furthermore, capital expansion often has been accompanied by an expansion of state power and force as a means of implementing and controlling new capital expansion policies. Instead of democracy, peoples typically have been met with authoritarianism and repression (Fagan, 1983; Mazrui, 1992). Thus, the capitalist state engages in behavior that not only deceives its citizenry and people of other developing states but also endorses repressive policies to prop up a system based on inequities, and a system dependent on political repression, torture, kidnappings, and countless murders, evidenced in recent reports of crimes committed by the U.S.-supported and -trained El Salvadoran Army during the 1980s. Such crimes typically are ignored except by independent human rights watch groups and social commentators. Nonetheless, these actions represent reprehensible behaviors, and here are considered crimes by the capitalist state certainly against workers but also against peasants and would-be workers.

Right-to-Work Laws

Workers have suffered in nearly every capitalist country in the world in the past two decades. Although a number of political decisions as well as the dynamics of economics explain these recent and detrimental changes, states' right-to-work laws account for much of the harm done to workers' collectives as they have attempted organizing and remaining organized. Right-to-work laws, emanating from recent conservative political dominance found in North America and western Europe, are official state policies designed to limit the power and membership of labor collectives. States that adopt such policies prohibit unions from collecting dues and representing workers who choose not to join. As a result, "union shops" are outlawed, the economic strength of the labor union is lessened, and its ability to bargain for the collective is weakened. The end result is that as labor finds itself unorganized or, at best, organized by an increasingly weaker union, laborers are left to represent themselves and no doubt have lost and will lose on key issues. Workers' most threatening bargaining chip—the strike—in many cases becomes a nonissue, since only union members will strike. In some cases, as few as 51 percent of a shop's employees may be unionized, leaving them with little strength for bargaining even with the threat of striking (e.g., Aulette and Michalowski, 1993: 181). Such recent changes that undoubtedly will harm workers in economic, physical, moral, and emotional terms are maintained by official state policies and are here treated as further state crimes against labor.

Similarly, the state has engaged in crimes against laborers by refusing to protect them as they have attempted negotiating in good faith with their employers. When negotiations have stalled and strikes have ensued, corporations over the past dozen years or so have increasingly relied on replacement workers (better known in capitalist countries as scabs). Until the 1980s, there was a general consensus about the role of replacement workers—they would be released when the strike was settled, as unionized laborers returned to work. Today, however, corporations are simply firing strikers and permanently replacing them with non-union workers, those who are somewhat antagonistic toward unions, and simply happy to find work in lean economic times. This corporate tactic of pitting worker against worker is an age-old strategy to keep labor divided and the working class absent of class consciousness (i.e., they fail to understand that their fundamental interests are class-based) (e.g., Lopreato and Hazelrigg, 1972). Workers have lobbied state legislatures and parliaments on their own behalf asking state managers to intervene by adopting legislation that prohibits the hiring of permanent replacement workers. They have been largely unsuccessful as state representatives have turned a deaf ear to this recent development in harmful activities against working-class men and women. (At this time [1994], a bill that would protect striking workers' jobs is pending in the U.S. Congress.) This represents another state crime against labor as the state refuses to act on behalf of millions of laborers.

Controlling State Crime

Media and public reaction to activities described in this chapter as state crime against labor are rarely critical, for evidently there is widespread trust in state managers to do what is morally right and legal. In the past, when confronted with state transgressions, the public has had difficulty constructing informed opinions about it, for, typically, media news propagates a state-sanctioned consensus and the assumption that state officials are trustworthy and capable of leading (e.g., Clinard and Quinney, 1978). Critical queries are rarely heard except in alternative news sources that lack both widespread credibility and a sizable audience. Also, there is ample documentation of the biased nature of news reporting in many capitalist states. The media saturate consumers with sensationalized reports of individual one-on-one crimes that usually involve violence rather than those on state crimes (e.g., Tunnell, 1992; Warr, 1991). The media's focus on personal crimes also keeps news consumers' attention fixed on street criminals, rather than state managers' misdeeds (e.g., Reiman, 1990). Thus, upperworld crimes of all varieties typically get little attention, and citizens of capitalist states continue to believe that grave threats to them come from individual predators rather than official state policies. As a result, state policies go unquestioned, as citizens believe that deviants are individual law violators rather than the state, its managers, and their policies.

Often state harms are ignored or dismissed out-of-hand, which is especially the case with state crimes against labor. Given the state's contradictory involvement as both offender and dispenser of justice, victims of state crime rarely are compensated or satisfied (Barak, 1991b). In order for victims to receive some type of compensation, the state must first recognize that its agents and policies are socially harmful. Even when the state has engaged in universally despicable behavior such as killing unarmed workers for protesting working conditions, or beating and killing students for protesting state war policies, it has not admitted its wrongdoing and simply dismissed its activities as the necessities for *sustaining* order. Since the state typically refuses to participate in a critical dialogue or investigation of its misdeeds, there is no official recognition of a crime.

Given these precedents, it is very difficult for any recognition of state crime to emerge, let alone any strategy for controlling it. But, specific transgressions are described in this chapter, and whether state managers recognize such activities as socially harmful, unavoidable, or as state crimes, citizens of capitalist countries can participate in strategies designed to control harmful state activities. The strategies offered here represent simply a starting point, as peoples throughout the capitalist world deal with state crimes against labor and modes of controlling such. Strategies offered here are not exhaustive and by design are not very concrete. Because there is such wide variance among countries and the types of crimes that emanate from capitalist states, these strategies are best served if presented as loose designs for controlling state transgressions against labor rather than a blueprint for action. Also, we must be mindful that strategies for controlling a particular capitalist state's misdeeds may not be generalizable to other countries. Particular cultures and ways of life play significant roles in giving rise to specific strategies for controlling state crime against labor. Undoubtedly, there are similarities for controlling state crime that cut across states, however, strategists must be mindful that variables other than mode of production may be just as important in the equation for controlling state crimes against labor. Thus, strategies alluded to here are loosely structured approaches for controlling this type of state crime, which has far-reaching social, economic, and physical consequences.

Regarding corporations moving from their home countries, especially in North America, workers recognize the complicitous role that the state plays in such crimes of omission and commission. As a result, workers and their representatives have mobilized to combat such capital/job flight. In 1992, the American Federation of Labor and the Congress of Industrial Organizations (AFL-CIO) joined forces in the United States with the environmental Sierra Club, Friends of the Earth, Greenpeace, and other grass-roots organizations to lobby against NAFTA. Canadian workers also have participated in such movements after learning first-hand the price tag that accompanies trade agreements. After their free-trade pact with the United States in 1989, Canada lost 460,000 jobs. Estimates are that the United States will lose 550,000 high-wage industrial jobs, about 3 percent of manufacturing (Greider, 1992a; 1992b). Companies allowed to move abroad will benefit by avoiding union labor, high wages, taxes, and regulatory laws on environmental pollution and worker safety. State managers pursued such free-trade agreements with little regard for the consequences that many predicted would befall workers. If the worst-case scenario comes to fruition, ultimately, more than workers will lose. States will also lose as the world economy undermines their ability and willingness to uphold their own regulatory laws as each is forced to compete in increasingly savvy ways including relaxing laws that protect workers' safety, their rights to organize, and their expectations of living in an environmentally safe world (e.g., Greider, 1992a; 1992b). Recently, workers and activists have suggested that to control these types of crime, countries should tightly control trade by banning products manufactured by corporations that are unfair to workers, that use child labor, and that have little regard for the environment (e.g., Greider, 1992a; 1992b). Such policies may encourage corporations to remain in their home countries, since moving abroad and operating with disregard for workers and the environment may not be as profitable as originally believed. Such strategies are being implemented today and represent starting points for controlling this type of state crime against labor.

Regarding state-corporate crime, the ground for this type of crime in the United States, Canada, and England was made fertile by the recent conservative dominance of government. A part of these conservative politics in the United States, for example, guaranteed individual state's rights. As a starting point for controlling this type of crime against labor, federal governments should discontinue the rights of states and provinces to govern themselves as freely as they have in the recent past. Federal regulation must be adopted that supersedes individual states' and provinces' regulations. Since 1970, the United States has had such legislation in place. Furthermore, a climate that places people before profits must be adopted as official state policies to ensure that workers will be afforded safe workplaces and that the mindless quest for profits will not overshadow the lives and safety of millions of laborers (e.g., Simon and Eitzen, 1982: 335).

In effect, this implies separating the very powerful institutions of the state and corporations. Such a mission may become a long-term objective for labor, although exactly how this could be accomplished is speculative. The state must internalize its role of caretaker of the populace rather than of the elite, placing human lives and safety over profits. This can happen only through an agenda of action, initiated by ideologically committed individuals toward "doing the right thing." To this end, labor must take a more active role in fielding and supporting political candidates who espouse these convictions and who would represent workers' and the masses' needs. In the United States and Canada, this may mean a departure from conservative AFL politics—doing the safe thing rather than right thing. This may also include supporting leftist candidates, those who consider themselves socialists, Marxists, or communists. In the state of Virginia, the Pittston coal miners fielded a fellow miner for political office who defeated the incumbent and today holds office. In Virginia (one tiny spot in the capitalist world) labor has at least one representative sympathetic to and understanding of their plight. Elsewhere in the United States, a socialist candidate won a seat in Congress in 1992, and was reelected in November 1994. The recently elected U.S. Congress and Senate are composed of more women and minorities (including Bobby Rush, the former deputy defense minister of the Black Panther Party) than at any time previously, and many of these representatives claim support for labor and working-class people. These recent victories are departures from politics as usual and represent the beginning of fielding candidates who voice opposition to state policies that are harmful particularly to working-class men and women. In Israel in 1992, labor parties won majorities over conservative "business as usual" politicians, and the 1993 elections in England, labor parties made a resurgence in their power (although still a minority). Likewise, socialist parties in Greece recently have made some gains. And South Africa's political future may indeed be dominated by those on the left who are sympathetic to workers' and peoples' struggles. Ongoing political changes such as strengthening labor parties and their running candidates are necessary for controlling state crime against labor.

In the United States, the National Labor Relations Act, passed in 1935, was a direct result of labor insurgency and state representatives' desire to both help workers and contain growing labor unrest. Ironically, its passage indirectly strengthened the AFL trade unions and weakened a growing leftist movement in the United States and ultimately Canada (Goldfield, 1989). AFL policies of forbidding communists from its ranks have kept the AFL unions, at best, politically liberal, which impedes their posing fundamental questions critical of an economic system based on inequalities and exploitation. Likewise, the labor movement in Canada and the Canadian Trades and Labor Congress became dominated by the American AFL, which proceeded to eliminate radicalism from its organizational agenda (Abella, 1978). Such a noncritical posture undoubtedly must change for workers to assert themselves in controlling state crimes against them.

Obviously the courts in capitalist states play a significant part in preserving order, enforcing the will of the state, limiting the activities of labor, and adjudicating conflicts between the state and labor. Recently, labor organizers and others involved in grass-roots activism have been subjected to a new form of lawsuit that is in effect an injunction for many—a Strategic Lawsuit Against Political Participation (SLAPP). A SLAPP is often a superfluous suit designed not so much to win effectively but simply to slow down or tire out workers involved in organizing and activist politics. But recently, workers' countersuits have resulted in dismissals of the original suits, while elsewhere work is being done to keep SLAPPs out of the increasingly strained courts. Some innovative laws award damages to those sued if the suit is dismissed. Such efforts led by labor and consumer groups, as well as progressive attorneys committed to peoples' struggles, may be effective in heading off such frivolous yet time- and resource-consuming suits and may be yet another step in the process of controlling state crime against labor (Cordes, 1992).

Currently, labor is puzzled over a strategy of how best to control harmful state activities. Labor seemingly is engaged in very little insurgency, for its political power certainly is at a low point in capitalist societies. Labor recently has taken a beating and as a result both is and considers itself less powerful than a generation ago. As a result, there presently is no method for determining the rate at which such controls are being implemented in combatting state crime against labor. At best, there are only isolated events that we can point to as examples of labor's attempts at controlling state crime. Although other types of state crime (e.g., terrorism, racism, and violence toward women) have grave consequences, state crimes against labor affect countless numbers of individuals, their livelihoods, ways of life, health, and future generations of laborers, yet is an offense that, at this time, rarely is publicly debated and remains uncontrolled.

NOTES

* An earlier version of this chapter was presented to the Academy of Criminal Justice Sciences, Kansas City, March 1993. This manuscript has benefited especially from the constructive comments of Jeffrey Ian Ross as well as the anonymous reviewers.

1. The focus of this work is specifically on crimes against labor by *capitalist* states. Doubtless, capitalist states do not have a monopoly on

both crimes against labor and the potential for crimes against labor. However, this work focuses on capitalist state crimes because these acts of commission and omission no doubt are conducted by the state in its resolve to maintain a particular socioeconomic order that, by design, is exploitative, as it expropriates wealth from those who have little choice but to serve as wage laborers. An inevitable consequence of such inequitable arrangements is class conflict, manifested in a variety of activities by labor, capitalists, and the mediator of such conflicts—the state. These conflicts often result in the state siding with capital both covertly and overtly to maintain capital accumulation, capitalist social order, and capital expansion. State actions that result in social harm to laborers (whether economic, physical, or psychological) are here treated as state crimes against working-class men and women.

2. During the American Airlines flight attendants' strike of 1993, just before the Thanksgiving holidays, U.S. President Bill Clinton personally intervened by asking both labor and management to begin negotiations again. Both sides agreed, the flight attendants returned to work, and bargaining is continuing at this time.

3. Unfortunately for the miners' union, during the strike a local judge fined them $50 million for refusing to obey various court orders. Under appeal since then, the Clinton administration, the same that intervened in the Flight Attendants' strike, just argued before the U.S. Supreme Court, in support of the lower court's ruling—that the union pay the fines. A decision is expected by the summer of 1994.

4. See Note 2.

References

Abella, Irving (1978) *The Canadian Labor Movement, 1902–1960.* Ottawa: Canadian Historical Association Booklet 28.

Aulette, Judy Root, and Raymond Michalowski (1993) "Fire in Hamlet: A Case Study of a State-Corporate Crime," in Kenneth D. Tunnell (ed.), *Political Crime in Contemporary America: A Critical Approach.* New York: Garland, pp. 171–206.

Barak, Gregg (1991a) *Gimme Shelter: A Social History of Homelessness in Contemporary America.* New York: Praeger.

———— (1991b) *Crimes by the Capitalist State*. Albany: State University of New York Press.

Bohm, Robert M. (1993) "Social Relationships That Arguably Should Be Criminal Although They Are Not: On the Political Economy of Crime," in Kenneth D. Tunnell (ed.), *Political Crime in Contemporary America: A Critical Approach.* New York: Garland, pp. 3–29.

Brake, Michael, and Ian Taylor (1984) "Community, Police, State: The Present Conjuncture in Britain and Canadian Paper presented to the American Society of Criminology, Cincinnati, November.

Cain, Maureen (1974) "The Main Theme of Marx and Engel's Sociology of Law." *British Journal of Law and Society* 1: 136–148.

Carnoy, Martin (1984) *The State and Political Theory*. Princeton, NJ: Princeton University Press.

Caulfield, Susan L. (1991) "Subcultures as Crime: The Theft of Legitimacy of Dissent in the United States," in Gregg Barak (ed.), *Crimes by the Capitalist State*. Albany: State University of New York Press, pp. 49–61.

————, and Nancy A. Wonders (1993) "Personal and Political: Violence Against Women and the Role of the State," in Kenneth D. Tunnell (ed.), *Political Crime in Contemporary America: A Critical Approach.* New York: Garland, pp. 79–100.

Chambliss, William J. (1976) "The State and Criminal Law," in W.J. Chambliss and M. Mankoff (eds.), *Whose Law, What Order?* New York: Wiley, pp. 66–106.

———— (1989) "State Organized Crime." *Criminology* 27: 183–208.

Chomsky, Noam (1988) *The Culture of Terrorism*. Boston: South End Press.

Christenson, Ron (1991) *Political Trials in History: From Antiquity to the Present*. New Brunswick, NJ: Transaction.

Churchill, Ward, and Jim V. Wall (1990) *The COINTELPRO Papers*. Boston: South End Press.

Clinard, Marshall, and Richard Quinney (1978) "Crime by Government," in David Ermann and Richard Lundman (eds.), *Corporate and Governmental Deviance*. New York: Oxford University Press, pp. 137–50.

Cordes, Helen (1992) "Get SLAPPed? SLAPP Back." *Utne Reader* 52 (July–August): 47.

Davis, James K. (1992) *Spying on America: The FBI's Domestic Counter-Intelligence Program*. New York: Praeger.

Ehrenreich, Barbara (1992) "Are You Middle Class?" *Utne Reader* 53 (September–October): 63–66.

Fagan, Richard R. (1983) "Theories of Development: The Question of Class Struggle." *Monthly Review* (September): 1324.

Gaventa, John (1980) *Power and Powerlessness*. Chicago: University of Illinois Press.

Geis, Gilbert (1974) "Upperworld Crimes," in Abraham Blumberg (ed.), *Current Perspectives on Criminal Behavior*. New York: Knopf, pp. 114–137.

Gold, David A., Clarence Y.H. Lo, and Erik Olin Wright (1975) "Recent Developments in Marxist Theories of the Capitalist State." *Monthly Review* (October): 29–42.

Goldfield, Michael (1989) "Worker Insurgency, Radical Organization, and New Deal Labor Legislation." *American Political Science Review* 83: 1257–1282.

Greider, William (1992a) "How We Export Jobs and Disease." *Rolling Stone* 638 (September 3): 32–33.

———— (1992b) *Who Will Tell the People? The Betrayal of American Democracy*. New York: Simon & Schuster.

Harring, Sidney L. (1981) "Policing a Cass Society: The Expansion of the Urban Police in the Late Nineteenth and Early Twentieth Centuries," in David F. Greenberg (ed.), *Crime and Capitalism*. Palo Alto, CA: Mayfield, pp. 292–313.

Henry, Stuart (1991) "The Informal Economy: A Crime of Omission by the State," in Gregg Barak (ed.), *Crimes by the Capitalist State*. Albany: State University of New York Press, pp. 253–270.

Kramer, Ronald C. (1992) "The Space Shuttle Challenger Explosion: A Case Study of State-Corporate Crime," in Kip Schlegel and David Weisburd (eds.), *White-Collar Crime Reconsidered*. Boston: Northeastern University Press, pp. 214–243.

Lopreato, Joseph, and Lawrence E. Hazelrigg (1972) *Class, Conflict, and Mobility*. San Francisco: Chandler.

Mazrui, Ali M. (1992) "Shaking Free of Colonialism." *Utne Reader* 54: 80–81.

Miliband, Ralph (1969) *The State in Capitalist Society*. New York: Basic Books.

Mokhiber, Russell (1988) *Corporate Crime and Violence*. San Francisco: Sierra Club.

Morris, Albert (1968) "Criminals in the Upperworld," in Gilbert Geis (ed.), *White Collar Criminal*. New York: Artherton Press, pp. 34–39.

Reiman, Jeffrey H. (1990) *The Rich Get Richer and the Poor Get Prison*, 3rd ed. New York: Macmillan.

Roebuck, Julian, and Stanley C. Weeber (1978) *Political Crime in the United States*. New York: Praeger.

Shanker, Albert (1992) "Where We Stand: The Hamlet, North Carolina Fire." *New York Times* (January 5): 7.

Simon, David R., and Stanley Eitzen (1982) *Elite Deviance*. Boston: Allyn and Bacon.

Szymanski, Albert (1978) *The Capitalist State and the Politics of Class*. Cambridge, MA: Winthrop.

Tunnell, Kenneth D. (1992) "Film at Eleven: Recent Developments in the Commodification of Crime." *Sociological Spectrum* 12: 293–313.

—— (1995a) "Silence of the Left: Reflections on Critical Criminology and Criminologists." *Social Justice* (forthcoming).

—— (1995b) "Worker Insurgency and Social Control: Violence By and Against Labor in Canada," in Jeffrey Ian Ross (ed.), *Violence in Canada*. Toronto: Oxford University Press (forthcoming).

Turk, Austin T. (1982) *Political Criminality: The Defiance and Defense of Authority*. Beverly Hills, CA: Sage.

Wallerstein, Immanuel (1974) *The Modern World-System*. New York: Academic Press.

Warr, Mark (1991) "America's Perceptions of Crime and Punishment," in Joseph F. Sheley (ed.), *Criminology*. Belmont, CA: Wadsworth, pp. 5–19.

Wright, Erik O. (1985) *Classes*. London: Verso.

——, Cynthia Costello, David Hachen, and Joey Sprague (1982) "The American Class Structure." *American Sociological Review* 47: 709–726.

Preventing State Crimes Against the Environment during Military Operations: The 1977 Environmental Modification Treaty*

Raymond A. Zilinskas

Introduction

International customary law limits the means by which a state may wage war. Thus, a country cannot use inhumane, indiscriminate, disproportionate, or treacherous weapons (Neier, 1992, Solf, 1986). To augment customary law, the international community has adopted specific laws of war that proscribe particular weapon systems or limits their use. For example, a series of specific arms control or limitation laws have been adopted by governments in the twentieth century to strengthen international customary law, including the 1925 Geneva Protocol (League of Nations, 1929), which bans the use of chemical and bacteriological weapons, and the 1972 Biological and Toxins Weapons Convention (BWC), which forbids the development, manufacture, testing, and storage of biological and toxin weapons (Anonymous, 1975b). But the focus of this chapter is on a third specific arms control treaty, namely the 1977 Convention on the Prohibition of Military or Any Other Hostile Use of Environmental Modification Techniques (ENMOD) (UN General Assembly, 1976). It was, and remains, a unique treaty because it seems to address a nonissue in that no state was known to have used such techniques in warfare and none appeared to be preparing for such an eventuality. Yet, it was to some extent grounded in reality because two trends, one military and the other civilian, were converging.

The first trend had its origin in the large-scale use of defoliation chemicals by the United States in Vietnam for military purposes. The U.S. defoliation program, which commenced in the late 1960s, was preceded by the tactical employment of defoliants by English forces in Malaysia in the 1950s, but unlike the British undertaking, that of the United States caused measurable damage to the environment. Some legal scholars therefore considered it a form of environmental modification warfare (Juda, 1978). The question arose whether combatants waging future conflicts would, as a matter of course, add defoliants to their arsenals. The second apparent trend was the increasing civilian research effort being devoted to deliberately alter the environment for some perceived benefit, such as to produce rain in regions suffering from drought, abort potentially destructive hurricanes and tornadoes, suppress hail, and divert north-flowing Siberian rivers from their normal course to bring waters to virgin agricultural lands in south Russia. If these trends were to merge, new possibilities for unconventional warfare might be created. For example, a technologically advanced country could seek to harness the power of nature for military aims to, for example, activate an earthquake, which might damage its enemy's cities; or to deflect rain-carrying clouds from crossing an enemy's territory, by that causing a drought destructive to vital crops. Faced with this possibility, the international arms control community acted to prevent military scientists of the future, possibly wielding technologies then deemed science fiction, from designing weapons that harness a meteorological phenomenon or other natural force to wreak destruction on an adversary.

Even though many conflicts have occurred since ENMOD came into force in 1978, no combatant appears to have violated the treaty, that is, until the Gulf War.[1] On August 2, 1990 Iraq invaded and occupied Kuwait. After an approximately five-month interlude, a coalition of military units from many countries, but acting under United Nations (UN) authority, mounted a military campaign called Desert Storm to repel the invader. A few days before the start of Desert Storm, Iraq's occupation army ignited about 150 Kuwaiti oil wells, sabotaged petroleum and natural gas processing facilities, opened oil pipelines, and discharged stored petroleum onto land and into the Persian Gulf. Iraqi destructive activities intensified after Desert Storm was launched. While these tactics did not greatly affect either the course of the battle or the war's outcome, they did damage the atmospheric, marine, and terrestrial environments. On the face of it, the government of Iraq therefore may have contravened ENMOD by having employed these tactics. Yet, no government or international legal authority has publicly indicted Iraq for having transgressed ENMOD. Why so? Was it because Iraq had not violated the treaty or, if it had, were there other forces at work that stopped the international community from prosecuting Iraq's government for having resorted to environmentally destructive tactics?

In this chapter, I attempt to determine whether Iraq in having employed tactics that damaged the Persian Gulf environment violated international law (particularly ENMOD), by using the environment as a means of warfare. To do so, it is necessary to review the intent and contents of ENMOD and to scrutinize military history for past events that hold lessons pertinent to this inquiry. Accordingly, the first section below describes and discusses ENMOD. In the second section, the Vietnam conflict is considered as it bears on ENMOD and its *raison d'être*. Third, Iraqi tactics that harmed the environment are described and analyzed to determine whether they contravened ENMOD. In the fourth section, international measures other than ENMOD that seek to protect the environment are outlined. Fifth, a simple schema for commencing the process of investigating crimes against the environment is set forth. Last, the implications of my findings for future attempts to prevent state crimes against the environment during military operations and for the future operation of ENMOD are examined.[2]

ENMOD

Briefly, ENMOD's Article I prohibits states from using techniques that could have widespread, long-lasting, or severe effects on the environment as means of destruction in war or for any other hostile purpose. Also, state actors are not allowed to help others use these so-called environmental modification techniques. The term *environmental modification techniques*, according to Article II, refers to any technique for manipulating natural processes that can be used to change the dynamics, composition, or structure of the earth, including its biota, atmosphere, hydrosphere, and lithosphere. Examples of such techniques include attempts to induce earthquakes or tsunamis (tidal waves), change the ecological balance of a geographic region, change climate or weather patterns, affect ocean currents, and alter the state of the ionosphere or ozone layer (U.S. Arms Control and Disarmament Agency, 1990). Because Article II forbids the use of "any technique for changing [the environment]—through the *deliberate manipulation* of natural processes," it appears to define environmental modification techniques in terms of intent and the scientific/technical capabilities to carry out that intent.

According to Article V, if the government of a state that has ratified ENMOD suspects another of having transgressed the convention, it can lodge a complaint with the UN, which then convenes a Consultative Committee of Experts (CCE) within one month to consider the charge. The CCE conducts an investigation and issues a report that shall be presented to the UN, which in turn distributes copies to all ENMOD signatories.[3] Alternatively, a state may lodge a complaint with the UN Security Council, which investigates and acts appropriately if the charge has merit. As of this writing, no state has made such a complaint to the UN or the UN Security Council. ENMOD's Article VIII enjoins states to organize a conference five years after ENMOD enters into force to review the operations of the treaty. Two review conferences have been held, in 1984 and 1992 (see below).

While ENMOD itself does not define the terms *widespread*, *long-lasting*, and *severe*, negotiations that led to ENMOD reached an understanding of these terms. They are interpreted as follows:

- *widespread:* encompasses an area on the scale of several hundred square kilometers (km²),
- *long-lasting:* lasting for months, or approximately a season, and;
- *severe:* involving serious or significant disruption or harm to human life, natural and economic resources, or other assets. (U.S. Arms Control and Disarmament Agency, 1990)

On May 18, 1977, U.S. Secretary of State C.R. Vance, Soviet Foreign Minister A.A. Gromyko, and representatives from 31 other states signed ENMOD (Johnston, 1977). The treaty entered into force on October 5, 1978. As of April 2, 1992, seventy-two states have signed ENMOD; of these, fifty-five also have ratified or acceded to the treaty, including Canada, the United Kingdom, and the United States. Iraq signed the convention in 1977, but has not ratified it.[4] Notable nonstate parties are China and France.

ENMOD's first review conference was held in 1984. The sense of this conference, which barely was noticed by the press or public, was that the treaty was operating well, but that more states should join it (UN, 1992a). A second review conference was held in September 1992 (UN, 1992b). It confirmed that Article I had been "faithfully observed by the state parties" and noted "with satisfaction that no state party had found it necessary to invoke the provisions of Article V dealing with international complaints" (UN, 1992b). However, the conference pointed out that relatively few states had ratified the treaty and requested the UN secretary-general to direct intensive efforts to induce nonstate parties to join the treaty.

ENMOD has been exhaustively analyzed by Goldblat (1975; 1977; 1984). In general, he determined that its weaknesses outweigh its strengths. Three major deficiencies in particular weaken ENMOD. First, only the use of techniques that cause "widespread, long-lasting or severe" effects are banned. Goldblat holds that the treaty should be made more comprehensive by forbidding any hostile use of environmental modification techniques. Second, ENMOD does not ban the preparation to use hostile environmental modification techniques (i.e., the research that necessarily precedes the development of illegal techniques). The treaty thus would be significantly strengthened if it enjoined states to, for example, place all relevant research and development (R&D) in the environmental field under civilian control and require that scientists from other countries be invited to observe or take part in them. Further, countries should be required to give advance notice of large experiments involving environmental modification. Third, the convention, which now covers only state actors, should have universal application (i.e., it should ban the hostile use of environmental modification techniques against any nation or subnational group, be they treaty parties or not). This absolute prohibition is needed because the effects of the hostile use of environmental modification techniques by definition most often cannot be confined within geographic boundaries.

As inferred by ENMOD's Article II, when the international community seeks to adjudicate whether a state has transgressed the treaty, the intent of its suspicious actions must be determined (Fauteux, 1992; UN, 1992b). They may ask whether the accused state deployed its scientific/technical capability deliberately to use the environment, or one of its processes, as part of its military tactics or strategies. Because the treaty's complaint process has not been tested, no one can discern how important the determination of intent will be when an adjudicating body, probably the UN Security Council, regards future violations of ENMOD. When such an occasion arises, two major problems may become apparent. First, it could be difficult to appraise if the questionable hostile or military activity coincidentally resulted in environmental damage or if it was, in fact, a deliberate manipulation of the environment for hostile purposes. Second, as events unfold, civilian and military leaders may explain war objectives in general terms, but almost always will keep secret reasons for employing particular military tactics or weapons systems. Inevitably it will be difficult for an outsider to ascertain the underlying reason for, or intent of, a military action or tactic that affected the environment.

The Vietnam Conflict and
Its Lessons for ENMOD

This section, and the next dealing with the Gulf War, are organized similarly: (1) the respective tactics or actions that damaged the environment are described; (2) the damages caused to the affected environments are assessed; (3) the intent of the environmentally destructive tactics or actions is determined; and (4) a conclusion is reached on whether the environmentally destructive tactics would have, or did, violate ENMOD.

1. Environmentally Destructive Tactics Employed in Vietnam

During the Vietnam conflict, U.S. military forces deployed a variety of what is commonly termed *conventional weapon systems*. Some of these were especially destructive—artillery barrages, carpet bombing, cluster bombs, and napalm caused extensive so-called "collateral" damage to the Vietnamese biota and environment (Westing, 1975). At times their effects on civilians horrified the world's public and raised questions about the legality and morality of their use (Trooboff, 1975). However, the environmental harm these weapons caused raised less controversy, possibly because conventional weapons have had a long history of use where their direct and collateral effects have been accepted as inevitable by-products of war. Similarly, the employment by U.S. forces of chemical riot control agents to flush Vietcong from caves, tunnels, and settlements were condemned by some as contravening international customary law and the Geneva Protocol (Neilands et al., 1972; Trooboff, 1975), but their environmental effects, if any, have not received public attention.

However, certain operations conducted for military reasons by U.S. forces in Vietnam and other parts of Southeast Asia during 1965–1971 caused widespread, long-lasting, or severe damage to the environment. As such, they collectively might be the only historic example of deliberately induced large-scale damage to the environment during military conflict. In particular, two tactics have been singled out for criticism—the large-scale employment of chemicals to defoliate or kill plants and the physical removal of ground cover so much so that one commentator equated the defoliation program with ecocide (Johnstone, 1971). After the war, when its details were revealed, a third program that affected the environment was revealed, namely, to use rainmaking for military purposes.[5] It is useful to analyze these operations in order to determine whether they would have violated ENMOD had the treaty been operational then, and to derive lessons useful for a similar analysis of Iraq's operations in the Gulf region.

The first operation, then, was defoliation. Defoliating chemicals (also known as defoliants) cause foliage to drop from the plants on which they are applied. If the dose is high, or if defoliants are used repeatedly, they can kill plants. The first defoliants, which were arsenical compounds, were developed during the 1920s, but saw limited use in agriculture because of their toxicity. However, in 1941 Allied scientists secretly developed a synthetic that chemically resembled a plant hormone. This agent, named 2,4,5-T for short, interfered with the metabolism of a narrow range of leafy plant and bush species, causing them to drop their leaves. It seemed not to harm nontarget plants or animals. Toward the end of World War II, preparations began to use the agent on Japan's crops, but the war's end terminated this plan.

After the war, 2,4,5-T became available on the open market. In the late 1940s, U.S. plantation owners employed it to defoliate cotton plants, thus making it easier for them to harvest cotton bolls mechanically. A few years later, during the early 1950s, health workers used defoliants in Kenya and Tanganyika to eliminate the tsetse fly, which prefers shady habitats and will therefore avoid defoliated areas. When Malaya was threatened by a destructive leaf disease caused by the fungus *Dothidella ulei*, plantation owners sprayed 2,4,5-T on diseased trees, which caused them to drop their leaves, but otherwise did little damage. After some months, new fungus-free leaves would form, and rubber production could resume. By the 1960s, the use of defoliants in world agriculture was common, encompassing such crops as seed legumes, potatoes, sugar cane, and tomatoes (Osborne, 1968).

In Malaya the properties of 2,4,5-T had been noted by the British military forces, who were trying to quell a dogged communist insurrection that had started in that country in 1948. Drawing on stocks stored to counter future outbreaks of *Dothidella ulei*, British troops began using the agent in 1955 to accomplish two military objectives. First, it was used to destroy the food crops of native peoples suspected of supporting the communist guerrillas. The food denial program was terminated rather quickly because it was perceived as counterproductive, having alienated friendly and neutral farmers. Second, surface vehicles equipped with sprayers were used to defoliate roadside vegetation, thereby reducing the risk of ambushes. In general, this program was deemed successful and continued to the end of the conflict in 1958[6] (Cecil, 1986; Osborne, 1968).

The Malaya lesson was not lost on the U.S. military conducting operations in Vietnam who faced many of the same field problems as had the British. First, a variety of known and candidate defoliants were first field-tested in the South Vietnamese jungles from December 1961 to February 1962 (Brown, 1962). After evaluating test results, the U.S. high command decided to initiate a defoliation program, code-named Ranch Hand, which eventually was conducted from 1965 to 1973.[7] Three commercial products were employed during Ranch Hand, nicknamed Agent Blue,[8] Agent Orange,[9] and Agent White (from the identifying bands marking the fifty-five-gallon drums used to store and transport the compounds).

The second environmentally damaging program was physical land-clearing, which was done by "Roman" plows and "Georgia" chains. Roman plows were armored tractors weighing 33,000 kilograms and equipped with huge blades capable of toppling the largest tree. They were organized in companies of 30 tractors each; a company could clear heavy jungle at the rate of 40 hectares (ha)[10] per day or light jungle at 160 ha per day (Westing, 1975). Georgia chains, on the other hand, were heavy-duty chains strung between tractors or Roman plows. When the vehicles advanced in unison, trees and bushes encountered between them were uprooted. Most of the land-clearing with

Roman plows and Georgia chains was done in Military Region III.[11]

Third, from March 20, 1967 to July 5, 1972, U.S. forces conducted a top secret rainmaking program in Southeast Asia. A detailed description of this program appeared first in 1978 when excerpts from a classified Senate hearing held in 1974 were published (U.S. Congress, 1978). Briefly, U.S. airplanes had seeded clouds over Vietnam and Laos with silver and lead iodide each monsoon season. The aim was to induce clouds to precipitate more rain than normal. The greater rainfall was expected to have three major effects: (1) the poor roads used by North Vietnamese forces would be soaked, making them unusable for vehicular traffic; (2) hillsides along roads would be destabilized, increasing the number of blocking landslides; and (3) enlarged water runoffs would create flooding conditions in rivers that would wash out bridges and river crossings. In addition, increased rainfall would saturate soils more thoroughly than usual, thereby extending drying time, lengthening the duration of difficult conditions. Three WC-130 and two RF-4c aircraft flew a total of 2,602 sorties over Laos, North Vietnam, and, to a lesser extent, Cambodia during which they dropped 47,409 seeding units.[12]

The U.S. Defense Intelligence Agency (DIA) claimed that rainfall in the area of operations increased 30 percent over normal and as a result the enemy experienced increased difficulties in moving supplies (U.S. Congress, 1978).[13]

2. Environmental Damage Caused by Defoliation, Land-clearing, and Rainmaking

As is discussed below, there is no information in the open literature on the long-term consequences of the military rainmaking during the Vietnam conflict. Conversely, several reputable institutions and independent researchers have investigated the ecological consequences of the large-scale use of defoliants and of land-clearing by Roman plows. In particular, reference is made to studies by the U.S. National Academy of Sciences (Committee on the Effects of Herbicides in Vietnam,

1974) and the American Association for the Advancement of Science (reprinted in U.S. Congress, 1978; pp. 120–124), as well as research performed by individuals (Westing, 1975; Cecil, 1986; Fyodorov, 1987). By consulting these sources, the "widespread, long-lasting or severe effects," of U.S. defoliation and land-clearing tactics on the Indochina environment may be analyzed in terms set forth in ENMOD.[14]

Widespread Effects

To sum up the findings of the authorities cited above, about 1.7 million ha, or 10 percent of Vietnam's total land area, was sprayed with defoliants at least once. However, some military regions that the U.S. military deemed important for strategic or tactical reasons were "treated" more widely and thoroughly. For example, 33 percent of the area constituting Military Region III was sprayed with defoliants, as was 19 percent of Military Region I. Beyond defoliation by chemicals, Roman plows and Georgia chains cleared over 325,000 ha of Vietnamese forest lands, representing about 2 percent of the country's land area. In view of about 12 percent of Vietnam's land area having been damaged by defoliants and land-clearing, it is reasonable to conclude that the effects of the defoliation and land-clearing operations indeed were widespread.

Long-lasting Effects

For the purpose of this chapter it is sufficient to limit discussion to four major types of long-lasting effects brought about by U.S. operations. Those processes include nutrient dumping, species replacement, mangrove destruction, and land erosion.

Nutrient dumping. When herbicide-mediated defoliation is deliberately brought on during the monsoon, the leaves that drop from trees and bushes are quickly flushed away by rains. The nutrients they contain are lost, impoverishing the soil. New growth of normal flora is thereby hindered, allowing competing, fast-growing weeds to gain a foothold in forests, mangroves, and other woodlands. It will usually take years to decades for nature to replace the lost nutrients; until then, biomass (the total organic matter that grows by the photosynthetic conversion of solar energy) is diminished, and the productivity of the affected area goes down.

Species replacement. In areas treated repeatedly with defoliants much of the normal, permanent vegetation was killed off. The loss of vegetation had two immediate major consequences. First, it provided opportunities for invasions by fast-growing grasses and brushes. These are in effect weeds that stay and dominate defoliated sites for many years. Second, most forms of wildlife that lived in the cleared forest were killed or, if they survived, were driven off, often ending up in habitats that were quite different from those to which they were adapted. Unable to defend themselves against unknown predators and facing competition from well-adapted indigenous species, the probability of survival and propagation in the alien territory was low for the displaced animals. In the longer term, loss of normal vegetation leads to the diminution of biodiversity; some species may become extinct. At best, in areas damaged by Ranch Hand operations, it will take decades to restore a balance among species approaching normality.

Mangrove destruction. Under normal conditions, mangrove forests are vital to the coastal environment since they have many essential functions: they protect coast lines from damage by typhoons and hurricanes; their root systems nurture and protect a large variety of marine organisms and provide breeding grounds for the newly hatched fry and larva of offshore fish and shellfish; and the canopy of a mangrove forest provides a habitat for a large variety of birds, mammals, invertebrates, and insects. However, because they hid enemy amphibious resupply routes, more so than anything else, coastal mangrove forests were targeted for Ranch Hand raids. The slow-growing plants that made up these forests proved especially susceptible to defoliant action. Since these highly specialized plants cannot be replaced by other species, and since wave and tidal action prevent the seeds that would grow into new plants from implanting themselves, it will take many decades to regenerate mangrove forests destroyed by defoliants. Until then, the coastal zone of Vietnam will remain unstable and largely unproductive.

Land erosion. Land cleared by Roman plows immediately underwent massive erosion, especially if the cleared land was on a hillside in areas subjected to heavy rains. Due to the unfavorable conditions created by erosion, cleared land was invaded by weeds, which cannot be displaced by plant species that once grew there. Areas that at once were favored with rich biodiversity and that sheltered a large variety of insect and animal life now resemble barren savanna. It is not known whether lands subjected to Roman plows can revive and reattain their original state. If so, it would take many decades.

Severe Effects

Of the treated areas, about 66 percent were sprayed once; 20 percent were sprayed twice; 10 percent, three times; and 4 percent, four or more times. The severity of the effects is related to the number of sprayings; a single spraying would kill about 10 percent of all vegetation; two sprays would kill 25 percent; three would kill 50 percent; and four or more would kill between 85 percent and almost 100 percent. The National Academy of Sciences study estimated that about 1.25 million square meters of "merchantable" timber (timber that may be harvested for economic gain) was destroyed by defoliants, as well as between 5 million and 11 million square meters of "nonmerchantable" timber (Committee on the Effects of Herbicides in Vietnam, 1974). Although affected areas were smaller, even heavier damage was caused to mangrove forests. Consequently, two types of severe effects from defoliation are discernible. First, forests and mangroves were damaged to a great degree in terms of areas affected and the number of plants killed or injured. Second, economic hardship was inflicted on Vietnam's population, since large quantities of what otherwise would have been merchantable timber were destroyed, precluding them from being harvested and processed for local use or export.[15] Further, the effects of the damage are likely to persist because so many saplings, which are the basis for tomorrow's merchantable timber, were killed off.

While the ecological consequences of herbicides and Roman plows described and analyzed in this chapter relate mainly to plant biota and soil, there was undoubtedly collateral damage to humans and animals who lived in or near treated or cleared areas. It is difficult to assess the extent of this damage, since there is no information available on the health of local civilian populations or indigenous animal species before their exposure to defoliants. A report by the Stockholm International Peace Research Institute (1975) alluded to possible long-term effects on humans: "The grim results will, however, only be made plain in the years and decades to come in the form of a rising cancer rate and an increasingly large number of deformed children."

3. Intent

The intent of the U.S. rainmaking program undertaken in Southeast Asia was made clear by a Department of Defense spokesperson who appeared before the Senate Committee on Foreign Relations in 1978. He testified that in 1966 the Office of Defense Research and Engineering proposed to test cloud-seeding over limited areas of Southeast Asia in order to find out if the additional rain would impede the enemy's logistic operations. During October 1966 a series of scientifically controlled cloud seeding tests were conducted in the Laos panhandle. The tests were terminated in early November 1966, and the Commander in Chief, Pacific (CINCPAC) decided that cloud seeding "to induce additional rain over infiltration routes in Laos could be used as a valuable tactical weapon" (U.S. Congress, 1978). On the basis of this testimony we can conclude that the tactical employment of this particular environmental modification technique was linked to achieving specific military objectives.

The intent of the U.S. defoliation program in Vietnam has been officially explained, but this has been discounted by at least one state. Officially, the twofold intent of defoliation is clearly stated in a U.S. military field manual of that time; it was employed, first, to achieve the "visual observation of enemy forces, facilities, roads, ambush sites, infiltration routes, and other enemy locations from the air, ground, or water" and, second, to destroy crops, by that decreasing the enemy's food resources and forcing him to divert scarce manpower to transport food from far-off supply depots (Department of the Army, 1971). As described above, the methods chosen by the U.S. military to accomplish these objectives depended on the large-scale dispersement of chemicals widely used throughout the world as defoliants or herbicides (although the formulation was designed for military purposes), and on land-clearing, which is similar to slash-and-burn, an age-old agricultural technique. If one considers together the objectives and methods used to achieve them, the link between cause and effect is clear and unmistakable; that is, the herbicide was applied, destroying the target crop, thereby making the crop unavailable to the enemy; or the defoliant was applied, the foliage that would otherwise hide the enemy was diminished or obliterated, thus affording less protection to enemy soldiers. The official U.S. view of the defoliation program is thus clear—the intent was to use defoliants to defoliate or destroy crops; it was not the use of the environment or one of its processes for military ends. A similarly compelling cause–effect linkage can be constructed as readily for the intent of tactics where Roman plows and Georgia chains were employed.

It is difficult to construct feasible alternative scenarios explaining the intent of the U.S. defoliation program. In fact, only one differing explanation of this program's intent has been published. This effort is illustrative of the difficulties inherent in determining whether environmental warfare has been employed and is therefore worth describing and analyzing.

In the early 1980s, it may be recalled, the Ronald Reagan administration had mounted a strong international campaign to convince the world that the Soviet Union was responsible for supplying mycotoxins to their Vietnamese ally, who allegedly employed them in the form of "yellow rain" to terrorize native tribes (U.S. Department of State, 1982a; 1982b). Put on the defensive, the Soviet government requested the USSR Academy of Sciences and Ministry of Health to investigate and clarify the matter. The results of their investigation were sent to the UN Secretary General for general distribution. The major finding is, "There is reason to assume that the main goal of the 'herbicide' war was to achieve . . . ecological change. A three-phase plan for altering the nature of the forests were [sic] developed and executed in South-East Asia" (UN General Assembly, 1982). Briefly, the Soviet scientists rationalized that Ranch Hand was mounted to kill off the normal species constituting jungle flora. U.S. forces then burned the dead wood with napalm, simultaneously sterilizing the soil. Much of the denuded land's topsoil was washed away by rain and flood waters, facilitating invasion by weeds. Taking advantage of this condition, U.S. aircraft seeded denuded areas with elephant grass. This plant incidentally harbored fungal species capable of producing mycotoxins, including trichothecene-producing *Fusarium* species. Winds carried fungal spores from contaminated elephant grass in Vietnam to Kampuchea and Laos, where the fungal species established themselves among the indigenous flora. Periodically, extensive outbreaks of plant diseases caused by the introduced fungus occurred during which large quantities of trichothecene toxins were produced. These toxins, the Soviet scientists claimed, were the actual etiology of yellow rain. Evidently, the United States itself was responsible for yellow rain and the damage it caused to indigenous people (UN General Assembly, 1982).

Neither scientists nor diplomats gave much credence to the Soviet attempt to link Ranch Hand and Roman plows with environmental destruction for military reasons. The problem with the study is that it asks the reader to believe that U.S. military planners of that era could direct scientific efforts to predict and manipulate complex natural meteorological phenomena for military ends beyond rainmaking, to affect, for example, wind force and wind direction. Further, they must also have had the capability purposefully to manipulate biological forces to introduce successfully foreign plant species into a new, alien environment and, after the introduced species established themselves, to deliberately colonize the introduced plants with exotic fungal species. Finally, after all this has been accomplished, a phenomenon occurs, which is unspecified in the Soviet report, whereby the toxins forming yellow rain are somehow concentrated and rendered airborne, transported to populated areas, and dispersed so it settles on humans and animals in sufficiently high doses to cause death or illness.

The two-pronged Soviet effort to convince the international community of its innocence and U.S. guilt in regard to yellow rain shows the difficulty with developing alternative theories to explain the intent of the defoliation and land-clearing programs. Alternative theories would, it seems, inevitably be convoluted, consisting of a series of improbable events with one leading to the next. The more reasonable explanation for intent thus should be allowed to prevail.

4. Would U.S. Tactics in Vietnam Have Violated ENMOD?

We have seen that in the case of rainmaking, the United States intentionally employed an environmental-modification technique to fulfill military objectives. However, the question remains whether it caused widespread, long-lasting, or severe damage to the environment. Even if we accept what could be a self-serving finding by the DIA, namely that the program succeeded in increasing local rainfall by 30 percent, it is not at all certain that the additional rain damaged Indochina's environment. No scientific studies have been published, as far as I can determine, whose results could support a claim of damage to the environment. Even if we recognize that the scientific evidence required to make such a claim probably could not have been compiled at the time because the affected states were unable to deploy the expertise to, for example, collect baseline ecologic and meteorologic data useful for long-term, comparative studies demonstrating environmental effects, this does not mean that legal requirements for acceptable evidence can be relaxed. Perhaps the requisite scientific expertise could now be mobilized to perform a retroactive investigation, but investigators would probably find it impossible to collect reliably the scientific data needed to reconstruct the state of the environment as it was twenty and more years ago, nor measure the effects of larger-than-normal quantities of rain that fell during long-past monsoons. In view of the lack of scientific data on possible environmental effects of the rainmaking program, no one can document that it caused widespread, long-lasting, or severe damage to the environment of the Indochina region. Therefore, a transgression of ENMOD by the United States may be suggested, but cannot be proven.

Unquestionably, the combination of defoliation and land-clearing methods used to destroy vegetation in the Indochina peninsula altered and damaged the region's terrestrial and marine environments. Further, information gleaned from scientifically conducted studies substantiate that these methods caused widespread, long-lasting, or severe damage to the terrestrial environment in Vietnam (and possibly to Cambodia and Laos as well). If no more was required to resolve whether the prospective ENMOD had been transgressed, the United States would have been condemned. But, as is pointed out above, before such a conclusion can be reached, an assessment also has to be made of the country's intent for having employed the questionable techniques.

As analyzed above, in view of the lack of plausible alternative explanations for the U.S. defoliation and land-clearing programs, the officially stated intent should be accepted (i.e., the intent of these programs was to defoliate or kill crop plants, not to affect the environment or to use the environment as a means of warfare). This conclusion is bolstered by examining how chemical defoliants and land-clearing equipment were used in the field to achieve limited tactical objectives. Although the totality of all defoliation and land-clearing operations had widespread, long-lasting, or severe effects, they cannot be considered environmental-modification techniques as defined in ENMOD or its supplementary understandings..For these reasons, the United States cannot be condemned as an ENMOD transgressor.

It is clear that some tactics used by the United States during the Vietnam War damaged the region's terrestrial environment and, possibly, its atmospheric and marine environments as well. However, my analysis of the events of the time indicates that these tactics did not contravene the prospective ENMOD. Leaping twenty years ahead, the government of Iraq also employed tactics before and during the Gulf War that had negative environmental effects. Did Iraq's government contravene ENMOD by having employed these tactics? I now attempt to answer this question, partly by using lessons gleaned from the U.S. involvement in Vietnam.

Iraq's Environmentally Destructive Tactics and ENMOD

Kuwait possesses vast petroleum and natural gas reserves, as well as the industrial infrastructure to process these raw materials. For example, Kuwait's petroleum reserves are the third largest in the world, containing about 94.5 billion barrels, and its refineries can process 2.5 million barrels of oil per day on a sustainable level, which is more than any other developing country except Saudi Arabia (UN Security Council, 1991). In view of the importance of its oil to energy-hungry European countries, Japan, and the United States, the maintenance of Kuwait's independence is vital to their national security and economic well-being.

Iraq invaded and occupied Kuwait on August 2, 1990. Iraq's occupation, however, was short-lived; on February 24, 1991, a coalition military force began a ground offensive, called Desert Storm, which "liberated" Kuwait in four days. For the purpose of this chapter, it is not necessary to dwell on the enormous damage that the Iraqi forces wrought on Kuwait's population and infrastructure (see, e.g., UN Security Council, 1991) or that Iraq itself suffered from coalition military activities (see, e.g., Aziz, 1992). Rather, following the format presented in the foregoing section, I review Iraqi tactics or activities that had an impact on the environment.

1. Iraq's Environmentally Destructive Tactics

An investigation conducted by Kuwaiti officials after the Gulf War indicated that during its occupation of Kuwait, Iraqi forces rigged most of the country's 1,330 oil wells, off-shore loading facilities, pipelines, and storage tanks with explosives. In late January 1991, possibly anticipating Desert Storm, Iraqi forces initiated a program of destruction by setting fire to oil installations in the Wafrah oil field. An estimated 150 wells were already on fire by the time Desert Storm commenced. Eventually, the Iraqis sabotaged 749 oil wells, of which 610 ignited, producing enormous quantities of smoke. After Kuwait was liberated, foreign fire-fighting firms were contracted to put out the oil well fires. During the spring and summer of 1991 progress was slow—fire fighters could extinguish only one or two fires per day. However, in August a machine called Big Wind was imported from Hungary. It was essentially a powerful jet engine generating a high velocity exhaust, which blew out fires at a rate of six per day. The last fire was extinguished during the first week of November 1991.

The total amount of oil that burned was about 500 million barrels (Readman et al., 1992), which is about the same as the total cargo carried by 2,000 *Exxon Valdez*–type supertankers. The oil fires of Kuwait produced enormous quantities of sooty smoke that polluted the atmosphere with oxides of carbon, sulphur, and nitrogen, and unburnt particulate matter. Scientists performing airborne studies during the spring of 1991, when about 4.6 million barrels of oil were burning per day, found that the fires were producing approximately 3,400 tons of smoke per day, which fanned out horizontally before reaching an altitude of six kilometers (Hobbs and Radke, 1992). The smoke was estimated to cause acid rain and photochemical smog within about 1,000 to 2,000 kms of Kuwait (Browning et. al., 1991). Winds carried smoke particles as far west as Wyoming and eastward to the Himalayan Mountains (Anonymous, 1991; Hobbs and Radke, 1992).

Concurrent to the fires, crude oil gushed from damaged wells and storage tanks onto land. Some of this oil came from wells that extinguished themselves, others from oil wells whose fires were put out by special engineering teams. Due to the natural drainage of the land, much of this oil flowed into the ocean at a rate of up to 80,000 barrels per day. The outpouring of oil reached a high point during the last part of March 1991, and then gradually diminished to almost nothing after November. Also, after March, Kuwaiti workers constructed barriers to prevent further discharge into the Gulf, but that led to the formation of large oil lakes on land. As gushing wells were capped, oil lakes ceased growing after November 1991.

In late January 1991, the beginning of what was to become a massive oil slick was observed in the Persian Gulf off Kuwait. Its origin were "farms" containing hundreds of oil storage tanks and artificial sea islands built to transfer oil from land-based tanks to ships whose contents the Iraqis discharged into the sea. These facilities were estimated to be holding 10.7 million barrels of petroleum at the time. After Desert Storm commenced, the Iraqis stepped up the release of stored oil. To hinder their efforts, the coalition's air force precision-bombed marine-based oil installations, to destroy the valves and nozzles through which petroleum flowed. Bombs were also used to set floating oil on fire, thereby limiting the size and movement of the oil slick. However, by the time the flow of oil was halted, about 6 million barrels had already been released into the ocean. In addition, Iraqi forces released oil from ships they captured in Kuwaiti harbors, which added approximately 4.2 million barrels to the slick (Anonymous, 1992a). Oil that flowed from gushing wells on land also contributed to the slick. Further, the quantity of airborne emissions from the burning oil wells that fell out in the Persian Gulf was great, in amount possibly surpassing spilled crude oil (Readman et al., 1992).

2. The Environmental Effects of Iraq's Activities

Soon after overt hostilities ended in the Gulf region, many environmental organizations and scientific teams initiated extensive investigations of various facets of the ecological disaster brought on by Iraq. Although at this writing only a little more than two years have passed since the last oil well fire was extinguished, and although remnants of the immense oil slick remain in the Persian Gulf, preliminary findings from this research have been published in four *New Scientist* review articles (Joyce and Charles, 1991; Pearce, 1991; Pearce and Pain, 1991; Sheppard and Price, 1991); two reports issued by Kuwaiti agencies (Kuwait Environment Protection Council, 1991; UN Security Council, 1991); the proceedings of an international scientific symposium on the environmental and health impacts of the oil fires (Al-Shatti and Harrington, 1992); and four scientific articles that address specific aspects of the Gulf environmental situation (Hobbs and Radke, 1992; Lee, Clark, and Thompson, 1992; Browning et al., 1991; Bakan et al., 1991). In addition, information about damage caused by the Iraqi occupiers has been issued by two Kuwaiti agencies (Environmental Sciences Division, n.d.; Kuwait News Agency, 1991) and a U.S. agency (Anonymous, 1991). These sources provide a detailed representation of how oil and smoke affected the Gulf's environment, thus allowing an analysis of ecological damage.

Widespread Effects

Shortly after the first oil fires were observed, some authorities postulated that they would produce sooty smoke that would enter the upper atmosphere, where it would be dispersed by jet winds and would shade over 100 million kms,[2] or one-fifth, of the world's surface (Pearce, 1991). If this had occurred, a situation akin to "nuclear winter" might have happened. Fortunately, the worst-case scenario of "nuclear winter" did not occur because the quantity of smoke generated was less than initially predicted, and none reached the upper atmosphere. Nevertheless, it caused substantial ecological effects (Sagan, 1991). The smoke columns emanating from fires combined a few kilometers southeast of Kuwait City, resulting in a dense plume, which was blown southeastward by prevailing winds. At its maximum size, the plume shaded the sun completely, causing a nightlike darkness on the ground during the day. Within about 200 kilometers of Kuwait, the smoke depressed the ground temperature about 10° Centigrade (C) (Browning et al., 1991). The decrease in surface air temperature for the entire Gulf region averaged 4° C (Bakan et al., 1991). For comparison, massive forest fires in Siberia during 1915 are estimated to have generated between 20 million and 40 million tons of smoke, which depressed the average day-time temperature of the region by an estimated 2° to 5° C (Pearce, 1991).

Iraqi actions caused more oil to be spilled onto land and into the ocean than any previous disasters. On land, over 240 oil lakes were formed, ranging in size from a few hundred to thousands of square meters (Chandler, 1993). The total spillage of oil onto land is estimated at 35 million to 150 million barrels (Pearce and Pain, 1991). In addition, large quantities of oil and other wastes that washed ashore or were skimmed off the ocean's surface of necessity had to be buried in the soil, debasing desert areas of as yet unspecified size.

In the ocean, the spill created the largest oil slick ever seen. Satellite photos taken on January 25, 1991, showed a slick that was 50 kilometers long and 8 kilometers wide, covering an area of approximately 400 square kilometers (UN Security Council, 1991). The main slick was estimated to contain 0.5 million to 2.5 million barrels (Joyce and Charles, 1991). However, as recounted above, the total amount of oil spillage during the Gulf War was undoubtedly much larger. For the sake of comparison, the largest accidental releases of oil until that time was the 1978 blow-out of the Ixtoc well in the Gulf of Mexico that spilled a total of 3.7 million barrels of oil, while the *Exxon Valdez* spilled 250,000 barrels into Prince William Sound in Alaska in 1989 (U.S. Congress, 1991). Besides the main slick, many smaller slicks were present in the Gulf, having either split from the main slick or originating from unique sources.

Referring to ENMOD terms of understanding, which defines *widespread* as encompassing several hundred square kilometers, the Iraqi tactics resulted in damages to the atmospheric and marine environments that were, and remain, widespread. Damage to the terrestrial environment probably is widespread, but this remains to be verified scientifically.

Long-lasting and Severe Effects

Little information as yet is available on whether the atmospheric pollution from the oil fires will cause long-lasting and severe effects on the environment. One can postulate that the smoke cover, which by now has dissipated, lowered the temperature of the region at the time, but it is not known how much lower than normal or its effects. Further, the smoke cover prevented sunlight from reaching the Persian Gulf's surface, which might have negatively affected marine primary producers, such as oxygen-generating plants and algae, but, if so, the baseline data required to measure the consequences is not available. It is also probable that some airborne pollutants will return to the earth or the sea as acid rain, but how much and its likely effects are unknown. Thus, as of this writing it is impossible to ascertain whether the smoke from oil fires has had, or will have, long-lasting or severe effects on the environment. Long-term scientific studies, some of which have already been started, may document such damage at some time in the future, so this issue remains unresolved.

In the marine environment, most of the oil slick that originated off Kuwait's coast has been pushed southward by currents and winds, moving to Qatar, a distance of over 400 kilometers. Initial observations by investigators suggest that the slick immediately smothered large areas of intertidal habitats, killing an unknown number of turtles, sea snakes, and wading birds, as well as threatening thousands of dugongs, dolphins, and whales. But the greatest threat posed by the spilled oil is to primary producers that live on the Gulf's shallow seabed. These organisms are at the beginning of many complex food chains, so if they died out, species further up the food chains, such as finfish and shellfish, would inevitably succumb. Eventually the fisheries of the Gulf's riparian nations would be affected, threatening the livelihood of coastal communities and inactivating the more than 1,000 small fishing boats that ply the Gulf (Sheppard and Price, 1991).

The full extent of the oil spill's damage that has been, and will be, caused to the Gulf is unknown. Lessons from past large oil spills suggest that affected areas indeed suffer long-lasting and severe damage; no one knows whether the Gulf's ecosystem is more or less vulnerable than other ecosystems. Adding difficulty to evaluating damage is that the Gulf's ecosystem is not well known to the scientific community, especially the eastern shore of the Gulf and the deep ocean bottom. An early study indicates that the Gulf may not be so badly damaged as first believed, but cautions that the full extent of damage cannot yet be made (Readman et al., 1992). A more recent report made to the 1993 Annual Meeting of the Geological Society of America was more pessimistic, finding that the aftereffects of the Gulf War caused "severe and lasting damage to Kuwait's desert, economic resources and ecosystems" (Chandler, 1993). In view of the uncertainties that still remain about the extent, reach, and persistence of damage caused to the Gulf environment by the war, a final tally of damage cannot be done for at least ten years.

Unlike the uncertainties regarding environmental harm, Kuwait's civilian population and economy undoubtedly suffered severe damage from Iraq's environmentally destructive tactics. At the height of the burning and gushing oil wells, between five and six million barrels of oil per day were lost, worth between $80 million and $100 million. The value of the total amount of oil lost by Kuwait is an estimated $8.5 billion. In addition, the Iraqi occupation force inflicted severe damage to the petrochemical infrastructure (i.e., oil wells, pipelines, processing facilities, storage tanks, loading and shipping facilities, etc.) and other purely civilian facilities and enterprises in agriculture, education, health delivery, manufacture, sewage disposal, and water treatment. By resorting to these tactics, Iraq's government extended the carnage past military bounds, to wreak long-lasting destruction on civilians.

3. Intent

In any discussion of state crime it is essential to determine intent. In general, no member of Iraq's leadership has provided information about its deliberations or reasons for decisions. Therefore the events in themselves have to be examined, to deduce intent. Thus, one might, for instance, postulate that Iraq's military ignited Kuwait's oil wells for defensive reasons, to create a thick smoke cloud that would hinder the coalition forces' air and ground operations. Similarly, oil might have been released into the ocean so it could be ignited at a propitious time, to prevent the coalition forces from undertaking amphibious operations, including landings. Alternatively, Iraq's leadership may have recognized that its armed forces would be unable to stem the coalition forces' headway, so a scorched-earth policy was adopted as a delaying tactic and to deny the enemy material required for future war making. Or, as suggested by Iraq's Deputy Prime Minister Tariz Aziz (Aziz, 1992), destruction may have been done in reprisal for the bombing of Iraq's petroleum facilities by coalition forces during the earlier Desert Shield phase of the war. Quite possibly we will never find out the reason behind Iraq's destructive stratagem. But in the final tally, regardless of how one tries to explain Iraq's logic, most probably it was not environmental modification for hostile use. Reaching this conclusion is not very complicated.

To begin, I refer to the military use of defoliants and land-clearing by the United States in Vietnam. Recall that the employment of actions or tactics that result in widespread, long-lasting, or severe environmental damage did not in itself mean a transgression of ENMOD. Before this determination can be made we have to find out the intent of the questionable activities according to Article II of ENMOD. Thus, we must ask the questions, Did Iraq's leadership intend to manipulate the environment for hostile purposes? Or, was it attempting to use one or more environmental-modification techniques for warfare? If we can answer either question positively, Iraq would be condemned for having breached ENMOD.

In order to answer these questions, Iraq's scientific/ technical capability with respect to environmental modification must be appraised. Aside from surprisingly advanced achievements in the nuclear weapons field (Smith and Frankel, 1991), technologies applicable to missile development and construction (Hull, 1991; Payne, 1992), and the petrochemical industry, Iraq is a third world country with limited capabilities in most scientific/technical areas. Referring to a possible scientific/technical capability that might have been present before the Gulf War to manipulate deliberately any aspect of the environment for whatever purpose, no relevant Iraqi research findings or claims of technical achievements can be found in the scientific/technical literature.[16] After the war, inspections carried out by the UN Special Commission (UNSCOM) of Iraq's industries, research institutions, military facilities and universities have divulged no information about capabilities for environmental manipulation, nor indicating that Iraqi scientists knew about environmental warfare or were trying to research the issue.[17] From this absence of information, it is reasonable to conclude that Iraq did not have the capability to manipulate environmental processes for civilian or military purposes, even if its leaders would have wished to do so.

Since Iraqi scientists were unable to modify deliberately the environment, what might have been the intent of Iraq's actions that damaged the Gulf's environment? A reasonable answer can be derived from examining the pattern of devastation wrought on Kuwait. It is important to note that the devastation of Kuwait's economically most important industry, including all or nearly all of Kuwait's oil wells, tank parks, and off-loading facilities, was only part of the picture, even if the most visually striking. Iraq's destructive campaign in fact affected nearly all of Kuwait's important or remarkable civilian institutions. For example, the Kuwait Institute for Scientific Research, perhaps the best-equipped and -housed research institution in the Middle East before the Gulf War, was stripped of everything removable, including the carpets covering the entryway and stairs (Hedén, 1992). That which could not be removed, such as large cold chambers and laboratory benches, was demolished. Perhaps even more poignant, most small- and medium-sized animals in the Kuwait Zoo were taken to Iraq, but larger animals, which could not be easily transported, or animals requiring special facilities were shot. Many other examples of how inclusive the destruction was can be specified.

The scenario, then, that best explains why Iraq embarked on wholesale destruction is a simple one. Anything that was movable and had potential artistic, economic, industrial, or scientific value was purloined and transported to Iraq. If an object was valuable for whatever reason but was immobile, it was destroyed (UN Security Council, 1991). By their nature, oil wells, refineries, tank parks, and loading facilities are immovable, so they were demolished by whatever methods would work quickly and efficiently. The means of demolition, as we know, caused smoke and discharged petroleum onto the land and into the sea, but this was incidental to the demolishing of Kuwait's infrastructure and therefore cannot be considered as environmental warfare.

We can hypothesize that this attempt at total destruction by theft or demolition indicated the Iraqi government's intent to gain as much as possible from its subjugation of Kuwait, while simultaneously causing so much damage to that country so that it would be unable to function as a viable state immediately or in the future.[18] Further, to ensure Kuwait's continued ruin, Iraq's leadership might have made what could have been an unprecedented decision, namely to induce the release of such massive quantities of toxic substances that Kuwait's environs would be converted into a wasteland shunned by human beings. Such destruction of a strategic part of the environment has been termed *strategic environmental terrorism*, which is the deliberate destruction of some part of the environment to gain strategic or tactical objectives (Kindt, 1993). However, even if this hypothesis is true, in having chosen its course of action, Iraq committed reprehensible deeds against civilians and the environment, but it cannot be condemned for having broken ENMOD because no environmental forces were directed to achieve military ends. Perhaps this is one of the treaty's most glaring weaknesses— parties to the treaty cannot employ environmental forces in warfare, but they can destroy the environment to achieve war objectives.

Protecting the Environment in the Time of War or Conflict

After having considered ENMOD and assessed its applicability to certain environmentally destructive tactics employed by combatants during the Vietnam conflict and the Gulf War, it is reasonable to conclude that ENMOD has limited utility for curtailing state crimes against the environment during war. Fortunately, some international laws address the issue of how to protect the environment during war or hostilities. In this regard, the findings of Goldblat (1982) and Sandoz (1992) may be summarized. Despite widespread and severe damage wrought on the environment by the mass employment of various weapons during World War I and World War II, the scope of the humanitarian law protecting nonmilitary targets did not include the environment. Several multilateral treaties have been designed to limit armaments or restrict their employment, in the process preventing indiscriminate damage to the environment, including the Geneva Convention of 1863, the Declarations of the

Hague Conferences of 1899 and 1907, the 1922 Washington Treaty, the 1925 Geneva Protocol, the 1949 Geneva Conventions, the 1972 BWC, the 1977 ENMOD, and, most recently, the 1993 Chemical Warfare Convention (CWC). In addition, more specialized or circumscribed treaties seek to protect circumscribed environments having special characteristics from destruction or damage from war or other military actions, including the 1959 Antarctic Treaty; the 1963 Treaty Banning Nuclear Weapon Tests in the Atmosphere, in Outer Space and Under Water; and the 1971 Treaty on the Prohibition of the Emplacement of Nuclear Weapons and Other Weapons of Mass Destruction on the Seabed and the Ocean Floor and in the Subsoil Thereof. Both the 1972 Declaration of the United Nations Conference on the Human Environment and the 1992 Declaration of the United Nations Conference on Environment and Development enunciated general principles for protecting the environment in war as well as in peace. However, the treaty having the highest relevance to the types of environmental damages discussed in this chapter are the Geneva Protocols of 1977, particularly Protocol I.

The basis for Protocol I lies with the 1972 United Nations Conference on the Human Environment. The Conference's declaration enunciated twenty-six principles, including some that explicitly seek to protect the environment. For example, Principle 2 states that "the natural resources of the earth, including the air, water, land, flora and fauna . . . must be safeguarded"; Principle 5 forbids "the discharge of toxic substances . . . in such quantities or concentrations as to exceed the capacity of the environment to render them harmless"; Principle 7 states that "states shall take all possible steps to prevent pollution of the seas by substances that are liable to create hazards to human health, to harm living resources and marine life"; and Principle 26 reads, "Man and his environment must be spared the effects of nuclear weapons and all other means of mass destruction" (Anonymous, 1975b). As a result of this conference, public awareness of ecology and environmental protection increased markedly (Taylhardat and Zilinskas, 1992).

The admonitions issued by the conference likely affected the negotiators who met in 1974 at the Diplomatic Conference on the Reaffirmation and Development of International Law Applicable in Armed Conflicts and eventually adopted the Geneva Protocols of 1977, since they included strong provisions for environmental protection in Protocol I. Protocol I reiterates the principle that states are limited in the means they use to wage war. The Protocol then enters new legal territory by expanding the protection that traditionally civilian populations retain, for example, from bombardments and air attacks; prohibiting the destruction of agricultural areas, drinking water facilities, irrigation works, and other objects indispensable for the survival of civilians; and extending special protection to dams, dikes, and nuclear power plants. More to the point of this chapter, Protocol I's Article 35 prohibits the use of "methods or means of warfare which are intended, or may be expected, to cause widespread, long-term and severe damage to the environment," while Article 48 states that "attacks against the natural environment by way of reprisal are prohibited." Perhaps most applicable to Iraq's tactics that damaged Kuwait's environment is Article 55, which enjoins "the use of methods or means of warfare which are intended or may be expected to cause such damage to the natural environment and thereby prejudice the health and survival of the population." Similar to its predecessor, the Geneva Conventions of 1949, breaches of the Protocols are to be reported to the UN Security Council, which then decides whether to investigate the matter and, if appropriate, put sanctions into effect. Due to their nature, the Protocols of 1977 apply to all conflicts whether or not the combatants are parties to the treaty (Neier, 1992). As noted by Solf (1986), the prohibitions prescribed in the Protocols of 1977 are so basic that they "must be construed as being inherent to a general principle of law and thus, general international law."

It can be seen that Protocol I complements ENMOD. ENMOD's main limitation is that it forbids states to use the environment itself, or its processes, as a weapon, which is most unlikely given the limitations of today's techniques; it does not forbid states to harm the environment during war, which is likely. As pointed out by former SIPRI director, Dr. Frank Barnaby (1976):

> . . . the impact of war on the environment in most urgent
> need of control is the damage, deliberate or incidental,
> done during combat. Particularly pernicious are military
> tactics involving deliberate damage caused to deny cover
> to enemy troops, to terrorize the enemy population, to
> destroy food crops, and so on.

Protocol I indeed forbids armies to wreak destruction on the environment during military operations, be they held in peace or war. Although some of its member states, such as the United States, are not parties to the Protocols of 1977, the North American Treaty Organization (NATO), for example, has taken heed of Protocol I provisions by elaborating a statement of principles that is expected to guide the actions of its member nations. It recognizes that "by their very nature, defense activities have the potential for adverse impacts on the environment. The need to protect the environment should be of critical concern to all Armed Forces and measures to achieve this are encouraged" (Committee on the Challenges of Modern Society, 1991). In view of this concern, nine recommendations are presented, to be taken up by member states. Included are such measures as performing environmental impact studies before conducting maneuvers or air operations, reducing noise at firing ranges, properly decontaminating staging areas, and appropriately de-arming munitions. There are no signs, however, of any government either inside or outside of NATO actually having incorporated these or similar principles into its military doctrine. Nevertheless it is a useful starting point in that never before have commanders shown a strong concern about the environment or the environmental effects of military activities.

Discussion

Most anyone who has experienced firsthand, or seen pictures or films of the oil-driven conflagrations in north and south Kuwait, the darkness of midnight at noon in the north Persian Gulf, the massive, ugly oil slick spreading over the Gulf's surface and coating its shores, and the exhaustive, spiteful destruction of waterworks, universities, and research institutes, industry, harbors, and other nonmilitary structures, cannot but believe that crimes of unsurpassed proportions have been committed against Kuwait's population and the atmospheric, marine, and terrestrial environments of the Gulf region. We can expect that an eventual peace settlement will adhere to the UN Security Council's Resolutions 674 and 687, which authorize reparations for the destruction Iraq's forces caused in and to Kuwait, although this has not happened so far. But what about the assault that Iraq's leaders ordered on the environment and the havoc it caused? Will Iraq's leaders be held responsible for these damages and for their redress?

So far, the international community's response to Iraq's abominable assault on the environment has been remarkably muted. Could it be a modern case of whom shall cast the first stone? After all, most states are themselves guilty of undertaking, promoting, or condoning activities that harm the environment. For instance, it is widely known that the United States with about 5 percent of the world's population produces almost 50 percent of its pollutants; the Japanese and Norwegian whaling fleets have succeeded in decimating some whale species; the Brazilian government does little to prevent its citizens from burning immense tracts of rain forests, and by doing so tolerates species extinctions on an extraordinary scale; the eastern European states have fostered unchecked industrial development that has monstrously polluted air, land, and water, in turn endangering the health of millions of citizens; and so forth. Would one of these states, by pointing an accusatory finger at Iraq, in the process open itself to accusations of having committed crimes against the environment?

Many governments have, of course, faced such accusations made by individuals and nongovernmental organizations. However, this does not mean that they risk being indicted by other governments. The difference between the environmentally harmful actions that states are responsible for or have condoned, and Iraq's assault on the environment is that the first were technically not illegal because they broke, or break, no international law, while the second, which stems from an act of aggression condemned as illegal by the international community, by definition was a criminal act. In view of this clear difference, being afraid to "cast the first stone" probably is not a reason for states being unwilling to bring a complaint to the United Nations.

A more difficult problem is the confusion presented by the large number of treaties and principles that may have been transgressed by Iraq's actions, some of which are named above, and the varying possibilities they present for achieving redress. Further, since no state has so far sought to have a perpetrator of environmental crimes indicted for having violated international law, this is uncharted legal territory. The head of the U.S. delegation at ENMOD's second review conference alluded to this problem:

> We believe environmental questions in warfare should be addressed. Indeed, it is for this reason that the United States is planning to propose a resolution in the sixth committee of the United Nations General Assembly to address specifically the question of what law applies to specific acts of war involving damage to the environment. A large body of treaty and customary law, including the Hague regulations [sic] and the Geneva conventions address the range of concerns associated with this issue. A broad forum such as the sixth committee is the appropriate place, we believe, where such concerns should be addressed. (Moodie, 1992)

To resolve the problem of confusing treaties and principles, a modest strategy for sorting out which treaties apply to an alleged criminal act against the environment perpetrated by a state is suggested. If a state suspects another one of causing damage to the environment or its processes, according to accepted principles it should present information to support its claim to the president of the UN Security Council. The president should not take it on herself or himself to judge the merits of the case, but should immediately establish a small ad hoc group with representatives from several countries to investigate the matter. This precludes the onus of the group's findings falling on one country. This group, rather than initially trying to determine whether a transgression of a treaty has taken place, should follow a plan that depends on going from the general to the specific by way of questions that are answered in the positive or negative, as follows:

1. Was the environmental damage under consideration caused by military activity? If no, refer to the declarations of the 1972 Conference of the Human Environment and the 1992 Conference on the Environment and Development. If yes, continue to 2.

2. Did the action or tactic damage a part of the environment covered by special treaties, such as the Antarctic, sea bottom, outer space, etc.? If no, continue to 3. If yes, refer to the provisions spelled out in treaties dealing with the specific environment, such as the 1959 Antarctic Treaty; the 1963 Treaty Banning Nuclear Weapon Tests in the Atmosphere, in Outer Space and Under Water; and the 1971 Treaty on the Prohibition of the Emplacement of Nuclear Weapons and Other Weapons of Mass Destruction on the Seabed and the Ocean Floor and in the Subsoil Thereof.

3. Was the damage widespread, long-lasting, or severe? If no, the matter is dropped. If yes, continue to 4.

4. Was the damage caused by the deliberate manipulation of the environment or its processes? If no, refer to the provisions of Protocol I of 1977. If the answer is perhaps or do not know, refer to ENMOD's Article 5 and Annex, which specifies that a CCE may be convened on request to investigate the matter. If yes, refer the matter to the UN Security Council for political redress, including sanctions.

Conclusion

Historically, the international community has sought to limit the extent of wars and put strictures on the means by which they are fought. One way of doing this is to define what constitutes a legitimate target for military operations and what is not. The legal principle that has evolved is that enemy soldiers can be targeted for wounding or killing but civilians cannot, even if citizens of the hostile state. By extension, the equipment of enemy soldiers, the facilities they inhabit, the area of land or sea they occupy, and the vegetation or other cover that hides them may be legally targeted for destruction. Conversely, civilian housing, equipment, farmland, and so forth are supposed to be protected from military activities by international law.

Even though the distinction of what is and is not a legitimate target erodes during wars, and the longer the war continues the worse the erosion, the legal principle remains: soldiers and military-related elements are legitimate targets for military operations, civilians and nonmilitary facilities and land are not. Therefore, weapons whose effects may harm only civilians, or soldiers and civilians alike, should be clearly identified and branded as illegal. So-called weapons of mass destruction fit this description, including nuclear, chemical, biological, and environmental weapons. These types of unconventional weapons,[19] then, have been marked for special attention by the international community, to be eliminated as soon as possible.

It can be seen that it is not accidental that many existing arms control treaties attempt to limit or eliminate weapons of mass destruction. Thus, in 1925 the Geneva Protocol forbade the use of chemical and bacteriological weapons. The former type of weapons used extensively during World War I had proven military utility; the latter was theoretically possible, but no state incorporated it in its arsenal. In 1972, two unconventional weapon systems with potential for mass destruction, those based on living organisms and toxins, were banned with the passage of the BWC. Three years later, ENMOD prohibited another unconventional weapon system whose military worth is uncertain—the use of environmental modification techniques for hostile purposes. In 1992 the CWC, which bans the development, manufacture, storage, and transfer of chemical weapons, was completed. The CWC, which in effect supersedes the Geneva Protocol, was signed by most of the world's states in early 1993 and is likely to come into force in 1994 (Drozdiak, 1993). The progression of treaties banning unconventional weapons is a promising, constructive trend of the post–Cold War era, but it is not the only one; new agreements are certain to be reached in the future that will eliminate one or another nuclear weapon system and that will decrease the number of nuclear weapons in existing arsenals. Next, perhaps, ballistic missiles and conventional weapon systems will be whittled away by special arms control treaties.

Concurrent to the process of controlling wars by limiting the means by which they can be pursued is an interesting and potentially destabilizing development: some weapon systems that in former times were deemed as unworkable or having limited military utility are resurging because scientific advances may be used to remove their shortcomings. Modern biotechnology, for example, may be turned to illicit purposes, to design, research, and develop biological and/or toxin weapons accessible to aggressive leaders of small countries or to terrorists (Zilinskas, 1990a; 1990b). New types of biological or toxin weapons could be developed tomorrow, or the day after, that would exhibit frighteningly powerful effects.

It can be seen that fate has played a cruel trick on security experts and arms control negotiators who followed that primary dictate of arms control—the more distant the applicability of a weapon system, the easier it is to eliminate. Because arms control negotiators perceived them to be experimental, inefficient, or unworkable, agreements to ban or curtail the development of weapons based on biologicals, toxins, and environmental-modification techniques were adopted without provisions for securing compliance, such as verification. As science advanced, and techniques were developed that can be applied to eliminate technical shortcomings that until now prevented them from having military utility, shortcomings inherent to treaties that address biologicals and toxins have become apparent (Zilinskas and Hedén, 1991). The problem of ensuring that countries are in compliance with the BWC is especially acute. In recognition of these problems, since 1986 international security experts have been laboring to strengthen the BWC, to the point where they are now trying to craft provisions for making certain that states are indeed adhering to it (Sims, 1991). For example, in April 1992 experts met in Geneva to consider the issue of how signatories of the BWC can verify that states are complying with its provisions without putting undue burdens on legitimate research and industrial activities. Much guidance in this regard will undoubtedly come from the operation of the newly developed CWC, which has strong provisions for verification (Trapp, 1991). However, apparently no initiatives to strengthen ENMOD are underway or planned.

The question may, of course, be raised whether one needs to worry about ENMOD and the efficiency of its operation. The techniques and weapons it was designed to prevent were distant possibilities in 1977 and seem almost as remote now. But is it possible, for example, that the equivalent of the biotechnology revolution might not occur in the environmental-modification field? If so, would the armed forces of some states be likely to take a second look, to assess whether advances may have military utility? While this possibility does not seem very likely from today's vantage point, revolutions in science periodically take place, and when they do, they tend to have unforeseeable consequences in the civilian and military spheres alike.

More likely, and therefore more threatening than unforeseen scientific advances, is that future wars will be fought over natural resources, rather than land, with the resources themselves potentially being used as weapons or being destroyed to deny them to the enemy. Most immediate is the possibility that a conflict over water resources will occur in the Middle East. The problem there, which now seems unsolvable, has two parts (Anonymous, 1992b). First, the underground water conifers supplying both Arab and Israeli lands are being depleted, and no means are available to resupply them adequately. Coterminously, the demand for water is growing as agriculture expands and populations grow. Second, governments of countries through which rivers flow are constructing dams and irrigation systems, thereby lessening the amount of water available to riparian states downriver. The latter, for understandable reasons, are protesting vigorously.

By denying water, one state may force another into submission, or provoke it to fight. The denial of water may become a military tactic; for example, the Jordan basin's water supply could be sabotaged relatively easily, by poison or explosion (Anderson, 1992). Since natural water resources indubitably are part of the environment, or its environmental processes, the problem of preventing environmental warfare will recur. If it does, the international community may face great difficulty in investigating allegations of ENMOD transgression. As demonstrated by the problem mentioned above of assessing the damage caused by the rainmaking program in Vietnam, the United Nations would find it a formidable, complicated task to mobilize a team having the scientific expertise required to investigate the suspicious events, to transport the team to the region where the alleged transgressions have occurred, to secure safe and adequate working conditions for the team in the field, to support the team for the long-term, and to access reliable baseline environmental and meteorological data.

States can also commit a crime against the environment by proxy. A number of terrorist organizations are supported by states, who may employ them to achieve political objectives. For example, much like Iraq's attacks on oil installations in Iran and Kuwait, a terrorist group supported by Iraq could be ordered to strike at oil platforms, tankers, and oil pipelines owned by a perceived enemy state to damage its environment and impair its economy. This *strategic environmental terrorism* (Kindt, 1993), would severely challenge the present international law regime for two reasons. First, only states are parties to treaties such as ENMOD and the Protocols of 1977, and only states are subject to their protection and prohibitions. An attack on the environment by terrorists would probably fall outside the purview of these treaties. Second, it probably would be very difficult to procure legally acceptable proof evidencing the responsibility of the state supporting the terrorists who perpetrated the attack against the environment. Without such proof, it would be impossible to prove that a state crime against the environment had been committed.

Whether a new development in military science, a resource conflict, or an occurrence of strategic environmental terrorism tests ENMOD matters little, since the treaty as it now stands is weak and therefore most likely would prove inadequate to meet the challenge. Clearly, ENMOD requires more effort to strengthen it than the international arms control community has given it so far, and this should be done before a possible violation tests it. The best and most immediate way to bring more attention to ENMOD and to begin the process of strengthening it is to establish a permanent CCE for ENMOD. A suggestion akin to this was made at ENMOD's second review conference, but was not acted on because several countries, including the United States, opposed the idea. Perhaps the main reason why the suggestion did not bear fruit was the vagueness of the proposal, which in part read, "in order to provide expert views relevant to clarifying the scope and application of the provisions of the convention" (United Nations, 1992b). This failing, however, could be corrected easily by giving the CCE a concrete first task—to consider whether Iraq violated ENMOD during the Gulf War. Although my analysis suggests that Iraq did not violate the treaty, ENMOD states may find otherwise. Alternatively, a CCE-led investigation could uncover new information about Iraq's intentions or capabilities that would change some important assumptions that underlie my assessment.

The importance of establishing the CCE transcends the necessity of appraising Iraq's actions. Even if the CCE concluded that Iraq's actions did not contravene ENMOD, the investigative process that led up to this conclusion could clarify alternative approaches for the international community to bring states that criminally assault the environment during war or other hostilities to justice, possibly through the mechanism of the Protocols of 1977. In addition, if not the CCE, by what mechanism will Iraq's crimes against the environment be adjudicated?[20] As it now stands Iraq's assault on the environment is likely to be disregarded or overlooked by the international community, much as what happened in the past when chemical weapons were used by Italy in Abyssinia, by Egypt in Yemen, and by Iraq against Iranian troops and Kurdish civilians. Inevitably, the unopposed breaking of international law not only invites disrespect for it, but it seems to favor a reoccurrence of the criminal act.

NOTES

*   The ideas and findings expressed in this chapter are the author's own and do not necessarily represent the viewpoint of the U.S. government or the U.S. Arms Control and Disarmament Agency.

1.   In this chapter the 1990–1991 conflict between Iraq and the coalition forces, comprising Desert Shield and Desert Storm, is called the Gulf War. This is in contradistinction to the 1980–1988 Iran–Iraq war, which some have named the Gulf War.

2.   The discussion and analysis that follows is limited largely to environmental considerations. Therefore, the horrendous human suffering that resulted from or accompanied the employment of various weapons is given only superficial coverage.

3.   The organization and duties of the CCE are set forth in an annex to the treaty.

4.   In general, a state indicates a willingness to observe a treaty by signing it. However, the state does not assume any of the treaty's legal obligations until its legislature has ratified or acceded to it. Therefore, Iraq is not a party to ENMOD and thus may choose to disregard its provisions. The state parties to ENMOD nevertheless could indict Iraq for its actions that may have contravened the objective and purpose of the treaty.

5.   Other techniques that some have termed environmental warfare were used by U.S. forces during the Vietnam conflict, such as spraying emulsifiers on asphalt roads to soften their surface or dispersing refractive chemicals from airplanes to confuse the enemy's radar. Not enough information is available on these activities to determine their effects on the environment.

6.   As far as I am aware, no scientist or professional organization has investigated the environmental consequences, if any, of these two programs.

7.   In addition to Ranch Hand, which was a U.S. Air Force program, U.S. and South Vietnamese ground forces used vehicle-mounted and hand-held sprayers to disperse large quantities of herbicides locally. Full information about ground-based defoliation operations remains to be published.

8.   Agent Blue's major constituent was sodium cacodylate; it contained over 15 percent arsenic. Agent Orange consisted of 2,4–dichlorophenoxyacetic acid and 2,4,5–trichlorophenoxyacetic acid.

Agent White's major ingredients were picloram and triiso-propanolamine salt of 2,4–dichlorophenoxyacetic acid. Small amounts of herbicides other than the "big three" were also employed in Vietnam, including "Green," "Pink," "Purple," and others. Some of these agents were not used in the field due to technical reasons, and others were strictly experimental.

9. After the Vietnam War ended several thousand service personnel who were exposed to Agent Orange claimed they suffered damage to their health as a result of either the agent itself, or a contaminant it contained—the extremely toxic chemical dioxin. It is beyond the scope of this chapter to consider whether these allegations have merit (see Cowan, 1993; Hanes, 1982; Jacobs and McNamara, 1986).

10. One hectare = 2.47 acres.

11. At the time of the Vietnamese conflict, South Vietnam was sectioned into four military regions by the U.S. high command, with the northernmost Military Region I bordering on North Vietnam and the southernmost Military Region IV encompassing the Mekong delta. Military Region III constituted the large, strategically important area north and east of South Vietnam's capital, Saigon.

12. Each seeding unit consisted of a 40-millimeter aluminum photoflash cartridge with primer and candle; when fired they produced silver iodide or lead iodide.

13. No independent confirmation of DIA's claim is possible, however, since meteorological baseline studies for the affected area are unavailable and war-time conditions precluded systematic attempts at the local level to measure precipitation and collect other meteorological data.

14. Vietnamese organizations and scientists may have studied the problem; if so, their findings are not readily available to analysts in the United States. The summation of effects found in this chapter therefore is based solely on Western sources.

15. Some may question whether "economic hardship" is part of ENMOD. On this matter, it is stated in the Understanding Regarding the Convention states that damage to "economic resources" is a factor when making a determination on how "severe" the damage to the environment (U.S. Arms Control and Disarmament Agency, 1990).

16. Iraq researchers have knowledge about pesticides, but this had no bearing on the Gulf War or its tactics.

17. UNSCOM inspections, according to the terms of UN Security Council Resolution 687, are carried out to discover Iraq's programs and facilities devoted to researching, developing and/or manufacturing

weapons of mass destruction and missile systems. I assume that if Iraq had a program devoted to environmental warfare, it would be discovered in the course of these inspections.

18. The reason why Iraq would seek to destroy Kuwait as a state probably stems from claims that previous Iraqi governments, as well as the present one, have made on territory that constitutes present-day Kuwait. In particular, Iraq has a what many international lawyers consider a strong claim for the greater part of the rich Ratga oil field, which is located just south of its border with Kuwait.

19. Unconventional weapons, as the designation suggests, are not usually part of nations' armories, nor have they been used with any frequency in past wars. Thus, in this century nuclear weapons were employed twice, chemical weapons were used in about ten conflicts, biological weapons were used several times by Japan during World War II, and an environmental weapon might have been used by the United States once in Vietnam.

20. Reportedly Kuwait will make a claim of $117 billion in compensation for losses from Iraq's occupation (Anonymous, 1993). This claim does not include lost oil revenues or destruction of oil installations. Neither does the claim have anything to do with the more general environmental damage to the Gulf's environment.

REFERENCES

Al-Shatti, A.K.S., and J.M. Harrington, eds. (1992) *The Environmental and Health Impact of the Kuwaiti Oil Fires. Proceedings of an International Symposium Held at the University of Birmingham, October 17, 1991.* University of Birmingham: Institute of Occupational Health.

Anderson, E. (1992) "Water Conflict in the Middle East—a New Initiative." *Jane's Intelligence Review* 4, 5: :227–230.

Anonymous (1975a) "Appendix. A Selection of Documents Mentioned in This Issue and Pertaining to War and the Environment." *Ambio* 4: 234–244.

Anonymous (1975b) "Convention on the Prohibition of the Development, Production and Stockpiling of Bacteriological (Biological) and Toxin Weapons and on Their Destruction, in U.S.

Department of State." *Treaties and International Agreements* Series No. 8062.

Anonymous (1991) Inferno: *The Legacy of Destruction in Kuwait*. Washington DC: U.S. Information Agency.

Anonymous (1992a) "Arab Experts See Water Shortage as National Security Issue." *Al-Watan Al-'Arabi* February 7: 26–28.

Anonymous (1992b) "Facts, Figures on Pollution in Gulf." *Al-Madinah* (Jeddah) August 16: 18.

Anonymous (1993) "Kuwait Makes Claim of $117 Billion." *Washington Times* December 5: 6.

Aziz, T. (1992) Address Given at the United Nations Conference on Environment and Development, Rio de Janeiro, Brazil, June 9.

Bakan, S., A. Chlond, U. Cubash, et al. (1991) "Climate Response to Smoke for the Burning Oil Wells in Kuwait." *Nature* 351: 367–371.

Barnaby, F. (1976) "Environmental Warfare." *Bulletin of the Atomic Scientists* 32: 37–43.

Brown, J.W. (1962) *Vegetational Spray Tests in South Vietnam*. Fort Detrick, MD: Biological Laboratories, U.S. Army Chemical Corps.

Browning, K.A., R.J. Allam, S.P. Ballard, et al. (1991) "Environmental Effects from Burning Oil Wells in Kuwait." *Nature* 351: 363–367.

Cecil, P.F. (1986) *Herbicidal Warfare: The Ranch Hand Project in Vietnam*. New York: Praeger.

Chandler, D.L. (1993) "Ecological Cost of Gulf War Documented." *Boston Globe* October 26: 16.

Committee on the Challenges of Modern Society (1991) *Pilot Study on Promotion of Environmental Awareness in the Armed Forces. Final Report*. Brussels, Belgium: North Atlantic Treaty Organization.

Committee on the Effects of Herbicides in Vietnam, National Research Council (1974) *The Effects of Herbicides in South Vietnam: Part A— Summary and Conclusions*. Washington, DC National Academy of Sciences.

Cowan, A.L. (1993) "Reopening of Defoliant Case Sought." *New York Times* November 30: D4.

Department of the Army (1971) *Tactical Employment of Herbicides*. FM 3–3.

Drozdiak, W. (1993) "Historic Treaty Bans Chemical Weapons." *Washington Post* January 14: A24.

Environmental Sciences Division, Kuwait Institute for Scientific Research (no date). *Kuwait's Ravaged Environment: A Global Issue.* Kuwait: Kuwait Institute for Scientific Research.

Fauteux, P. (1992) "The Gulf War, the ENMOD Convention and the Review Conference." *UNIDIR Newsletter* No. 18: 6–12.

Fyodorov, Y. (1987) *The Silent Death.* Moscow, USSR: Progress Publishers.

Goldblat, J. (1975) "The Prohibition of Environmental Warfare." *Ambio* 4: 186–190.

—— (1977) "The Environmental Warfare Convention: How Meaningful Is It?" *Ambio* 6: 216–221.

—— (1982) *Agreements for Arms Control: A Critical Survey.* London: Taylor & Francis Ltd.

——(1984) "The Environmental Modification Convention of 1977: An Analysis," in A.H. Westing (ed.), *Environmental Warfare: A Technical, Legal & Policy Appraisal.* London: Taylor & Francis, pp. 53–64.

Hanes, J.H. (1982) "Agent Orange Liability of Federal Contractors." *University of Toledo Law Review* 13, 4: 1271–1280.

Hedén, C.-G. (1992) "The Persian Gulf War: Implications for Biological Arms Control," in R.A. Zilinskas (ed.), *The Microbiologist and Biological Defense Research: Ethics, Politics and International Security,* pp. 1–9, Annals of the New York Academy of Sciences, Vol. 666.

Hobbs, P.V., and L.F. Radke (1992) "Airborne Studies of the Smoke from the Kuwait Oil Fires." *Science* 256: 987–991.

Hull, A. (1991) "The Role of Ballistic Missiles in Third World Defence Strategies." *Jane's Intelligence Review* 3, 10: 464–470.

Jacobs, J.B., and D. McNamara (1986) "Vietnam Veterans and the Agent Orange Controversy." *Armed Forces & Society* 12: 57–77.

Johnston, O. (1977) "Arms Talks Resume with Cautious Hint That Some Real Bargaining Has Begun." *Los Angeles Times* May 19: 5.

Johnstone, L.C. (1971) "Ecocide and the Geneva Protocol." *Foreign Affairs* 49: 711–720.

Joyce, C., and D. Charles (1991) "The Battle to Stop the Gulf from Choking." *New Scientist* 129: 20–21.

Juda, L. (1978) "Negotiating a Treaty on Environmental Modification Warfare: The Convention on Environmental Warfare and Its Impacts upon Arms Control Negotiations." *International Organization* 32, 4: 25–41.

Kindt, J.W. (1993) "Environmental Terrorism: A Strategic Assault on Public Order." *Sea Technology* 34, 2: 105.

Kuwait Environment Protection Council (1991) *State of the Environment Report: A Case Study of Iraqi Regime Crimes Against the Environment.*

Kuwait News Agency (1991) *The Mother of Crimes Against Kuwait in Pictures.* Kuwait.

League of Nations (1929) "Protocol for the Prohibition of the Use in War of Asphyxiating, Poisonous or Other Gases, and of Bacterial Methods of Warfare." *Treaty Series* 94 (2138).

Lee, T.F., J. Clark, and M. Thompson (1992) "Multispectral Image Enhancement Reveals Kuwaiti Oil Plumes." *Naval Research Reviews* 44, 2: 22–26.

Moodie, M. (1992) "Address Made to the Plenary Session of the Second Review Conference of ENMOD" (September 15). (Draft provided by the U.S. Arms Control and Disarmament Agency.)

Neier, A. (1992) "Laws Protecting Victims of Warfare." *Physicians for Human Rights Record* 5, 2: 7.

Neilands, J.B., G.H. Orians, E.W. Pfeiffer, A. Vennema, and A.H. Westing (1972) *Harvest of Death: Chemical Warfare in Vietnam and Cambodia.* New York: The Free Press.

Osborne, D.J. (1968) "Defoliation and Defoliants." *Nature* 219: 564–567.

Payne, K.B. (1992) "Defense Against Missile Proliferation." *Jane's Intelligence Review* 4, 5: 235–239.

Pearce, F. (1991) "Desert Fires Cast a Shadow over Asia." *New Scientist* 129, 30–31.

———, and S. Pain (1991) "Oil from Kuwaiti Wells Still Pouring into the Desert." *New Scientist* 132: 14.

Readman, J.W., S.W. Fowler, J.-P. Villeneuve, C. Cattini, B. Oregioni, and L.D. Mee (1992) "Oil and Combustion-product Contamination of the Gulf Marine Environment Following the War." *Nature* 358: 662–665.

Sagan, C. (1991) "Kuwait Fires and Nuclear Winter" (letter). *Science* 254: 1434.

Sandoz, Y. (1992) "Protection of the Environment in Time of War." *UNIDIR Newsletter* No. 18: 12–14.

Sheppard, C., and A. Price (1991) "Will Marine Life Survive the Gulf War?" *New Scientist* 129: 36–40.

Sims, N. (1991) "Achievements and Failure at the Third Review Conference." *Chemical Weapons Convention Bulletin* No. 14: 2–5.

Smith, R.J., and G. Frankel (1991) "Saddam's Nuclear-Weapons Dream: A Lingering Nightmare." *Washington Post* October 13: A1, A44.

Solf, W.A. (1986) "Protection of Civilians Against the Effects of Hostilities Under Customary International Law and Under Protocol I." *American University Journal of International Law and Policy* 1: 117–135.

Stockholm International Peace Research Institute (1975) *Delayed Toxic Effects of Chemical Warfare Agents.* Stockholm and New York: Almqvist & Wiksell International.

Taylhardat, A.R., and R.A. Zilinskas (1992) *The ICGEB and Agenda 21: Biotechnology at the United Nations Conference on Environment and Development.* Vienna, Austria: UNIDO document CRP. 4, February 19.

Trapp, R. (1991) "Applicable Verification Lessons from the Negotiations on the Chemical Weapons Convention," in S.J. Lundin (ed.), *Views on Possible Verification Measures for the Biological Weapons Convention.* New York: Oxford University Press, pp. 26–36.

Trooboff, P.D., ed. (1975) *Law and Responsibility in Warfare: The Vietnam Experience.* Chapel Hill: University of North Carolina Press.

United Nations, First Review Conference of the Convention on the Prohibition of Military and Any Other Hostile Use of Environmental Modification Techniques (1992a) "Final Declaration" (September 20, 1984). *UNIDIR Newsletter* No. 18: 19.

United Nations, Second Review Conference of the Convention on the Prohibition of Military and Any Other Hostile Use of Environmental Modification Techniques (1992b) "Final Declaration" (September 18, 1992). (Draft provided by the U.S. Arms Control and Disarmament Agency.)

United Nations General Assembly (1976) *Resolution adopted by the General Assembly. 31/72. Convention on the Prohibition of Military and Any Other Hostile Use of Environmental Modification Techniques.* A/RES/31/72.

United Nations General Assembly (1982) *Chemical and Bacteriological (Biological) Weapons. Letter Dated 20 May 1982 from the Permanent Representative of the Union of the Soviet Socialist Republics to the United Nations Addressed to the Secretary-General.* A/37/233.

United Nations Security Council (1991) *Report of a Mission on the Damage Sustained by the Infrastructure and Economy of Kuwait During Iraqi Occupation*. Document S/22535.

U.S. Arms Control and Disarmament Agency (1990) Arms Control and Disarmament Agreements: *Texts and Histories of the Negotiations*. Washington, DC: U.S. Arms Control and Disarmament Agency.

U.S. Congress, Office of Technology Assessment (1991) *Bioremediation for Marine Oil Spills*. Washington, DC: Office of Technology Assessment.

U.S. Congress, Senate Committee on Foreign Relations (1978) Environmental Modification Treaty. *Hearing Before the Committee on Foreign Relations, 95th Congress, Second Session, Held October 3, 1978*. Washington, DC: U.S. Government Printing Office.

U.S. Department of State (1982a) *Chemical Warfare in Southeast Asia and Afghanistan. Report to the Congress from Secretary of State Alexander M. Haig, Jr., March 22, 1982* (Special Report No. 98). Washington, DC: U.S. Department of State.

U.S. Department of State (1982b) Chemical Warfare in Southeast Asia and Afghanistan: *An Update. Report From Secretary of State George P. Shultz, November 1982 (Special Report No. 104)*. Washington, DC: U.S. Department of State.

Westing, A.H. (1975) "Environmental Consequences of the Second Indochina War: A Case Study." *Ambio* 4: 216–222.

Zilinskas, R.A. (1990a) "Biological Warfare and the Third World." *Politics and the Life Sciences* 9, 1: 59–76.

———(1990b) "Terrorism and Biological Weapons: Inevitable Alliance?" *Perspectives in Biology and Medicine* 34, 1: 44–72.

———, and C.G. Hedén (1991) "The Biological Weapons Convention: A Vehicle for International Co-operation," in S.J. Lundin (ed.), *Views on Possible Verification Measures for the Biological Weapons Convention*. New York: Oxford University Press, pp. 71–97.

International State-Sponsored Organizations to Control State Crime: The European Convention on Human Rights

Leon Hurwitz

Introduction

Although many societies provide domestic procedures to control state crime and illegal behavior, as described in other chapters in this book, more than a few situations exist in which individuals still believe their own government has violated their civil, political, and human rights, and the prescribed internal controls have not been able to adequately deal with the complaint. Most often, these situations involve human rights questions, but the individual is unable to secure redress from the state because the action of the government was judged to be entirely "legal" under domestic standards and thus permissible according to internal legislation.

Recognizing the inherent limitations of a country's internal controls and procedures, however impartial and effective they may be—even the classical Scandinavian ombudsman cannot, for example, investigate complaints directed at parliamentary decisions (Gellhorn, 1966)—some societies have progressed one step beyond these domestic mechanisms into the area of collective international guarantees against state crime. If, after all the internal procedures have been exhausted, the individual still believes that his or her rights have been violated by state action, the person can then "appeal" to a "higher authority"—a supranational institution.

This chapter discusses one of the best-known state-sponsored international organizations to control state crime: the European Commission on Human Rights and the European Court of Human Rights, created by the Council of Europe's European Convention on Human Rights. To be sure, a United Nations Commission on Human Rights exists, but it is not nearly as effective as the European process (Carey, 1970). The UN Commission may have lofty ideals and good intentions, but it has very little power or influence in protecting an individual from illegal state behavior (see Molina, this volume).

These supranational organizations, although dealing specifically with "human rights" and not with bureaucratic impoliteness or insensitivity like an ombudsman, nonetheless are an important and significant part of any discussion of controls over state "crime" and of the ability of an individual to press complaints against the state or to seek redress for alleged mistreatment. As discussed in this chapter, the European Court of Human Rights has in many instances placed a sovereign state in the position of defendant and has ruled that an individual has priority over the dubious concept of sovereign immunity (Anderson, 1978).

The European process has effective power and legitimacy, especially in relation to those Council of Europe states that have accepted the compulsory jurisdiction of the European Court. This chapter rests on the view that violations of human rights are most assuredly "crimes" and that physical violence is not a requirement to be classified as such. The argument will be made that the European Convention on Human Rights process represents a later developmental stage in the slow transformation of the nature of the relationship between the individual and the state. International state-sponsored organizations to control state crime—and, again, violations by the state of individual human rights *are* crimes—presents an extraterritorial jurisdiction and is slowly eroding national juridical self-sufficiency and sovereignty.

The European Convention on Human Rights

Background

The institutionalization of human rights protection in Europe can be traced to May 1948 when ten western European countries established the Congress of Europe, a rather loose organization in which areas of common concern could be discussed. The Congress of Europe met at The Hague with approximately 700 delegates and observers. It was to provide encouragement to the nascent European unification and cooperative process, and to offer recommendations on how to achieve such cooperation. The Congress of Europe received a report from the International Committee of the Movements for European Unity, and this report formed the basis of a very significant Congressional resolution.

The 1948 Congress of Europe's resolution, titled "A Message to Europeans," reviewed the evils of nationalism and then called upon the European countries to transfer some sovereignty to an international organization. Adopted at the final session, the resolution also contained the following statement: "We desire a charter of human rights guaranteeing liberty of thought, assembly and expression as well as the right to form a political opposition . . . [and] a Court of Justice with adequate sanctions for the implementation of this Charter."

The recommendations from the Congress of Europe at The Hague were then submitted to the newly established Consultative Council of the Brussels Treaty Organization and eventually led to the signing of the statute of the Council of Europe in May 1949. This 1949 Statute had a direct and immediate impact on the development of the European Convention on Human Rights. Article 1 of the Statute of the Council of Europe specified that one of the means by which the Council's aims were to be pursued would be "the maintenance and further realization of human rights and fundamental freedoms," and Article 3 placed the maintenance of human rights and respect for the rule of law as a condition of membership in the Council of Europe.[1]

Based in Strasbourg since 1949, the Council of Europe has grown from its original ten members to a current twenty-four European states.[2] The Council's major objectives are to achieve greater unity among its members, to increase economic and social progress, and to protect the principles of parliamentary democracy. The Council of Europe should not be confused with the European Community (EC). Each is a separate inter-governmental organization whose legal existence rests upon different treaties and texts; the 12 European Community countries all belong to the Council of Europe and the Council has an additional 12 members who are not currently within the EC framework. The Council of Europe is composed of a Council of Ministers,[3] a Committee of Permanent Representatives/Ministers' Deputies,[4] and a Parliamentary Assembly.[5]

The Council of Europe's major success has not been in the area of political integration; rather, it is within the domain of the harmonization across Europe of certain laws and standards and operating procedures. The Council has passed over 100 conventions or general agreements (some are yet to enter into force) on a wide range of issues. Some of these issues are in the domains of social welfare, migrant workers, youth and sport, the environment, and monuments and historical sites.[6]

The European Convention on Human Rights

The area of human rights protection was an important element in the 1948 Congress and the 1949 Statute of the Council of Europe. The Council strongly endorsed the protection of human rights at that time for two fundamental reasons. One stimulus was the then acute and dangerous ideological conflict between eastern and western Europe. Not only was European unity seen as a desirable goal in itself, but it was also a defensive strategy directed at the then very real Communist threat. It must be recalled that during the short space of time between the Congress of Europe at The Hague (May 1948) and the signing of the Statute of the Council of Europe (May 1949), several events occurred, including the Communist coup and seizure of power in Czechoslovakia, the beginning of the Greek civil war, and the Berlin blockade. It was in response to these overt actions that the

European nations felt the need to reassert their own ideological standards for the protection of individual human rights.

The second reason evolved more from the stream of historical consciousness than from the immediate political events. Europe had just emerged from the barbarism of the Holocaust, the utter absence of any concern whatsoever for individual human rights, and the protection of the individual from state actions. One of the first steps in the march toward a totalitarian system is the denial of individual rights, and it is difficult to reverse this process before it reaches an inevitable end point, as was demonstrated in Auschwitz and Treblinka.

Those Europeans who drafted, signed, and abided by the European Convention on Human Rights believed that if they specified in advance what basic human rights were to be protected and what governments could not do to individuals, the first step might not ever arise again. The envisaged protection of individual human rights involved the establishment of an international mechanism to monitor the protection of human rights, and if any state were to violate such rights, this international mechanism could then be put into operation to restore the rule of law and the protection of individuals. The European Convention did not meet these envisaged goals—no "monitoring" device and no means of automatic international intervention were created—although these goals were influential in the creation of the actual institutions and processes.

When the Council of Europe met for its inaugural session in August 1949, the Consultative Assembly placed on its agenda an item titled "Measures for the fulfillment of the declared aim of the Council of Europe, in accordance with Article 1 of the Statute, in regard to the maintenance and further realization of human rights and fundamental freedoms." The Council's Committee of Ministers was called upon to authorize the drafting of a convention to provide a collective European guarantee designed to secure the rights and freedoms contained in the Universal Declaration of Human Rights, adopted by the UN General Assembly in December 1948.[7]

General debate on the question began in August 1949, and the entire matter was referred to the Committee on Legal and Administrative Questions. Using the UN Universal Declaration of Human Rights as a basis for its own deliberations, the Committee identified a list of fundamental rights that it proposed as the content of this collective European guarantee. The Committee then proposed how this guarantee would be established and enforced. First, all members of the Council of Europe would commit themselves to respect the fundamental principles of democracy and to hold free elections at reasonable intervals, employing universal suffrage and secret ballots. It was, however, left to each state, subject to certain guidelines, to determine the rules and processes by which these guaranteed rights would be protected within its territory. Second, to implement this collective guarantee, the Committee proposed the establishment of a Commission and a Human Rights Court. These institutions would administer the guarantee and adjudicate alleged violations of the rights contained in the Convention.

A revised draft of the Convention was adopted by the Council's Committee of Ministers during its fifth session in August 1950. This text was, however, considerably weaker in two major areas compared to the original document proposed by the Committee on Legal and Administrative Matters. First, the revised draft made the rights of the individual conditional upon certain processes rather than as absolute, and second, the jurisdiction of the proposed court was made optional at the discretion of each state rather than as compulsory for any state that signed the convention. This revised draft was signed in Rome on November 4, 1950, and the European Convention on Human Rights entered into force on September 3, 1953. The rights and freedoms cited below are not, however, absolute; practically every article has its disclaimer, exception, exclusion, or condition. Be that as it may, the Convention is an honorable document that pays more than lip service to the rights of individuals and the protection of individuals from state behavior. Most of the described rights are in the nature of what governments "shall not do" to individuals, although, as mentioned above, these prohibitions are not absolute due to the presence of the exclusions and exceptions.

Citizens of those countries who have signed the Convention have their right to life protected by law, and no one shall be deprived of life intentionally except in the execution of a European Court decision (article 2); no one shall be subjected to torture or to inhuman or degrading treatment or punishment (article 3); no one shall be held in slavery or servitude or be required to perform forced or compulsory labor (article 4); everyone has the right to liberty and security of person, and anyone who is arrested shall be informed, in a language he or she understands, of any charge and is entitled to trial within a reasonable time (article 5); everyone charged with a criminal offense shall be presumed innocent until proved guilty and shall have the right to legal counsel or be given it free (article 6); states shall not enforce ex post facto laws (article 7);[8] everyone has the right to respect privacy and family life, home, and correspondence (article 8); everyone has the freedom of thought, conscience, religion, expression, and peaceful assembly (articles 9, 10, 11); everyone has the right to marry and to found a family (article 12); and article 14 reads that the above rights and freedoms shall be secured without discrimination on any ground such as sex, race, color, language, religion, political or other opinion, national or social origin, association with a national minority, property, birth, or other status.

Even the concept of sovereign immunity is restricted, for the Convention explicitly requires each country to have an avenue of redress available for its citizens to complain against the state. Article 13 states that everyone whose rights and freedoms are violated shall have an effective remedy before a national authority notwithstanding that the violation has been committed by persons acting in an official capacity. Article 13 thus strengthened the position of the individual in relation to his or her own government and, at least for Europe, was perhaps the final blow against sovereign immunity and recognized that the king and/or his agents could do wrong, and therefore, they were to be held accountable for their actions.

The original Convention had five protocols. The first protocol, "Enforcement of Certain Rights and Freedoms not included in Section I of the Convention," was signed in Paris on March 20, 1952, and became effective on May 18, 1954. These additional rights are that every person is entitled to the peaceful enjoyment of possessions (article 1); no person shall be denied the right to education (article 2); and the signatory states are required to hold free elections at reasonable intervals by secret ballot, under conditions that will insure the free expression of the opinion of the people in the choice of the legislature (article 3).

The fourth protocol, "Protecting Certain Additional Rights," was signed in Strasbourg on September 16, 1963, and became effective on May 2, 1968. These additional rights state that no one shall be deprived of liberty merely on the grounds of inability to fulfill a contractual obligation (article 1); everyone within the territory of a state shall have the right to liberty of movement and freedom to choose one's residence, and anyone shall be free to leave any country, including his or her own (article 2); and collective expulsion of aliens is prohibited (article 4).

The rights and freedoms contained in the Convention and the Protocols are, however, not absolute. The rights are most of the time qualified by statements such as "except in accordance with law and justified by the public interest in a democratic society" or "except when it is necessary in a democratic society in the interests of national security, public safety, or territorial integrity." Thus, if any individual wants to pursue a complaint under the terms of the Convention, he or she might be faced with the "national security" defense. But if such acts are not "justifiable by the public interest in a democratic society"—as some complaints clearly demonstrated—the state is indeed the defendant and is to be held accountable for its actions and treatment of the individual.

Institutions

To insure the observance of the rights contained in the Convention, two bodies were established: the European Commission on Human Rights and a European Court of Human Rights. These two institutions, along with the Council of

Europe's Committee of Ministers, compose the formal organizations. The Committee of Ministers was not created by the Convention but derives its existence from the Statute of the Council of Europe. The Committee, however, was given a substantial role to play in the protection of human rights, and the Committee is an integral part of the process. The Committee of Ministers is the basic executive organ or "governing board" of the Council of Europe. Each member of the Council has one seat and vote on the Committee, and thus some countries participate in the application of the Convention through this Committee of Ministers even though the country has not yet signed the Convention. The specific ministers are to be those for foreign affairs, although representatives may participate.

The Convention provides the actual powers of the Committee in relationship to the application of this collective guarantee of human rights. The Committee is responsible for electing members of the Commission from a list provided by the Council's Consultative Assembly. The Committee also has the responsibility to decide whether a violation of the Convention has occurred if a case, after being deemed admissible by the Commission, has not been settled by the Commission itself or referred to the European Court by the Commission. Sohn and Buergenthal (1973: 1100) believe this authority was granted to the Committee because the governments refused to establish a court whose jurisdiction would be compulsory, and the European Court itself did not come into existence until some time after the Convention became applicable. A decision by the Committee of Ministers is stated (article 32) to be binding on the signatory countries. Such a decision requires a two-thirds majority vote, but the Committee has, in the past, seldom agreed to censure one of its own number.

The Commission is the workhorse of the system, because it receives all complaints. The number of commissioners is equal to the number of states that have signed the Convention, and no two members can be nationals of the same state. Elected by the Committee of Ministers, members sit for six-year terms and can be reelected. Article 23 states that the commissioners shall sit in their individual capacity; thus they are to be independent of the Committee that elected them as well as their governments. The

Commission, which sits in Strasbourg, decides by majority vote, determines its own rules of procedure, and is funded by the Council of Europe.

As mentioned above, the original draft of the Convention envisaged the European Court as having compulsory jurisdiction, but this concept provoked strong opposition. The very idea of having such a body also brought about some opposition. Thus the jurisdiction of the Court was made optional. The Court could not be established formally until at least eight Convention signatories declared that they "recognize as compulsory *ipso facto* and without special agreement the jurisdiction of the Court in all matters concerning the interpretation and application of the Convention" (article 46). This requirement of eight was not attained until September 3, 1958—five years after the Convention entered in force and eight years after the signing of the document. Thus the activity that was done in applying the Convention from 1953 to late 1958 did not involve the Court.

The judges are elected for a nine-year term and can be reelected.[9] The Consultative Assembly of the Council of Europe elects the judges from a list of nominations submitted by the Council's members, and the number of jurists is equal to that of the members of the Council, but no two can be nationals of the same state. Thus two judges on the current European Court are nationals of states that have not ratified the Convention, and an additional four are nationals of states that have not accepted the compulsory jurisdiction of the Court itself.

The Convention is relatively silent on the degree of judicial independence the European Court possesses, although it appears that the judges act in their "individual capacity," and little criticism has arisen about the Court being only the outward extension of the various governments. The judges may be nominated by their governments, but the Consultative Assembly appoints them; the Court chooses its own president and vice president; it draws up its own rules and determines its own procedure; and in place of an annual salary, the judges receive a per diem fee. Thus the position is in reality part-time, and the judges are not dependent on the few pounds, francs, or marks they may receive. One would have to conclude that the Court and judges are "independent," and they have not hesitated to rule against a government when, in fact, a violation of the Convention occurred.

The full European Court does not usually hear the cases referred to it; the actual hearing is performed by a seven-judge chamber.[10] This chamber is chosen by lot before the case begins, except "there shall sit as an *ex officio* member of the Chamber the judge who is a national of any State party concerned" (article 43). Similar to the procedure with the U.S. Supreme Court, a majority vote is required, with an allowance for concurring and/or dissenting opinions. No appeal from the European Court's decision is permitted—it is final—and it is the responsibility of the Committee of Ministers to supervise the execution of the Court's decisions. The Court also sits in Strasbourg and is funded by the Council of Europe.

Procedures

The formal procedures employed in the handling and disposal of a complaint filed under the Convention are relatively straightforward, although they do not readily lend themselves to speedy decisions, and a petitioner must overcome several obstacles before the merits of the complaint can actually be argued. Since the Convention makes the Commission the "gatekeeper," or the primary decision-making unit, in the process, the Commission is thus the "workhorse" of the system and is the recipient of all complaints and petitions. Petitions cannot be submitted directly to the Committee of Ministers and/or the European Court. Any person, nongovernmental organization, or group of individuals who allege to have been a victim of a violation are entitled to submit a petition. However, this applies only to alleged violations by member countries of the Convention; it does not apply to the Council of Europe's entire membership. Article 24 of the Convention entitles any signatory government to complain about a violation of the Convention by any other signatory government. Governmental complaints are not as numerous as individual complaints, but because of their nature, they receive far greater publicity and media coverage than individual petitions.[11]

Summary figures through 1991 show that approximately 14,160 complaints and petitions had been filed with the Commission since its establishment. However, only 560, or 4.0 percent were judged "admissible" by the Commission. The Commission thus routinely rejects 96 percent of all the petitions it receives. The grounds for mandatory inadmissibility are numerous. As mentioned above, Article 25 requires that the accused government must be a signatory of the Convention. This article also requires that the signatory government against whom the complaint is lodged "recognize the competence of the Commission to receive such petitions." Thus no complaints by individuals can be received by the Commission if they are directed against one of the four states that have yet to allow such individual petitions (viz., Cyprus, Malta, Turkey, and Hungary). However, those countries that do recognize the Commission's competence in receiving individuals' petitions have the added obligation of not "hindering in any way the effective exercise" of this right of petition. One application of this right is that, even though certain countries maintain some censorship over prison inmates' correspondence, a request to the Commission must be forwarded by the prison administration.

Article 26 specifically mandates as inadmissible any petition that has not progressed through all domestic avenues of redress or review. This means that any individual who believes his or her rights as contained in the Convention have been violated must have exhausted all avenues of review and appeal within the state itself before turning to the Commission for relief. The Commission is thus not perceived to be a parallel structure for the redress of grievances, but, rather, the state itself, through whatever process it makes available, is a prior independent process of review that has to run its entire course before the Commission can be involved. Article 26 does require, however, that a petition must be submitted to the Commission within six months from the date on which the final domestic decision was taken.

Article 27 mandates as inadmissible any petition that is anonymous or that is substantially the same as a matter previously examined by the Commission. This exclusion of "previously examined" questions can include those that have been ruled either admissible or inadmissible. Thus, for an individual who submits a petition claiming a violation of the Convention, if a similar case in the past were accepted and a decision reached against a state, this petition would be ruled inadmissible and the individual could not rely upon the Commission for redress. In such situations, the individual either does not receive redress or, depending upon the way Commission and European Court decisions are seen to be part of domestic legislation—a question dealt with below—is dependent upon the goodwill of the national government to once again review its actions in light of Court decisions. Article 27 also categorizes as inadmissible a petition that has already been submitted to another international procedure of settlement, but only if the petition contains no relevant new information. If a petition does contain "relevant new information," the fact that it was previously submitted to a different international review process will not automatically render it inadmissible. The above grounds for inadmissibility may be broad, but at least they are precisely stated and they have meaning. However, Article 27 also contains some vague and undefined grounds for mandatory inadmissibility, which can be regarded as a political obstacle. These additional obstacles read that the Commission shall view as inadmissible any petition that it considers "incompatible with the provisions of the Convention, manifestly ill-founded, or an abuse of the right of petition." However, a petition that in reality meets the requirements of Articles 25, 26, and 27(1) cannot be "manifestly ill-founded" or an "abuse of the right of petition." Be that as it may, for the above reasons (and, perhaps, for unstated reasons), the Commission routinely rejects as inadmissible approximately 23 of 24 petitions received.

The Commission as gatekeeper thus has a very small opening through which petitions must squeeze. What is the next stage in the process, once the eye of the needle has been successfully negotiated? The first goal of the Commission, after accepting a petition and ruling it admissible, is to appoint a seven-person sub-Commission (each of the parties involved in the complaint can appoint someone of their own choice to this sub-Commission) to investigate the "facts" and to attempt to reach a "friendly settlement." With our figures above, of the 560 petitions ruled admissible, 460 were resolved at this stage through a "friendly settlement." The friendly settlement, however, must be based on "respect for human rights" as defined in the Convention.

However, in the remaining 100 cases, the Commission was unable to use its good offices to reach a "friendly settlement." The entire Commission had an important option: it could submit the unresolved dispute either to the Committee of Ministers *or* to the European Court. [12] Of these 100, the Commission referred 36 cases to the Committee and 64 to the Court. When sent to the former, a decision about whether the Convention was violated is made by a two-thirds vote of the entire Committee. If a violation is deemed to have occurred, the Committee of Ministers prescribes what has to be done by the state. The signatory states to the Convention have "undertaken to regard as binding on them any decision" of the Committee, although the Convention recognizes that this may not be automatic. If the "guilty" state does not take the prescribed measures, the Committee may meet again to decide how to effect its original decision, and publicity is one of the methods mentioned in the Convention. The Committee is hesitant, however, to censure one of its own members, and a "friendly settlement" is usually attained at this stage in the process.

Our figures leave 64 petitions that were neither resolved at the Commission level nor referred to the Committee. The individual petitioner does not bring the case to the European Court, but, rather, it is the Commission or the signatory state against which the complaint is lodged. Once a case leaves the Commission—either referred to the Committee or the Court—it cannot be withdrawn by the individual petitioner and/or the signatory state. The arguments—oral and written—are presented to the Court from each party in the dispute, and it is the Commission that usually acts as the "prosecuting attorney," and the state is the "defendant." The Court's decision is sent to the Committee of Ministers, which supervises the execution of any decision. No situation has yet occurred where a state has refused to abide by the Court's decision, although only a few of the cases that did reach the Court ruled against the state. Be that as it may, the state is certainly a "defendant" in the Court, and it is held liable for its behavior.

Illustrative Selected Cases

The European Court's caseload has increased remarkably over the years. This is primarily a result of the Commission ruling more petitions as admissible and, if unable to achieve a "friendly settlement," choosing the option of referring the case to the Court rather than to the Committee of Ministers. The Commission is choosing the Court over the Committee because as Marc-Andre Eissen, a former registrar of the Commission, said: "The Commission and the governments both feel these days that alleged human rights violations should be judged by the Strasbourg Court and not by politicians." Another factor in this increased activity is the rising salience that human rights enjoys; the protection of human rights has been elevated to a meaningful international level, and more people have become aware of the Convention and the Commission. In the 1990s, the Commission and especially the Court are much more active than previously.

Denmark, Norway, Sweden, and the Netherlands Versus Greece (1967)

Governments themselves have the right to submit complaints to the Commission. Article 24 of the Convention entitles any signatory country to complain about a violation of the Convention by any other signatory government. Government complaints are not as numerous as individual complaints, but because of their very nature, they receive far greater publicity and media coverage than individual petitions. One of the best known of these governmental complaints was *Denmark, Norway, Sweden, and the Netherlands v. Greece* filed in September 1967. This case concerned the situation in Greece after the April 1967 military coup d'état.

In May 1967, one month after the coup d'état, the Greek representative to the Council of Europe stated that the new Greek government was invoking Article 15 of the Convention and, by so doing, was suspending various human rights protection clauses in the Greek constitution. Article 15 of the Convention is the "escape clause," if a government is faced with internal dangers threatening public order and the security of the state.[13]

In September 1967, the governments of Denmark, Norway, and Sweden (joined by the Netherlands in October of that same year), filed a formal complaint with the Commission claiming that the Greek government had failed to justify its claim that Article 15 was necessary and, therefore, the actions of the Greek junta violated several articles of the Convention (e.g., arrest and detention; fair trial; right to privacy; and freedom of thought, expression, and peaceful assembly). The Greek government, in its response to the Commission's process of determining the admissibility of the complaint, argued that it was the prerogative of the government involved to determine whether or not the political situation in the country justified invoking Article 15 and to determine the appropriate measures to deal with the situation.

The Commission refused to accept the Greek position that only the government involved could determine the existence of a "public emergency threatening the life of the nation." The Commission's position was that an "uncontrolled" power of decision to declare a national emergency would make it possible for any government to do such at any time for the most tenuous reasons and the collective guarantee of the Convention would therefore be rendered useless just at the precise time it was needed most. The Commission did not reach this position with the Greek case, it was announced in 1956:

> The Commission . . . has the competence and the duty under Article 15 to examine and pronounce upon a Government's determination of the existence of a public emergency threatening the life of the nation for the purpose of . . . Article [15]; but some discretion and some margin of appreciation must be allowed to a Government in determining whether there exists a public emergency which threatens the life of the nation and which must be

dealt with by exceptional measures derogating from its normal obligations under the Convention.[14]

Once the Commission had decided that it would not accept the Greek claim prima facie, it had to determine whether or not a bona fide "public emergency" did exist; if it did, the Greek government obviously would have had greater legitimacy for its actions and would have undermined the complaint by Denmark, Norway, Sweden, and the Netherlands.

In January 1968, the Commission announced that the complaint was admissible and that there was "probable cause" for further investigation. This decision was based on the Commission's view that invoking Article 15 was not justified. The Commission applied a fourfold test to the Greek claim and found it wanting because:

1. the public emergency must be actual or imminent;
2. its effects must involve the whole nation;
3. the continuance of the organized life of the community must be threatened; and
4. the crisis or danger must be exceptional, in that the normal measures permitted by the Convention for the maintenance of public safety, health, and order are plainly inadequate.

The Commission then embarked on an eighteen-month investigation, which took place both in Strasbourg and at various locations in Greece (with a very mixed level of cooperation from the Greek government). A substantial part of the Commission's report dealt with allegations of torture and mistreatment of political prisoners. The Greek government was given every opportunity to refute the allegations, and the Commission was very careful to examine whether or not the allegations of torture were deliberate falsehoods in order to discredit the Greek government. The Commission found that it

> . . . cannot ignore the sheer number of complaints. The International Red Cross reported that, at one stage, out of 131 prisoners, forty-six complained of torture or ill-treatment, and it apparently later investigated certain further torture allegations, but the respondent Government has failed to submit the report on those

investigations. In the present proceedings allegations have been made concerning the treatment of 213 named detainees; thirty of these cases had been examined to some substantial degree before the proceedings were terminated following the respondent Government's refusal to make possible the hearing of a number of further witnesses detained in Greece.

Since the Commission considers that in eleven of the cases which were examined torture or ill-treatment has been established and that in seventeen others there is at least some evidence corroborating the Complaint, it is not able to reject the whole as a conspiracy by Communist and anti-Government groups to discredit the Government and the police. It cannot but regard the actual number of complaints brought before it as strong indication that acts of torture or ill-treatment are not isolated or exceptional, nor limited to one place. (*Yearbook*, 1969: 502)

The Commission announced its findings in November 1969: (1) there was not a "public emergency" in Greece and thus the derogations under Article 15 were invalid; (2) there was a practice of torture and mistreatment by the Greek security forces of people arrested for political reasons; (3) the Greek government had failed to investigate and/or remedy (1) and (2) above; and (4) Articles 5, 6, 8, 9, 10, 11, 13, and 14 of the Convention were also violated. These conclusions were then given to the Committee of Ministers and were duly endorsed. The Consultative Assembly of the Council of Europe had, in the meantime, passed a resolution that recommended that Greece be suspended from Council membership. In December 1969, while the Committee of Ministers was debating both the nature of sanctions to be applied to Greece for the violations and the recommendation of the Assembly to expel Greece from membership, the Permanent Representative of Greece to the Council of Europe informed the Council that the country, (1) denounced the European Convention on Human Rights, (2) denounced the Statute of the Council of Europe, and (3) was withdrawing from all further deliberations of the Council and its subsidiary agencies.[15]

The Convention and the decisions of the Commission and Assembly may have brought unwanted publicity to the military junta, but it had little real influence on the protection of human rights in Greece under the Papadopoulos regime. One would be hard put to argue that the process in Strasbourg by the Commission and the Committee of Ministers had any linkage to the eventual restoration of democratic government and civil liberties in Greece.

Ireland Versus the United Kingdom (1971)

One of the most bitterly contested, longest, and politically explosive cases decided by the European Court was another interstate complaint, *Ireland v. United Kingdom*. The Irish petition to the Commission was formally submitted in December 1971, but the process was not completed until January 1978, when the Court announced its decision. This time period witnessed investigations, recriminations, hostile international propaganda, secret rendezvous, charges of obstructing justice and countercharges, and a chilled relationship between Ireland and the United Kingdom. Although the Irish petition contained a series of charges and demands, the most important and significant component of the Irish petition was the allegation that the British security forces in Northern Ireland "tortured" suspected Irish Republican Army (IRA) internees.

The major issue concerned the methods employed by the British security forces in the "interrogation" of suspected IRA internees. These methods were termed "sensory-deprivation" (prolonged wall standing, loud noises, hooding, and deprivation of food, water, and sleep), and they were designed to elicit desired information from the internees.[16] The interrogations involved fourteen internees at an undisclosed security facility somewhere in Northern Ireland in August and October 1971. The British government did not deny the application of such methods, and thus one of the major issues was not whether these occurred, but, rather, whether such behavior and additional actions by the British government constituted a violation of the European Convention.

The 1971 Irish petition to the Commission contained allegations of several other Convention violations, as well as demands that the British government take further action to "atone" for or rectify such violations. The Irish government charged that the "sensory-deprivation" techniques violated Article 3 (no one shall be subjected to torture or to inhuman or degrading treatment or punishment); that such treatment was a formal administrative policy of the British that was applied beyond the documented fourteen individual cases; that the British practice of interning IRA suspects violated Article 5 (detainees are entitled to a trial within a reasonable time or to be released on bail); that Article 50 should be invoked ("just satisfaction" or compensation to the injured party); and, not least, that the British government prosecute those people responsible for the actual violations (the police and security forces) *and* those responsible for the decision to violate the Convention (the politicians themselves, starting with the British prime minister). These were indeed serious allegations and demands, particularly since most of the "facts" were not in dispute (the British *were* interning people and they *were* practicing "sensory deprivation" on at least fourteen individuals).

The Commission ruled the petition admissible in 1972, but did not announce its findings until 1977. The investigation of the charges was long and costly for both sides and contained elements of B-grade espionage novels with a secret rendezvous and unidentified witnesses. Approximately 120 witnesses appeared before the Commission, and their testimony ran to 4,500 "closely typed" pages.[17] Some members of the Commission accused the British government of deliberately obstructing the investigation to minimize adverse publicity. Such a charge arose out of Britain's initial refusal to allow members of its security forces to appear as witnesses.[18] Several three-sided meetings (Ireland, the United Kingdom, and the Commission) were held, both publicly and privately, and the controversy dominated and chilled Irish–British relations.

As usual, the Commission attempted to achieve a "friendly settlement" between the two parties, and, for a while, it appeared that a settlement could be reached because Great Britain "confessed." The British government admitted fault, stopped the practice of sensory deprivation, gave assurances that it would not be resumed, and made compensation of up to

£25,000 to those subjected to the special interrogation techniques. But the Irish government was not prepared to negotiate a "friendly settlement," although the Commission, in no uncertain terms, labeled the sensory-deprivation techniques as torture, and, moreover, the British government did *not* contest the Commission's finding (in a sense, the British government pleaded "guilty" to the charge of "torture"). The Commission thus finally ruled in favor of Ireland, and the controversy might have ended at this point if Ireland had accepted the "friendly settlement." But Ireland did not, and an editorial from *The London Times* (January 19, 1978: 17) commented on the British perception and interpretation of the Irish government's decision:

> It was difficult to avoid the supposition that the Irish Government (it was not Mr. Lynch's but its predecessor) persisted for domestic political reasons and in order to maximize a propaganda advantage over Britain. The reasons which it published or supplied were of course higher sounding: the implication of the case for the security of human rights were of an order that *called for the authoritative judgment of a Court over and above the findings of a Commission;* and there were other claims arising out of the proceedings with which it did not succeed before the Commission and which it wished to pursue before the Court in the name of justice.

Accordingly, the Irish government made use of its prerogative under the Convention and appealed the case to the European Court. The Court received written and oral arguments in 1977, and the Irish position basically was identical to its original petition and arguments before the Commission. The British government, however, did not contest the Commission's finding of "torture" in front of the Court, although, since the Irish argued that it was torture, the British government did defend itself at the hearing. The Court announced its verdict in an eighty-three-page decision on January 18, 1978. The Court's decision, given what had been decided previously and given that Great Britain really did not contest the Commission's findings but, rather, had admitted the offense and had compensated the victims, came as a surprise to the Irish and British governments.

The European Court, either unanimously or by an overwhelming majority, *rejected* all but one of the Irish claims and demands. The sole allegation upheld by the Court was that "sensory deprivation" was inhuman and degrading treatment, *not* torture, and Great Britain was "cleared" of all other charges. The initial reaction of the Irish government was muted disappointment, while the British government and its elite press were pleased at the Irish government's embarrassment and loss of prestige. To Britain's satisfaction, the Court unanimously ruled that, although certain violations were not contested (the unanimous finding of the Commission that the administrative practice of sensory deprivation did indeed constitute "torture"), the Court nonetheless should rule on the merits of such posited violations. This meant the Court would reopen the question of whether sensory deprivation was, in fact, torture, although Ireland, the United Kingdom, and the Commission all previously accepted it as such.[19] The Court thus examined the issue of torture and by a vote of thirteen to four found that "sensory deprivation" did not constitute torture, but it did, by a vote of sixteen to one, find that it constituted a practice of inhuman and degrading treatment and, therefore, was a violation of Article 3.

Majority opinion held (by a vote of thirteen to four), in rejecting the allegation of torture, that the techniques of sensory deprivation did not cause "suffering of the particular intensity and cruelty implied by the word 'torture.'" The practice was, however, by a vote of sixteen to one, judged to be "inhuman" treatment and thus a violation of Article 3. It was the British judge who dissented from the "inhuman" treatment decision; for this judge, sensory-deprivation techniques were not inhuman or degrading. The majority view on the torture issue apparently was that "torture" is reserved for acts such as having electrical shocks applied to one's genitals or having one's fingernails torn out one at a time; being forced to stand against a wall for twenty-four hours was, in the Court's view, essentially something else— something unpleasant and "inhuman" but definitely not "torture."

Such reasoning was immediately accepted and praised by the jubilant British government and the press. In a lead editorial titled "A Dispassionate Judgment," the usually staid *London*

Times rushed to endorse the view that "torture" could only take place under the Spanish Inquisition in some dark, smelly dungeon or by the SS in Auschwitz; if such activity were done at other times by other methods, it could not be torture. The *Times* (January 19, 1978: 17) editorial neatly made this distinction, and it reflected the Court's opinion:

> 'Torture' never was the right word for the treatment. . . . 'Torture' is an ultimate word. It denotes those practices, like the rack, electric shock, beating to the point of surrender, the purpose of which is to inflict such pain that terror of its continuation or repetition breaks the victim's will to resist interrogation.
>
> That is not the purpose of . . . sensory deprivation. . . . The purpose is to induce a state of temporary disorientation and distraction of the will in which the victim may be more easily led by his interrogator. *It induces stress, it inflicts pain, its effects may not wholly disappear when the pressure is lifted . . . but it is less than torture*, and it is a good thing the Court . . . has said so.

Four judges dissented from this verbal legerdemain: the Austrian, Greek, Cypriot, and, not surprisingly, the Irish judge. In a separate opinion against the majority view, Philip O'Donoghue, the Irish judge, stated: "One is not bound to regard torture as only present in a medieval dungeon where the appliance of rack and thumbscrew, or similar devices were employed. Indeed, in the present-day world, there can be little doubt that torture may be inflicted in the mental sphere."

Sensory deprivation may indeed not be torture like that of the Gestapo or the Inquisition, but Judge O'Donoghue viewed torture also could be mental or psychological. Raised to new heights in the second half of the twentieth century, brainwashing and other psychological techniques have, in the main, replaced the rather crude rack or portable electrodes. Such practices induce stress, inflict pain, and do not always disappear when the pressure is lifted, and with these practices the will is distracted. Great pain can be deliberately inflicted to the mind, and it is unfortunate that the Court refused to look beyond the thumbscrew and, in the words of the Northern Ireland Civil Rights Association, refused "to call a spade a spade." Britain could no longer be accused of *torturing* the internees—a term that is headline material—but only for engaging in the more acceptable and less interesting practice of "inhuman" and "degrading" treatment.

The Irish government was understandably surprised and disappointed with the European Court's decision, especially since the Commission previously ruled by a unanimous vote on the torture issue and since Great Britain did not contest the Commission's ruling. The official Irish position, however, was that its view was indeed upheld, since the practices in question *were* a violation of Article 3 (inhuman treatment). The Court's verdict was a very hollow "victory" for Ireland.[20]

All of the other allegations and demands in the Irish petition were rejected by the European Court, each by an overwhelming majority. The Court ruled that it was not established that the practice in question (sensory deprivation) continued beyond the autumn of 1971, nor was it proven that other ill treatment occurred at the unidentified interrogation centers. By a unanimous decision, the Court ruled that it could not direct Great Britain to institute judicial proceedings against those security personnel who actually administered the sensory deprivation or against those who "tolerated" the practice (for example, the British politicians). Thus, although Britain was "guilty" of inhuman treatment, the Court declined to press for any punishment of those who committed the violations. The Court also ruled unanimously that Article 50 (just payments to the victims) was not to be applied, and whatever compensation Great Britain might have offered in the past was sufficient. Ireland also alleged a violation of Article 14 (religious discrimination), since most of the people interned by the British were Roman Catholics. The Court simply ruled (fifteen to two) that no such discrimination existed. Finally, it was the unanimous decision that whatever measures Britain applied (excepting sensory deprivation) in Northern Ireland, especially the practice of interning suspected IRA sympathizers, were not in violation of Articles 5 and 6. The Court cited Article 15 as Britain's justification for the activities. Article 15 is the escape clause: in time of public emergency threatening the life of a nation, measures derogating from the Convention to the extent required by the situation are permissible. The Court, including even the Irish judge, ruled that, indeed, a public emergency existed, and the measures taken by Great Britain were required by the situation.

But what can be said about the protection of an individual's rights vis-à-vis state behavior after a reading of the Irish–British case? The existence of the Commission and the European Court obviously did not help the fourteen people subjected to sensory deprivation, except, perhaps, international publicity was given to their experience, and Britain was chastised for its behavior. The British government gave its assurance that the practice will not be repeated, and no reason can be found to doubt the government's promise. But other European countries may face a public emergency threatening the existence of their country to, of course, a less immediate degree than the British in Northern Ireland. These governments might be more hesitant to employ techniques such as sensory deprivation, knowing full well that it has been condemned as inhuman treatment and, as well, is a violation of the Convention. The impact of the British case was more to prevent future occurrences than to punish past behaviors.

Conclusions

Avoiding spectacular or dramatic actions, the Court's process has influenced the relationship of the individual vis-à-vis the state, provided an additional means to control state crime against its population, and enshrined the principle that the state is indeed responsible and accountable for its actions. The European Convention was the first real collective international agreement giving specific legal content and protection to the individual in relation to one's government as well as establishing the necessary machinery for its supervision and enforcement. This European system may very well serve as a model for other geographical groupings of states that want to set up a similar process.

The European system has strengthened the position of the individual by clearly requiring the establishment of domestic avenues to adjudicate individual complaints against state mistreatment. Article 13 of the Convention clearly rejects the notion that official acts are immune from accountability (everyone should have "an effective remedy before a national authority notwithstanding that the violation has been committed by persons acting in an official capacity"), and this alone would be a significant and important contribution.

In addition, Article 57 authorizes the secretary-general of the Council of Europe to receive an explanation of how the internal domestic law of any signatory state "ensures the effective implementation" of the Convention. The Convention and its institutions thus may question domestic law, uncover those segments of domestic law that are possibly in violation of the Convention, and prevent further so-called state crimes. The anomalies in domestic law regarding human rights are being "exposed," and national legislation has been amended in light of the Court's decisions. The Court, as long as the governments continue to recognize its jurisdiction and accept its decisions as legitimate, will insure that national legislation is coherent with the provisions of the Convention. The Commission itself has an important function. The process of a "friendly settlement" serves to mediate conflict and, rather than having the punishment of past behavior as the main—or only—objective, attempts to prevent future occurrences. This low-key and muted conflict-management process serves the individual well and can protect individuals from governmental mistreatment.

But the above comments are not to be interpreted as saying no problems or shortcomings exist with the European Convention process. The formal proceedings are, to say the least, ponderous and time-consuming. Several years usually elapse between the original filing of a complaint and the final decision. Part of the problem stems from the necessity of treating each stage of the process as a "new" situation; oral and written arguments are presented on the complaint's admissibility and are repeated in front of both the Commission and the European Court. Recent attempts to streamline and therefore shorten the process have been made, but the unduly lengthy bureaucratic procedure does not serve the individual's best interest.

The most serious shortcoming is that protected rights are not absolute; that is, ample leeway exists for states to violate the Convention and not be held accountable for their actions. Article 15 can be invoked (successfully in the *Ireland v. United Kingdom* case, unsuccessfully in the *Denmark, Norway, Sweden, and the Netherlands v. Greece* case) as a justifiable defense to what would otherwise be a clear violation of the Convention. Article 15 allows the states, in time of war or other public emergency threatening the life of the nation, to take measures derogating from its obligations under the Convention. It is, however, *precisely* during such "public emergencies" that individuals need added protection from state mistreatment rather than allowing the state to do as it sees fit. If the "exigencies" of the situation justify the need for a "national emergency," the mistreatment of individuals can then be justified by the vague notion of a "public emergency" (e.g., the internment camps for the Japanese in the United States during World War II).

In conclusion, the European Convention on Human Rights process represents a later development in the nature of the relationship between an individual and the state's apparatus. The Commission and Court of Human Rights injects an extraterritorial jurisdiction and is slowly eroding national juridical self-sufficiency. Such international collective guarantee to control state crime, while not foolproof (short of an armed intervention, the Council of Europe had very little ability to influence the behavior of the Greek colonels), can nonetheless reduce the incidence of such behavior.

NOTES

1. Article 3 of the Statute of the Council of Europe reads, inter alia: "Every member of the Council of Europe must accept the principles of the rule of the law and of the enjoyment of all persons within its jurisdiction of human rights and fundamental freedoms, and collaborate sincerely and effectively in [their] realization."

2. The current members of the Council of Europe are Austria, Belgium, Cyprus, Denmark, Finland, France, Germany, Greece, Hungary, Iceland, Ireland, Italy, Liechtenstein, Luxembourg, Malta, The Netherlands, Norway, Portugal, San Marino, Spain, Sweden, Switzerland, Turkey, and the United Kingdom. Czechoslovakia and Poland applied for full membership in 1990, and Bulgaria and Romania declared their intention to apply. Former Yugoslavia also applied for full membership in 1990, but its application is in abeyance.

3. The Council of Ministers consists of the foreign ministers from each of the twenty-four members. The Council is the formal decision-making unit within the framework and can make various recommendations to the member governments; it also must approve any of the conventions passed before putting them before the member governments for ratification. The Council of Ministers meets about twice a year (usually in May and December) for a short period.

4. This Committee consists of twenty-four senior diplomats (one from each member government) who are accredited to the Council of Europe. These diplomats deal with the routine matters at monthly meetings and prepare for the Council of Ministers' meetings, and any decision taken by this group has the same binding effect as those taken by the Council of Ministers.

5. The Assembly has 183 members, distributed as follows: France, Germany, Italy, and the United Kingdom—18 each; Spain and Turkey—12 each; Belgium, Greece, the Netherlands, and Portugal—7 each; Austria, Hungary, Sweden, and Switzerland—6 each; Denmark, Finland, and Norway—5 each; Ireland—4; Cyprus, Iceland, Luxembourg, and Malta—3 each; Liechtenstein and San Marino—2 each. Israel has permanent "observer" status in the Parliamentary Assembly and Bulgaria, Czechoslovakia, and Poland have "guest" status. The former USSR and former Yugoslavia also had "guest" status, but these linkages are now open to question. Albania was an "observer" in 1990 and 1991. The members of the Assembly are appointed by and from their own national parliaments according to the strength of each national political party; there are currently five major transnational party groupings represented (Socialist, Christian Democrat, European Democrat [Conservative], Liberal, and Communist). The Assembly meets several times a year in Strasbourg, and it is basically a consultative body without any real legislative powers, although it does elect several Council officials, including the judges who sit on the European Court of Human Rights. There are fourteen standing Committees: political, economic and development, social and health, legal, culture and education, science and technology, regional planning

and local authorities, rules of procedure, agriculture, relations with non-member European countries, parliamentary and public relations, migration, refugees and demography, and budget.

6. Some of the Conventions passed by the Council of Europe include European Social Charter, European Code of Social Security, Convention on the Elaboration of a European Pharmacopoeia, Convention on the Legal Status of Migrants, and the Convention on the Conservation of European Wildlife and Natural Habitats.

7. The UN Universal Declaration of Human Rights proclaimed all human beings "free and equal in dignity and rights." Invoking many inalienable rights and consisting of some thirty articles, the Declaration emphasized the right to life, liberty, security, nationality, property ownership; freedom of thought, conscience, religion; freedom from arbitrary arrest, detention, exile; freedom of movement, residence, and freedom of peaceful assembly and association. Although an admirable document, the Declaration's practical effect in protecting human rights has been minimal at best and nonexistent at worst.

8. Although article 7(1) prohibits ex post facto legislation, article 7(2) reads that 7(1) "shall not prejudice the trial and punishment of any person for any act or omission which, at the time when it was committed, was criminal according to the general principles of law recognized by civilized nations." It is obvious that article 7(2) refers to Nazi war crimes, and the Convention thus permits the prosecution and punishment of such crimes. It is significant, however, that the German Federal Republic made the following reservation when ratifying the Convention: "[The German Federal Republic] will only apply the provisions of Article 7(2) of the Convention within the limits of Article 103, Clause 2, of the Basic Law of the German Federal Republic. This provides that 'any act is only punishable if it was so by law before the offense was committed.'"

9. Article 39(3) lists the necessary qualifications: "The candidates shall be of high moral character and must either possess the qualifications required for appointment to high judicial office or be jurisconsults of recognized competence."

10. Recent practice by the Court, however, has had the full Court hearing a greater number of cases. In addition, article 3(1) of Protocol 2 has the full Court responding to the Committee's request for an advisory opinion.

11. Approximately ten such interstate complaints have been filed. One of these, *Cyprus v. Turkey* (1974), illustrates a shortcoming of the process. Cyprus filed the petition, alleging that Turkey violated

numerous Convention articles when Turkey invaded Cyprus in 1974. However, since neither Cyprus nor Turkey had recognized the Court's jurisdiction, the case was referred to the Committee of Ministers, which usually shies away from such "political" decisions.

12. Article 32 requires the referral of the case to the Committee if the Commission does not send it to the Court within three months or if one of the states involved does not recognize the Court's jurisdiction. A state always has the prerogative, however, to refer a Commission decision to the Court.

13. Article 15 reads as follows:

> 1. In time of war or other public emergency threatening the life of the nation, any High Contracting Party may take measures derogating from its obligations under this Convention to the extent strictly required by the exigencies of the situation, provided that such measures are not inconsistent with its other obligations under international law.

> 2. No derogation from Article 2 [right to life], except in respect of deaths resulting from acts of war, or from Articles 3 [prohibiting torture, inhuman or degrading treatment], 4 (paragraph 1) [prohibiting servitude] and 7 [prohibiting ex post facto punishment] shall be made under this provision.

14. This pronouncement was made by the Commission in *Greece v. United Kingdom* (1956), concerning the actions of the British government in Cyprus while the island was still a British colony.

15. Excerpts from the statement by the Greek government are reproduced as follows:

> *Considering* that the system of collective implementation of human rights and fundamental freedoms, established under the European Convention on Human Rights and Fundamental Freedoms, failed in its aims and became, under the influence of political considerations, unable to secure the equal and effective observance of Conventional stipulations;

> *Considering* that the European Commission of Human Rights has in the most unacceptable and intolerable manner indulged in a series of violations of the procedure . . . and has been motivated not by

principles of law but by purely political considerations;

Considering that the organs set up by the European Convention on Human Rights failed to secure equality of treatment for all signatory nationals, small and big, and became tools of injustice in the hands of certain powers;

Reaffirms its profound belief in the fundamental human rights and freedoms ... and its determination to safeguard them according to the provisions on human rights of the Greek Constitution;

Denounces, according to the provisions of Article 65 of the Convention, the Convention for the Protection of Human Rights and Fundamental Freedoms and the additional Protocol of the Convention, the Convention for the Protection of Human Rights and Fundamental Freedoms, serving the notification o. denouncement as of today [December 12, 1969]. (*Yearbook* 1969: 502)

16. *The London Times* presented a brief description of sensory deprivation:

Some of the Irish witnesses demonstrated to the Commissioners how they were spreadeagled against a wall, their legs spread apart and their weight forced on to their fingertips. One man said to have remained like that for 29 hours. The hoods used on the 14 men were described as black or navy-blue bags and the noise to which they were subjected was 'a continuous, loud hissing sound.' They were denied sleep and given a restricted diet consisting of a round of bread and a pint of water every six hours." (*The London Times* [January 19, 1978]: 5)

17. The Commission's document was and still is cloaked in secrecy: only two copies exist, and all parties have agreed not to publish the full document; in the Commission's 500-page public report, witnesses are identified by code names only.

18. Some of the proceedings appear to have been lifted from the cloak-and-dagger script of the "Mission Impossible" TV series: several members of the British security forces were flown by the RAF to Sola on the Norwegian coast to be interviewed by the Commission, and the witnesses appeared behind screens to protect their identity.

19. The British judge, Sir Gerald Fitzmaurice, severely chastised the British government for not contesting the Commission's original finding that sensory deprivation was torture. Sir Gerald stated: "Had the Court accepted the United Kingdom's contention that it need not and should not pronounce upon the non-contested allegations, the Commission's findings as to torture would have constituted the last word on the subject and . . . the United Kingdom would have stood convicted . . . of that grave charge" *The London Times* (January 19, 1978: 5).

20. The Irish government attempted to retrieve the situation by issuing several platitudinous statements about "inhuman" treatment, but its real reaction was probably summed up by an unidentified Irish spokesman in reference to Britain not contesting the Commission's finding of torture but having the Court decide otherwise: "it is akin to someone pleading guilty in court and being overruled."

REFERENCES

Anderson, Perry (1978) *Lineages of the Absolutist State.* New York: NLB/Schocken Books.

Berger, Vincent (1989) *Case Law of the European Court of Human Rights.* Sarasota, FL: UNIFO.

Carey, John (1970) *UN Protection of Civil and Political Rights.* Syracuse, NY: Syracuse University Press.

Council of Europe (n.d.) *Convention for the Protection of Human Rights and Fundamental Freedoms with Protocols Nos. I and IV and Selected Reservations/Convention de Sauvegarde des Droits de l'homme et des Libertés Fondamentales accompagnée des Protocoles Nos I et IV et d'un choix de réserves.* Strasbourg: Council of Europe.

—— (1957–) *Yearbook of the Commission on Human Rights.* The Hague: Council of Europe.

European Commission on Human Rights (1957–) *Annual Review.* Strasbourg: Council of Europe.

Gellhorn, Walter (1966) *Ombudsmen and Others: Citizens' Protectors in Nine Countries.* Cambridge: Harvard University Press.

Gibson, John S. (1991) *International Organizations, Constitutional Law, and Human Rights.* New York: Praeger.

Hurwitz, Leon (1981) *The State as Defendant: Governmental Accountability and the Redress of Individual Grievances.* Westport, CT: Greenwood Press.

Janis, Mark W. (1990) *European Human Rights Law.* Hartford, CT: Foundation Press.

Kamminga, Menno T. (1992) *Inter-State Accountability for Violations of Human Rights.* Philadelphia: University of Pennsylvania Press.

Kinley, David (1993) *The European Convention on Human Rights: Compliance Without Incorporation.* Aldershot, UK: Dartmouth.

Merrills, J.G. (1988) *The Development of International Law by the European Court of Human Rights.* Manchester, UK: Manchester University Press.

Mikaelsen, Laurids (1990) *European Protection of Human Rights: The Practice and Procedure of the European Commission of Human Rights on the Admissibility of Applications from Individuals and States.* Alphen aan den Rijn: Sijthoff a Noordhoff.

Mower, A. Glenn (1991) *Regional Human Rights: A Comparative Study of the West European and Inter-American Systems.* New York: Greenwood Press.

Oraa, Jaime (1992) *Human Rights in States of Emergency in International Law.* Oxford: Clarendon Press.

Robertson, A.H. (1977) *Human Rights in Europe.* Manchester, UK: Manchester University Press.

Sohn, Louis B., and Buergenthal, Thomas (1973) *International Protection of Human Rights.* New York: Bobbs-Merrill.

A New Role for the International Court of Justice: Adjudicator of International and State Transnational Crimes*

Barbara M. Yarnold

Theoretical Framework: State Crimes

A good starting place for an inquiry into controlling state criminality is with Gregg Barak's edited book entitled *Crimes by the Capitalist State: An Introduction to State Criminality* (1991), one of the first scholarly books on the subject of state criminality. According to Barak (1991: 6), a framework must be developed for conceptualizing crimes committed by states. Although state crimes are most often associated with overt military action, which Barak labels "proactive state criminality," there is a second category that is scarcely mentioned in the literature on state criminality that includes crimes of omission (Barak, 1991: 6). Examples of proactive state crimes include the U.S. government's activities in the course of the Iran-Contra affair. On the other hand, a state crime of omission may involve a state's denial of adequate housing and economic opportunities to a segment of the population, which induces criminal behavior on the part of the economically displaced (Barak, 1991: 6; Henry, 1991). Roebuck and Weeber (1978) similarly acknowledged, over a decade earlier, that governments violate the law by omission or commission.

Complicating the conceptualization of state criminality is that, as with white-collar criminals, the perpetrators of the crime (agents and organizations) tend to have attained social status and political power within the state (Barak, 1991: 7). These state agents attempt to obscure the criminality of their actions through appeals to ideology and to "national" and "public" interests.

Barak suggests,

> Crimes by the state involve violence and property and include such diverse behaviors as murder, rape, espionage, coverup, burglary, illegal wiretapping, illegal break-in, disinformation, kidnapping, piracy, as-sassination, counter- and state terrorism, bankrupting and destroying whole economies, secrecy, unaccountability, corruption, exporting arms illegally, obstruction of justice, perjury, deception, fraud, conspiracy, and the general violation of both domestic and international law. They also include behaviors which cause social injury and therefore violate universally defined human rights (e.g., food, shelter, self-determination, etc.). (Barak 1991: 274)

Ross (1992: 352) believes that Barak is overinclusive in listing as state crimes such actions as counterterrorism, secrecy, and destroying whole economies. Ross suggests that counterterrorism is appropriate state action when states act within legal boundaries. Similarly, with regard to state secrecy, Ross maintains that this is an inevitable consequence of sovereignty and concerns that most states could not survive without maintaining some level of secrecy (Ross, 1992: 353). Finally, the problem with labeling "destroying state economies" as a state crime is that it is "vague and problematic" (Ross, 1992: 353). Is it justifiable to label a state's action criminal when it makes business investments that have an adverse impact on the economies of other states?

Roebuck and Weeber (1978), while acknowledging that governments violate law by omission and commission, go beyond Barak in terms of the number of state crimes they identify. Roebuck and Weeber add as state crimes, for example, drug, behavioral, and bacterial experiments; destruction of the environment; manipulating the unemployment rate; militant lobbying; and engineering the domestic arms race (1978: 68).

What links all of these state crimes, Barak suggests, is the motive. Hence, "these acts committed by and/or on behalf of the state and its dominant ruling elites are political crimes essentially because they have been rationalized or justified in order to preserve and maintain the status quo" (Barak, 1991: 275).

Similarly, Roebuck and Weeber (1978) argue that political crime is endemic to all contemporary states and consists of violations of the law by the government "in order to maintain and enhance the existing political and economic systems" (1978: iv.). According to Turk (1982), the "legal norms defining political offenses . . . are publicly justified as defenses of the polity and its governmental structure, and assert or imply the primacy of collective or ruling group interests over subcollectivity or individual interests" (1982: 54–55).

If one accepts Barak's argument that through their political crimes states seek to maintain the status quo, it is highly unlikely that states will adopt internal mechanisms that will control their criminality. Hence, external controls may be the only viable alternative in controlling state crime.

Barak (1991: 275) seems to acknowledge this, in his brief discussion on controlling state criminality, where he makes vague reference to the need for multilateral cooperation and decreasing the power of state political police apparatuses.

This chapter proposes an external methodology, rooted in international law, for controlling state crimes, committed against both individuals and other states. This proposal involves reforming current practices for dealing with international extradition and international adjudication, whether the criminal activity is engaged in by states, their agents, or private individuals.

To give due credit to states, it should be noted that external controls on states, including international law, are produced through the self-interested actions of individual states. As states enter into bilateral and multilateral treaties that codify international crimes and establish and recognize international organizations, external controls on state criminality eventually emerge out of this piecemeal and gradual process, proving once again that the whole is indeed greater than the sum of its parts.

Controlling State and Individual Crimes:
A Proposal

International extradition deserves immediate world attention due to the repeated threats to international security as states increasingly violate extradition agreements and engage in extralegal extradition (Yarnold, 1991).

International extradition is the delivery of an individual, usually a fugitive from justice, by one state to another. This process results from explicit agreements in the form of treaties among states, or from reciprocity or comity (Bassiouni, 1987: 8). Extradition agreements most often apply to common criminals (those who violate domestic laws of individual states). However, also included are those who engage in international crimes (e.g., torture, genocide, and apartheid) (Blakesly, 1981). International crimes have been codified in various international agreements, many of which (e.g., multilateral treaties) provide that signatory states must either prosecute or extradite international criminals within their territories (Bassiouni, 1987: 13).

Extradition has an extended history. Some writers trace its origins to ancient civilizations, including ancient Egypt (Blakesly, 1981). In fact, the oldest recorded extradition agreement is dated 1280 B.C., after the Egyptian pharaoh foiled an attempted Hittite invasion. The subsequent peace treaty provided that the sovereigns of both nations would deliver certain individuals who had fled for shelter back to their own respective countries (Bassiouni, 1983; Blakesly, 1981).

Though current extradition treaties often recognize a "political offense" exception to extradition, the earliest extradition agreements were primarily for the purpose of delivering political and religious offenders to sovereigns (Bassiouni, 1983; Farrell, 1985; O'Higgins, 1964). By the eighteenth century, and lasting until 1832, extradition had become a tool for the delivery of military offenders. The period 1833–1948 is marked by a significant change in extradition practice; it came to be utilized during this time for the exchange of "common criminals" (Bassiouni, 1983: 7), defined as those charged with having violated the domestic law of individual states. Since 1948, extradition has still been primarily concerned with common crimes against states, although it is increasingly subjected to international human rights and due process standards (Bassiouni, 1983: 7).

A general rule in the world community of states that governs contemporary extradition practices is that there is no duty to extradite in the absence of a treaty, yet some states voluntarily extradite individuals, even in the absence of a treaty (Bassiouni 1987: 12; Blakesly 1981). Although there are multilateral conventions on extradition, most extradition agreements are bilateral (Bassiouni, 1987: 56; Gilbert, 1991: 20).

Coinciding with the increased number of states that emerged in the post–World War II period in the wake of anti-colonial movements within countries (Calvacoressi, 1987; Hoffmann, 1968; Robertson, 1975), the number of bilateral extradition treaties has increased dramatically (Bassiouni, 1987: 56); from 1945 to 1973, the number increased from 60 to over 130 (Pearson and Rochester, 1988: 56–57). Newly formed states typically enter into bilateral extradition treaties as an exercise of state sovereignty, and to escape the treaty obligations of the colonial states that preceded them (Bassiouni, 1987: 97; O'Connell, 1967).

Bilateral extradition treaties tend to be quite complex and require extensive negotiation. One critic of bilateral extradition treaties notes that if each of the 154 member states of the United Nations (in 1983) entered into bilateral extradition treaties with all other members, there would be 6,776 total bilateral extradition treaties (Bassiouni, 1987). The United States is a good example of a state that relies greatly (but not exclusively) on bilateral extradition treaties. By 1989 the United States had signed such treaties with over 100 other countries (Bassiouni, 1987: 57), and the trend of reliance on bilateral extradition agreements continues into the 1990s (Gilbert, 1991: 20).

In spite of many problems encountered with bilateral extradition agreements, they remain the primary means through which states extradite individuals charged with law violations.

Major Problems: Extradition Agreements

One limitation of extradition treaties, whether multilateral or bilateral, is that they bind only signatory states (i.e., states that have entered into an extradition agreement). Further, the general rule is that no duty to extradite exists in the absence of a treaty (Bassiouni, 1987: 10). Hence, the most obvious barrier to effective international extradition is that there is no requirement that states cooperate with others in delivering fugitives to states where they are charged with a crime. Also, to the extent that extradition takes place, it is likely to lack uniformity. This tends to diminish the legitimacy of extradition and states' willingness to comply with such agreements.

For example, the Extradition Act 18 U.S.C.S. 3184 sets forth the responsibilities of the United States with respect to international extradition:

> Whenever there is a treaty or convention for extradition between the United States and any foreign government, any justice or judge of the United States . . . may, upon complaint made under oath, charging any person found within his jurisdiction, with having committed within the jurisdiction of any such foreign government any of the crimes provided for by such treaty or convention, issue his warrant for the apprehension of the person so charged, that he may be brought before such justice, judge, or magistrate, to the end that the evidence of criminality may be heard and considered. (As amended Nov. 18, 1988, P. L. 100–690, Title VII, Subtitle B, section 7087, 102 Stat. 4409)

Hence, the statute conditions the transfer of fugitives if an extradition treaty or convention exists between the United States and the requesting state. Most American federal courts that have considered this issue have arrived at the same conclusion, namely that there is no duty to extradite in the absence of a treaty or convention. The U.S. Supreme Court adopted this position in an early case, *Factor* v. *Laubenheimer*, 290 U.S. 276 (1933), where it stated that principles of international law recognize no right to extradition apart from treaty. The Supreme Court reaffirmed this position three years later in *Valentine* v. *United States*, 299 U.S. 5 (1936). Lower federal courts in the

United States have generally followed the lead of the Supreme Court, suggesting that the right of foreign states to demand the transfer of one accused of a crime exists only when allowed by treaty (*Ramos v. Rodriguez Diaz*, 179 F. Supp. 459 [D.C. Fla. 1959]; *Re Edmondson*, 352 F. Supp. 22 [D.C. Minn. 1972]; *Re United States*, 713 F.2d 105 [5th Cir. 1983]).

There have been instances, though few in number, in which extradition was granted by the United States in the absence of a treaty usually on the basis of comity or reciprocity (Bassiouni, 1987: 59). One such case occurred in 1864, when the United States sent Arguelles, an officer in the Spanish army, to Spain, in the absence of a treaty, for selling individuals into slavery (an international crime) (Bassiouni, 1987: 60).

Although states that have civil law systems traditionally have relied upon comity and reciprocity as bases for international extradition, they too, like countries with common law systems, since World War II, have increased their reliance on bilateral treaties (Bassiouni, 1987: 11).

The United States, for example, relies almost exclusively on bilateral treaties for extradition, though it is a party to multilateral ones. As such, it is subject to all of the problems that normally plague states that rely to a great extent on bilateral agreements in extradition matters, including (1) state succession, (2) the severing of diplomatic relations, (3) war, and (4) "the perennial dilemma of maintaining a network of treaties with over one hundred states" (Bassiouni, 1987: 37). With regard to the last point, each treaty that is renegotiated must be approved by the U.S. Senate.

In *Argento v. Horn*, 241 F.2d 258 (6th Cir. 1957), *cert. denied*, 355 U.S. 818, *rehearing denied*, 355 U.S. 885 (1957), a U.S. court of appeals, in considering an extradition request, was confronted with the argument that a treaty which provided for the transfer of fugitives between Italy and the United States was terminated during the war against Italy declared by the U.S. Congress on December 11, 1941. The court held that the treaty was suspended during the war merely so that extradition might still proceed between the two states.

In *Sabatier v. Dabrowski*, 586 F.2d 866 (1st Cir. 1978), a circuit court of appeals was called upon to address the question of whether a treaty (providing for extradition) entered into by Great Britain and the United States in 1842 was inherited by Canada, having been a colony of Great Britain. The court held that Canada did in fact inherit the treaty obligations of Great Britain and could seek extradition from the United States pursuant to the treaty.

These cases merely suggest the multiplicity of problems that arise from reliance on bilateral extradition treaties. These problems also pertain to multilateral treaties. They appear to be endemic to an international extradition system that is formed by the piecemeal treaty-making powers of individual states over time.

Another difficulty is that extradition treaties often set forth defenses. Bassiouni (1987: 381–383) suggests that there are four major grounds for denials of requests for extradition. These bases for denial relate to (1) the offense charged, (2) the individual whose extradition is sought, (3) the nature of the criminal charge or the prosecution of the charge, and (4) the penalty or punishment which may be applied to the individual extradited.

One of the most controversial exceptions, or "defenses," to extradition is the political offense exception. Nevertheless, it is currently included in virtually every extradition treaty and in the domestic laws of many states (Evans, 1963; Kelly, 1987). In spite of its wide usage in extradition treaties, the political offense exception has not been well defined (Bassiouni, 1987: 383–394; Kelly, 1987). For example, a 1978 extradition treaty between the United States and Japan provides that

> [e]xtradition shall not be granted under this Treaty in any of the following circumstances: . . . when the offense for which extradition is requested is a political offense or when it appears that the request for extradition is made with a view to prosecuting, trying or punishing the person sought for a political offense. (Extradition Treaty Between United States and Japan)

The interpretation of the political offense exception has been left largely to courts within states (Deere, 1933; Evans, 1963; Garcia-Mora, 1953). As a result of vague legal standards (Yarnold, 1991; 1992), domestic courts have great discretion in these cases, the decisions of which are likely influenced by local political and environmental factors. Hence, one expects that their decisions will vary.

Bassiouni (1987), a noted international law scholar, suggests that there is local variance in judicial interpretation of the political offense exception.[1] Of course, state courts not only decide whether the political offense exception applies, but are given much broader authority in extradition cases.

Recent contributions in criminology, particularly work that has distinguished between political crimes and other types of crime, are useful in determining who is eligible for the political offense exception to extradition. Although recognizing that crime is a relative concept, Schafer (1974) distinguishes between ordinary offenses and political crimes on the basis that political crimes target "the ruling power's value system as a whole, rather than a part or an issue of it" (p. 29). Further, the political criminal acts in the name of justice are often perpetrated by those willing to suffer a personal loss to promote his or her ideology.

In agreement with Schafer's typology, Minor (1975) similarly defined *political crime* as politically-motivated lawbreaking by idealists. Turk (1975) describes political criminals as those who have been identified by authorities as potential political threats because their values and/or actions challenge the system. Political criminals often become targets of political policing (Turk, 1975; 1982).

Schafer warns, however, that for the purposes of determining the proper official response, the convictional political criminal must be distinguished from the ordinary criminal and the pseudoconvictional criminal, both of whom promote selfish goals and not altruism through their criminality (Schafer, 1974: 146, 154–155). Applying Schafer's typology, for example, the International Court of Justice and individual states should recognize only the political offense exception to extradition in cases involving convictional political criminals.

Contributing greatly to the delay, confusion, and lack of uniformity that characterizes contemporary extradition practices is that the task of enforcing and interpreting international treaties and conventions relating to extradition is given to the courts of individual states (Bassiouni, 1987: 77). These courts typically handle domestic matters, whether criminal or civil, and lack the necessary expertise to deal adequately with international law and extradition issues. In fact, most courts are rarely faced with an international extradition case (Kester, 1988). When they must adjudicate an extradition matter, the substantive and procedural rights of individuals subject to extradition are not clearly specified in the governing statute or treaty (Kester, 1988).

Hence, decisions of state courts on extradition requests are conflicting and may be "politicized" by political factors relevant to the state in question. For example, in one analysis of U.S. federal district court cases that dealt with extradition during the period of 1932–1990 (Yarnold, 1991: 27–30), the courts were seemingly influenced by ethnic politics in the United States. Irish fugitives linked to the Irish Republican Army, who had the support of a powerful ethnic lobby in the United States, tended to prevail in these cases to a far greater extent than fugitives who lacked such a lobby (including fugitives linked to the Palestine Liberation Organization). Hence, there is some danger that the decisions rendered by state courts on international extradition requests may be arbitrary. At a bare minimum, they give little guidance to individuals subject to extradition proceedings and may consequently violate national and international standards of due process, to the extent that these protections exist in extradition proceedings (Harris, 1967).

Let us take, however, the "best case" scenario: extradition proceeds in accordance with a treaty that clearly binds two states, and sets forth crimes for which extradition might proceed. After extradition takes place, new problems of greater magnitude arise. Even if extradition goes smoothly, the individual who has been extradited may not receive a fair trial in the state to which he or she is extradited, or that person may fall victim to excessive punishment and other violations of national and international human rights standards (Banoff and Pyle, 1984; Kester, 1988).

For all of these reasons—the requirement of a treaty, the enormous barriers to treaty formation; the inherent ambiguities in treaty application; the many loopholes to extradition, including the political offense exception; the need correctly to classify political criminals, the barriers to extradition; and the danger that extradited individuals will not receive a fair trial and may be subject to human rights violations—a fairly safe observation is that contemporary extradition procedures are not adequate and should be replaced.

The inadequacy of existing international extradition procedures is borne out by many instances of self-help measures taken by states in which they flagrantly circumvent legal procedures. Bassiouni (1987: 190) refers to such practices as "extralegal extradition." One of the most celebrated instances involved the 1960 kidnapping of the notorious Nazi war criminal Adolf Eichmann from Argentina by Israeli security forces. A second example was the "disguised extradition" of fugitives through use of immigration laws. Bassiouni (1987: 163–164) notes that since World War II, the United States employed this strategy with Nazi War criminals in the United States. There is also evidence that the United States has also employed this strategy in the case of Irish fugitives in the late 1970s and 1980s, as a way to rid the United States of members of the Irish Republican Army (Farrell, 1985; Yarnold, 1991). More recently, in 1989, the United States engaged in what I refer to as "gunboat extradition" (Yarnold, 1991), where a military invasion of another state (Panama) was launched in order to obtain a fugitive, in this case General Manuel Noriega, who was later convicted of violating U.S. drug laws.

These acts of extralegal extradition were accomplished in spite of the fact that the states engaging in these acts had valid treaties with the offended state. These actions tended to increase the risk of international conflict, since they involved violations of the sovereignty of other states and breaches of existing treaty obligations. Since contemporary extradition practices, for a variety of reasons, are not working, it is necessary to design a new international extradition process.

The International Court of Justice as an Adjudicator of International and State Transnational Crimes

There are two main proposals for changing present extradition practices. First, authority for the adjudication of international crimes should be transferred to the International Court of Justice (ICJ). This proposal is the less controversial of the two; various international law scholars and practitioners have made this suggestion (Bridge, 1964; Eagleton, 1957; Golt, 1966). For this reason, I will not dwell upon it, except to add that it is unreasonable to expect that state courts, specialists in domestic law and subject to local influences (Yarnold, 1991; 1992), are able to adequately adjudicate international law cases. Further, it is unfair that those few states, such as Israel, that attempt to enforce international criminal law (e.g., the 1960 kidnapping and trial of Nazi war criminal Adolf Eichmann), incur the wrath and ingratitude of the international community (Arendt, 1963; Kuzmanovic, 1987; Leavy, 1962; Pearlman, 1963; Rosenne, 1973; Yarnold, 1991). Hence, the ICJ would have jurisdiction over all violations of international law and human rights standards, whether the perpetrator is an individual, a person or an organization working on the behalf of the state, or the country itself. Of course, individuals and states would be able to bring their claims to the World Court, and states might be sued by their own citizens for international law violations.

A more controversial suggestion is that the ICJ be given jurisdiction over state crimes when fugitives have crossed national boundaries and are outside of the state in which they committed their illegal acts. Currently, the state whose criminal law was violated seeks to have the fugitive extradited, and the fugitive's state of refuge, through its judicial and executive branches, determines whether to extradite the fugitive to the requesting state.

The role states currently play in the extradition process should be eliminated. First, the determination as to whether a "relator" (the person whose extradition is sought) should be extradited (this determination is usually made by state courts, through a probable cause hearing) should be made by the ICJ.

During the extradition hearing, the ICJ should determine whether the defendant engaged in a political crime; if so, then no further proceedings should commence, and the defendant will be allowed to remain in the country in which he or she is located. If extradition is found to be reasonable and legal, then the defendant should be delivered to the ICJ for subsequent proceedings. Second, jurisdiction over the state crime itself should also be transferred to the ICJ, since the crime has assumed an international or transnational character through the fugitive's flight from the state in which a crime was committed to a second state.

Hence, I suggest that the ICJ be transformed into an adjudicator of international crimes and state transnational crimes. One issue that requires attention is whether it is advisable to create a new international criminal tribunal, rather than, as suggested, utilizing the ICJ.

The ICJ is the best forum for the adjudication of state and international crimes for several reasons. First, the world community has been socialized into the concept of international adjudication through the ICJ and its precursor, the Permanent Court of International Justice. Although the ICJ has not been used much in recent years, it has commanded the respect of many states in the world community, due to its presumed expertise and impartiality (Lissitzyn, 1972; Rosenne, 1973). Hence, the ICJ already has some minimal level of legitimacy and support among states.

Second, the concept of a new international tribunal may be more difficult to sell to the world community than simply transferring new responsibilities to a preexisting international tribunal, the ICJ. Third, the community of states has already invested enormous resources in creating and developing the ICJ, though it is a vastly underutilized international forum (Hudson, 1943; 1969; Pearson and Rochester, 1988; Rosenne, 1973). The Statute of the ICJ would not be discarded. Instead, where necessary, the Statute would require only amendment.

This recommendation, that the ICJ be given jurisdiction over international crimes and state crimes where fugitives have crossed national borders, will be opposed by those superpowers in the world community that historically have favored the use of force over the rule of law (Rosenne, 1973). However, given the contemporary climate, in which superpowers are quickly losing their preeminence, it may be possible to implement these proposals.

A Framework

The following suggestions are very much based upon what U.S. federal courts typically do in "diversity cases" (i.e., cases that involve the citizens of more than one state): apply the procedures of the forum and the substantive law of states (Moore, 1982; *Erie R. Co. v. Tompkins*, 1938; Article III, Section 2 of the U.S. Constitution). The procedures used by U.S. federal courts in diversity cases are able to accommodate conflicting demands made by states, which have an interest in the enforcement of their substantive laws; the forum, which seeks to ensure that proper procedures are followed; and litigants, who seek a fair and timely resolution of the underlying dispute.

What follows is a suggested framework for the adjudication of both state and international crimes by the ICJ, including the substantive law that might apply, procedures for the ICJ, identification of appropriate adjudicators for this international forum, and provisions for penalties and bail.

Substantive Law

International Crimes

When the ICJ exercises jurisdiction over an international crime, the substantive law to be applied is, quite simply speaking, international criminal law. Of course, one problem that arises is how to discover the underlying sources of international crimes, since various conventions, treaties, and other agreements purport to establish the existence of international crimes. Hence, the first problem, that of identifying international crimes, is not an insignificant one.

Article 38 of the Statute of the International Court of Justice sets forth the "sources" of international law that are to be applied by the ICJ:

    a. international conventions, whether general or particular, establishing rules expressly recognized by the contesting states;

    b. international custom, as evidence of a general practice accepted as law;

    c. the general principles of law recognized by civilized nations;

    d. subject to the provisions of Article 59, judicial decisions and the teachings of the most highly qualified publicists of the various nations, as subsidiary means for the determination of rules of law.

Article 59 of the ICJ Statute, referred to in the last paragraph of Article 38, provides that: "[t]he decision of the Court has no binding force except between the parties and in respect of that particular case." Article 59 thus places a limitation upon the use of prior cases adjudicated by the ICJ as precedents, an unfortunate result. It would be quite useful to have the rule of *stare decisis* apply in the context of international criminal adjudication by the ICJ; the use of common law in this manner would inject some measure of predictability into the process and give those who are subject to international criminal proceedings the benefit of advance notice that their activity may be criminal. If Article 59 continues in effect, this leaves the development of international criminal law to the courts of the various nations, which are subject to domestic biases and certainly less qualified to decide international law issues than the ICJ.

In the post–World War II period, there was great movement toward the establishment of an international criminal court, which would have jurisdiction over international crimes (Bridge, 1964; Golt, 1966). Although these ideas have not yet come to fruition, they led to the development of a draft code for an international criminal court (Golt, 1966; United Nations Documents A/2136 and A/2624). This code has been modified over the years.

Bassiouni (1987) contributed to this process through drawing up a "Draft International Criminal Code and Draft Statute for An International Criminal Tribunal," by consolidating existing international instruments. He suggests that in the period of 1815–1985, 22 categories of international crimes were set forth in 312 multilateral instruments. The groups of crimes include, for example, aggression, war crimes, the unlawful use of weapons and the unlawful emplacement of weapons (Bassiouni, 1987). [2]

As a result of these combined efforts, the problem of identifying the substantive law to be applied in international criminal adjudications by the ICJ has been largely resolved.

State Crimes

When the ICJ has jurisdiction over a state criminal case, the appropriate law to apply is (as in U.S. federal court diversity cases) the substantive law of the state which files a complaint against an individual. Hence, for example, if Great Britain is the complaining party, British criminal law would be used, that might include statutes, regulations, decisions of British courts, and constitutional provisions.

Of course, one obvious barrier is that states have vastly diverse legal systems and laws. One of the greatest differences that arises in state criminal law systems is that between states which rely upon the common law, as opposed to states which rely to a greater degree upon codes. This problem, however, may be overcome by ensuring that judges who serve on the ICJ are trained in comparative law and are cognizant of the major differences that exist in state criminal law systems.

Procedures

Many of the procedures to be followed by the ICJ in international criminal adjudications have already been codified in the Statute of the ICJ. Where the Statute is silent on an issue, it might be supplemented in the manner suggested below.

States would initiate proceedings before the ICJ through filing a complaint (or "memorial") alleging a violation of either (1) the domestic law of the state or (2) international criminal law.

In either case, the complaint should state the facts and the law upon which the complaint is based, the identity of the party against whom the complaint is filed (whether the defendant is another state or an individual), and the location of the defendant (if known). This complaint would thus conform with the requirements of Article 40 of the Statute of the ICJ; which provides "the subject of the dispute and the parties shall be indicated." After filing the complaint, the Registrar of the Court would give notice of the filing to all concerned, including states and individuals (ICJ, Statute, Article 40). A more far-reaching revision would also allow individuals to file complaints with the ICJ, based on violations of international law. The defendants would again be either states or individuals.

Where the complaint is based on a violation of either international criminal law or the domestic criminal law of a state, after notice had been given to the defendant and he or she filed an answer to the complaint (or "countermemorial"), the ICJ would then preside over a probable cause hearing, with the objective of determining whether a reasonable basis exists to believe (1) that a crime was committed and (2) that the defendant named in the complaint committed the crime. The burden of proof in such a case would be on the complaining party. These proceedings would be based on documents, including pleadings and affidavits, but would not require the presence of the defendant or the plaintiff, although both could appear if they so desired. In this way, the role currently played by states in extradition proceedings (through their courts and/or executive branch officials) would be eliminated.

If the ICJ finds probable cause lacking, the matter ends at this point. However, if it is found to exist, an arrest warrant requesting extradition will be issued and forwarded to the state in which the fugitive is located. The defendant will be extradited to a confinement center (specifically constructed for this purpose) at The Hague. The proximity of the confinement center would ensure that defendants would not be detained indefinitely. Within forty-eight hours after the extradition of the fugitive, a preliminary hearing would proceed, for the purpose of formally charging the defendant, allowing the fugitive to enter a plea (guilty or not guilty), setting a trial date, and deciding whether to grant bail. The trial would begin a short time after the preliminary hearing. At all stages in these proceedings, defendants are entitled to the assistance of counsel. If the defending party is an individual, and is unable to hire an attorney, the ICJ will appoint counsel.

The hearing itself is subject to the terms set forth in Articles 39 through 64 of the Statute of the ICJ. Pursuant to Article 43, the procedure consists of two parts, one written and the other oral. The hearings are public (Article 46) and minutes are kept by the registrar of the ICJ (Article 47). All questions are decided by a majority of the judges present. In the event that votes are tied, the president or the person who acts in his place has the final vote (Article 55).

Article 59 provides that the decisions of the ICJ have no binding force except between the parties and in respect of the particular case. In short, these decisions do not serve as precedents. Article 59 should be substituted for one which expressly provides that decisions of the ICJ form precedents which are binding in subsequent cases before the ICJ and in state court cases which consider international law issues. It would foster the rule of law to have an international criminal court, through its adjudications, contribute to the development of a body of common law. Also, making decisions of the ICJ binding precedents would satisfy minimal due process requirements for criminal defendants, since these decisions would put them on notice as to what actions might be deemed criminal.

Articles 39 through 64 of the Statute of the ICJ set forth procedures currently employed by the ICJ. There is no apparent reason why they cannot be successfully employed, with the suggested revisions, in criminal cases that might arise before the ICJ. They reflect the combined wisdom of all of the disparate legal systems of the world community and the labor of international and national scholars and statesmen who united at a critical point in history to draft a statute—the Statute of the International Court of Justice—for a court that would, through its adjudications, enhance the prospects of world peace. These same procedures may be employed in state and international criminal cases adjudicated by the ICJ. The prospects for international peace and security may thereby be increased.

The Adjudicators: Judges Versus Jury

The Statute of the ICJ contains elaborate provisions for the selection of judges. The ICJ consists of fifteen members, no two of whom may be nationals of the same state, thereby ensuring some degree of representation of the various members of the world community (Article 3). Members of the ICJ must have good moral character and the necessary expertise; they have to be either "jurisconsults of recognized competence in international law" or possess the requirements in their states for appointment to the highest judicial office (Article 2). Nominees for positions on the ICJ are made by national groups of the Permanent Court of Arbitration or, if a state is not represented on this tribunal, by national groups appointed by their governments (Article 4). National groups may nominate up to four candidates; no more than two of these may be of the same nationality as the national group (Article 5).

The nominations made by national groups are submitted to the ICJ General Assembly and the Security Council, which vote independently for nominees. To be successful, a candidate must receive an absolute majority of the vote in each organization. If selected, judges sit for nine years and are eligible for reelection. The terms of judges on the ICJ are staggered, so that five judgeships come to an end every three years (Rosenne, 1973).

In searching for candidates, Article 9 suggests that national groups should seek to ensure that the ICJ as a whole represents the main forms of civilization and the principal legal systems of the world. An additional, unwritten rule that guides judicial selection is that each of the five permanent members of the ICJ Security Council is entitled to have a judge of its nationality on the ICJ (Rosenne, 1973).

Once again, the Statute of the ICJ has established an excellent framework for adjudication by the ICJ and, more specifically, the selection of the members of the ICJ. Although some have suggested that the members of the ICJ should be selected for life, instead of a nine-year period (Lissitzyn, 1972), the current nine-year period is probably preferable. It is of a long enough duration that it enables judges to become expert and somewhat detached from their states. It also ensures, however, that a member of the ICJ who is arbitrary may be eliminated after his appointment.

If, however, the ICJ becomes involved in the adjudication of international and state transnational crimes, it may be that where the right to a jury trial for the crime in question is guaranteed by state or international law, new measures will have to be adopted to allow for the selection of an "international jury" that will make factual findings as to, for example, the guilt or innocence of a criminal defendant. Of course, the jury should not be composed of nationals of the state that filed the complaint, since one of the primary objectives in giving jurisdiction over state crimes to the ICJ is to ensure that the defendant receives a fair trial, which may not occur if a defendant is tried by a jury or judge in the complaining state.

The international jury could be selected in a similar manner to the judges of the ICJ, namely through national groups associated with the Permanent Court of Arbitration, or by national groups appointed for this purpose (Article 4). However, these national groups would select jurors from a much broader cross section of their states, excluding elected officials, government employees, government administrators, lawyers, and judges. The use of nonstate actors on the international jury will enhance the legitimacy of the jury and its decisions. In short, the appointees to the jury would not need to have a background in law, and should be, as much as possible, private individuals, not affiliated with governments within their states or their legal systems. They should have a minimum level of education (to ensure literacy) and be of good moral character.

Each national group should be responsible for selecting ten prospective jury members. These ten candidates would be included on a list of international jurors, and through random assignment, they would be appointed to cases that come before the ICJ. This random assignment of jurors to cases would promote the representativeness of juries and refute any charges of selection bias that might be raised, while simultaneously enhancing the legitimacy of the international jury. The jury would not, as in the case of the judges of the ICJ, be subject to the limitation of Article 3, namely that the ICJ shall consist of fifteen members, no two of whom may be nationals of the same state. A panel of jurors includes twelve members, and a majority vote of the jury would be required for each decision. After serving on one criminal case, the members of the jury would be thereafter barred from sitting on another jury of the ICJ. Although their experience might make them valued future jurors, former jurors would be excluded with the goal of avoiding even the appearance of impropriety in the conduct of cases. Their expenses would be paid by the ICJ. In order to maintain a sufficient number of prospective jurors, national groups would be responsible for maintaining a list of ten additional jury members at all times, and they could be included only on such a list for five years.

The jury of twelve international jurors would thus adjudicate in those cases where state or international law provides that a defendant is entitled to have a jury. The defendant may waive this right, and have judges of the ICJ act as the decision-makers. The defendant would have the opportunity to reject three jurors, without having to make any explanation as to the cause. If jurors indicate that they are unable to decide a case impartially, the defendant may also object, with no limitation upon the number of such objections. If the ICJ agrees with the defendant's claim, a juror will be excluded. These final provisions promote the legitimacy of international jury as a fair and impartial decision-maker and may, due to the concern showed for the defendant's interests, promote voluntary compliance with final ICJ orders.

The Application of Penalties

Imprisonment

When the jury or judges of the ICJ find a defendant who is an individual guilty of a state crime, and (pursuant to state substantive law) the judges of the ICJ give to the defendant a sentence of imprisonment, the defendant may be returned to the complaining state to serve the duration of his incarceration. If the ICJ finds, however, that the defendant's imprisonment would be cruel or a violation of international human rights, as described in various international agreements, the defendant could be imprisoned in a special international prison located near the ICJ. When the defendant, again an individual, is found guilty of an international crime, and receives a prison sentence, the defendant could also be incarcerated in the international prison. In the event that it is not possible to agree upon the creation of an international prison, the defendant could be imprisoned in a neutral state, not involved in the criminal court proceedings, if the prisons of that neutral state conform with minimum requirements for the treatment of prisoners.

It would also be necessary to create an international jail, located near the ICJ, for the purpose of holding defendants who are not eligible for bail prior to trial and for detaining convicted defendants who are awaiting sentencing.

Other Penalties

Where the substantive criminal law of a state provides for penalties other than imprisonment, such as capital punishment, the defendant is to be sent to the plaintiff country unless the penalty provided under state law and made applicable to the prisoner would violate international human rights standards and those relating to the treatment of prisoners. In the event that a state's penalties do violate such international human rights standards, the defendant should instead be subject to sentencing to a term of imprisonment by the judges of the ICJ, pursuant to guidelines set forth in the laws of civilized states, and to previous sentences imposed by the ICJ in similar cases. The defendant would thereafter be confined in an international prison or in the prison system of a neutral third state.

Restitution

Where the defendant in an international criminal case is a state, the ICJ will also have the authority to render judgments. If it is found to have committed an international crime, the court may order the offending country to pay restitution to the complaining party, where this is appropriate. Alternately, it may order the country to refrain from the actions that constitute an international crime and order it to take measures to correct injuries that have already been inflicted.

Bail

The defendant in a case involving a violation of either international or state criminal law is generally entitled to bail, to be granted during the course of a preliminary hearing. Bail is to be set by judges of the ICJ and may not be excessive. The objective in granting bail is to ensure that the defendant will be available for trial. Bail may be posted by the defendant, or by any individual or organization on his or her behalf, if the defendant consents. Bail will not be granted if the ICJ finds, during a preliminary hearing, that the individual poses a substantial danger to individuals in the world community or where there is a substantial risk that the individual will not appear for trial. In the event that bail is denied, the defendant will be incarcerated in an international jail until the time that the trial commences.

Establishing the Jurisdiction of the International Court of Justice over International and State Transnational Crimes

The proposal set forth above is that the ICJ be granted jurisdiction over both international and state transnational crimes. One issue that immediately arises is whether it is appropriate for the ICJ to exercise jurisdiction over such matters. Arguably, it is appropriate for an international tribunal, the ICJ, to exercise jurisdiction over international crimes. However, the more problematic issue has to do with the proposed jurisdiction of the ICJ over state crimes.

An immediate clarification is in order. It has been stressed throughout that the ICJ should exercise jurisdiction over a state crime only when the offender of national law has fled that country's borders. Hence, a local affair, namely the violation of a state's criminal laws, becomes a transnational issue and of international concern because the fugitive has escaped into another country, where he has taken refuge. It is of immense international interest at this point because the attempts of the offended state to obtain the fugitive may threaten world peace and security. Hence, the assertion of jurisdiction by the ICJ is appropriate when the crime in question is an international crime or a state crime that is accompanied with the flight of a fugitive from the offended country.

Another issue that arises relates to the implementation of this suggestion. Obviously, the only way in which to carry out this proposal is through a multilateral treaty between the world community of states that would supersede all existing bilateral and multilateral extradition treaties existing between states. The treaty itself would have to grant to the ICJ jurisdiction over the adjudication of international crimes and state crimes that have a transnational element (through the flight of fugitives to another country). The treaty would also have to recognize that the ICJ has compulsory jurisdiction over these cases, that states do not have concurrent authority over these matters, and that both countries and individuals may be involved in these proceedings, as plaintiffs and as defendants.

The best way to accomplish this change would be through amending the Statute of the ICJ, in these particulars and in the manner discussed above; this would, of course, require a revision of the United Nations Charter. Of course, proposals of this type, which would inject the rule of law into relations between states and aid in controlling state criminality, have always been opposed by the superpowers of the day, which prefer to settle disputes through force and coercion. Hence, the contemporary disintegration of the superpowers bodes well for the application of the rule of law to international affairs.

NOTES

* This is a revised version of Barbara M. Yarnold (1991), *International Fugitives: A New Role for the International Court of Justice*. New York: Praeger.

1. Bassiouni (1987) suggests that Anglo-American courts have adopted a "political-incidence theory" in determining whether the political offense exception applies, which is quite different from the European courts' "injured rights approach," which again contrasts with the "political motivation approach" of the courts of Switzerland and the Netherlands.

2. The twenty-two categories of crimes are: aggression, war crimes, unlawful use of weapons and unlawful emplacement of weapons, crimes against humanity, genocide, racial discrimination and apartheid, slavery and related crimes, torture, unlawful human experimentation, piracy, hijacking of aircraft, threat and use of force against internationally protected persons, taking civilian hostages, drug offenses, international traffic in obscene publications, destruction and/or theft of national treasures, environmental protection, unlawful use of the mails, interference with submarine cables, falsification and counterfeiting, bribery of a foreign public official, and theft of nuclear materials (Bassiouni, 1987).

REFERENCES

Anand, R.P. (1976) "Role of International Adjudication," in Leo Gross (ed.), *The Future of the International Court of Justice*. Vol. 1. New York: Oceana Publications, pp. 1–21.

Arendt, Hannah (1963) *Eichmann in Jerusalem*. New York: Viking Press.

Banoff, Barbara, and Christopher Pyle (1984) "To Surrender Political Offenders: The Political Offense Exception to Extradition in United States Law." *New York University Journal of International Law and Politics*, 16: 169–210.

Barak, Gregg (1990) "Crime, Criminology and Human Rights: Toward an Understanding of State Criminality." *The Journal of Human Justice* 2, 1: 11–28.

——— (1991) *Crimes by the Capitalist State: An Introduction to State Criminality*. Albany: State University of New York Press.

Bassiouni, M. Cherif (1983) *International Extradition*. New York: Oceana Publications.

——— (1987) *A Draft International Criminal Code and Draft Statute for an International Criminal Tribunal*. Boston: Kluwer Academic Publishers.

Blakesly, Christopher L. (1981) "The Practice of Extradition from Antiquity to Modern France and the United States: A Brief History." *Boston College International and Comparative Law Review* 4: 39–60.

Bohm, Bob (1993) "Social Relationships That Arguably Should Be Criminal Although They Are Not: On the Political Economy of Crime," in Kenneth Tunnell (ed.), *Political Crime*. New York: Garland, pp. 2–29.

Bridge, John W. (1964) "The Case for an International Court of Criminal Justice and the Formulation of International Criminal Law." *International and Comparative Law Quarterly* 13: 1255–1281.

Calvacoressi, Peter (1987) *World Politics Since 1945*. New York: Longman.

Clinard, Marshall, and Richard Quinney (1978) "Crime by Government," in David Ermann and Richard Lundman (eds.), *Corporate and Governmental Deviance*. New York: Oxford University Press, pp. 137–150.

Cohn, Norman (1967) *Warrant for Genocide*. New York: Harper & Row.

Cowen, Jon C. (1988) "The Omnibus Diplomatic Security and Antiterrorism Act of 1986: Faulty Drafting May Defeat Efforts to Bring Terrorists to Justice." *Cornell International Law Journal* 21: 127–146.

Deere, Lora L. (1933) "Political Offenses in the Law and Practice of Extradition." *American Journal of International Law* 27: 247–270.

Deutsch, Eberhard P. (1972) "The International Court of Justice." *Cornell International Law Journal* 5: pp. 35–41.

Eagleton, Clyde (1957) *International Government*. New York: Ronald Press.

The Economist (1990) "The Logic of Intervention: Plenty of Provocation." *World Press Review,* February: 19–20.

Erie R. Co. v. Tompkins (1938) 304 U.S. 64.

Evans, Alona E. (1963) "Reflections Upon the Political Offenses in the Law of Extradition and Asylum." *American Journal of International Law* 57: 1–24.

Extradition Act of U.S., 18 U.S.C. 3184–3190; as amended November 18, 1988, P.L. 100–690, Title VII, Subtitle B, Section 7087, 102 Stat. 4409.

Extradition Treaty Between United States and Japan, entered into force, September 1, 1978, T.I.A.S. No. 9625.

Farrell, Michael (1985) *Sheltering the Fugitive?* Dublin, Ireland: The Mercier Press.

Fischer, Dana D. (1982) "Decisions to Use the International Court of Justice." *International Studies Quarterly* 26: 251–277.

Fleming, Denna F. (1968) *The United States and the World Court, 1920–1966.* New York: Russell & Russell.

Fuentes, Carlos (1990) "Some Lessons from Panama: A Strong Latin Condemnation." *World Press Review* (February): 17–19.

Fuller, Steven N. (1988) "Extradition of Terrorists: An Executive Solution to the Limitations of the Political Offense Exception in the Context of Contemporary Judicial Interpretations of American Extradition Law." *Suffolk Transnational Law Journal* 11: 351–385.

Garcia-Mora, Manuel R. (1953) "The Present Status of Political Offenses in the Law of Extradition and Asylum." *University of Pittsburgh Law Review* 14: pp. 371–396.

Gilbert, Geoff (1991) *Aspects of Extradition Law.* Norwell, MA: Kluwer Academic Publishers.

Golt, Maynard B. (1966) "The Necessity of an International Court of Criminal Justice." *Washburn Law Journal* 6: 13–23.

Grabosky, Peter N. (1989) *Wayward Governance: Illegality and Its Control in the Public Sector.* Canberra: Australian Institute of Criminology.

Graham, Robert (1990) "Grounds for Doubt." *World Press Review* (February): 180.

Groarke, John P. (1985) "Revolutionaries Beware: The Erosion of the Political Offense Exception Under the 1986 United States–United Kingdom Supplementary Extradition Treaty." *University of Pennsylvania Law Review* 136: 1515–1545.

Gross, Leo (1969) *International Law in the Twentieth Century*. New York: Appleton-Century-Crofts.

—— (1976) "The International Court of Justice: Consideration of Requirements for Enhancing Its Role in the International Legal Order," in Leo Gross (ed.), *The Future of the International Court of Justice*, Vol. 1. New York: Oceana Publications, Inc., pp. 22–104.

—— (1976) *The Future of the International Court of Justice*, Volumes I and II. New York: Oceana Publications.

Gurovitsch, Kerry Ann (1987) "Legal Obstacles to Combatting International State-Sponsored Terrorism." *Houston Journal of International Law* 10: 159–180.

Hall, Jeffrey A. (1987) "A Recommended Approach to Bail in International Extradition Cases." *Michigan Law Review* 86: 599–619.

Harris, David (1967) "The Right to a Fair Trial in Criminal Proceedings as a Human Right." *International and Comparative Law Quarterly* 16: 352–378.

Henry, Stuart (1991) "The Informal Economy: A Crime of Omission by the State," in Gregg Barak (ed.), *Crimes by the Capitalist State*. Albany: State University of New York Press, pp. 253–272.

Higgins, Rosalyn (1963) *The Development of International Law Through the Political Organs of the United Nations*. New York: Oxford University Press.

Hoffmann, Stanley (1968) *Gulliver's Troubles, Or the Setting of American Foreign Policy*. New York: McGraw-Hill.

Hudson, Manley O. (1943) *The Permanent Court of International Justice*. New York: Macmillan.

—— (1969) "The Twenty-Fourth Year of the World Court," in Leo Gross (ed.), *International Law in the Twentieth Century*. New York: Meredith Corporation.

Ingraham, Barton L. (1979) *Political Crime in Europe*. Berkeley, California: University of California Press.

International Court of Justice (Date?) Statute.

Jenks, C. Wilfred (1964) *The Prospects of International Adjudication*. New York: Oceana Publications, Inc.

Kelly, Nancy P. (1987) "The Political Offense Exemption to Extradition: Protecting the Right of Rebellion in an Era of International Political Violence." *Oregon Law Review* 66: 405–428.

Kester, John G. (1988) "Some Myths of United States Extradition Law." *Georgetown Law Journal* 76: 1441–1493.

Kuzmanovic, Tomislav Z. (1987) "The Artukovic Case: Do the Means Justify the End?" *Wisconsin International Law Journal* 6: 155–172.

Lauterpacht, H. (1933) *The Function of Law in the International Community*. Oxford: Clarendon Press.

Leavy, Zad (1962) "The Eichmann Trial and the Role of Law." *American Bar Association Journal* 48: 820–825.

Lissitzyn, Oliver J. (1972) *The International Court of Justice*. New York: Octagon Books.

Minor, William W. (1975) "Political Crime, Political Justice, and Political Prisoners." *Criminology* 12: 385–398.

Moore, James (1982) *Moore's Federal Practice*. 2nd ed. Vol. 1A, parts 1 and 2. New York: Matthew Bender.

Mullally, Kathe F. (1986) "Combatting International Terrorism: Limiting the Political Exception Doctrine in Order to Prevent 'One Man's Terrorism from Becoming Another Man's Heroism'." *Villanova Law Review* 31: 1495–1547.

Nerone, F. Regan (1965–1966) "The Legality of Nuremberg." *Duquesne University Law Review* 4: 146–162.

O'Connell, D.P. (1967) *State Succession in Municipal Law and International Law* (2 volumes).

O'Higgins (1964) "The History of Extradition in British Practice, 1174–1794." *Indian Year Book of International Affairs* 13: 80.

Ostrihansky, Rudolf (1988) "Chambers of the International Court of Justice." *International and Comparative Law Quarterly* 37: 30–52.

Pearlman, Moshe (1963) *The Capture and Trial of Adolf Eichmann*. New York: Simon & Schuster.

Pearson, Frederic S., and Martin J. Rochester (1988) *International Relations*. New York: Random House.

Robertson, Charles L. (1975) *International Politics Since World War II: A Short History*. New York: Wiley.

Roebuck, Julian, and Stanley C. Weeber (1978) *Political Crime in the United States*. New York: Praeger.

Ropp, Steve C. (1990) "Military Retrenchment and Decay in Panama." *Current History* 89 (January): 17–20.

Rosenne, Shabtai (1973) *The World Court*. Dobbs Ferry, NY: A.W. Sijthoff-Leiden, Oceana Publications.

Ross, Jeffrey Ian (1992) Review of Gregg Barak, *Crimes by the Capitalist State*. *Justice Quarterly* 9, 2: 347–354.

Russell of Liverpool, E. (1963) *The Trial of Adolph Eichmann*. London: Transworld Publishers.

Schafer, Stephen (1974) *The Political Criminal*. New York: Free Press.

Scott, Sterling (1985) "Codification of State Responsibility in International Law: A Review and Assessment." *ASILS International Law Journal* 9: 1–36.

Siemens, Jochen (1990) "Cover Story Panama." *World Press Review*, February: 15–16.

Simon, Michael P. (1988) "The Political Offense Exception: Recent Changes in Extradition Law Appertaining to the Northern Ireland Conflict." *Arizona Journal of International and Comparative Law* 5: 244–258.

Strauss, Francine R. (1987) "Demjanjuk v. Petrovsky: An Analysis of Extradition." *Maryland Journal of International Law and Trade*, 12: 65–80.

Sweeney, Joseph M., Covey T. Oliver, and Noyes E. Leech (1981) *The International Legal System*. Mineola, NY: Foundation Press.

Turk, Austin T. (1975) *Political Criminality and Political Policing*. New York: MSS Modular Publishers.

———— (1982) *Political Criminality*. Beverly Hills, CA: Sage.

United Nations (1983) *UN Chronicle* 20: 47–53.

U.S. Constitution, Article III, Section 2.

Vasilyev, Gennady (1990) "The View from Moscow: Back to the Future?" *World Press Review*, February: 22–23.

Vines, K.N. (1963) "The Role of Circuit Courts of Appeal in the Federal Judicial Process: A Case Study." *Midwest Journal of Political Science* 7: 305–319.

von Lang, Jochen, and Sibyll Claus (1983) *Eichmann Interrogated*. New York: Farrar, Straus & Giroux.

von Mangoldt, Hans (1982) "Arbitration and Conciliation," in Joseph M. Sweeney, Covey T. Oliver, and Noyes E. Leech (eds.), *The International Legal System*. Mineola, NY: Foundation Press.

Yarnold, Barbara M. (1991) *International Fugitives: A New Role for the International Court of Justice*. New York: Praeger.

————— (1992) *Politics and the Courts: Toward a General Theory of Public Law*. New York: Praeger.

Can States Commit Crimes? The Limits of Formal International Law

*Luis F. Molina**

In a strict sense, the term *state crime* is almost, but not quite, an oxymoron, a legal absurdity. A crime is, tautologically, a wrongful act only insofar as it is a violation of criminal law that is punishable by a state,[1] and sovereign states have generally been unwilling to expose themselves to sanction by other countries or by international tribunals. Under only two treaties have states contemplated ceding their sovereignty to an international body that would have the authority to identify and prosecute international crimes.[2] Under no circumstance has any state agreed to international criminal prosecution, although individuals who have acted in their official capacities have been prosecuted before international tribunals. Moreover, despite some recent impetus encouraging identification and prosecution of state crimes under formal international law, it is unlikely that international prosecutorial courts to assess state reponsibility for criminal conduct will be created in the foreseeable future.

Nonetheless, there are actions perpetrated by state authorities that are normatively criminal, and despite problems in enforcement, the international community is not entirely without recourse. A broad range of measures, including legal ones, are available to respond to reprehensible actions by states against individuals. At the international level, these legal measures are chiefly provided through international criminal justice and human rights instruments under the auspices of human rights bodies and initiatives.

In this chapter, I will first show that international condemnation of states allowing or promoting consensually reprehensible acts has not been achieved through recourse to a formal international legal system. Second, to overcome the implications of the definitional and practical problems embedded in a concept of "state crime," including international enforcement, I outline some forces that provide a philosophical basis for a circumvention of these problems. Third, I describe situations in which human rights procedures, not criminal proceedings, have effectively addressed normatively criminal acts by violative states.[3] Finally, I discuss existing formal legal and human rights–based international developments and instruments which may eventually form part of a comprehensive approach to curtail state actions that are both crimes and human rights violations. These approaches are useful in themselves and could also serve as complementary strategies if an international criminal tribunal were eventually established.

The Identification of International Criminals

Rather than hold states criminally responsible for international criminal acts, the trend in international criminal law since World War II has been the opposite: to hold individuals internationally accountable for wrongful acts, even if state governments are thought to be culpable.[4]

States as Juridical Subjects: Can States Commit Crimes?

There are clear doctrinal constraints on the use of international law to deal with crimes committed by states. As a result, states have not been subject to prosecution for their criminal actions by international law (Munch, 1986: 127).

The *doctrine of sovereignty* is the principal tenet of international law, and politically constructed entities identified as sovereign states are its primary focus (MacLean, 1989).[5] The legal rights and duties of states are predicated on the doctrine of sovereignty, according to which states are independent and have an equal status as participants in the international forum. As such, international law is comprised of rules which states agree will be valid. Under international law, states are accountable[6] for their actions according either to treaty or customary international law.[7] Under a treaty, obligations are binding on a state once the government of that state has ratified the treaty. Therefore, the state clearly controls the treaty obligations it undertakes. One example of a treaty according to which certain states have ceded jurisdiction in cases between themselves is the Statute of the International Court of Justice, and there are regional examples as well.

The second method of accountability, norms of customary international law, emerge through the acts of states. However, before a norm of customary international law is recognized, the community of states through consistent and uniform practice, based on a conscious duty to act, must accept the particular custom.[8] However, a state will not be bound by a rule of customary international law if it shows its opposition to the rule from the time of the rule's inception. This self-definition is rooted in the principle of nonintervention, articulated in Article 2(7) of the Charter of the United Nations (hereafter "Charter") which stipulates that:

> [n]othing contained in the present Charter shall authorize the United Nations to intervene in matters which are essentially within the domestic jurisdiction of any state or shall require the Members to submit such matters to settlement under the present Charter; but this principle shall not prejudice the application of enforcement measures under Chapter VII.[9]

The International Court of Justice

The International Court of Justice (ICJ), popularly called the World Court, was established under the Statute of the International Court of Justice, an annex of the Charter of the United Nations in 1945, and is the most important authority for the resolution of disputes between states.[10] However, it has no criminal jurisdiction, and even if it did, there is no international law enforcement authority (Article 59). Further, an important precondition of any dispute brought before the ICJ, flowing from the doctrine of state sovereignty, is that states involved in a dispute must consent to the jurisdiction of the World Court.[11] In recent years, the most publicized example of the need for consent was demonstrated when the United States rescinded its declaration of compulsory jurisdiction during the World Court's consideration of *Nicaragua v. United States*, although the ICJ went on to render its decision anyway (ICJ, 1986: 14).[12] Likely because of the requirement for consent, the World Court gave judgments on only fifty-one cases, and offered twenty-one advisory opinions, in the period 1946–1990 (ICJ, 1990: 3–6).[13]

The Individual as an International Criminal

The decision to hold individuals criminally responsible under international law was first formulated in the Moscow Declaration of 1943 (UN War Crimes Commission, 1948: 270), codified in Article 7 of the Nürnberg Charter,[14] and articulated during opening statements at the Nürnberg Trials by the U.S. chief of Counsel, Justice Robert H. Jackson, who stated,

> Crimes against international law are committed by men, not by abstract entities, and only by punishing individuals who commit such crimes can the provisions of international law be enforced.[15]

Hence the effects of the Charter of Nürnberg Tribunal and the judgments against individuals that followed it were profound:

> [they] proclaimed the criminality of offenses against humanity, i.e. of such offenses against the fundamental rights of man to life and liberty, even if committed in obedience to the law of the State. To that extent, in a different sphere, positive law has recognised the individual as endowed, under international law, with rights the violation of which is a criminal act. (Harris, 1991: 146).

Since World War II, multilateral conventions provide the basis to find individuals responsible for acts that are internationally defined as crimes. As a result of these multilateral treaties, a large number of states have identified crimes, including genocide, slavery, apartheid, torture, and "terrorist" offenses such as aircraft hijacking, attacks on diplomats, and hostage-taking.[16] These conventions are evidence of a general consensus by states that certain criminal acts damage values held by the international community, and that individual perpetrators should be prosecuted in the country where the offenses took place, or be extradited to a state that has the jurisdiction to prosecute them for these offenses under national law. Because states have not been able to agree on direct enforcement mechanisms, for example, an international criminal court, Bassiouni terms the duty of a signatory state to prosecute or extradite the "indirect enforcement system" in international criminal law (Bassiouni, 1986: 1–6). This indirect enforcement system is an imperfect one, however, because it depends on the inclusion of specific "prosecute or extradite" provisions in international criminal law conventions, and not on some overarching principle or practice of international law acceptable to all states.

The treaties that identify international crimes potentially permit all states to prosecute individuals for these offenses under national criminal law. The notion is that if enough states co-operate to exercise their own national criminal jurisdictions, which for some crimes may extend beyond territorial venue according to the conventions, individuals responsible for certain serious forms of transnational crime will not go unpunished. However, one exceptional addition to the reliance on national criminal justice systems to curtail transnational crime can be found in Article IV of the *Convention on the Prevention and Punishment of the Crime of Genocide:* "[p]ersons committing genocide or any of the other acts enumerated in Article III shall be punished, whether they are constitutionally responsible rulers, public officials or private individuals." Further, the treaty goes on to specify that "[p]ersons charged with genocide . . . shall be tried by a competent tribunal of the State in the territory of which the Act was committed, *or by such international penal tribunal as may have jurisdiction with respect to those Contracting Parties which shall have accepted its jurisdiction*" (United

Nations, 1948, emphasis added). Bassiouni explains the conundrum as follows:

> [t]he only convention that refers to an international criminal court is the Genocide Convention, which provides only for the jurisdiction of an international criminal court for the crime of genocide in the event that such a court exists, but it does not require or mandate the establishment of such a court. (1987: 10)[17]

At the same time, this unique treaty provision leaves open the possibility, on an international level, of deciding whether officials of a given state are guity of genocide, but does not mention prosecution of the state itself.

The preference for pursuing individual accountability at the international level is also demonstrated through the development of the *Draft Code of Crimes Against the Peace and Security of Mankind* (hereafter "*Draft Code*").[18] For various reasons, the *Draft Code* received little attention from 1950, when it was submitted to the International Law Commission (ILC),[19] until 1981, when the General Assembly invited resumption of work on the document (United Nations 1981).[20] Shortly thereafter, in 1983, the ILC clarified that the Draft Code would be limited to the criminal responsibility of individuals, not states (United Nations, 1985).[21] Then, in 1988, the ILC adopted a commentary to Article 11 of the Draft Code, which rejects immunity for officials who commit certain crimes, affirming its intention as follows: "the very essence of the code [was]: to pierce the veil of the State and prosecute those who were materially responsible for crimes committed on behalf of the State as an abstract entity" (United Nations, 1988: 289). Malekian writes "consensus has grown, that prosecution of a criminal state is possible through the punishment of its official individuals, economy, armed forces or other state entities" (1988: 195), and reviews the historically perceived impracticality of assigning criminal responsibility to a state entity (177–181).[22]

A recent (1991) and significant articulation of the Draft Code of Crimes, the *Code of Talloires* (hereafter Code), proposes the establishment of an international criminal court and identifies individuals as the proper subject of such a court. According to the Code, the liability of states "shall be governed by applicable international instruments" (Foundation for the Establishment of an International Criminal Court and International Criminal Law Commission, 1991: 18). The Code does not propose states as international juridical subjects, and it intentionally "drive[s] back outdated notions of sovereignty and enhanc[es] the role of the individual. . . . [I]ndividuals are subjects of the international community first, not of any particular sovereign entity."[23]

The juridical reality remains, however, that since the Nürnberg and Tokyo tribunals no individuals have been tried by a competent international court.[24] States are the recognized subjects of international criminal law, but generally cannot be prosecuted for crimes. There is a philosophical rationale behind this paradox, and a brief overview of that reasoning, and an alternative perspective, will help form a basis for understanding the current obstacles to international criminal prosecution. This alternative perspective, realized only since 1945, has enabled the effective sanctioning of states under rights-based criminal justice instruments.

The Dumb Ox Revised

Criminal law is considered to be positive law in most of the major legal systems of the world.[25] Since the time of John Austin (1790–1859), "positive law" has meant law as the command of a sovereign backed by force, where "laws in any observed system are such just by being enacted by the procedures accepted in the system" (Braybrooke, 1989: 2). Kelsen, for example, writes that "[i]t is the essential characteristic of the law as a coercive order to establish a community monopoly of force"(1944: 3). Justice Holmes wrote that law "does not exist without some definite authority behind it" (*Black & White Taxicab & Transfer Co.*, 1928). Positivists would argue that international criminal law should "unite all individual States or, at least, as many as possible, into a World State, to concentrate all their means of power, their armed forces, and put them at the disposal of a world government under laws created by a world parliament" (Kelsen, 1944: 5). Fisher writes that

[i]t is fair to say that most reformers in the field of international law have accepted the notion that the basic way of enforcing law is by a policeman, and the way to improve compliance with international law is to establish an international police force strong enough to impose the law upon any country. (1981: 13)

But what is the effect if a supranational system, like the United Nations, normally cannot exercise coercive authority? Can such an agency effect a change in state "criminal" practices? There is reason to believe that it can. The basis for compliance, though, is not likely to be achieved through formal, positive juridical procedures.

An opposing legal philosophy stems from a belief in natural law, but because "natural law" is often an oversimplified term, some explanation is required. As it is generally considered to have been first articulated by Thomas Aquinas,[26] the term included a legal *weltanschauung* that was based on the law of God, which was therefore immutable. In the seventeenth century, this general philosophy began to be importantly modified to be a secular, human accountability,[27] but still consensual: natural law was, and is, normative law.[28] In the eighteenth century, when positivism became essentially hegemonic in all academic pursuits, including "legal science,"[29] a "natural law" view of law and jurisprudence was virtually extinguished, at least in Western society, for almost two hundred years. The renaissance of natural law took different forms, and had different entrepreneurs in Europe and North America, but basically by World War II dichotomous legal philosophy, at least in broad terms, was conceivable. The problem, for adherents of a more fluid, human-based, value-recognizing form of law and jurisprudence was that most (Western) superior courts were presided over by judges who believed that legal science was formal, value-free, and impartial. The Permanent Court of International Justice, and later the early ICJ, were no exceptions to this positivistic view of the basis of law.

In international criminal law, the atrocities of World War II motivated an exceptional jurisprudence, in positivist terms, to deal with the previously sacrosanct tenets of state sovereignty that, since articulated in *Lotus*, had been unquestioned.

Humphrey writes that "*[j]us inter gentes*, the law traditionally governing the relations between states, now extended its reach to other entities, including individual men and women, who, for a long time objects of the law, now became its subjects." However, once Western collective retribution was expiated, and vengeance exacted, international jurisprudence returned, more or less, to the presumed predictability of rule-based law, at least until 1966.[30] But by establishing individual criminal responsibility, the World War II tribunals and other forces had begun to penetrate the "shield" of state sovereignty which dictated that "each member of the system was to be its own judge concerning questions relating to compliance with international prescriptions" (Young, 1979: 45). This erosion was largely ignored by legal positivists, but did not go unnoticed by human rights advocates.

The international metamorphosis of human rights into a postwar world order was achieved in 1945 through the Charter of the United Nations. The Charter specifically refers to human rights in its Preamble and six of its articles (Humphrey, 1989: 59–71; McGoldrick, 1991: 2). In contrast, in the Covenant of the League of Nations, the term "human rights" does not appear at all (e.g., Humphrey, 1984: 11, McGoldrick, 1991: 25). Under Article 68 of the Charter,[31] the Economic and Social Council is empowered to "set up commissions in economic and social fields and for the promotion of human rights." The most important of these is the Commission on Human Rights, which held its first session January 27–February 10, 1947, and which was charged with drafting the Universal Declaration of Human Rights (UDHR).

Adopted by the General Assembly on December 10, 1948, the UDHR is the keystone document of the International Bill of Human Rights. The other two documents are the International Covenant on Civil and Political Rights (ICCPR), with its Optional Protocol (OP),[32] and the International Covenant on Economic, Social and Cultural Rights. These documents establish a superior normative order by which the actions of states toward their residents can be judged, reflecting a natural law common to all people.[33]

Under provisions of the International Bill of Human Rights states cannot commit "crimes"; they can, however, violate provisions of Covenants to which they have solemnly agreed, and as I will illustrate below, there can be effective remedies to violations.

The International Legal Response to State Crime

The Script, Setting and Actors

The most demonstrable, effective international instrument for the abolition or prohibition of wrongful acts by state authorities has been the ICCPR and its OP. It is effective because Article 28 of the ICCPR establishes a Human Rights Committee (HRC) consisting of eighteen members who are nationals of states that have ratified the ICCPR,[34] who have "recognized competence in the field of human rights," and who serve in their personal capacities. The HRC is empowered to hear complaints from states' parties to the ICCPR alleging violations of the ICCPR by other states' parties (Article 41), receive periodic reports from states' parties on measures adopted to give effect to the rights recognized by the ICCPR, and, most importantly, states' parties to the OP empower the HRC "to receive and consider . . . communications from individuals claiming to be victims of violations of any of the rights set forth in the Covenant" (OP Preamble).[35] Those rights are enumerated in Articles 1 through 27 of the ICCPR and include the rights not to be arbitrarily deprived of life (Article 6), tortured (Article 7), or enslaved (Article 8), actions that are unequivocally and normatively criminal. Article 2(3) of the ICCPR reads as follows:

> 3. Each State Party to the present Covenant undertakes:
> (a) To ensure that any person whose rights or freedoms as herein recognized are violated shall have an effective remedy, notwithstanding that the violation has been committed by persons acting in an official capacity;
> (b) To ensure that any person claiming such a remedy shall have his right thereto determined by competent judicial, administrative or legislative authorities, or by any

other competent authority provided for by the legal system of the State, and to develop the possibilities of judicial remedy;

(c) To ensure that the competent authorities shall enforce such remedies when granted.

Although no state has agreed to an international criminal authority, fifty-five countries have acceded authority to the United Nations Human Rights Committee to receive complaints alleging violations of the ICCPR.[36]

The HRC was, and is, not a court. Allegations accepted for investigation are "complaints," not indictments. The HRC is careful to offer "views," not judgments, and the effect of its views is persuasive, not binding, upon states.[37] The task of the HRC is to use its tools, the ICCPR and the OP, to establish a field of symbolic force, "to cast into sensible form a concept of what, together, [we are] supposed to make of [ourselves]" (Geertz, 1980: 102). The views expressed by the HRC exemplify Gusfield's theoretical position that "public presentations assume significance because they convey a description of what is the public order, even though it is not the governing order of interpersonal and routine actions" (1981: 180).

In the year after the first expression of its views, which was in 1979 against Uruguay, the HRC began to realize the importance of publicity for its decisions.[38] Greater efforts to provide public awareness were made, and the HRC argued for additional reporting media.[39] Justice Tarnapolsky has written that

> [i]t has to be recognized that the Human Rights Committee has no enforcement powers for its supervising mandate, except the pressure of world public opinion. . . . [A consequence of this is that] the Human Rights Committee is the only international forum from which the [former] Warsaw Pact countries have accepted questioning on their human rights record and to which they have responded. (1987: 613, 621)[40]

Clearly, publicity can produce desired results.

The Results

As of July 26, 1991, after 12 years of operation, the HRC has adopted views regarding 119 communications and found violations of the ICCPR in 93 of them.[41] The overwhelming violative state has been Uruguay, with 78 complaints received, and 45 views adopted, regarding the state since the first expression of views by the HRC in 1979,[42] although it must be stressed that since the restoration of democracy in Uruguay on March 1, 1985, complaints have virtually ceased.[43] The second greatest number of complaints to the HRC has alleged violations of the ICCPR in Canada, although 80 percent of the forty-five complaints have been declared inadmissible or withdrawn (United Nations, 1990: 229).

Earlier in this chapter I identified three rights violations that are unequivocally crimes: enslavement, torture, and murder. Of the three, torture is the crime that has been most frequently condemned in the views of the HRC. No published complaints of enslavement exist, and murder is a crime requiring evidentiary proof, which would be difficult, if not impossible, to present to the HRC because the committee does not conduct criminal trials. The term *disappearance*, though, has been accepted by the HRC as a basis for complaints.[44]

Article 6 : "Every Human Being Has the Inherent Right to Life"

The right to life is one of the rights under the ICCPR from which derogation is not permitted, even during times of public emergency.[45] Only Article 6 has been the subject of two general comments by the HRC.[46]

Views expressed by the HRC concerning Article 6 (deprivation of life) can be understood in two ways.[47] First, in several cases the HRC has condemned state parties for failing to protect the right to life,[48] or for failing to protect individuals from the violation of that right by the police.[49] Second, flowing from "[perhaps] the most significant decision of the HRC concerning Article 6" (McGoldrick, 1991: 345), *Mbenge v. Zaire,*[50] the HRC has combined the provisions of ICCPR Article 14, which is the right to a fair trial, with the imposition of a death penalty, so that

> [t]his requires that both the substantive and the procedural law in the application of which the death penalty was imposed was not contrary to the provisions of the Covenant and also that the death penalty was imposed in accordance with that law and therefore with the provisions of the Covenant.

This expression of views has been reinforced in subsequent decisions by the HRC.[51] McGoldrick emphasizes the "enormous significance" of the decision, because "the failure of the substantive or procedural law of a State party to comply with any provision of the Covenant will render any death penalty imposed a violation of article 6(2)" (1991: 346).

Article 7: "No One Shall Be Subjected to Torture or to Cruel, Inhuman or Degrading Treatment or Punishment"

Article 7, like Article 6, is nonderogable, and it was the subject of an important 1982 general comment by the HRC in which it linked Article 7 to Article 10(1) of the ICCPR, an article which requires that prisoners be "treated with humanity and with respect for the inherent dignity of the human person." This linkage by the HRC is important because it broadens the scope of conditions under which torture can be found to have occurred, and affords a standard of prisoner treatment consistent with the European Convention on Human Rights.[52]

Prior to 1990, the HRC's views concerning Article 7 failed to define specific actions that constitute violations of the right to be free from torture.[53] This lack of clarity was a serious obstacle in mandating compliance with the Article, but the HRC has now begun to specify actions which constitute torture.[54] The HRC has, however, used article 7 to condemn actions that clearly would be criminal including electric shock and physical beatings,[55] mock burials,[56] mock executions,[57] and treatment by state authorities resulting in permanent physical injury.[58]

A major expansion in the international protection against torture, and a provision for increased condemnation of offending states, occurred in 1987 when the Convention against Torture and Other Cruel, Inhuman or Degrading Treatment or Punishment (UNCAT) entered into force.[59] Following the model of the ICCPR, UNCAT established a Committee against Torture (hereafter "Committee"),[60] and it also provides both state-to-state and individual complaint mechanisms, the latter virtually identical to the HRC.[61] As well, there is a progressive system to handle complaints of a "systematic practice" of torture in the territory of a state party, which goes beyond the traditional notions of state sovereignty. If such complaints are received, the Committee can conduct an investigation, discuss findings with the state party, and use the force of publicity by publishing a summary account of the results.[62]

As of 1991, the Committee received seven individual complaints, five of which it declared inadmissible and two were under consideration as additional depositions.[63] At that time, the Committee was also considering the first communication alleging the systematic practice of torture by a state party.[64]

The Effects: International Condemnation of State Crimes

The important question, of course, is whether the views of the HRC contribute to an alteration in state practices? The answer, as with sanctions imposed on individuals, is "sometimes." Since Canada and Uruguay are the two countries against which the greatest number of complaints have been lodged (United Nations, 1990: 229), some effects of the HRC's views on those two states will be described.[65]

Canada: An Example of Influence

Canada ratified the ICCPR and the OP in May 1976, and the documents entered into force three months later.[66] Under the terms of Article 40 of the ICCPR, all states' parties to the treaty must provide a report on "measures they have adopted which give effect to the rights recognized herein and on the progress made in the enjoyment of those rights." Canada responded enthusiastically, in 1979, with a 468-page report.[67]

There have not been any published complaints to the HRC from Canadian residents alleging violations of Articles 6 and 7. There have been complaints of violations of the ICCPR, however, and a consideration of the domestic effects of one of these complaints illustrates the persuasive force and significant effects that the HRC can have, and has had, in Canada.

On December 29, 1977, a Maliseet Indian, Sandra Nicholas Lovelace, complained to the HRC that she had lost her Indian status as a result of her marriage to a non-Indian on May 23, 1970. She alleged that the Canadian legislation under which the discriminatory disentitlement occurred, then s. 12(1)(b) of the *Indian Act*,[68] contravened Article 27 of the ICCPR.[69] On July 30, 1981, the HRC agreed that the Canadian legislation contravened Article 27, and a supplementary individual opinion also found violation of Articles 2(1), 3, 23(1) and (4), and 26.[70]

These domestic events followed:

1. In April 1982, the *Canadian Charter of Rights and Freedoms* became law. The *Charter* included an "equality provision," which entered into effect three years later.[71]

2. In September 1982, a Canadian Parliamentary *Subcommittee on Indian Women and the Indian Act* began hearings to study "the provisions of the Indian Act dealing with band membership and Indian Status, with a view to recommending how the Act might be amended to remove those provisions that discriminate against women on the basis of sex."[72] In the ten days of Subcommittee proceedings, there were at least thirteen discussions of *Lovelace* and its implications for Canada, including the testimony of an international law expert who said, "In the eyes of the world [*Lovelace*] is a severe embarrassment to a nation that claims to base a great deal of its foreign policy on human rights determinations."[73]

3. On April 17, 1985, amendments to the *Indian Act* took effect that, among other things, abrogated section 12(1)(b), and any woman who had lost her status under the repealed section was able to be registered as an Indian.[74]

4. On June 6, 1983, Canada wrote to the HRC regarding the views adopted by it in *Lovelace*. Although Canada acknowledged that it was in violation of Article 27 of the ICCPR, even before discussing remedies to the finding, Canada noted that it was not found in violation of Article 26.[75] Canada's response to the HRC was carefully framed to establish Canadian compliance with both Articles 26 and 27.

5. In their presentation of the second and third reports of the government of Canada to the HRC in 1990,[76] representatives of Canada reported that "some 76,000 persons had since acquired Indian status as a result of that amendment [to the *Indian Act*]."[77]

Uruguay: An Example of Probable Influence

As discussed earlier, until 1988 Uruguay had the greatest number of complaints registered against it by the HRC, and was determined by the HRC as the most violative state.[78] In 1984 the Lawyers Committee for International Human Rights wrote that

> [d]uring the last decade Uruguay's military police and detention authorities have earned a reputation for savagery that is matched by few anywhere. Torture is widespread and continues despite its prohibition under Article 26 of the Uruguayan Constitution and Article 7 of the International Covenant on Civil and Political Rights. . . . It typically occurs in the period immediately following arrest. In that period, detainees are routinely beaten; hung from their knees, wrists and ankles; submerged in tanks of urine, dirty water or other liquid until they are nearly drowned (submarino); forced to straddle wooden or iron bars which cut the groin (caballete); and given extensive electric shock torture to sensitive parts of their bodies. (1984: 17)

After twelve years of military dictatorship, Uruguay's 1985 return to democratic political rule has been fragile. President Julio Maria Sanguinetti's successful campaign compromised with the military, guaranteeing no civilian trials for human rights abuses during military rule, and no military dismissals (Weinstein, 1988: 90, 104–12). On December 22, 1986, that compromise was enshrined in the *Expiry Law*, which "grant[s] exemption from punishment to all police and military personnel responsible for human rights violations committed before March 1, 1985 if such acts were carried out for political motives or in fulfilment of orders" (Amnesty International, 1988: 209). On April 16, 1989, the electorate voted (58 percent) to not repeal the 1986 Expiry Law which had legalized prosecutorial immunity for the military. As well, President Luis Alberto Lacalle, who assumed office on March 1, 1990, repudiated an announcement by his foreign minister that those responsible for the disappearance of Elena Quinteros, a highly publicized person who had "disappeared," would be brought to justice, and stated that he does not support a "reinvestigation of the past" (Amnesty International, 1992: 244). These examples support Weinstein's comment that "[t]he culture of fear produced by the dictatorship continues to haunt the minds of politicians and workers alike. The various intelligence services of the armed forces have deliberately kept up activities that are designed to intimidate the population" (1988: 109).

On the other hand, on February 4, 1985, Uruguay signed the UNCAT, and it came into force on June 26, 1987. Uruguay's first periodic report to the Committee against Torture was due on June 25, 1988, but as of May 3, 1991, had not submitted its report.[79] In February 1990, Uruguay signed the Second Optional Protocol to the ICCPR, but had not ratified it by December 31, 1990 (Amnesty International, 1992: 243).

Notwithstanding these mixed signals, which President Lacalle characterizes as a healing process, Uruguay renewed its formal dialogue with the HRC through the submission of its second report on July 28, 1988.[80] During the discussion of that report in 1989, the Uruguayan representative stated that the "national tragedy" of military dictatorship was overcome, and that "democratic Uruguay expected to resume its active role in the international defence of human rights."[81] He reported to the HRC that only one complaint was lodged with the American Commission on Human Rights for an alleged violation of the American Convention on Human Rights.[82] HRC members "expressed admiration for Uruguay's efforts to restore democracy and welcomed the impressive progress that had been achieved in restoring democratic institutions and respect for human rights."[83] Amnesty International has not reported any recent civilian disappearances or allegations of torture, but there have been complaints of ill treatment of prisoners (Amnesty International, 1992: 244–5).

In summary, notwithstanding the general accuracy of McGoldrick's point that "[i]t is very difficult to provide positive evidence that the existence of the Covenant and the work of the HRC [has] any concrete and positive effect on the human rights position[s] in the states parties" (1991: 504), there are nonetheless some clear and important signs of effect and influence. In addition to the two state party examples given above, recently the Dominican Republic,[84] Ecuador,[85] Mauritius,[86] the Netherlands,[87] Colombia,[88] Peru,[89] Trinidad and Tobago,[90] and notably Finland,[91] have all communicated to the HRC assurances of legislative or other remedies following expressions of views by the HRC. Moreover, in 1991 the HRC continued its initiative to hold state parties accountable to report on actions taken as a result of views expressed by the HRC against that country. Progress has been achieved, and the HRC has indicated that the initiative will be maintained.[92]

A Possible Future: Article 19 of the Draft Articles on State Responsibility

No successful prosecutions of criminal state responsibility under a formal legal process have succeeded and no prosecutions are likely to occur in the immediate future. As discussed above, state criminal culpability has been achieved by characterizing consensually criminal acts by state agents as human rights violations under existing international treaties and by providing declarations of international condemnation of violative states from a credible source, the UNHRC.

However, there is some current international institutional momentum for the establishment of a formal legal regime that should not be ignored. In 1976 the International Law Commission adopted Article 19 of the Draft Articles on State Responsibility (hereafter "Draft Articles"),[93] which "established international criminal responsibility of states and gives recognition to the concept of state criminality" (Malekian, 1985: 190). In an earlier commentary to Article 19, the ILC asserted that

> [t]he obligation to punish personally individuals who are organs of the State and are guilty of crimes against the peace, against humanity, and so on does not, in the Commission's view, constitute a form of international responsibility of the State, and such punishment certainly does not exhaust the prosecution of the international responsibility incumbent upon the State for internationally wrongful acts which are attributed to it in such cases by reason of the conduct of its organs. (Amnesty International, 1976: 104)

The Draft Articles define four actions or categories of actions as examples of international crimes: aggression; colonial domination; slavery, genocide, and apartheid; and massive pollution of the atmosphere or of the seas. Even though these examples are not exhaustive, they are an attempt by the ILC to reflect some possible consequences of an international crime by a state. It is the definition of the criminal behavior that is significant: for example, the criminal behavior that might lead to aggression is defined as "a serious breach of an international obligation of essential importance for the maintenance of international peace and security."[94]

Within these lofty phrases is embedded the problem of enforcement: what organ, for example, defines an "international obligation of essential importance?"[95] The ILC was unable to take a position, although the United Nations Security Council, and General Assembly, were proposed as possible organs, either together or separately (Spinedi, 1989: 112–114).

Because of the irresolution of any sanctioning body for international crimes as proposed in the Draft Articles, but somewhat unfortunately, the ILC then went on in its extensive commentary to "resist the temptation to give any indication at the present time . . . as to . . . the régime of responsibility [sanctions] applicable to . . . 'international crimes'" (Amnesty International, 1976: 117).

It remains to be determined whether the Gulf War and its consequences, or the continuing Balkan tragedy, will be construed as a demonstration of international enforcement of violations of the Draft Articles, since a case could be made for a violation by several states of sections of the four exemplary crimes. In a review of these issues, Steinhart, somewhat pessimistically but probably correctly, writes that "state crimes will remain inherently political crimes, in the same sense that international law has generally been deemed political by its various and irreconcilable observers" (1991: 619).[96]

Conclusion

Given the rapid proliferation of international treaties and reporting bodies concerned with normatively criminal acts defined as rights violations, it would be foolish to predict the future, but some trends can be identified. First, it is not likely that prosecution of states, as entities, for international crimes will occur in the near future under the jurisdiction of an international criminal court. In fact, the secretary-general of the United Nations, in his recommendation to the Security Council on the establishment of an international criminal tribunal for the prosecution of serious violations of international law in the former Yugoslavia since January 1, 1991, recommends that the jurisdiction of the proposed tribunal extend to natural persons, not states, regardless of their official capacities.[97]

Secondly, note should be taken of the increasing number of important nontreaty instruments that have been adopted in the recent past, many of them under the aegis of the United Nations Committee on Crime Prevention and Control (CCPC), and quinquennial United Nations congresses on the Prevention of Crime and Treatment of Offenders.[98] A former member of the CCPC,[99] Clark, has written that the CCPC:

has been expanding its role as a standard-creating catalyst in the broad criminal justice area. Increasingly as well, it is devoting its attention beyond standard setting to follow-up, or implementation, a tentative step down the road that other human rights bodies describe as "enforcement." (1989: 69)

As an example of this increasing emphasis on "follow-up," in 1991 a group of experts reviewing the problems of implementation of international criminal justice standards discussed the feasibility of several compliance mechanisms, including the possibility of appointing special rapporteurs to monitor compliance.[100] There is likely to be increased emphasis on member states that have consensually adopted international criminal justice instruments, at the quinquennial UN congresses, to account for the enforcement of those standards. While international review will not assume the persuasive force of HRC views, increased compliance will result.[101]

Finally, protection of the environment against damage by state organs may be an area where international criminal law will evolve, but the problems in effecting criminal remedies are formidable.[102] There are two possibilities. First, there is the possibility of treaties that entail jurisdictional accession to, for example, the ICJ,[103] but there are the consequent enforcement difficulties. Second, there is the difficult problem of determining the locus of violation of the "global commons," areas including the high seas, the deep seabed, the ozone layer, and outer space (Boyle, 1991: 69).[104] He writes that "[t]he problems of using state responsibility as a tool for resolving transboundary environmental disputes on a basis of customary law are already severe; application of the concept to the environment of the global commons merely accentuates the difficulty."[105]

Boyle's comment was reinforced at the United Nations Conference on Environment and Development (UNCED) in June 1992.[106] At the UNCED there were calls for "the further development of international law on sustainable development," and "the need to clarify and strengthen the relationship between existing international agreements."[107] In terms of substantive developments, the UNCED agreed on the (nonbinding) Rio Declaration on Environment and Development,[108] and there was one agreement regarding forest conservation and management tellingly titled a "Non-Legally Binding Authoritative Statement of Principles." [109]

If it was not previously apparent, recent global events have emphasized the need for proactive measures in the prosecution and sanction of both individuals and states. One can only hope that substantive, not only rhetorical, progress will continue, and that more effective mechanisms will soon be developed that will enable the swift and certain prosecution of international criminals.

NOTES

* I gratefully acknowledge the reviews, comments and suggestions on earlier drafts of this work from Roger S. Clark, Marcia V.J. Kran, Jeffrey Ian Ross, and three anonymous reviewers. That I may not have entirely incorporated their valuable views remains my sole responsibility. Finally, thanks to Paul R. Bond, for his excellent research assistance.

1. Although criminological texts recognize and discuss the social construction of crime from various theoretical or legal perspectives (e.g., Inciardi, 1983, Nettler, 1983), even Quinney, a respected contributor to the "radical criminology" school allows that the "definition of crime which is perhaps the most acceptable" is the following: "[t]he essential characteristic of crime is that it is behaviour which is prohibited by the State as an injury to the State and against which the State may react, at least as a last resort, by punishment" (1971: 4); see also Sutherland's classic definition (1949: 31).

2. The two are the *International Convention on the Suppression and Punishment of the Crime of Apartheid*, General Assembly resolution 3068 (XXVII) (November, 1973), and the *Convention on the Prevention and Punishment of the Crime of Genocide*, General Assembly resolution 260 A (III) (December 9, 1948). See discussion in text below.

3. Of course, these formal procedures are most effective if used in addition to political and other actions not only by states, but also by individuals and organizations. See, for example, Sands (1991: 61–68).

4. Individual criminal accountability was established in two international tribunals since World War II: The International Military Tribunal at Nürnburg in 1945–1946, and The International Military Tribunal For the Far East at Tokyo in 1946–1948. See the United Nations War Crimes Commission (1948: 188, 461–475). For a comprehensive review of the legal mechanisms under which individuals are culpable through nineteen international treaties since World War II, see Clark (1988: 49).

5. According to the general principle of state sovereignty, states had virtually exclusive authority to sanction crimes committed within their jurisdiction until after World War II: "[n]ow the first and foremost restriction imposed by international law upon a State is that—failing the existence of a permissive rule to the contrary—it may not exercise its power in any form in the territory of another State": see *The Lotus Case (France v. Turkey)* 1927, PCIJ Reports, series A, No. 10. The "Principle of Sovereign Equality of States" is also part of the *General Assembly Declaration on Principles of International Law Concerning Friendly Relations and Co-operation Among States in Accordance with the Charter of the United Nations 1970* GA Res 2625 (XXV) (October 24, 1970).

6. The terms *accountable* and *responsible* have special meanings in international law that are discussed in Kamminga (1992) and reviewed by Theo van Boven in *Human Rights Quarterly* 14 (1992): 561.

7. Article 38 of the Statute of the International Court of Justice (ICJ) (hereinafter "Statute") lists another source, general principles of law recognized by civilized nations, but that phrase is currently not often invoked in legal arguments. Its *importance*, although probatively difficult, has been recognized and articulated by Judge Nagendra Singh, former president of the ICJ. See Singh (1989: 144, 258).

8. See *Colombia v. Peru*, 1950, ICJ Reports, *United Kingdom v. Norway*, 1951, ICJ Reports and *Federal Republic of Germany v. Denmark; Federal Republic of Germany v. The Netherlands*, 1969, ICJ Reports. Also see Cohen and Bayefsky (1983: 283–284).

9. The provisions of the exception, Chapter VII, are discussed in the text *infra*. For the history of the noninterventionist clause, see Jones (1979: 18–32). This Charter clause was reinforced by the General Assembly in 1965 when it declared that "no state has the right to intervene directly or indirectly, for any reason whatsoever, in the internal or external affairs of any other state" (United Nations, 1965).

Implicit in the notion of sovereignty is that one state cannot use its criminal law to punish another state for criminal activity. In other words, "the State has over it no authority other than that of international law" (Anzilotti, 1931: 57). The doctrine of state sovereignty, however, does not preclude a state from voluntarily assuming responsibility for past actions that are arguably criminal and providing compensation for those actions, as the government of Canada did in 1988 when it compensated Japanese Canadians who had been interned in Canada during World War II.

10. There are two points here. First, only two United Nations organs have the authority to enact decisions binding on member states: the Security Council under the Charter of the United Nations and, if states consent, the ICJ.

Second, there are courts of international jurisdiction in two of the three "regional" arrangements in place in the world. One is the European Court, in Strasbourg, France, which is the judicial organ of the Council of Europe, and the other is the Inter-American Court of Human Rights, in San Jose, Costa Rica, which is the judicial organ of the Organization of American States. There is no court for the Organization of African Unity, although, like the others, there is a strong human rights declaration.

11. See Statute, Article 36, para. 2. As of July 31, 1990, fifty-one states accepted some measure of compulsory jurisdiction. Of the five permanent members of the UN Security Council, only Britain has accepted compulsory jurisdiction.

12. See *Military and Paramilitary Activities in and Against Nicaragua, Merits, Judgement* ICJ Reports 1986, p. 14. McWhinney argues that two World Court decisions have greatly influenced the international credibility of the Court. The first was *South West Africa, Second Phase* (1966), and the second was *Nicaragua v. United States* (1984, 1986) see McWhinney (1991: xiii-46). On the trial itself, see Gill (1989: 339–342) and, generally, D'Amato (1985).

13. There were also eight cases referred to the World Court in which the respondent refused the invitation to litigate. Readable, accessible summaries of all judgments given by the ICJ are provided in Rosenne (1989: 155–232).

14. Article 7 reads as follows: "[t]he official position of defendants, whether as heads of State or responsible officials in government departments, shall not be considered as freeing them from responsibility or mitigating punishment."

15. Trial of the major war criminals before the International Military Tribunal, *Proceedings* (Vol. 1), Nürnberg, 1947 at p. 34. For the most recent first-person account, see Taylor (1992). For a discussion of the international law that influenced Nürnberg, see United Nations War Crimes Commission (1948: 262–274). Also see Morgan (1988: 40)

16. International criminal law conventions are thoroughly classified, and cross-referenced, in two very valuable works by Bassiouni (1986: 135–163; 1987: 357–467).

17. Subsequent to the adoption of the Genocide Convention, Graefath reports that "many states which voted against an international criminal court in the context of the *Genocide Convention* subsequently declared that in principle they had nothing against the establishment of such a court; they claimed they did not vote for it at the time because it was a mere hope, not a possible reality" (1990: 69). Also see Malekian (1985: 162–164). In Resolution 260B (III) (December 9, 1948), the second part of the Genocide Convention, the General Assembly "request[ed] the International Law Commission, in carrying out [the international trial of persons], to pay attention to the possibility of establishing a Criminal Chamber of the International Court of Justice." Article V of the Apartheid Convention (1976) also provides for the creation of an international criminal jurisdiction, and Bassiouni drafted one as a special rapporteur for the UN Commission on Human Rights, but no action has been taken since the draft statute was submitted in 1980.

18. This document was initiated in 1947 by General Assembly resolution 177(II) of November 21, 1947. There are domestic examples also. A common domestic criminal codification, which devolves from Article 8 of the Nürnberg Charter, is the elimination of the defense by an individual acting in an official capacity for the illegal application of force (torture) as a consequence of "superior orders." See UN War Crimes Commission (1948: 283).

19. Submitted by the special rapporteur Jean Spiropoulos: see United Nations, 1950. Originally titled the Draft Code of Offenses Against the Peace and Security of Mankind, the term *crimes* was substituted for *offenses* in 1987: see United Nations (1987).

20. The history of the delay is discussed by Williams (1986: 109–116).

21. This distinction became important for the development of the Draft Articles on State Responsibility, discussed in the text below.

22. These definitions include the arguments that punishment should not fall upon the whole population because they have not all committed crimes, that the punishment could become brutal, and that it is impractical.

23. The Code was adopted at a meeting in Talloires, France, May 18–20, 1991, which was sponsored by the Foundation for the Establishment of an International Criminal Court and International Criminal Law Commission, an international nongovernmental

organization. The meeting was attended by thirty legal experts from twenty-five countries representing the world's principal legal systems and major geographical areas. They included members of the ILC, the Sixth Committee of the United Nations General Assembly, the United Nations Office of Legal Affairs, and United Nations missions.

24. At the International Military Tribunal at Nürnburg, twenty-four former Nazis were indicted, twenty-two tried, nineteen convicted, and twelve of them sentenced to death. At Tokyo, twenty-five defendants were tried, all convicted, and seven were sentenced to death.

25. I am considering that there are six major systems: "common," "civil," socialist, Islamic, African, and Chinese. The one that is not arguably based on positivistic legal principles is African.

26. Thomas Aquinas was called the "Dumb Ox" because fellow students thought he was dim-witted and because of his size. He was over six and a half feet tall and weighed more than three hundred pounds (Morris, 1959: 56).

27. Braybrooke captures the essence as "to retire God to at most a role speaking offstage" (1989: 1).

28. But international customary law should not be equated with "common law." For the distinction, see Henkin (1991: 311–312) and D'Amato (1985: 662–664)

29. I say "eighteenth century" because the "father of positivism," August Comte (1798–1857), was heavily influenced by the previous generation, including Fourier, Lerox, and Proudhon and his major influence, Saint-Simon. There are many accounts, but one of the most authoritative is Levy-Bruhl (1924: 357–364).

30. I say "1966" because that was arguably the year in which consensual, normative international law began to replace a rule-based, positive law at the ICJ, as reflected in *South West Africa. Second Phase, Judgement* (ICJ Reports, 1966, p. 6). This decision, a single-vote majority "denying the Court's jurisdiction to rule on the substantive legal issues, must be properly directed to its basic premise, and to the particular philosophy of law (legal positivism) and to the particular conception of the role of the judge (absolute divorcement between Law and Society) inherent in it" (McWhinney, 1991: 21). Following a storm of protest, five years later, in 1971, the Court reversed itself in *Namibia* and declared that "[the Court's] interpretation cannot remain unaffected by the subsequent development of law, through the Charter of the United Nations and by way of customary law." This trend in ICJ jurisprudence has continued until the present, although Anthony D'Amato has argued that the Court did not go far enough in *Nicaragua* (1985). See *Legal*

Consequences for States of the Continued Presence of South Africa in Namibia (South West Africa) notwithstanding Security Council Resolution 276 (1970), Advisory Opinion ICJ Reports 1971, p. 6, and D'Amato (1985: 661). Also on the subject see Henkin (1989: 37–39).

31. The Economic and Social Council is established as one of the principal organs of the United Nations in the Charter, Article 7, and the duties of ECOSOC are detailed in Chapter X, Articles 61–72.

32. When the ICCPR entered into force in 1976, it had attached an Optional Protocol that allows certain procedures which will be discussed in the text below. On December 15, 1989, a second Optional Protocol to this Covenant was also adopted, and it entered into force on July 11, 1991. Member states that have ratified it agree to the abolition of the death penalty, except for the possibility of certain circumstances during wartime (United Nations, 1989).

33. The first and former Canadian director of the United Nations Human Rights Directorate (1946–1966), John Humphrey, wrote that "the Universal Declaration of Human Rights is now part of the customary law of nations and therefore binding on all states" (1984: 66,44,75; 1989: 71,155,160,164). However, a leading Canadian international lawyer, L.C. Green, disagrees: "if this were true, there would be little need for the variety of treaty instruments on human rights that exist and we might have seen more efforts by "obedient" states to secure judicial condemnation of the "lawbreakers" (1991: 255). The issue of whether human rights as customary law are *jus cogens* is also addressed by Schachter (1991: 343–344).

34. Members of the HRC are nominated and elected by state parties to the ICCPR. It is interesting that a draft ICCPR proposed that the members of the HRC would be appointed by the ICJ: this draft was replaced by the current election procedure, according to McGoldrick, as "an adverse reaction to the judgement of the ICJ in the *South West Africa Cases*" (1991: 9,29 [n.88]).

35. Individuals filing complaints must meet certain tests which, among others, preclude unsigned complaints and require that an individual must have exhausted all domestic remedies for the complaint (Articles 2,3). If a complaint is deemed admissible, after certain exchanges between the individual and the State Party (Article 5), the HRC may offer its views on the complaint.

36. As of July 26, 1991, there were ninety-five states' parties to the ICCPR and fifty-five states' parties to the OP. As of the same date there were also thirty-one states' parties that have accepted Article 41 of the ICCPR, which allows complaints against them by other states' parties

who have accepted Article 41. Canada has ratified Article 41. Note: update as of the last date possible, UN Treaty Section 212–963–5467.

37. The HRC has stated that it "applies the provisions of the Covenant and of the Optional Protocol in a judicial spirit," see United Nations (1990) *Selected Decisions of the Human Rights Committee Under the Optional Protocol* (Vol 2). New York: United Nations, 1990) at p. 1 (UN doc CCPR/C/OP/2), hereinafter "SD2" (United Nations, 1990: 1).

38. The first acknowledgment of the importance of publicity was in 1980, but in 1981 the HRC issued a general comment which was much more prescriptive:

> it is very important that individuals should know what their rights are under the Covenant (and the Optional Protocol, as the case may be) and also that all administrative and judicial authorities should be aware of the obligations which the State party has assumed under the Covenant. To this end, the Covenant should be publicized in all official languages of the State and steps should be taken to familiarize the authorities concerned with the contents as part of their training.

See *Report of the Human Rights Committee* (UN doc A/36/40), General Comment 3/13, at p. 109. Note: Hereafter the annual *Report of the Human Rights Committee* will be cited by session number: e.g., "36, General Comment 3/13, at p. 109."

39. 36, pp. 5–6; 38, pp. 5–6, 106; 39, pp. 5–6; 40, p. 3. The function of publicity for the European Convention on Human Rights in Sweden, presumably applicable to the HRC, has been documented by Sundberg (1987: 649–659).

40. Tarnapolsky's observations can be contrasted with Graefrath's equally correct observation that "although the Soviet Union and other socialist countries emphatically support international cooperation of states to coordinate criminal prosecution of crimes against peace and humanity, from the outset they have repeatedly rejected the creation of an international criminal court as a supranational institution" (Graefath, 1990: 74).

41. 46, at p. 173. This is 25 percent of the 468 complaints received as of that date. The status of the most recent balance of submissions was as follows: declared inadmissible, 124 (26 percent); discontinued or withdrawn, 70 (15 percent); declared admissible but not yet concluded, 46 (9 percent); pending at the pre-admissibility stage, 109 (23 percent): see UN doc GA a/46/40, at p. 160. The caseload of the HRC has grown

dramatically in the last few years. Before 1987, the greatest number of annual complaints received annually was 30 (1981). In 1988, the number soared to 80; in most ensuing years has been comparatively high: 75 (1989), 27 (1990), and 50 (1991).

42. The last published breakdown of complaints by states' parties was as at June 30, 1988 (United Nations, 1990: 229). I have used the figure reported in 1988 and added from subsequent annual reports.

43. There was a military government in Uruguay during 1973–1985. Since the assumption of power by President Julio Maria Sanguinetti on March 1, 1985, Uruguay proclaimed an amnesty for political prisoners (March 8, 1985) and enacted a number of rights guarantees, including the ratification and entry into force of the United Nations Convention Against Torture and Other Cruel, Inhuman or Degrading Treatment or Punishment (October 26, 1986/June 26, 1987).

44. The term "disappeared" is a translation from the Spanish *desaparecido*, which was first used to describe crimes in Guatemala in 1966. It became part of the worldwide human rights vocabulary following the military coup in Chile in 1973 (Amnesty International, 1981: 75; Berman and Clark, 1992: 531).

45. Article 4 of the ICCPR stipulates that Articles 6, 7, 8 (paras. 1 and 2), 11, 15, 16 and 18 are non-derogable.

46. 37, pp. 93–94; 40, pp. 162–163. In both comments the HRC addressed the issue of nuclear armament in context, but most specifically in the second, declaring that "[t]he production, testing, possession, deployment and use of nuclear weapons should be prohibited and recognized as crimes against humanity": see p. 162.

47. *Status juris*: July 26, 1991.

48. *Guillerma Ignacia Dermit Barbato and Hugo Haroldo Dermit Barbato v. Uruguay* 38, p. 124: "the Uruguayan authorities failed to take appropriate measures to protect his life while he was in custody," at p. 13; *Miango v. Zaire* 43, p. 218 "the State party has the duty to investigate in good faith all allegations of violations of the Covenant made against it and its authorities, and to furnish to the Committee the information available to it," at p. 220; *A. and H. Sanjúan Arévalo v. Columbia* 45, p. 31: "the right[s] to life . . . [and] liberty . . . and security of the person . . . have not been effectively protected by the State of Colombia," at p. 36.

49. *Guerro v. Colombia* 37, p. 137: "the law must strictly control and limit the circumstances in which a person may be deprived of his life by the authorities of a State" at p. 146; *Baboeram and Others v. Suriname* 40,

p. 187: the same quote, at p. 194. Both these cases are also discussed in Rodley (1987: 149–150, 155–156).

50. 38, p. 134. Daniel Monquya Mbenge was tried *in absentia* for "treason" and "conspiracy" by the government of Zaire and twice sentenced to death. The HRC concluded, among other things, that the government of Zaire had not taken necessary steps to notify the accused of the charges against him, which effectively extinguished his rights to a fair trial under provisions of Article 14.

51. *Earl Pratt and Ivan Morgan v. Jamaica*, 44, p. 222 at 231; *Daniel Pinto v. Trinidad and Tobago*, 45, p. 69 at 74 (dissent at p. 75); *Carlton Reid v. Jamaica*, 45, p. 85 at 92 (dissent at p. 94); *Paul Kelly v. Jamaica* 46, p. 241 at 248 (dissent at p. 250).

52. Specifically, Article 3 of the ECHR.

53. The first expression of views by the HRC was against Uruguay and concerned Article 7, *Ambrosini, Valentini de Massera and Massera v. Uruguay*, 34, p. 124 at 129. Further important decisions against Uruguay concerning violations of Article 7 were *Lanza and Perdoma v. Uruguay*, 35, p. 111 at 118; *Weinberger v. Uruguay*, 36, p. 114 at 119; *Antonaccio v. Uruguay*, 37, p. 114 at 120; *Izquierdo v. Uruguay*, 37, p. 179 at 186.

54. This failure began to be remedied in 1990, when the HRC defined "inhuman treatment as "depriv[ation] of food and drink for four days . . . [and] interned under unacceptable sanitary conditions" (*Birhashwirwa and Mulumba v. Zaire*, 45, p. 77 at 84).

55. *Lopez Burgos v. Uruguay*, 36, p. 176 at 177, *Cariboni v. Uruguay*, CCPR/C/OP/2, p. 189 at 190.

56. *Lewenhoff and de Bleier v. Uruguay*, 37, p. 130 at 131.

57. *Muteba v. Zaire*, 39 at 182.

58. *Supra, Ambrosini*, note 58.

59. GA res 39/46 (December 10, 1984). UNCAT entered into force one month after the tenth ratification, on June 26, 1987. As of May 3, 1991, there were fifty-five states' parties to UNCAT.

60. Article 17.

61. Articles 21 and 22. Among other things, states' parties to UNCAT must make a declaration of competence under these articles. As at May 3, 1991, twenty-six states' parties had declared under Article 21, and twenty-five states' parties had declared under Article 22: see 46T, pp. 55, 59–62. Note: Hereafter the reference system is the same as the annual *Report of the Human Rights Committee*, using the UN session number, but with a "T" following: e.g., *Report of the Committee Against Torture* (A/46/46) is given as "46T."

62. Article 20. For the relevant rules, see 44T, Annex IV, pp. 50–55.

63. 46T, p. 56.

64. 46T, p. 54. All such deliberations are confidential.

65. Because the views of the HRC and the Committee are not binding, the degree to which views expressed have been influential can be determined only through two sources: 1) reports of the states themselves and 2) assessments by nongovernmental organizations and individuals.

66. Pursuant to provisions of the ICCPR, Article 49(2); OP, Article 9(2).

67. The report was due on August 18, 1977 and was submitted on April 18, 1979: see 34, p. 117. Nolan writes that Canada's report "was by far the longest and most comprehensive report prepared by any State" (1988: 108).

68. R.S.C. 1970, c. I-6.

69. Article 27 reads as follows: "[i]n those States in which ethnic, religious or linguistic minorities exist, persons belonging to such minorities shall not be denied the right, in community with the other members of their group, to enjoy their own culture, to profess and practise their own religion, or to use their own language."

70. 36, pp. 166–175. Article 26 of the ICCPR reads as follows: "[a]ll persons are equal before the law and are entitled without any discrimination to the equal protection of the law. In this respect, the law shall prohibit any discrimination and guarantee to all persons equal and effective protection against discrimination on any ground such as race, colour, sex, language, religion, political or other opinion, national or social origin, property, birth or other status."

71. *Constitution Act, 1982* Section 15(1) reads as follows: "Every individual is equal before and under the law and has the right to the equal protection and equal benefit of the law without discrimination and, in particular, without discrimination based on race, national or ethnic origin, colour, religion, sex, age or mental or physical disability."

72. *Minutes of Proceedings and Evidence of the Sub-committee on Indian Women and the Indian Act*, First Session of the Thirty-Second Parliament, 1980–81–82 (House of Commons, Issues No. 1–5) at p. 1.

73. *Ibid.*, vol. 2, p. 99.

74. R.S.C. 1985, c. 32 (1st sup.), s. 6.

75. 38, p. 249.

76.   The second report was due on April 8, 1988 (submitted July 28, 1989), and the third report was due April 4, 1990 (submitted August 20, 1990). Both reports were considered by the HRC on October 23 and 24, 1990: see 46, pp. 10–24.

77.   *Ibid.*, p. 14. Also, although not directly related to *Lovelace*, it is interesting to note that since the patriation of Canada's Constitution in 1982, there have been several domestic constitutional cases that have cited Canada's accession to twenty-five international human rights instruments.

78.   77, or 26 percent of the 288 total (See United Nations, 1990: 229).

79.   See 40T, p. 9; 46T, p. 64.

80.   The report was due on 21 March 1983.

81.   44, pp. 61–71 at p. 61.

82.   *Ibid.*, p. 63.

83.   *Ibid.*, p. 71.

84.   45(II), pp. 207–208.

85.   45(II), p. 209.

86.   *Supra,* note 64, SD2, at p. 226.

87.   46, p. 174.

88.   *Ibid.*, p. 174.

89.   *Ibid.*, p. 174.

90.   *Ibid.*, p. 174.

91.   44, p. 149; 45(II), pp. 209–210; SD2, p. 226. I say "notably" because the HRC has published more responses indicating compliance from Finland than from any other country.

92.   46, p. 174.

93.   *Yearbook of the International Law Commission 1976* Volume II, Part 2, UN doc A/CN.4/SER.A/1976/Add.1(Part 2) (hereinafter "*Yearbook*") at p. 73. Article 19 reads in part:

> 2. An internationally wrongful act which results from the breach by a State of an international obligation so essential for the protection of fundamental interests of the international community that its breach is recognized as a crime by that community as a whole, constitutes an international crime.

94.   Article 19 (3)(a).

95. The legal issues surrounding distinctions between international crimes and delicts, the limitations of *erga onmes* (the obligations of a state toward the international community), and *jus cogens* (a peremptory norm of international conduct), in relation to Article 19 are thoroughly discussed in Spinedi (1989: 135–138), and Gaja (1989: 151–160).

96. This article is a review of Weiler et al. (1989).

97. *Report of the Secretary-General Pursuant to Paragraph 2 of Security Council Resolution 808 (1993)* of May 3, 1993 (UN Doc S/25704) at p. 14.

98. The first Congress was held in Geneva in 1955, and they have been held every five years since.

99. As a result of the conclusions of a Ministerial Meeting on the Creation of an Effective United Nations Crime Prevention and Criminal Justice Programme (Paris, November 21–23, 1991), on February 6, 1992 the Economic and Social Council dissolved the Committee and created a Commission on Crime Prevention and Criminal Justice (ECOSOC res 1992/1). This Commission consists of forty member state representatives, and had its inaugural meeting from April 21–30, 1992 in Vienna.

100. United Nations Expert Meeting on Implementation of UN Norms and Standards in Criminal Justice, October 14–16, 1991, Vienna, Austria.

101. A "non-HRC" example is the March 4, 1992, attempted censure by the United Nations Commission on Human Rights of China for human rights violations in Tibet. It was reported that China successfully lobbied Third World support against the proposed censure because "Beijing . . . [was] fearful that condemnation could affect its international trading position" (see *Globe and Mail*, March 5, 1992, at A9).

102. The first ICJ decision, the *Corfu Channel* (*United Kingdom v. Albania*) case (1949), helped pave the ideological path for the development of international environmental law, notably at the United Nations Conference on the Human Environment held in Stockholm in 1972. In *Corfu Channel*, the ICJ referred to "certain general and well-recognized principles" that supported "every State's obligation not to allow knowingly its territory to be used for acts contrary to the rights of other States" (see *U.K.* v. *Albania*, ICJ Reports 1949, at p. 4 et seq.; also Schachter [1991: 363], and, generally, Chapter 16, "Protecting the Environment."

103. *Supra*, note 15, for an explanation.

104.   See also the discussion of the ILC on the topic of the global commons in *Report of the International Law Commission* (May 1–July 20, 1990) UN doc A/45/10 at pp. 282–285.

105.   The ILC has drafted a relatively unhelpful proposed Article 26 to the *Draft Code of Crimes*, which, consistently, identifies *individual* responsibility: "[a]n individual who wilfully causes or orders the causing of widespread, long-term and severe damage to the natural environment shall, on conviction thereof, be sentenced [to . . .]" see *Report of the International Law Commission* (April 29–July 19, 1991) UN doc A/46/10 at pp. 275–276. In a Recommendation and Report on the Protection of the Environment adopted by the American Bar Association's House of Delegates in August, 1991 the ABA has encouraged only "further discussions and appropriate action" (1992: 289).

106.   The UNCECD was held in Rio de Janeiro, Brazil from June 3–14, 1992: see UN doc A/CONF.151/26 [Vols. I–V].

107.   *Ibid.*, Vol. III (Chapter 39: International Legal Instruments and Mechanisms), at p. 100.

108.   *Ibid.*, Vol. I (Annex I), at p. 8.

109.   *Ibid.*, Vol. III, at p. 111. At least one international conference, the International High Seas Fishing Conference held in New York in April 1993, has resulted from UNCED.

REFERENCES

American Bar Association (1992) "Recommendations and Reports." *The International Lawyer* 26: 281–290.

Amnesty International (1981) *'Disappearances': A Workbook*. New York: Amnesty International USA.

———— (1988) *Report 1987*. London: Amnesty International.

———— (1991) *Report 1990*. London: Amnesty International.

———— (1992) *Report 1991*. London: Amnesty International.

Anzilotti, J. (1931) *Advisory Opinion: Customs Regime Between Germany and Austria*, PCIJ Reports, Series A/B, No. 41.

Bassiouni, M. Cherif, ed. (1987) *A Draft International Code and Draft Statute for an International Criminal Tribunal*. London: Martinus Nijhoff.

—— (1986, 1987) *International Criminal Law (Volumes 1–3)*. New York: Transnational Publishers.

Berman, Maureen R., and Roger S. Clark (1992) "State Terrorism: Disappearances." *Rutgers Law Journal* 13: 531–577.

Black & White Taxicab & Transfer Co. v. Brown & Yellow Taxicab & Transfer Co. (1928) 276 U.S. 518, 533 (dissenting).

Boyle, Alan E. (1991) "State Responsibility for Breach of Obligations to protect the Global Environment," in W.E. Butler (ed.), *Control over Compliance with International Law*. Netherlands: Kluwer, pp. 69–81.

Braybrooke, David (1989) *Natural Law Theory: The Link Between Its Descriptive Strength and Its Prescriptive Strength*. Paper presented at the Legal Theory Workshop, Faculty of Law, University of Toronto on October 25, 1989.

Clark, Roger S. (1988) "Offences of International Concern: Multilateral State Treaty Practice in the Forty Years Since Nuremburg." *Nordic Journal of International Law* 57: 49–118.

—— (1989) "Human Rights and the UN Committee on Crime Prevention and Control." *The Annals of the American Academy of Political and Social Science* 506: 68–84.

Cohen, Maxwell, and Anne F. Bayefsky (1983) "The Canadian Charter of Rights and Freedoms and Public International Law." *Canadian Bar Review* 61: 265–313.

D'Amato, Anthony (1985) "Nicaragua and International Law: The 'Academic' and the 'Real.'" *American Journal of International Law* 79: 657–664.

The Economist (1992) "A World Criminal Court?" *The Economist* (March 28, 1992): pp. 13–14.

Fisher, Roger (1981) *Improving Compliance with International Law*. Charlottesville: University Press of Virginia.

Foundation for the Establishment of an International Criminal Court and International Criminal Law Commission (1991) *The Code of Talloires: On an Interim International Criminal Trial Mechanism, a Permanent International Criminal Court, a Code of Crimes and Universal Criminal Jurisdiction*. Report of the Seminar on an International Code of Crimes and Universal Criminal Jurisdiction at the International Diplomatic Symposium of 1991 at the Tufts European Conference Center in Talloires, France, May 18–20.

Gaja, Giorgio (1989) "Obligations of *Erga Omnes*, International Crimes and *Jus Cogens*: A Tentative Analysis of Three Related Concepts," in Joseph H.H. Weiler, Antonio Cassese, and Marina Spinedi (eds.), *International Crimes of State: A Critical Analysis of the ILC's Draft Article 19 on State Responsibility*. Berlin/New York: Walter de Gruyter.

Green, L.C. (1991) "Review of *No Distant Millennium.*" *McGill Law Journal* 36: 244–256.

Geertz, Clifford (1980) *Negara: The Theatre State in Nineteenth Century Bali*. Princeton, NJ: Princeton University Press.

Gill, Terry D. (1989) *Litigation Strategy at the International Court: A Case Study of the Nicaragua v. United States Dispute*. London: Martinus Nijhoff.

Graefrath, Bernhard (1990) "Universal Criminal Jurisdiction and an International Criminal Court." *European Journal of International Law* 1: 67–88.

Gusfield, Joseph R. (1981) *The Culture of Public Problems: Drinking-Driving and the Symbolic Order*. Chicago: University of Chicago Press.

Harris, D.J. (1991) *Cases and Materials on International Law*, 4th ed. London: Sweet and Maxwell.

Henkin, Louis (1989a) *Right v. Might: International Law and the Use of Force*. New York: Council on Foreign Relations Press.

——— (1991) "The Invasion of Panama Under International Law: A Gross Violation." *Columbia Journal of Transnational Law* 29: 293–311.

Henkin, Louis, ed. (1989b) "Use of Force: Law and U.S. Policy," in Henkin (ed.), *Right v. Might: International Law and the Use of Force*. New York: Council on Foreign Relations Press, pp. 37–69.

HEUNI (1990) *Criminal Justice Systems in Europe and North America (Report 17)*. Helsinki: HEUNI.

Humphrey, John P. (1984) *Human Rights & the United Nations: A Great Adventure*. Dobbs Ferry, NY: Transnational Publishers.

——— (1989) *No Distant Millennium: The International Law of Human Rights*. Paris: UNESCO.

International Court of Justice (1990) *Yearbook 1989–90 (No. 44)*. The Hague: ICJ.

Jones, Goronwy J. (1979) *The United Nations and the Domestic Jurisdiction of States: Interpretations and Applications of the Non-Interventionist Principle.* Cardiff: University of Wales Press.

Kamminga, Menno T. (1992) *Inter-State Accountability for Violations of Human Rights.* Philadelphia: University of Pennsylvania Press.

Kelsen, Hans (1944) *Peace Through Law.* Chapel Hill: University of North Carolina Press.

Lawyers Committee for International Human Rights (1984) *Uruguay: The End of a Nightmare? A Report on Human Rights Based on a Mission of Inquiry.* New York: Lawyers Committee for International Human Rights.

Levy-Bruhl, Lucien (1924) *History of Modern Philosophy in France.* Chicago: Open Court Publishing.

Lutz, Robert E., II (1991) "Perspectives on the World Court, the United States, and International Dispute Resolution in a Changing World." *The International Lawyer* 25: 675–711.

McGoldrick, Dominic (1991) *The Human Rights Committee: Its Role in the Development of the International Covenant in Civil and Political Rights.* Oxford, Eng.: Clarendon Press.

MacLean, Robert M. (1989) "The Proper Function of International Law in the Determination of Global Behaviour." *The Canadian Yearbook of International Law* 27: 57–79.

McWhinney, Edward (1991) *Judicial Settlement of International Disputes: Jurisdiction Justiciability and Judicial Law-making on the Contemporary International Court.* London: Martinus Nijhoff.

Malekian, Farhad (1985) *International Criminal Responsibility of States.* Stockholm: University of Stockholm.

Morgan, Edward M. (1988) "Retributory Theatre." *American University Journal of International Law and Policy* 3: 1–64.

Morris, Clarence, ed. (1959) *The Great Legal Philosophers: Selected Reading in Jurisprudence.* Philadelphia: University of Pennsylvania Press.

Munch, Fritz (1986) "Criminal Responsibility of States," in M. Cherif Bassiouni (ed.), *International Criminal Law (Volume 1: Crimes).* New York: Transnational Publishers, pp. 123–127.

Nolan, Cathral J. (1988) "The Human Rights Committee," in Robert O. Matthews and Cranford Pratt (eds.), *Human Rights in Canadian Foreign Policy.* Kingston: McGill-Queen's University Press, pp. 101–114.

Quinney, Richard (1971) *The Problem of Crime*. New York: Dodd, Mead & Company.

Rodley, Nigel (1987) *The Treatment of Prisoners Under International Law*. Oxford, Eng.: Clarendon Press.

Rogers, William S. (1989) "The Principles of Force, the Force of Principles," in Henkin (ed.), *Right v. Might*. New York: Council on Foreign Relations Press, pp. 95–107.

Röhl, K.F. (1991) "The Globalization of Legal Phenomena: Preliminary Considerations for a Legal Sociological Approach." Paper prepared for the Law and Society Meetings in Amsterdam, Holland, June 26–29 , 1991.

Rosenne, Shabtai, with Terry D. Gill (1989) *The World Court: What It is and How It Works*, 4th ed. London: Martinus Nijhoff.

Sands, P.J. (1991) "The Role of Non-Governmental Organizations in Enforcing International Environmental Law," in W.E. Butler (ed.), *Control over Compliance with International Law*. Netherlands: Kluwer, pp. 61–81.

Schachter, Oscar (1991) *International Law in Theory and Practice*. Netherlands: Martinus Nijhoff.

Scheffer, David J. (1989) "Introduction: The Great Debate of the 1980s," in Henkin (ed.), *Right v. Might*. New York: Council on Foreign Relations Press, pp. 1–17.

Singh, Nagendra (1989) *The Role and Record of the International Court of Justice*. London: Martinus Nijhoff.

Spinedi, Marina (1989) "International Crimes of State: The Legislative History," in Joseph H.H. Weiler, Antonio Cassese, and Marina Spinedi (eds.), *International Crimes of State: A Critical Analysis of the ILC's Draft Article 19 on State Responsibility*. Berlin/New York: Walter de Gruyter, pp. 7–138.

Steinhardt, Ralph G. (1991) "State Criminality and the 'New' World Order." *Criminal Law Forum* 2: 607–619.

Sutherland, Edwin H. (1949) *White Collar Crime*. New York: Holt, Rinehart and Winston.

Sundberg, Jacob W.F. (1987) "The Swedish Experience of the European Convention: The View from Beneath." *Akron Law Review* 20: 649–670.

Tarnopolsky, Walter (1987) "The Canadian Experience with the International Covenant on Civil and Political Rights Seen from the Perspective of a Former Member of the Human Rights Committee." *Akron Law Review* 20: 611–628.

Taylor, Telford (1992) *The Anatomy of the Nuremberg Trials: A Personal Memoir*. New York: Knopf.

Tusca and Tusca (1983) *The Nürnberg Trial*. London: Macmillan.

United Nations General Assembly (1948) *Convention on the Prevention and Punishment of the Crime of Genocide*. Resolution 260A (III) (December 9).

———— (1947) *Draft Code of Crimes Against the Peace and Security of Mankind*. Resolution 177(II) of November 21.

———— (1950) *II Yearbook International Law Commission*. UN Doc A/CN.4 (April 25–26).

———— (1965) General Assembly Resolution 2131(XX) of December 21.

———— (1976) *Yearbook of the International Law Commission 1976, Volume II*, Part 2 UN doc A/CN.4/SER.A/1976/Add.1(Part 2).

———— (1980) *Report of the Human Rights Committee*. UN doc A/35/40.

———— (1981) Resolution 36/106 of December 10.

———— (1985) *Report of the International Law Commission*. May 2–July 21, UN Doc A/44/10, p. 129.

———— (1987a) *Draft Code of Crimes Against the Peace and Security of Mankind*. Resolution 42/151 of December 7.

———— (1987b) *Status of the International Covenants on Human Rights*. UN doc E/CN.4/1987/NGO/50 (February 20, 1987).

———— (1988) *Yearbook of the International Law Commission (Vol. 1)*, UN doc A/CN.4/SER.A/1988.

———— (1989) Resolution 44/128 (December 15, 1989).

———— (1990) *Selected Decisions of the Human Rights Committee Under the Optional Protocol (Vol. 2)*. (UN doc CCPR/C/OP/2) New York: United Nations.

United Nations War Crimes Commission (1948) *History of the United Nations War Crimes Commission and the Development of the Laws of War*. London: His Majesty's Stationery Office.

Weiler, Joseph H.H., Antonio Cassese, and Marina Spinedi, eds. (1989) *International Crimes of State: A Critical Analysis of the ILC's Draft Article 19 on State Responsibility*. Berlin/New York: Walter de Gruyter.

Weinstein, Martin (1988) *Uruguay: Democracy at the Crossroads*. Boulder, CO: Westview Press.

Williams, Sharon A. (1986) "The Draft Code of Offences Against the Peace and Security of Mankind," in W. Cherif Bassiouni (ed.),

International Criminal Law (Volume 1). New York: Transnational Publishers, pp. 109–16.

Woetzel, Robert W., et al., eds. (1970) *Toward a Feasible International Criminal Court*. Geneva: World Peace Through Law Center.

Young, Oran R. (1979) *Compliance and Public Authority: A Theory with International Implications*. London: Johns Hopkins University Press.

Eliminating State Crime by Abolishing the State

*Brian Martin**

State crime seems inevitable as long as there are states. In the well-known formulation by Weber (1947), states are communities based on a monopoly over "legitimate" violence within a territory. What makes violence "legitimate" is that it is sanctioned by the state itself. This violence is perpetrated by a variety of state actors. There is no higher power to ensure that this monopoly over violence is used for the greater good, and, indeed, it is regularly used for the aggrandizement of ruling elites at the expense of the general population.

Is it really feasible to expect that crimes by the state can be overcome by reform measures such as international agreements, laws, regulations, oversight committees, or even the organized action of community groups? Such efforts, however laudable, may only mask the problem, which is the underlying structure of the state itself. Consider an analogy. When slavery was widespread and generally accepted, was there a point in trying to reform the practice? Did it make sense to prosecute a few of the slaveowners who were excessively brutal, to pass laws about hours of work or about the buying and selling of slaves? Surely, such reform efforts helped the lot of many slaves. But as well, it was essential to oppose the practice of slavery itself.

In this chapter, I proceed by examining five possible goals or visions of a world without states—namely, communism, world government, small size, libertarianism, and anarchism— and strategies for achieving these goals. In each case, I discuss whether the goal and its associated strategy would be likely to reduce or eliminate state crime. I do not argue that states must be abolished to eliminate state crime, nor that the problem of state crime is sufficiently serious to warrant abolishing the state. (In both cases, the nature of the alternative to the state is crucial to the argument. Rather, I make the more modest claim that action toward the goal of abolishing the state offers *one* strategy for dealing with state crime. Personally, I believe that this strategy is important, but only future initiatives can determine its efficacy.

Abolishing the state, in my view, is not a process of achieving social change and then finding that social problems have been eliminated. This assumes a dichotomy between revolution and reform. Rather, the process of challenging and replacing the state should be linked to immediate challenges to state crime. More generally, abolishing the state is a process, not an end point (Gowan et al., 1976: 2).[1] Nor is it likely that a world without states will be free of crimes and other social problems. There will continue to be a need for struggles to achieve a world without oppression.

Approach 1: Communism

Communists claim that their ultimate aim is a society without the state (namely communism in its original sense, before the term was used to denote bureaucratic state systems and their official ideology). Their usual method is to capture state power in order to destroy the capitalist state. Historically, however, Leninist practice has produced enormously powerful states that have shown no signs of withering away. Theoretically, the Marxist tradition has devoted little attention to the social organization of a stateless world or how to get there. Most Marxist critiques of the state are of the *capitalist* state and how to abolish it (Wright, 1979), not how to abolish the state per se. Most Marxists focus on crimes linked to capitalism and the capitalist state but show relatively little interest in state crime not linked to capitalism. For these reasons, the communist approach offers little to aid the project of challenging state crime via strategies toward a stateless world.[2]

Approach 2: World Government

Another approach to the abolition of states is the creation of a world government, namely a single state. To those who promote this alternative, the problem with the present state system is its "anarchy," namely its lack of any higher authority to adjudicate and control unruly and criminal members of the international community.

The League of Nations and the United Nations are well-known attempts to develop controls over the actions of governments. Arguably though, these organizations serve more to legitimate states than to restrain their excesses (Yeselson and Gaglione, 1974). In the case of genocide, for example, the UN has generally taken a hands-off policy so long as the killings remain within a single country, as in Bangladesh in 1971 and Cambodia in 1975–1979 (Kuper, 1981). When the UN does act, it is usually at the behest of dominant states (most commonly the United States government).

Perhaps more promising for the prospect of world government is the process of European unification, in which economic and political controls are gradually ceded to central bodies. Imagining this process succeeding and spreading through the world, the end result might resemble a world parliament and a world administration, with varying degrees of autonomy still resting in entities similar in area and population to present-day countries. Present states then might become similar to provinces in current federal systems.

Central administrative control would certainly provide the potential to intervene against local administrative crimes in various parts of the world. But is this likely? All the evidence today suggests that much locally organized, nominally non-state crime—such as private crime syndicates, vigilantes, and death squads—survives and thrives through open or tacit collusion with state bodies (Chambliss, 1989). Why would this be any different under a world state?

Another fundamental problem with the world state is that it might itself engage in state crime. The advocates of world government have not explained how to overcome this problem. Both psychological and sociological studies show that the greater the concentration of power, the more likely it is to be misused (Comfort, 1950; Kipnis, 1990; Sorokin and Lunden, 1959).

Finally, what is the strategy for achieving world government? Most of the arguments seem to assume that because it is a good idea, people (or at least present elites) will support it. There certainly is no program of action that links a transition to world government with systematic challenges to state crime.

Although the usual idea is that world government will result from an evolution toward world unity led by public-spirited elites, in practice it is much more likely that it will result from a world war. Methods of bureaucratic social organization and associated technologies have made possible increasingly larger empires; a world empire is entirely feasible today. The aftermath of nuclear war or collapse of the world economy could well lead to world domination by a single power (the United States is the prime candidate). In this scenario, the prospects for benevolent world rule are remote (Martin, 1984: 124, 258–261).

In summary, the vision of world government is flawed as a direction to challenge state crime. Local government crime could still persist, and the world government itself could become a world oppressor. Just as problematic, proponents of world government have no strategy that links strongly with challenges to present-day state crime.

Approach 3: Small Size

According to one school of thought, the primary source of problems with modern social institutions is their large size (see, for example, the journal *Fourth World Review*; Kohr, 1957; Sale, 1980). A big organization is susceptible to inequalities of power, usually with a small dominating elite. Bureaucracy is the standard form of large organizations, and hierarchy is a defining characteristic of bureaucracy (Perrow, 1979). States commonly involve the rule of millions or even hundreds of millions of people. The opportunities for exploitative rule, crime, and many other evils are due to the scale at which power may be exerted—or so, at least, say the critics of large size. A more moderate position is that big size exacerbates many of the problems associated with social institutions. Certainly it seems that egalitarian social relations are easier to establish and maintain in small, face-to-face groups (Mansbridge, 1980).

For the purposes of the discussion here, it is not necessary to decide whether or not large size is responsible for social problems. All that is necessary is a vision of a world without states, achieved by reducing the size of political units and hence the scale of governance from millions of people to perhaps thousands or tens of thousands, small enough so that the apparatuses associated with the state become unsustainable or too small to operate oppressively.

But what exactly is the vision of a world without states? There are various images presented, including the ancient Greek democracies, New England towns (governed through town-hall meetings), and, more recently, bioregions. Setting aside the internal workings of these models of society, a key issue is the relation between the small units and, in particular, how they can act against aggression and repression, two central state crimes.

One often-cited model is Swiss-style democracy, based on autonomous cantons and a weak central government. Switzerland is known as one of the most enlightened and nonrepressive countries in the world today. Militarily it is neutral and has avoided the major European wars of this century (Lloyd, 1980). Its system of local control has a degree of conservatism (illustrated by some cantons refusing the vote to women much longer than in other parts of the world), but also a degree of participation much greater than most societies (Barber, 1988).

Switzerland is still criticized for being home to banks and multinational corporations that are exploitative. Although the central military command is weak, the society itself is highly militarized. Switzerland has a thriving arms industry, including a substantial export business.

The case for small size does not depend solely on the Swiss example. The positive features of Swiss society can be used as a basis for a vision—or, more properly, a range of visions—that can be used in various parts of the world. One example of this is the work of Kendall and Louw (1987, 1989) that draws from the

Swiss example to propose a canton-style model for South Africa. In their model, the autonomous cantons can choose for themselves their form of social organization. For example, there might be socialist, laissez-faire, radical white and black nationalist cantons (Kendall and Louw, 1987: 123–134). So long as people are free to emigrate and immigrate and cantons can secede or be expelled from the system, choice will be maximized and oppression limited.

Although Kendall and Louw propose that South Africa be decomposed into a multitude of cantons, they still envisage a role for a South African state, to carry out certain collective functions such as military defense. Needless to say, this raises some serious problems. What is to stop the military forces from aligning themselves with particular groups and intervening internally against certain cantons? Who will guard the guardians? What is to ensure that the "minimal state" remains minimal?

The discussion so far suggests that small size may be more hospitable to a society without oppression, but it is hardly a guarantee. The nature of the small units needs to be better specified. Small is not necessarily beautiful. After all, many more children are battered by family members (most commonly fathers) than by the remote state apparatus. Smallness needs to be linked to appropriate forms of social organization. Some possibilities are mentioned later.

So much for the goal of small size. What about a strategy toward this goal? Can a strategy to promote small-scale associations be part of a challenge to state crime? The big problem here is that proponents of small size have no strategy. Kohr, guru of this movement, argues the case through many chapters in his 1957 book *The Breakdown of Nations*. One chapter is titled "But Will It Be Done?," the text of which has one word: "No!" With this pessimistic attitude, it is not surprising that Kohr presents no strategy.

Likewise, Sale presents a vast amount of evidence for small scale in his mammoth book *Human Scale* (1980). But on the question of how to move toward human scale, he says that people will have to work out the methods themselves—on a small scale.

It seems that the basic technique used by proponents of small size is the power of argument. They seem to think that if the evidence is presented, people will be persuaded and proceed, in their own way, to bring about the alternative. This is not the first movement to imagine that good ideas are sufficient in themselves to bring about social change. If this were actually the case, the world would long ago have been blessed with universal peace and prosperity.

The vision of small size does have some implications for practice. One is that the organizations and activities to bring about smaller social institutions should themselves be small and decentralized. This implication draws on an assumption common in "prefigurative politics," namely, the practice of trying to behave according to the ideal that the activity is aimed at achieving. This principle can also be called "turning the ends into means," or "living the alternative." As will be described later, this principle has a varied application.

Approach 4: Libertarianism

Many libertarians are intensely hostile to the state. Market-oriented libertarians, found in greatest numbers in the United States, oppose state regulation of the capitalist market. Instead, they favor extension of the market to areas such as education, prisons, pollution, roads, professions, organ transplants, drugs, telecommunications, and many other areas that are state-run or state-regulated in many countries. Although some libertarians are comfortable with the existence of large corporations, others want a free market without the distortions of either government or corporate monopolies.

There is much controversy among libertarians about the exact form of their ideal society, but for the purposes here it is necessary to mention only the role of the state. The usual solution is to propose a "minimal state" to carry out only those functions necessary to protect the radically extended market (Nozick, 1974). Two key elements of the minimal state are the military, for defense against external threat, and the legal system (with police or military enforcement), for ensuring compliance with market principles. The foundation of the market is private property, which must be protected against theft, blackmail, and so forth.

There are a number of criticisms that can be made against the radical extension of the market. One fundamental criticism is that an unregulated market is unstable, in the sense that there is nothing to prevent massive inequalities from developing. Some individuals may become extremely rich and powerful, while underprivileged groups may be unable to survive. Private charities may help the disadvantaged, but one likely result of severe inequalities is collapse of support for the market and political agitation for some sort of change. There is a body of literature arguing that the state is essential for the survival of capitalism (Moran and Wright, 1991). The political and economic instabilities engendered by the market require constant intervention in order to maintain some sort of stability.

Another big problem is the minimal state itself. Why should the military and legal functionaries sit primly in their restricted domain, stick entirely to regulating the market, and refuse to use their power in other ways? The capacity to use violence for warfare is closely linked to the use of violence for internal repression (Gurr, 1988; Tilly, 1985). What would stop the military from joining with powerful entrepreneurs to build their own power?

The evidence from many countries today is that the military and police are strongly political, usually supporting the most powerful economic groups (large landowners, large corporations) and opposing populist movements. The rise of modern states in earlier centuries was a process intimately linked with the rise of capitalism as well as the concentration of means for organized coercion (Tilly, 1975; 1990). The supporters of libertarian capitalism have not shown how the state can be kept at some minimal level.

The goal of the minimal-state libertarians seems insufficient to eliminate the state and, therefore, state crime. But what about the methods to achieve this goal? Can they contribute to reducing state crime?

There are a number of strategies used by libertarians. A primary one is continual promotion of the libertarian message through newsletters, radio, magazines, and meetings. Another is lobbying and agitation against various government functions.

These behaviors can play a role in challenging state crime. Libertarian critics of the state have often played a key role in exposing crimes, such as actions by spy agencies and harassment of citizens by police and taxation officials (see, for example, the journals *Inquiry* and *The Pragmatist*). It should be noted that many libertarians see measures such as taxation and compulsory schooling as forms of state crime, and they seek to convince others of this perspective.

Another strategy that can be used by libertarians is to establish a political party. Most successful in this regard is the Libertarian Party in the United States, which in recent years received the third-most votes after the Republicans and Democrats. A political party typically seeks to increase mass support and, ultimately, obtain political power to implement its program. Although a small party such as the Libertarian one may have no immediate prospect of victory, its efforts can apply pressure on other parties to adopt some of its policies. If a few representatives can be elected, they can play a powerful propaganda role and, if by chance they hold the balance of power, be influential in terms of legislation.

But there seems to be an inherent contradiction in a libertarian movement, premised on reducing the role of the state, seeking access to state power through a political party. There is no example of a party seriously implementing a program that eliminates central bases of state power, leaving a skeleton state to administer a market-driven society. Indeed, all the evidence is that political parties, as they grow and become serious contenders, become adapted to the goals of the state. In Europe since 1945, the state has grown under all types of governments (McEachern 1990). The Libertarian Party in the United States has not developed an organizational strategy that would resist this process.

Perhaps, it could be argued, however, that the Libertarian Party is mainly a vehicle for libertarian ideas, not a serious party of government. Even so, simply by constituting itself as a party and participating in the process of elections, the Libertarian

Party legitimates the representative system of government and, in turn, the state (Ginsberg, 1982).

For these reasons, some libertarians reject the Libertarian Party and, more generally, participation in activities that provide support or legitimation for the state. This perspective is boldly articulated and elaborated in the journal *The Voluntaryist*. Voluntaryists reject the state entirely—including the minimal state—and propose in its place a society based entirely on voluntary agreements. The economic system is one based on exchange, namely, a market, but one without central regulation. All standards, regulations, and procedures are developed through voluntary processes, such as the development of time zones by the railways in the United States, prior to government control.

With no state, there is no taxation, and hence all health, education, and welfare services must be organized from the community. With no state, there is no military. The voluntaryists recognize that the military is the foundation of state power. They advocate the use of nonviolent action as a replacement for military force.

Clearly, the voluntaryist vision of a world without states is one in which state crimes have been eliminated, and also one in which there is no power base for other sorts of crimes. What then of the practice, of the strategy for getting there? Does it hold potential for challenging state crimes?

A total commitment to voluntaryist principles in one's life means living as a voluntaryist today, and that means noncooperation with all aspects of the state. This means, for example, accepting no payments from the state, using private health and education services, and refusing to pay tax, join a political party, or vote. Most difficult is refusing to pay tax. One way to avoid paying income tax is to obtain goods and services through private barter arrangements.

There are limits, of course, to what individuals can and want to do to avoid supporting the state. Only a few would adopt a policy of noncooperation in every area immediately. But the more who do, the easier it is for others. For example, the expansion of private, cooperative education or barter arrangements gives people experience in voluntary approaches;

the continued operation of viable alternatives to state-run systems gives credibility to voluntaryism. Both the experience and credibility can encourage others to participate.

The basic strategy of voluntaryists in relation to state power is to withdraw consent and participation. This can be a powerful method if enough people join in, but what will encourage them to do so? Voluntaryists have only their personal example and small efforts at communicating their viewpoints. In the face of the massive shaping of beliefs and behaviors by mammoth government bodies, it would seem that voluntaryists have little prospect of winning significant numbers of converts.

More generally, the strategy of withdrawal of support is seldom enough to challenge crimes. State crimes can occur as long as enough people are willing to participate in them. That a minority refuses to join in is an inconvenience but not a fundamental obstacle. Generally, a more active stance is needed to challenge the crimes.

The great value of noncooperation is its symbolism. Even if only a few people refuse to cooperate, others will then be encouraged to do the same. But the power of the symbol depends on circumstances. If the noncooperators are isolated and obscure, their acts will have little influence. In order to have a greater practical impact, voluntaryist principles for a transitional practice need to be worked out. Should every soldier and government employee who comes to believe in voluntaryism immediately drop out of their job? Or is there some method of action that allows promotion of voluntaryism from inside the system?

To these arguments, voluntaryists might respond that their primary concern is to take a principled position against cooperation with the state, not to develop an elaborate strategy. In the case of state crimes, voluntaryists would be alert to the danger of becoming part of the crimes or committing new crimes to stop the state's crimes, both of which are dangers if one is cooperating with the state. Rather than attempting to develop a grand strategy, voluntaryists have faith that if individuals act according to their consciences, using the proper means (voluntary, nonviolent action), great things can result.

Approach 5: Anarchism

In its classical formulation, anarchism is a political philosophy that sees the state as the primary source of oppression. But some classical anarchists and many contemporary anarchists oppose not just the state but all forms of hierarchy. In such a view the state is not necessarily seen as a more fundamental or crucial form of hierarchy. This broader conception of anarchism incorporates critiques of capitalism, patriarchy, professions, liberal democracy, and domination of nature. In short, anarchist society is a society without rulers or domination (Ward, 1982).

Whereas libertarians and voluntaryists favor a large role for the market in a society with a minimal or no state, anarchists generally see a lesser or nonexistent role for the market. The overlap and distinction between the two orientations is indicated by some terminology: "libertarian socialism" is generally considered synonymous with anarchism, whereas the radical variety of libertarianism where the state is entirely eliminated is called "anarcho-capitalism," or "free-market anarchism." An important difference is that anarchists are far stronger than libertarians in their critique of capitalism and, more generally, market systems. In relation to state crime, the important point is that anarchists wish to abolish the state and replace it by systems of governance that minimize the ability of any part of society to exercise power over others.

The number of groups that call themselves anarchist is not large. Furthermore, relatively few people know about these groups or understand their philosophy. However, the anarchist conception of the world has a much wider sway than suggested by the impact of anarchist groups. Many members of environmental, feminist, nonviolent action and other community groups have beliefs that could be described as anarchist (although they themselves may not describe their beliefs this way). They are opposed to systems of rule, whether capitalist, communist, or liberal democratic, and support instead methods of direct democracy such as consensus. They reject reform solutions of achieving power through individual advancement or parliamentary election, seeing bureaucratic hierarchies as part of the problem. Their aim is to empower individuals and communities rather than to gain power and use that power to "help" others.

This type of anarchist "sensibility" is widespread. Activists would agree that in many countries anarchism has much more support than do vanguard left parties (which seek to capture state power). This sensibility is seldom due to the direct influence of anarchists or anarchist writings. Rather, it appears to be a response to hierarchical systems of power; it reflects a belief that a more egalitarian society is both possible and desirable. [3]

Because most intellectuals are tied to dominant social institutions—universities, governments, mass media, professions, corporations—they are likely to adopt or develop sets of ideas compatible with the interests of those institutions, and especially with the interests of intellectuals themselves (Cabrera, this volume; Gouldner, 1979). Support for the state is overwhelming among intellectuals, including those subscribing to Marxism, the main dissident political perspective in universities. As a consequence, there has been relatively little development of anarchist theory compared both to dominant perspectives such as liberal democracy and neoclassical economics and also to challenging perspectives such as Marxism and feminism.

Many anarchists do not believe in trying to envisage the, ideal nonhierarchical society, except in very general terms. They have faith in people's ability to develop a self-managing society and do not want to inhibit the creativity of the people by specifying in advance what should be achieved. This is not very helpful for developing strategies against state crime, which necessitates a look at anarchist methods and visions.

A central anarchist principle is that the means should incorporate the ends. If the goal is a society without bosses, then it is foolish to put faith in bosses (including politicians and trade union leaders) to bring it about. If the goal is a society without violence, then it is foolish to try to bring it about using violence. Anarchists reject the Leninist project of gaining state power in order to lay the basis for the eventual withering away of the state. Because of the anarchist commitment to making means reflect ends, it becomes fruitful to assess anarchist methods and their potential for challenging state crime.

To further explore anarchism, I will briefly outline four visions of anarchist society and the methods used to get there, and then comment on the implications of these visions and methods for challenging state crime today. Many anarchists would see the first vision discussed here, federations of self-managing collectives, as identical with anarchism itself. I prefer a broader picture, incorporating under the banner of anarchism a variety of ways of organizing society without hierarchy.

Federations of Self-Managing Collectives

The most common picture in the European anarchist tradition is self-management and federations. *Self-management* refers to some form of direct democracy for a workplace or community, such as voting in mass meetings or consensus. The model is inspired by the practical experiences of collectives, soviets, and communes, especially those developing in periods of revolution or crisis, such as the 1871 Paris commune, soviets in Russia in 1917–1918; soldiers' councils in Germany in 1918–1919; collectives in Spain in 1936–1939; and egalitarian movements in Hungary in 1956, Czechoslovakia in 1968, and France in 1968. People on these and other occasions have shown the capacity to organize work and life without politicians and managers (Guérin, 1970).

Direct democracy sounds fine for a community of hundreds or thousands of people. But what about a million people? How is coordination to occur? The usual solution proposed is federations. Each self-managing group would choose a delegate for a decision-making body at a higher level. The delegates could be elected, but they would be bound to represent the views of the collective, unlike the more familiar elected representatives, who are free to break election promises and to vote against the wishes of electors. Delegates can be replaced at any time, following a decision of the self-managing group, again unlike most elected representatives. Finally, the task of delegates is to coordinate decisions made at the local level, not, as in the case of representatives, to make decisions that are implemented from above. Delegates would examine alternatives and take them back to local groups to approve or reject. Finally, in a federation of self-managing collectives, most decisions would be made at the local level. Only a few decisions would require meetings of delegate groups or, at higher levels, federations of federations and delegates from delegate groups.

Sarvodaya

The Gandhian vision of *sarvodaya* or village self-management, falls squarely within the anarchist tradition (Kantowsky, 1980; Ostergaard, 1985; Ostergaard and Currell, 1971). Gandhi was opposed to all types of hierarchies, including caste, gender, capitalist, and state hierarchies. He opposed the process of Western-style industralization and "modernization" through which Indian elites mimicked European economic and political institutions. Instead, he supported village-level direct democracy as the basis for society. Gandhi's successors have pursued this vision.

Today, Gandhians vary in their attitudes to the state. Although some of them support state intervention on at least some issues, others support Gandhi's focus on grassroots issues. The Gandhian "positive programme" contains a radical rejection of Western-style economic development. One reason for this rejection is the oppression that seems inevitably associated with the division of labor in modern industry: specialization and large scale are linked with the need for management, and this opens opportunities for control by elites (whether corporate or government). An alternative is "bread labor," in which individuals participate in the direct production of goods for local use.

There have been significant *sarvodaya* movements in India and Sri Lanka for decades that have had numerous committed adherents and that have pioneered innovative projects. Yet progress toward *sarvodaya* remains slow at best; Western-style industrialization has been the dominant force in "development" in these countries. Furthermore, much of the Gandhian movement in India has been institutionalized, for example, becoming part of the educational establishment.

Demarchy

Burnheim (1985), in his book *Is Democracy Possible?* presents a different model for organizing society without the state and without bureaucracy, both of which he sees as incompatible with participatory democracy. Burnheim argues that the usual models of participatory democracy cannot deal with the problem of time and complexity. If everyone has to be involved in every decision, they will not have enough time to become properly informed about the issues.

Burnheim proposes that decisions be made in communities by "functional groups," namely, groups of people dealing with such issues as education, industry, land development, garbage collection, and so forth. There would be groups for all such functions in each community of perhaps tens of thousands of people. There would be no state and no government bureaucracies: the functional groups would make decisions and implement them directly. In order to avoid the usual tyranny of the majority, political parties, vote-trading, and other pathologies of representative democracy, the groups should not be elected. He proposes instead that group members be chosen randomly from volunteers, as in the selection of a jury.

As yet, no demarchy movement exists. There are experiments taking place in Germany and the United States that show the effectiveness of randomly selected groups for decision-making (Crosby, 1990; Crosby, Kelly, and Schaefer, 1986; Dienel, 1988; 1989), and there are a small number of individuals who are promoting the idea of demarchy and projects related to it. It remains to be seen whether demarchy can be turned into a process for social change to replace state and bureaucratic structures.

Networks

Self-organized networks are commonplace. There are networks of stamp collectors, computer enthusiasts, engineers, and advocates of world government. The success of such networks raises the question, is central authority necessary? If networking can accomplish everything needed, perhaps the state can be superseded.

The word *network* is a bit of jargon, of course. Most of the entities called networks could just as easily be called organizations, associations, or collectives. There is some difference, though. Most traditional organizations are based around a locality: employees at a workplace, residents in a community, local people with a common interest. Networks remove the requirement of locality, as they can include people from countries around the world. Secondly, networks come with a minimum of bureaucracy and centralized control.

Could a thoroughly networked society do without the state? The details have not been worked out, but certainly this is a potential direction for developing an alternative (Andrews, 1984). What seems to be lacking is any idea of the institutions for economic and political life. But then again, perhaps the idea of "institutions" is part of the problem. With networks, people decide what they want to do rather than being forced to act within a rigid framework. As long as there are numerous networks in any area of interest, and it is easy to start a new network if the existing ones are unsatisfactory, there should be ample scope for individuals to choose and shape their own lives.

How to Bring About the Change

The above are brief accounts of four models of society that could be characterized as anarchist. They give an idea of how society could be organized around cooperation and participation. These models do away with the state and, thereby, state crime. But what is the transitional practice?

Anarchists promote their visions through several means. One is by spreading the ideas of anarchism through leaflets, magazines, and books. Anarchists believe in persuasion through rational argument. They do not want to manipulate individuals through clever advertisements, moral appeals (to guilt or self-interest), or special tricks of group dynamics. They believe that most people, given the opportunity to make a rational and informed choice, would prefer a society without the state or other hierarchies (see, for example, the journals *Freedom, Kick It*

Over, *Our Generation*, and *Social Anarchism*). Of course, the world is dominated by hierarchies, so only a few individuals are willing to push for such an alternative against the status quo.

But once people do come to believe that anarchism is a good idea, what do they do? Basically, they do what they can in their own life to oppose hierarchies and increase the degree of self-management. They can treat others as equals, regardless of sex, race, wealth, degrees and so on. They can oppose bosses of various sorts, including politicians, police, government bureaucrats, business executives, and church leaders. They can refuse to participate in armies. They can join a variety of community organizations and actions that involve people taking control over their own lives: action against male violence, cooperatives for production and distribution of goods and services, environmental action, peace action.

From this list of activities, it appears that anarchists (whether or not they use this label) help provide a direction for many grassroots campaigns that challenge rather than accommodate or reinforce the state.

Whereas liberal feminists support an increased role for women within existing hierarchies, including the state, anarcha-feminists oppose the state, seeing it as an oppressive institution that reinforces and is reinforced by patriarchy. Anarcha-feminists (like radical feminists) support feminist strategies that empower all women and especially those with the least power.

Whereas reform environmentalists welcome the intervention of the state against environmental destruction and seek this intervention through lobbying and support for certain politicians and political parties, environmentalists of an anarchist orientation seek first and foremost to empower local communities to help create an environmentally sound society, through direct action against threats and through community action for renewable energy, and so on; they are suspicious of methods that rely on governments to protect the environment.

In these and other areas, the role of anarchists (or those with anarchist inclinations) is to push campaigns in the direction of self-management (or, to use a different jargon, grassroots empowerment) and to withdraw support from campaigns that rely on or reinforce the power of dominant institutions, especially the state.

How effective are these efforts? Have they made any impact on state crime? Such questions are very difficult to answer. But there is a plausible case to be made that (1) social movements' central strength comes from their ability to convince and mobilize large numbers of people rather than to persuade a few people at the top and (2) social movements have sometimes had a major restraining effect on state crime.

Galtung (1991) argues that the strength of the peace movement in the West made it possible for Gorbachev to be elected head of the Central Committee and subsequently proceed with *perestroika* in the Soviet Union. Without the Western peace movement as a restraint on the Western military threat, Soviet hardliners might have been able to argue more successfully against Gorbachev and his initiatives. Thus, it can be argued that the subsequent collapse of Soviet-type regimes in eastern Europe owed much to the political space made possible by the peace movement.

Of course, the Western peace movement in the 1980s included people from all parts of the political spectrum. But those of anarchist persuasion, such as within War Resisters' International, have long played a crucial role in peace movements. Arguably, their efforts in this instance helped open the space for the collapse of European state socialism and its associated state crimes (see reports in *Peace News*).[4]

Another example is nuclear power. The movement against nuclear power has been a grassroots one, involving groups as diverse as farmers in France, fishing communities in Japan, and suburbanites in the United States (Falk, 1982). Although the most prominent arguments against nuclear power have been reactor accidents, long-lived radioactive waste, nuclear proliferation and other such hazards, a number of activists became involved because they opposed the expansion of state power that would inevitably accompany a nuclear society (Friends of the Earth, 1986). To protect against terrorist and criminal use of nuclear materials, strict policing would be required; in other words, a nuclear society would involve increasing the power of the state and pose grave threats to civil liberties (Jungk, 1979).

Rather than becoming an all-pervasive energy source as envisaged by its advocates, nuclear power has been stopped in its tracks. Campaigning against nuclear power has been so effective that people in most countries are acutely aware of its dangers. Some part of this success can be attributed to activists with an anarchist sensibility (Falk, 1982). This is perhaps most apparent among advocates of renewable energy and alternative technology, which are seen as both technological and social alternatives to nuclear power and fossil fuels (Boyle and Harper, 1976; the journal *Undercurrents*).

Another test of anarchist influence comes when there is a social crisis undermining the credibility of existing state structures, such as during the revolutionary periods mentioned earlier. Anarchists, by spreading ideas of egalitarian alternatives and encouraging initiatives that give people experience in nonhierarchical social arrangements, can help to encourage people's action against the state and toward self-management in the event of a crisis. For example, when socialist regimes in eastern Europe collapsed in 1989, the only alternative perceived by most people was Western-style capitalism and parliamentary democracy. Because there had been very little anarchist activity—state socialists are intensely hostile to anarchism, so most efforts to promote anarchism were repressed—few people were familiar with anarchist ideas or ready to act on them. Anarchists hope that, if anarchist ideas become more widely understood, on future occasions it will be possible to "seize the moment" to make significant steps toward an egalitarian society.

Abolishing the Military

The military is central to the power of the state and also a key instrument of some of the most horrific state crimes, including war and genocide. Abolishing the state requires abolishing the military. How is this to occur? What, if anything, is to replace the military?

Some pacifists believe that the solution is to eliminate the sources of conflict in society: the inequalities, the injustice, the indoctrination into ethnic and national chauvinisms. They favor conflict resolution, win-win solutions to problems, and enlightened educational practices. An alternative approach is to accept the inevitability of conflict and to develop nonviolent methods of waging conflict. The techniques of nonviolent action include symbolic behaviors such as petitions and fasts, noncooperation such as strikes and boycotts, and intervention such as sit-ins and alternative institutions (Sharp, 1973).

Organized, preplanned nonviolent action by members of a community, proposed as an alternative to military defense, primarily is called social defense, and is alternatively referred to as nonviolent defense, civilian defense, and civilian-based defense. The basic idea is that people oppose aggression and repression using a range of nonviolent methods and that this capacity for nonviolent struggle replaces or eliminates the need for military forces (Boserup and Mack, 1974; Sharp and Jenkins, 1990).

Among the proponents of social defense are two orientations of interest. The first is "elite reform." In this model, social defense is national defense—defense of the state using people's nonviolent action—which will be introduced because it is perceived by elites as a more effective form of defense. Setting aside arguments against the elite reform scenario, it is clear that this model retains the state. Of course, a state with no military would be incapable of many of the most serious state crimes and would undoubtedly be a great improvement over typical states today.

For the purposes of this discussion, the focus here will be on the second orientation, grassroots initiative. In this approach, social defense is likely to be introduced only as a consequence of many local initiatives that develop the capacity and skill of people to wage nonviolent struggle. This includes workers, environmentalists, feminists, antiracist activists, and others learning the methods of nonviolent action for their own struggles. Their efforts could then be combined against state aggression and repression (Martin 1993).

The grassroots approach to social defense contains its own built-in transitional practice: grassroots nonviolent action is both the goal and the method to achieve the goal.

Wars and states are a center of attention in many histories. The largely nonviolent people's struggles are usually omitted. Yet there are some dramatic examples of nonviolent action against even the most repressive regimes. These include the passive resistance by Finns to Russian attempts at tightening control in 1898–1905; campaigns in India, led by Gandhi, against the British in the 1920s and 1930s; the nonviolent resistance to the Nazi occupations in Norway, Denmark, and the Netherlands; the toppling of military dictatorships in Guatemala and El Salvador in 1944 by "nonviolent insurrection;" the collapse of the Algerian Generals' Revolt in 1961 due to noncooperation by soldiers and civilians; the remarkable nonviolent resistance by the Czechoslovak people to the Soviet invasion of 1968, the Iranian Revolution of 1978–1979, a largely nonviolent people's resistance that was successful against a horrifically brutal regime; and the collapse of the communist regimes of eastern Europe in 1989.

These historical examples suggest that nonviolent action has considerable potential for opposing aggression and repression. They certainly do not prove that social defense would always be successful. Indeed, in many of the examples, nonviolent action toppled one violent one but could not stop the rise of a new violent one (as in the case of the Iranian Revolution). It can be expected that if social defense is introduced as a preplanned and well-organized defense system, it will work better than the largely spontaneous efforts noted above. Even so, no method can always be successful. Certainly, military defense regularly fails.

Nonviolent action is a potent challenge to crimes of violence precisely because most people abhor violence. If both sides in a dispute use violence, it is possible to discredit the other one. If one side remains nonviolent, it can win more sympathy. This explains why the killing of thousands of guerrillas and peasants in the course of a guerrilla war may cause little comment, whereas the killing of unarmed protesters (e.g., Sharpeville, South Africa, 1960; Beijing, China, 1989; and Dili, East Timor, 1991), can generate international outrage and change the balance of forces. In these cases, communication of information about the events to outsiders is crucial. Reliable and authoritative information about crimes is essential to nonviolent struggle. It is the foundation of the important work of Amnesty International and would be central to any system of social defense.

The evidence suggests that nonviolent action is one of the most effective means for opposing state crimes (Sharp, 1980). Social defense is the institutionalization of nonviolent action, and hence would be a system for preventing state crime.

Although social defense is normally presented simply as an alternative to the military, it is a serious threat to the power of the state as well. Social defense requires developing the skills and willingness of members of the population to take action against hostile elites. These same skills can also be used against other forms of oppression. For example, if workers learn how to shut down their factories in order to oppose an aggressor, they will also know how to act against their employers. If government employees learn how to destroy files and liaise with citizens in order to oppose an aggressor, they will also be better able to help movements against the government. Social defense is, therefore, a logical part of many strategies against the state.

Among the libertarian and anarchist opponents of the state, there is a range of views about the military. Some libertarians support a minimal state, which usually includes the military. On the other hand, some libertarians and anarchists favor abolishing the army and arming the people. Finally, voluntaryists, Gandhians, and probably a majority of anarchists (see the debate in the journal *Freedom* throughout its 1992 issues) favor nonviolent methods and goals. Furthermore, almost all the social movements that include people with a vision of self-managed society, such as feminists and environmentalists, rely exclusively on nonviolent methods.

Conclusion

When examples of state crime are mentioned, few critics think that the solution is to abolish the state. The state is so much a part of contemporary thinking that reform is usually the only approach considered. Partly as a result of this neglect, visions of society without the state have not been given much attention. The libertarian and anarchist models that do exist are sketchy.

Similarly, there is not much social action that is explicitly linked to the aim of abolishing the state. But on closer scrutiny, there is quite a lot of action that is compatible with a program for abolishing the state. This includes challenges to state initiatives and development of self-managing groups, networks, and campaigns using non-violent action.

A large gap exists here: a gap between the ambitious goal of abolishing the state and the diverse local initiatives that strengthen self-reliance and withdraw power from the state. To fill this gap, strategies and campaigns need to be developed. This would both sharpen the visions of society without the state and focus the campaigns that are relevant to moving toward them.

Abolishing the state is obviously a long-term project and to some people may seem implausible or impossible. In this chapter many of the difficulties facing challenges to the state have been emphasized. In order to decide whether this is nevertheless a useful direction for social action depends on an assessment of alternative strategies, namely, reform solutions that seek to control, rather than eliminate, state crime. Given that state crime seems inevitable whenever states exist, and that some essential functions of states, such as military forces and taxation, can be considered criminal under some definitions, in the long run the reform agenda may actually be more utopian than the task of abolishing the state.

NOTES

* I thank Sharon Beder, Robert Burrowes, Richard Gosden, James Green, Val Plumwood, Jeffrey Ian Ross, Ralph Summy, Joe Toscano, Carl Watner, John Zube and two anonymous referees for helpful comments.

1. On "nonreformist reforms," which provide a process for transforming the state, see Gorz (1967: 6–8).

2 Marxism undoubtedly can offer insights and inspiration for challenging various types of state crime. However, the concern here is how to challenge state crime via abolishing the state, and the Marxist tradition provides very little in this endeavor. There is not a single well-known Marxist discussion on strategies to abolish the state. Marx's own works can be interpreted in Leninist, social democratic, and anarchist directions. Of these, only the anarchist tradition provides much guidance for the task of abolishing the state. This explains the emphasis on anarchist rather than Leninist or liberal strategies in this chapter.

3. The statements in the previous two paragraphs are recognized by many activists, but appear seldom to have been "authenticated" by scholars (exceptions include Epstein, 1990; Falk, 1982). Because the professional interests of most intellectuals are linked to the state (Gouldner, 1979, 1985), the presence of anarchist sensibility is least apparent in academic journals. It is more apparent in movement journals, such as *Chain Reaction* (magazine of Friends of the Earth Australia), *Earth First!, Green Revolution,* and *Peace News* (now produced in cooperation with War Resisters' International), although even in these forums only an articulate minority is represented. Newsletters put out by organizations are more likely to represent the views of ordinary activists, but these seldom are circulated beyond the local area and thus have low visibility by scholars. Three highly experienced and theoretically knowledgeable activists support the points made here about anarchist sensibility: Robert Burrowes, a leading nonviolent activist; Felice and Jack Cohen-Joppa, editors of *The Nuclear Resister;* and Val Plumwood, a prominent philosopher and environmentalist (personal communications).

4. There are, of course, other interpretations of the rise of Gorbachev and the events of 1989 in Europe. This is not the place to present or adjudicate between such interpretations, since the aim here is to argue only that there is a case that social movements have played some sole in restraining state crime through their ability to persuade and mobilize people at the grassroots. On the impact of social movements, see for example Ash (1972), Foss and Larkin (1986), and Piven and Cloward (1979).

REFERENCES

Andrews, David (1984) *The IRG Solution: Hierarchical Incompetence and How to Overcome It.* London: Souvenir Press.

Ash, Roberta (1972) *Social Movements in America.* Chicago: Markham.

Barber, Benjamin (1988) "Participation and Swiss Democracy." *Government and Opposition* 23, 1: 31–50.

Boserup, Anders, and Andrew Mack (1974) *War Without Weapons: Non-violence in National Defence.* London: Frances Pinter.

Boyle, Godfrey, Peter Harper, and the editors of *Undercurrents*, eds. (1976) *Radical Technology.* London: Wildwood House.

Burnheim, John (1985) *Is Democracy Possible? The Alternative to Electoral Politics.* Cambridge: Polity Press.

Chain Reaction, P.O. Box 45, O'Connor ACT 2601, Australia.

Chambliss, William J. (1989) "State-organized Crime." *Criminology* 27, 1: 183–208.

Comfort, Alex (1950) *Authority and Delinquency in the Modern State: A Criminological Approach to the Problem of Power.* London: Routledge and Kegan Paul.

Crosby, Ned (1990) "The Peace Movement and New Democratic Processes." *Social Alternatives* 8, 4: 33–37.

———, Janet M. Kelly, and Paul Schaefer (1986) "Citizen Panels: A New Approach to Citizen Participation." *Public Administration Review* 46 March–April: 170–178.

Dienel, P.C. (1988) *Die Planungszelle: Eine Alternative zur Establishment-Demokratie.* Opladen: Westdeutscher Verlag, second edition.

——— (1989) "Contributing to Social Decision Methodology: Citizen Reports on Technological Projects," in Charles Vlek and George Cvetkovich (eds.), *Social Decision Methodology for Technological Projects.* Dordrecht: Kluwer Academic Publishers, pp. 133–151.

Earth First!, P.O. Box 5176, Missoula, MT 59806, USA.

Epstein, Barbara (1990) "Rethinking Social Movement Theory." *Socialist Review* 20, 1: 35–65.

Falk, Jim (1982) *Global Fission: The Battle over Nuclear Power.* Melbourne: Oxford University Press.

Foss, Daniel A., and Ralph Larkin (1986) *Beyond Revolution: A New Theory of Social Movements.* South Hadley, MA: Bergin and Garvey.

Fourth World Review, 24 Abercorn Place, London NW8 9XP, England.

Freedom, 84b Whitechapel High Street, London E1 7QX, England.

Friends of the Earth (Canberra) (1986) "Strategy Against Nuclear Power." *Social Alternatives* 5, 2: 9–16.

Galtung, Johan (1991) Europe 1989. Lecture at the University of Queensland, July 17.

Ginsberg, Benjamin (1982) *The Consequences of Consent: Elections, Citizen Control and Popular Acquiescence.* Reading, MA: Addison-Wesley.

Gorz, André (1967) *Strategy for Labor: A Radical Proposal.* Boston: Beacon Press.

Gouldner, Alvin W. (1979) *The Future of Intellectuals and the Rise of the New Class.* London: Macmillan.

——— (1985) *Against Fragmentation: The Origins of Marxism and the Sociology of Intellectuals.* New York: Oxford University Press.

Gowan, Susanne, George Lakey, William Moyer, and Richard Taylor (1976) *Moving Toward a New Society.* Philadelphia: New Society Press.

Green Revolution, School of Living, RD 1 Box 185A, Cochranville, PA 19330, USA.

Guérin, Daniel (1970) *Anarchism: From Theory to Practice.* New York: Monthly Review Press.

Gurr, Ted Robert (1988) "War, Revolution, and the Growth of the Coercive State." *Comparative Political Studies* 21, 1: 45–65.

Inquiry, published by the Libertarian Review Foundation, 1977–1984.

Jungk, Robert (1979) *The New Tyranny: How Nuclear Power Enslaves Us.* New York: Grosset and Dunlap.

Kantowsky, Detlef (1980) *Sarvodaya: The Other Development.* New Delhi, India: Vikas.

Kendall, Frances, and Leon Louw (1987) *After Apartheid: The Solution for South Africa.* San Francisco: ICS Press.

——— (1989) *Let the People Govern.* Ciskei: Amagi.

Kick It Over, PO Box 5811, Station A, Toronto, Ontario M5W 1P2, Canada.

Kipnis, David (1990) *Technology and Power.* New York: Springer-Verlag.

Kohr, Leopold (1957) *The Breakdown of Nations*. London: Routledge and Kegan Paul.

Kuper, Leo (1981) *Genocide*. Harmondsworth: Penguin.

Lloyd, William Bross, Jr. (1980) *Waging Peace: The Swiss Experience*. Westport, CT: Greenwood Press.

McEachern, Doug (1990) *The Expanding State: Class and Economy in Europe Since 1945*. New York: Harvester Wheatsheaf.

Mansbridge, Jane J. (1980) *Beyond Adversary Democracy*. New York: Basic Books.

Martin, Brian (1984) *Uprooting War*. London: Freedom Press.

—— (1993) *Social Defence, Social Change*. London: Freedom Press.

Moran, Michael, and Maurice Wright, eds. (1991) *The Market and the State: Studies in Interdependence*. London: Macmillan.

Nozick, Robert (1974) *Anarchy, State, and Utopia*. Oxford: Basil Blackwell.

Nuclear Resister, P.O. Box 43383, Tucson, AZ 85733–3383, USA.

Ostergaard, Geoffrey (1985) *Nonviolent Revolution in India*. New Delhi: Gandhi Peace Foundation.

——, and Melville Currell (1971) *The Gentle Anarchists: A Study of the Leaders of the Sarvodaya Movement for Non-Violent Revolution in India*. Oxford: Clarendon Press.

Our Generation, 3981 boul. St-Laurent, Suite 444, Montréal, Québec H2W 1Y5, Canada.

Peace News, 55 Dawes Street, London SE17 1EL, England.

Perrow, Charles (1979) *Complex Organizations: A Critical Essay*. Glenview, IL: Scott, Foresman.

Piven, Frances Fox, and Richard A. Cloward (1979) *Poor People's Movements: Why They Succeed, How They Fail*. New York: Vintage.

The Pragmatist, P.O. Box 392, Forest Grove, PA 18922, USA.

Sale, Kirkpatrick (1980) *Human Scale*. New York: Coward, McCann and Geoghegan.

Sharp, Gene (1973) *The Politics of Nonviolent Action*. Boston: Porter Sargent.

—— (1980) *Social Power and Political Freedom*. Boston: Porter Sargent.

——, with Bruce Jenkins (1990) *Civilian-based Defense: A Post-military Weapons System*. Princeton, NJ: Princeton University Press.

Social Anarchism, 2743 Maryland Avenue, Baltimore, MD 21218, USA.

Sorokin, Pitirim A., and Walter A. Lunden (1959) *Power and Morality: Who Shall Guard the Guardians?* Boston: Porter Sargent.

Tilly, Charles, ed. 1975. *The Formation of National States in Western Europe.* Princeton: Princeton University Press.

────── (1985) "War Making and State Making as Organized Crime," in Peter B. Evans, Dietrich Rueschemeyer, and Theda Skocpol (eds.), *Bringing the State Back In.* Cambridge, Eng.: Cambridge University Press, pp. 169–191.

────── (1990) *Coercion, Capital, and European States, AD 990–1990.* Cambridge, MA: Basil Blackwell.

Undercurrents, London, 1972–1984.

The Voluntaryist, P.O. Box 1275, Gramling, SC 29348, USA.

Ward, Colin (1982) *Anarchy in Action.* London: Freedom Press.

Weber, Max (1947) *The Theory of Social and Economic Organization.* New York: Free Press.

Wright, E.O. (1979) *Class, Crisis and the State.* London: Verso.

Yeselson, Abraham, and Anthony Gaglione (1974) *A Dangerous Place: The United Nations as a Weapon in World Politics.* New York: Grossman.

The Future of Controlling State Crime: Where Do We Go from Here?*

Jeffrey Ian Ross

Introduction

Despite some researchers' difficulty and eloquent argument against the use of the term *state crime* (e.g., Sharkansky), the study of this subject, as this book attests, is achieving a dominant position in several domains. Although there is considerable variability in how state crimes are defined, there is also consensus among the contributors to this book with respect to which actions should be labeled "state crimes." [All references are to chapters in this book.] Consequently, a number of practices to control these state crimes have been articulated and analyzed in this volume. In an effort to put some closure on this research, in the following pages I summarize these control practices and put them into a theoretical perspective. Because each action produced a reaction, I also look at the unintended effects of these controls. Finally, I outline a series of areas of research that might be pursued in the future.

Reviewing the Controls

In general, the controls articulated in this book can be divided into state-driven or public-initiated mechanisms. This dichotomy is made while recognizing that there are no hard and fast demarcations between these two contexts. Typically, either public complaints against the government or the state's own fear of losing legitimacy will motivate the government to engage in what appears to be controls against state crimes. State-driven mechanisms include a number of diverse processes. For example, Gill and Sharkansky mention judicial or legislative commissions of inquiry that were instituted when there was some suspicion of wrongdoing, or, to use our term, state crime. These inquiries typically produced reports that made a series of recommendations and occasionally forced the resignations of those under investigation, the restructuring of criminogenic organizations, or the adoption of new policies. Others, such as Friedrichs, Ross, and Yarnold, referred to the use of criminal and military trials, and in some cases convictions of a number of "civil servants" (e.g., U.S. Army's Lt. William Calley, Panama's Manuel Noriega, etc.) who engaged in state crimes. Clear guidelines or policies, concerning contentious actions that may lead to criminal activities, is another alternative that state criminogenic agencies may adopt (e.g., Menzies).

Another state-driven mechanism to improve control is training of state actors, in the general discipline of philosophy with a particular emphasis in ethics and morality (e.g., Menzies). Victimization studies of citizens affected by state crimes may help them prevent possible acts of state crime or deal with acts of state crime before they become more severe (e.g., Menzies). Special agencies, supervisory bodies, or social auditors could monitor state criminogenic actors (e.g., Gill, Menzies). Moreover, building on the Madisonian framework (e.g., *Federalist* 10), criminogenic organizations should serve several masters, not just one (e.g., Gill, Menzies). Finally, in some, but not all, cases, international law has served as a symbolic motivator to countries that engage in state crimes to change their contentious behaviors (e.g., Molina) and is one of many tools in the state's arsenal to control other state crimes.

Few of the contributors suggest the implementation of public-driven actions. Since the creation of the modern state, the burden for control has traditionally been left to the state itself, with occasional input from citizens and organized nonstate actors. When actions by the public have been taken, they have either been violent or nonviolent, either legal or illegal. On the violent side of the spectrum we see such behaviors as oppositional political terrorism, guerrilla warfare, assassination, and collective violence. On the nonviolent end of the spectrum, we have "Publicity . . . and access to files of state" criminogenic agencies (Gill). In some cases, actors (i.e., individuals or groups) have broken into the offices of state criminogenic organizations and stolen materials that would prove the state was illegally interfering with their group (e.g., Gill). Others suggest legal nonviolent actions. These behaviors include forming alliances with other nonstate groups. Tunnell, for example, documented how North American labor has become allies with environmental organizations. This activism can extend to boycotting the products and services of corporations that have benefited from state crimes (e.g., Tunnell), supporting opponents (e.g., activists, politicians, candidates) who are capable or advocate controlling state crimes (e.g., Tunnell), launching civil suits against governments and corporations that have profited from state crimes (e.g., Tunnell), and social defense and civil disobedience (e.g., Martin). However, some responses (e.g., protest, secession of regions from states that may contain a dominant minority in the total state) can be both violent and nonviolent depending on the immediate conditions (e.g., Friedrichs).

Also embedded in this discussion is a tension between controls initiated inside a country versus those implemented from beyond the state's borders. It is argued that, in many situations, it is not possible to implement controls inside countries, but external controls suffer from problems connected to a state's sovereignty. Part of the solution then lies in reforming international law and processes, such as the International Court of Justice (e.g., Yarnold).

A discussion of controls must be context-specific to be meaningful. Gill, for example, suggests that "effective control and oversight [of national security agencies] require some mechanism at each level. It does not specify that any particular institutional form will be universally superior; such mechanisms must be rooted within their own culture" (Gill).   He adds,

"Elegant structures of control and oversight may be erected but may be worthless if those responsible for them see their role as providing no more than a modicum of public reassurance that previous problem-areas of government are under control" (Gill). This approach helps us to determine whether oversight structures are real or merely symbolic.

The Adverse Effects of Controls or the Irony of Controlling State Crime

Controls on state criminogenic agencies and practices can have unintended and undesirable effects. For example, controls can lead to unplanned censure of activist politicians by more powerful governmental forces. Additionally, when governments produce reports of inquiries, occasionally some portions are considered to be so secret, preventing full exposure (e.g., Sharkansky). Moreover, sometimes the internal inquiries "have narrow terms of reference," which prevents the revelation of contentious issues that the general populace considers to be state crimes, or prevents those found culpable to ultimately be held responsible (e.g., Gill). Both governmental commissions and the reports they produce give critics of the state (e.g., activists) and victims of state crimes the impression that governments examine their crimes, but it is often interpreted simply as a symbolic gesture, if the whole report cannot be released.

Occasionally trials and convictions of state criminals are "widely criticized [for] deflecting attention from the far more substantial crimes of those higher in the chain of command" (Friedrichs). Although launching complaints with official bodies is an oft-recommended policy, one should be sensitive to the policies and practices that state criminogenic agencies themselves have established for resolution. Some of these institutional follow-ups may have undesirable consequences, including punishing the wrong person, unjustly singling out the agent who is accused of a state crime, inconveniencing, hampering, or ruining the agent's career by an unfounded complaint (e.g., Cabrera). This may encourage unaccountability in some segments of the public bureaucracy.

Rejection of "judgements of an international judiciary concerning [a country's] military actions, even if it supports an international court with more limited jurisdiction" is another unintended effect (Friedrichs). This is the frequently cited reaction of the United States when, in 1986, it was accused of placing mines in the Managuan harbor. The frustration of international law is abundantly documented by contributors such as Molina, Hurwitz, and Yarnold. Moreover, broadly based recruitment of individuals from sectors of the community who are traditional victims of state crime is not a panacea. Problems may result from "people's self-imposed conformity in the face of some perceived organisational 'dominant ideology'." (Gill).

Although mass media exposure of state crimes is an essential component of the process of control, its involvement may be circumscribed. For example, the media are generally owned by large corporations that are ideologically aligned with the state or lack access or ability to provide informed analysis of state transgressions (e.g., Tunnell). The problem is not circumvented with the alternative media because they are simply too underfinanced or do not have a large enough readership/viewership to inform enough members of the public (e.g., Tunnell).

Better training of government actors (especially the coercive agents) can be seen as an improvement (e.g., Menzies), but it is not clear in what areas and how we should educate and retrain these individuals. Alternatively, professionalism is advocated by pro-government organizations and the criminogenic state actors themselves, but this mechanism is criticized as investing the police, military, or national security organizations with too much power to identify what they define as the important factors for their organization's mission. Unfortunately, professionalism can also isolate the criminogenic organization from public control.

Locus of control is another suggestion that is hotly contested. Local democratic control is problematic, as Menzies argues, because it might lead to a "tyranny of the majority" and may ignore the more subtle ways by which state criminals carry out their mandate. Finally, while some states have implemented legislation to protect whistleblowers, as Gill states, "the main hazard faced by civil servants everywhere has been the variety of internal administrative 'punishments' that might be inflicted upon them." Add to this the fact that formal methods of control are time-consuming, and the result is a powerful motivation to remain silent (e.g., Hurwitz).

Perhaps the most radical critique of the problems with controlling state crime was provided by Martin. He generally suggested that reforms are often piecemeal, and what we need is simply the dismantling of the state as we currently know and experience it.

Conclusion

All contributors to the book share the view that state crime should be controlled, and most have articulated a series of controls that have or should be used. This book is an important first step toward this effort. Future research must build on previous work. Apart from exploring the topics identified in this book that are lacking research, the next step in this research agenda is to examine the methods that public and private organizations have used to control state crime in individual countries. One way to achieve this is by compiling an extensive set of case studies written by a number of country experts. These data would provide the raw material for a more sophisticated comparative treatment of controlling state crime. Ideally, research on this subject should be based on a contextual, rather than a geographical, rationale. This selection strategy recognizes the centrality of political and economic forces in the commission and control of state crime. In practice, analysts should begin by systematically analyzing advanced industrialized democracies, as they are most amenable to investigation because of the relative openness of their governmental bureaucracies.

The next logical step should be a systematic investigation of controlling state crime in lesser developed contexts using the same carefully documented sources and style of investigation used in this project. This may involve an analysis of controlling state crime in Caribbean, Central American, South American, Middle Eastern, African, and Asian states. Finally, we need to examine the process of controlling state crime in the communist, or formerly communist, countries, also known as second world, or transitional, contexts. Because of the changing nature of these countries they should be tackled last in order to take into account the processes and mechanisms put in place by these embryonic new governments to control their citizens and states.

Only the most frequent types of state crime occurring in a variety of states experiencing a high level of state crimes should be reviewed. There should be a systematic effort not to include only those cases that are the most readily available. This precaution would add more generalizability to the findings. A comparative approach requires adequate rationale for the selection of different cases or processes. Contributions should also demonstrate historical depth; research needs to deal with events and processes that are connected to overt and covert causes that may otherwise be overlooked. The genesis of these state crimes as well as the success or failure, if any, of solutions implemented to control such crimes should also be integral components of this proposed research agenda.

An analysis of state crime in individual states provides a better contextual and more comprehensive approach to the subject of state crime. Research of this nature represents the basis of all further theory development, testing, analysis, and, perhaps more important, policy formation and implementation. In short, this type of research should soon be recognized as an important building block in the emerging study of state crime and in the broader area of political crime. I believe this volume is an important contribution to this endeavor.

NOTE

* Special thanks to Natasha J. Cabrera, Frank Williams III, and anonymous internal reviewers for comments.

Contributors

Natasha J. Cabrera is an Educational Psychologist and Study Director for the Roundtable on Head Start Research for the National Research Council in Washington. She has taught at Centennial College (Montreal), Lethbridge Community College, and University of Lethbridge. She has published in *Education Research Quarterly* and has a forthcoming chapter in another book. Her research focuses on learning processes and social aspects of education.

David O. Friedrichs is professor of Sociology and Criminal Justice at the University of Scranton. Some fifty articles and essays of his, on sociological, criminological, and legal topics, have been published in various books and journals, including *Social Research*, *Social Problems*, *Crime and Delinquency*, *Justice Quarterly*, *Criminal Justice Review*, and the *Journal of Legal Education*. During 1985–1989, he served as editor of *Legal Studies Forum*, the official journal of the American Legal Studies Association. He is currently working on a book on white collar crime.

Pete Gill is a senior lecturer in Politics and Criminal Justice at Liverpool John Moores University, UK. He is the author of *Policing Politics: Security Intelligence and the Liberal Democratic State* and has published several articles on the oversight of Canadian security intelligence. He is also co-author of *Introduction to Politics* and is currently researching further into police and security intelligence processes.

Leon Hurwitz is Professor of Political Science and an associate dean, College of Arts and Sciences, at Cleveland State University. He has published articles in several scholarly journals and written and has edited ten books, including *Introduction to Politics, Contemporary Perspectives on European Integration, The State as Defendant, International Organizations, The Harmonization of European Public Policy, Historical Dictionary of Censorship in the United States, The European Community and the Management of International Cooperation, The Free Circulation of Physicians Within the European Community,* and *The State of European Community.*

Brian Martin is Senior Lecturer in Science and Technology at the University of Wollingong (Australia). He has been active for many years in the environmental and peace movements, with a special interest in nonviolent alternatives to military systems. He is the author of *The Bias of Science, Uprooting War, Scientific Knowledge in Controversy,* and *Social Defence, Social Change,* co-editor of *Intellectual Suppression;* and author of over 100 articles in a wide range of science and social science journals.

Ken Menzies is a professor at the University of Guelph. He has written two books on sociological theory, the most recent being *Sociological Theory in Use.* He has also written articles on refuges for battered wives, community service orders, and welfare fraud. Currently, he is writing a book on what is the best realistically feasible society from the point of view of liberal social democratic values.

Luis F. Molina is an international criminologist and former professional officer with the United Nations Crime Prevention and Criminal Justice Branch at the United Nations Office in Vienna, Austria. He has written on comparative and international criminal justice practices in the *Third World Legal Studies Journal,* the *Canadian Journal of Law and Society,* and United Nations publications, and currently has editorial responsibility for a forthcoming United Nations publication surveying global crime trends. He and his partner provide consulting services on international justice issues from Vancouver, Canada.

Jeffrey Ian Ross is an assistant professor at Kent State University and has an appointment with George Washington University. He has conducted research, written, and lectured on political and criminal violence and policing for over a decade. His work has appeared in academic journals such as *Canadian Journal of Political Science*, *Comparative Politics*, *Conflict Quarterly*, *Contemporary Sociology*, *International Journal of Group Tensions*, *Journal of Peace Research*, *Justice Quarterly*, *Local Government Studies*, *Low Intensity Conflict and Law Enforcement*, *Peace and Change*, *Police Studies*, *Terrorism*, *Terrorism and Political Violence*, and a variety of chapters in academic books, as well as articles in popular magazines in Canada and the United States. Ross is the editor of *Violence in Canada: Sociopolitical Perspectives* (forthcoming). In 1986, Ross was the lead expert witness for the Canadian Senate of Canada's Special Committee on Terrorism and Public Safety.

Ira Sharkansky is a professor of Political Science and Public Administration at the Hebrew University of Jerusalem. His books include *The Routines of Politics*, *The United States: A Study of a Developing Country*, and *Ancient and Modern Israel: An Exploration of Political Parallels*.

Kenneth D. Tunnell is an associate professor at Eastern Kentucky University. He received his PhD in Sociology at the University of Tennessee in 1988. He has published in *Justice Quarterly*, *Qualitative Sociology*, *Sociological Spectrum*, *Journal of Criminal Justice Education*, and *Journal of Popular Culture*. He is the author of the recent *Choosing Crime: The Criminal Calculus of Property Offenders*, and the editor of *Political Crime in Contemporary America: A Critical Approach*. His ongoing research interests are in qualitative approaches to understanding crime and criminals and the political economy of crime and social control.

Austin T. Turk is professor and chair of Sociology at the University of California, Riverside. His research and writing focus primarily on relationships among law, power, inequality, and social conflict. Major publications include *Criminality and Legal Order*, *Legal Sanctioning and Social Control*, and *Political Criminality: The Defiance and Defense of Authority*. Turk is a Fellow and former President of the American Society of Criminology. He has been a Trustee of the Law and Society Association, as well as Chair of the American Sociological Association's Section on Crime, Law, and Deviance.

Barbara M. Yarnold is an assistant professor and attorney, Department of Public Administration at Florida International University, and an attorney licensed in Florida and Illinois, who has practiced immigration and corporate law, among others. She has been recognized as an expert by members of the U.S. Congress and has offered expert testimony during immigration hearings. She has presented her research at regional, national, and international conferences on law, political science, international relations, and criminal justice and has published articles in political science journals, including, *American Politics Quarterly*, *Policy Sciences*, *Policy Studies Review*, and *Southeastern Political Review*. She has published four books: *Refugees Without Refuge*, *International Fugitives: A New Role for the International Court of Justice*, *Politics and the Courts: Toward a General Theory of Public Law*, and *Abortion Politics in the Federal Courts: Right Versus Right*, and was the editor and contributed an article to a fifth book entitled, *The Role of Religious Organizations in Social Movements*.

Raymond A. Zilinskas is a research associate professor with the Center for Public Issues in Biotechnology, Maryland Biotechnology Institute and an Adjunct Assistant Professor at the School of Hygiene and Public Health, Johns Hopkins University. He is the author of numerous articles on biotechnology vis-à-vis the Third World, biological and toxin warfare, and biotechnology in the former USSR. He co-edited the book *The Gene Splicing Wars: Reflections on the Recombinant DNA Controversy*.

Index